QUEER BRITISH ART

1861–1967

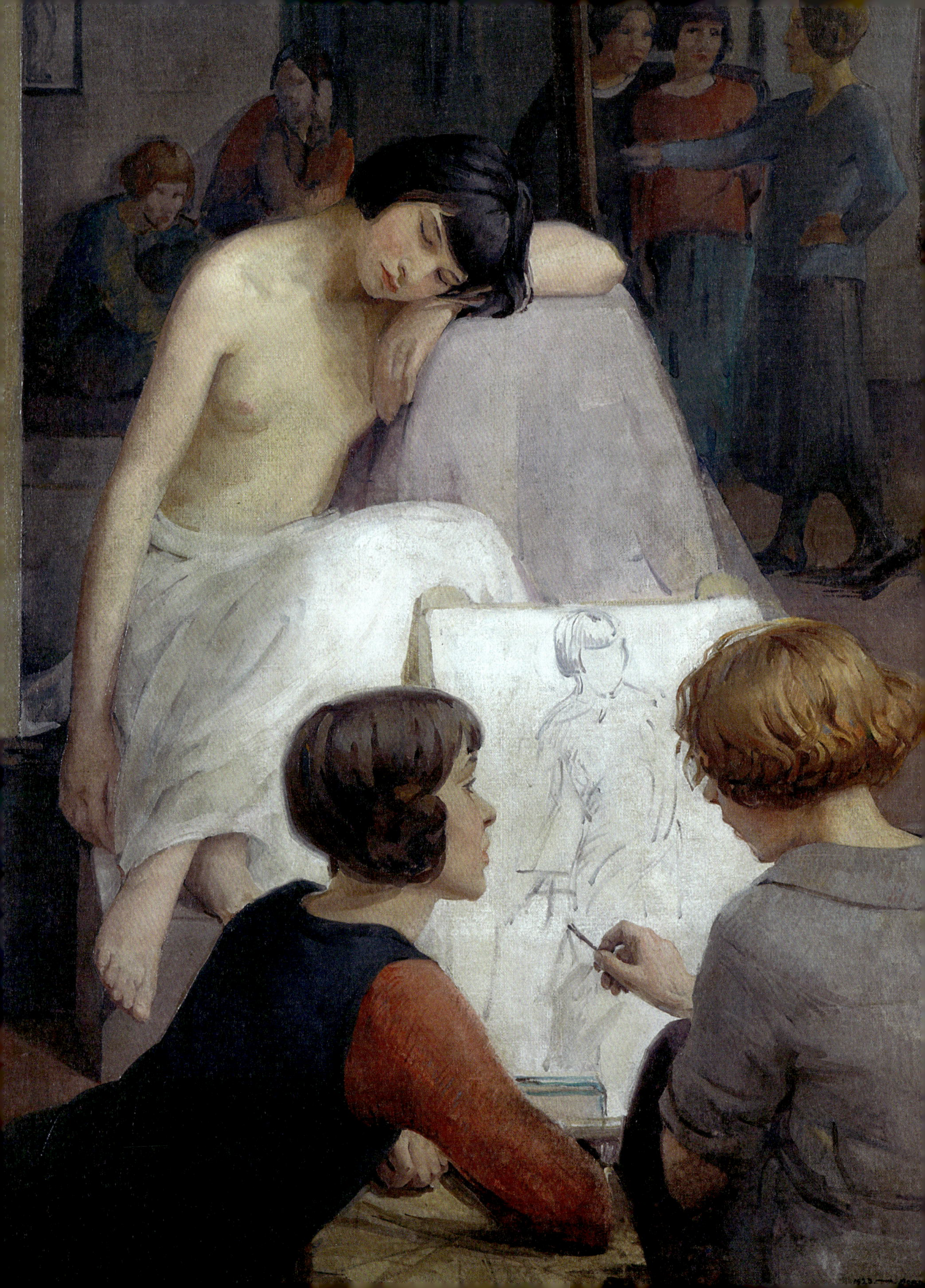

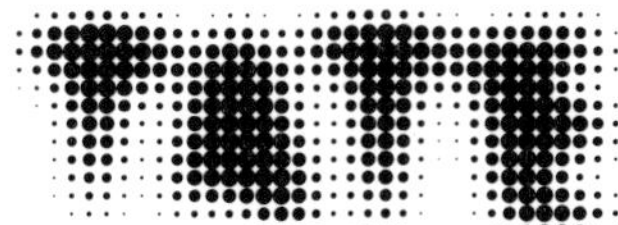

QUEER BRITISH ART

1861–1967

EDITED BY CLARE BARLOW

First published 2017 by order of the Tate Trustees
by Tate Publishing, a division of Tate Enterprises Ltd,
Millbank, London SW1P 4RG
www.tate.org.uk/publishing

on the occasion of the exhibition
Queer British Art 1861–1967

Tate Britain, London
5 April–1 October 2017

Supported by the Queer British Art Exhibition Supporters Circle, with additional
support from Tate Patrons

A catalogue record for this book is available from the British Library

ISBN 978-1-84976-452-0

Distributed in the United States and Canada by ABRAMS, New York
Library of Congress Control Number: applied for

Designed by Peter Dawson, Alice Kennedy-Owen, www.gradedesign.com
Colour reproduction by DL Imaging Ltd, London
Printed and bound in UK by Cambrian Printers

Front cover: Gluck *Self-portrait* 1942. See pp.18, 116
Back cover: Angus McBean *Quentin Crisp* 1941. See pp.152–3
Frontispiece: Dorothy Johnstone *Rest Time in the Life Class* 1923. See pp.126–7

Measurements of artworks are given in centimetres, height before width

CONTENTS

CHAIRMAN'S FOREWORD

When I turned eighteen in 1966, consensual sex between two men was a crime. The following year, the Sexual Offences Act became law, decriminalising sex between consenting men in England and Wales. The sex was no longer illegal, but any normal interaction that might have led to it remained a criminal offence. In this context, and coupled with my mother's experience as an Auschwitz survivor persecuted for being an identifiable member of a minority, I resolved to keep my sexuality a secret. I remained in the closet, hiding my true identity, until 2007.

I had failed to recognise that public opinion of gay people in business was changing around me. But the secular shift in attitudes in the last fifty years has been slow in coming. The year 1967 did not represent the end of a process begun in 1861 with the repeal of the death penalty for sodomy. Rather it was another – albeit important – step in a gradual and hard-fought movement towards greater acceptance. And it was not all forward progress: in 1988, the promotion of homosexuality by local authorities was banned. It took fourteen years to repeal the infamous Section 28. It was nine years after they were granted the right to a civil partnership that same-sex couples were accepted into the institution of marriage.

This progress has only been possible through the leadership of individuals and organisations working together to create a society in which everyone can be themselves, and where everyone is included. And inclusion is at the core of Tate's mission. Our role is to reflect the nation in the diversity of the artists and art forms we display, the teams we employ and the audiences we engage. It is therefore absolutely right that we should take a prominent role by putting on this exhibition.

Our ability to bring together a collection of queer British art and to expose our audience to a once taboo topic demonstrates the progress made in the last fifty years. But the fact that this is the first exhibition of its kind shows that society has yet to fully accept LGBTQ+ culture. Until it has, Tate will continue to lead.

Lord Browne of Madingley
Chairman, Tate

DIRECTOR'S FOREWORD

Tate Britain is proud to mark the fiftieth anniversary of the Sexual Offences Act, 1967, with the first exhibition to explore over a century of queer British art. Beginning in 1861, when the death penalty for sodomy was abolished, this landmark show reflects gay and lesbian identities, and 'queer' experience more broadly. It reveals how this experience – often necessarily concealed or disguised – belongs to the mainstream of British art history, as well as some of its more fascinating margins. The exhibition touches on Pre-Raphaelitism and English impressionism, *fin-de-siècle* aestheticism and Bloomsbury Group modernism, surrealism and neo-romanticism, pop and kinetic art.

We now live in a society in which sexual difference is at least officially recognised, if not always accepted. In the past few decades LGBTQ+ artists have made a prominent contribution to the development of contemporary art, as major collections of contemporary art attest. *Queer British Art* offers a pre-history of this queer present, one that is in part necessarily speculative: many of the artists featured we know were gay, others we think may have been, while others almost certainly weren't. Nevertheless each work in the exhibition speaks in some way or other to the experience of sexual difference. The use of the word 'queer' in the title aims to capture the diversity and ambiguity of its artist-protagonists. Once a pejorative, the communities against which it was used have since reclaimed and transformed it into an expression of affirmation and self-empowerment. Its intentionally anachronistic use in the exhibition title suggests how excavating these hidden histories can help us better understand our present.

Queer British Art is as much a human history as it is an art history, and its emotional terrain is as varied as the artistic tendencies it encompasses: we are taken through scenes of isolation as well as community, of love and longing, tragedy and comedy, melancholy and defiance, lust and romance, and of intimacy and spectacle. Art and life merge. *Queer British Art*, likewise, is more than an exhibition; it is a celebration of a social and legal turning point, and also over 100 years of queer creativity.

My first thanks and congratulations go to Clare Barlow, Assistant Curator, British Art 1750–1830, for a meticulously researched, innovative and heartfelt exhibition. Amy Concannon, Assistant Curator, British Art 1790–1850, worked with Clare on the curation and organisation of the exhibition, and Eleanor Jones, AHRC Collaborative Doctoral Partnership student, offered further assistance.

I would like to thank our colleagues across Tate, who have contributed to making the exhibition a success, in particular our LGBTQ+ network from whose discussions the original idea arose, and who have been an unfailing source of help and support to their colleagues. Thanks also to Jack Halberstam, Colin Cruise, Laura Doan, Joseph Bristow, Neil Bartlett, Neil McKenna, Kobena Mercer, Caroline Gonda, Linsey Young, Andrew Stephenson, Gerard Hastings, Ilsa Colsell, Dominic Janes, Rupert Smith and Catherine Howe for enriching this publication with their insightful scholarship.

Exhibitions on this scale rely on the interest and generosity of a great many lenders and supporters: we owe all who have kindly assisted a sincere debt of gratitude. *Queer British Art* has been made possible by the provision of insurance through the Government Indemnity Scheme, for which we are grateful to HM Government and the Department for Culture, Media and Sport and Arts Council England for arranging the indemnity. We would also like to thank the Paul Mellon Centre for funding and hosting a research seminar at the early stages of the exhibition's development and the Queer British Art Exhibition Supporters Circle and Tate Patrons for their kind and generous support. Finally, we would like to express our gratitude to members of the public, particularly the LGBTQ+ community, whose feedback has helped shaped the project. Tate Britain is honoured to participate in the celebration of this milestone in British social history.

Alex Farquharson
Director, Tate Britain

ACKNOWLEDGEMENTS

We are grateful to everyone who has assisted with this show. Firstly, we would like to thank the many private lenders, who have kindly shared their artworks and their expertise with us. We are also grateful to our colleagues in other institutions who have loaned works and shared insights from their research. Particular thanks are due to Mark Aston, Victoria Avery, Darren Clarke, Patrick Elliott, Clare Freestone, Barbara Fuchs, Adrian George, Hope Kingsley, Simon Martin, Simon McCallum, Fiona McKellar, Ellen McAdam, Neil Parkinson, David Pratt, Paul Rousseau, Nina Schneider, Simon Sladen, Duncan Walker and Melanie Unwin. The exhibition has also benefited from many discussions with members of the public and organisations including Stonewall, Opening Doors, Rukus! and Pride In London. Many thanks to all.

I am personally indebted to Andrew Stephenson, who has supported me every step of the way with his wisdom, advice and encouragement. I am grateful to Neil Bartlett, Joseph Bristow, Ilsa Colsell, Colin Cruise, Laura Doan, Caroline Gonda, Gerard Hastings, Catherine Howe, Dominic Janes, Eleanor Jones, Neil McKenna, Kobena Mercer, Rupert Smith and Linsey Young for their contributions to this book. Thanks are also due to Martin Beisly, Lorna Booth, Guy Burch, Ian Collins, Whitney Davis, Hilary Fraser, James Gardiner, Roy Gluckstein, James Gordon, Michael Hatt, Charles Hart, Paul Heber-Percy, Thomas Holman, Reina Lewis, Robert Peden, Terence Pepper, Ian Massey, Richard Meyer, Simon Moretti, Sarah Moss, Richard Riley, Leon Robinson, Richard Selby, Matt Smith, Kim Thomas, Jon Lys Turner, Mark Turner, Simon Wilson and Viktor Wynd and all at the Paul Mellon Centre, particularly Mark Hallett and Sarah Turner.

At Tate, my PhD student Eleanor Jones and Assistant Curator Amy Concannon have my heartfelt thanks. I am also grateful to Catherine Howe, CHASE fellow, and Juliette Wallace, who assisted as intern. Thanks are also due to Alex Farquharson, Penelope Curtis, Alison Smith, Martin Myrone, Andrew Wilson, Chris Stephens and to the project teams, including Carolyn Kerr, Abi Laughton, Sara Warsama, Madeleine Keep, Emma Poulter, Emma O'Neill, Bill Jones, Mikei Hall, Juleigh Gordon-Orr, Andy Sheil, the conservators and the art installation team. Finally, a huge debt of gratitude is owed to Tate's LGBTQ+ network, particularly Alex Pilcher, Vilma Nikolaidou, and Emma Green.

Clare Barlow
Assistant Curator, British Art 1750–1830, Tate

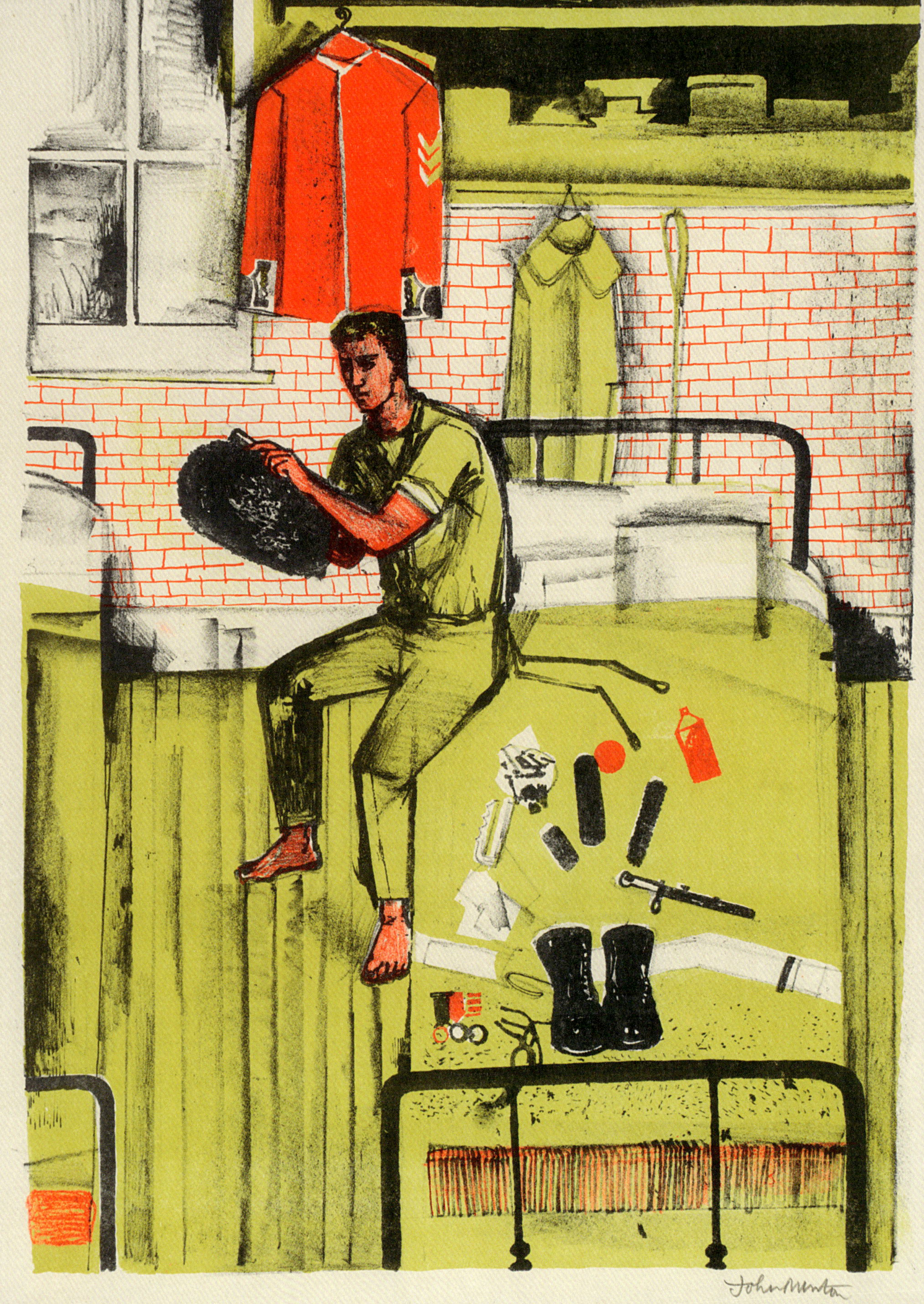

INTRODUCTION

CLARE BARLOW

John Minton 1917–57

Horseguards in their
Dressing Rooms at
Whitehall 1953

Lithograph on paper
42.3 x 30
Tate. Purchased 1990

In 1953, John Minton (1917–57) made *Horseguards in their Dressing Rooms at Whitehall* (opposite), one in a series of prints that was commissioned by the Royal College of Art to mark the coronation of Queen Elizabeth II. Unlike other representations of guardsmen in this series, Minton depicts a young guardsman in barracks, sitting on the side of his bed to brush his bearskin headdress in a scene of easy domesticity. The guardsman's braces are shown trailing across the bed behind him while his bare feet give the image a striking intimacy. Such details do not, perhaps, amount to much in themselves. However, in the 1950s, off-duty guardsmen had a widespread reputation as being willing participants in what historian Matt Houlbrook has described as 'an institutionalised erotic trade'. It is therefore hardly surprising that the War Office's memorandum to the Committee on Homosexual Offences and Prostitution stated 'persons afflicted with homosexual tendencies are strongly attracted towards soldiers ... particularly [those] of the physical requirements and standards of deportment required by the Guards'. Minton was himself attracted to men and had many casual erotic encounters of his own. In this context the intimacy of this scene and the potentially fetishistic range of objects laid out on the bed, including the prominently displayed boots, what appears to be a truncheon, and a tube of some unspecified product, might well take on a more erotic significance in the eyes of certain informed viewers. Such an interpretation of the image would have been accessible only to those who were open to it: the work appears to have passed the Royal College of Art's commissioners without comment. Yet awareness of the diverse cultural meanings of guardsmen in this period has the power to transform how we interpret the image and the insight it offers into the past, moving it from being a somewhat bland official commission into something transgressive and potentially far more personal.

Such are the possibilities of queer interpretations: readings of bodies and objects that foreground connections with same-sex or gender-variant desires, lives, cultures, identities or perspectives. Interpretations of this kind have often been excluded from the history of art or squeezed to its margins. In contrast, this book offers the chance to see what happens when such interpretations are given centre stage. What possibilities open up? What new understandings are gained? What new connections or themes emerge? What new questions are we prompted to ask? In this context, it should be stated that the queer readings offered here are not the only possible approaches. As with Minton's guardsman, objects can be read in a number of different ways, meaning, of course, that it is perfectly possible

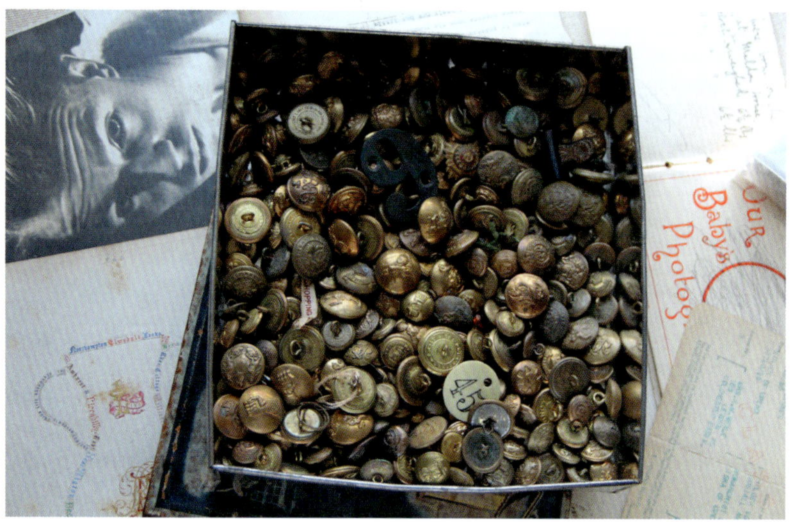

to look at these artworks without considerations of gender or sexuality crossing your mind. Ultimately, it is up to you, the viewer, to decide whether or not the queer interpretations that the authors of this volume have proposed add to your appreciation or understanding of the works illustrated. You may feel that in some cases the possible queerness has been overstated or, alternatively, you may come up with your own innovative queer interpretations that go beyond anything that has previously been imagined. This book is published to accompany an exhibition that is the first to tell this story for British art. As such, the selection of artists and works should not be interpreted as a definitive canon – this would, in any case, be somewhat counter-intuitive, given the expansive, playful and, at times, transgressive nature of queerness. Rather, this is a step towards a conversation, presenting a number of objects that have been considered to hold queer meanings in a range of different ways by certain people at certain times.

'For me, to use the word "queer" is a liberation; it was a word that frightened me, but no longer', wrote the artist and film director Derek Jarman (1942–94). Jarman's words have been one of the key starting points for our thinking about the narrative of this book. The past contains many stories of the oppression of gay, lesbian, bisexual, trans and other related identities (LGBTQ+). This book begins in 1861 with the abolition of the death penalty for sodomy and ends with the 1967 partial decriminalisation of male homosexuality in England and Wales, only fifty years ago. Several of the artists and subjects discussed here consequently suffered from legal persecution, including Simeon Solomon (1840–1905), Oscar Wilde (1854–1900) and Angus McBean (1904–90). Yet this is also a story about liberation – about people finding themselves and each other, about friendships and lovers, staying in and going out and, above all, about a community developing its distinctive voice.

As Jarman's words suggest, 'queer' as an umbrella term for same-sex desire and gender-variant identities has a complex history. If this book addressed identities today, 'queer' would sit alongside other terms such as 'gay', 'lesbian', 'bisexual', 'trans' and 'asexual' but these words either did not exist or were not

These buttons were collected by the artists Denis Wirth-Miller and Richard ('Dickie') Chopping (opposite) as mementos of their liaisons with guardsmen, who were stationed near their home in Wivenhoe, Essex. Private collection

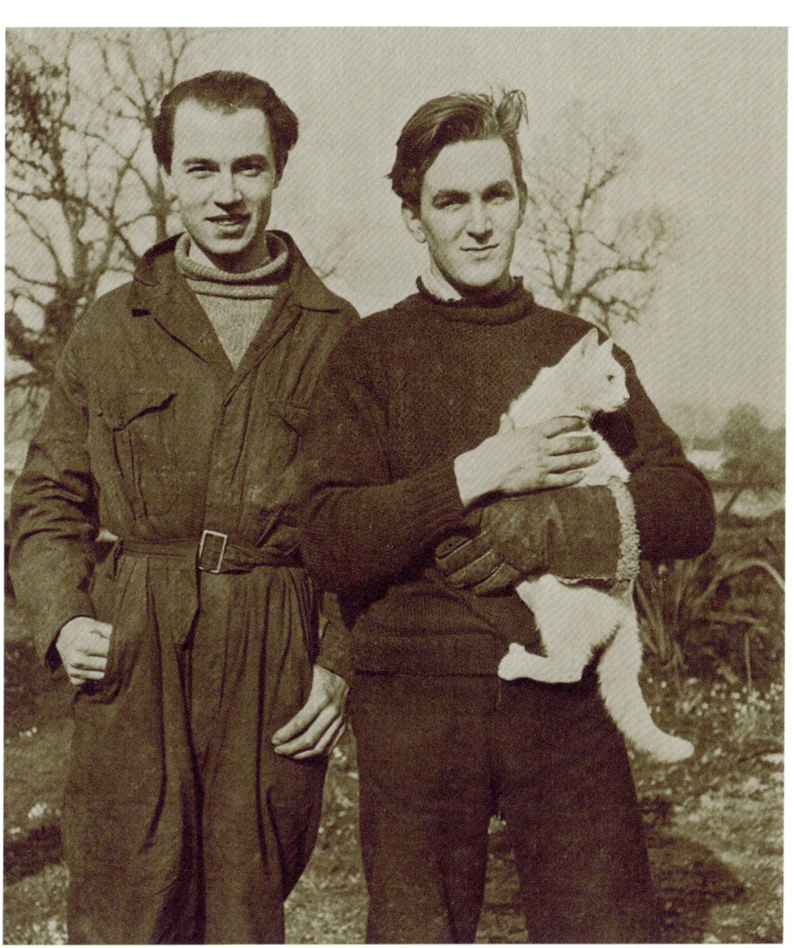

Artists Denis Wirth-Miller (1915–2010) and Richard ('Dickie') Chopping (1917–2008). The couple met in 1937 and celebrated their civil partnership in 2005. Private collection

widely recognised for most of the period explored here. Alongside its original meaning of 'strange' or 'eccentric', queer was initially used as a term for people in same-sex relationships in the 1890s, around the same time that the medical term 'homosexual' entered the lexicon. It was often an insult although there are examples of it being used in more positive ways. Fred 'Jester' Barnes (1885–1938), notorious for his relationships with men, sang in his 1907 hit 'The Black Sheep of the Family', 'It's a queer, queer world we live in and Dame Nature plays a funny game, / Some get all the sunshine, others get the shame.' Was this a deliberate double entendre or simply an example of the other meaning of queer, meaning 'odd'? By this point, both interpretations would have been possible. The long history of queer being employed as an insult contributed to its reclamation in the 1970s and 1980s, as a badge of protest. In the early 1990s, Queer Theory began to emerge, pioneered by scholars such as Judith Butler (b.1956) and Eve Sedgwick (1950–2009), influenced in part by the writings of Michel Foucault (1926–84). Their work radically critiqued concepts of gender and sexual identity, and suggested new methodologies that privileged transgression, subversion and the unsettling of established norms.[1] More recently, queer has been adopted as an elastic term, which encompasses a spectrum of identities and approaches that are not straight and/or that do not conform to what are sometimes regarded as traditional models of gender difference.

Some historians of sexuality and scholars in Queer Studies have argued that the inclusive imprecision of queer is helpful and empowering. The term queer foregrounds non-conforming sexualities and gender identities but avoids imposing identity labels on people that they themselves would not recognise and have not chosen. Many people in the past developed nuanced understandings of their identities that do not fit easily into modern categories. One example is the couple who were born Edith Cooper (1862–1913) and Katherine Bradley (1846–1914) but who took the single name Michael Field, creating an identity that sat at a crossroads between gender, sexuality and, somewhat surprisingly, professional authorship. Michael Field were lovers who often (but not exclusively) used male pronouns to refer to themselves. They were also successful poets who presented co-authorship as a fundamental aspect of their relationship (see p.63). Acknowledging the queerness of this identity allows us to consider its complexities without trying to define it further. Even in examples where an identity might initially look familiar, as in the case of Radclyffe Hall (1880–1943), there are dangers in making too swift an association across time. It can be very tempting to ignore the radical shifts in the ways gender and sexuality were understood so as to reassure ourselves that there were people like us in the past. However, as Laura Doan's essay (pp.48–53) in this volume argues, there may be advantages to setting this viewpoint aside, allowing us to appreciate approaches to sexuality and gender identity that are radically different from our own.

In addition to complex identities, there are also many people and relationships about which little is known for certain. The 'smoking gun' letter or diary, saying who did what to whom, and what they thought about it, is incredibly rare. Few couples in straight relationships left such accounts, so it is perhaps somewhat unfair to expect them from people in same-sex relationships, who often had more to risk from exposure. Sometimes this absence of evidence has been used as a justification to present everyone in the past as straight and cis (non-trans) unless 'proven' otherwise. This approach makes the fundamental error of assuming that the queer and the not-queer are closed categories that do not intermesh, ignoring the multifaceted ways in which even otherwise straight lives might be tinged with queerness. In the case of nineteenth-century women, for example, research by Sharon Marcus (b.1966) has shown that moments of queer eroticism can be found in such surprising places as *The Englishwoman's Domestic Magazine*, a publication aimed at middle-class housewives.[2] Here, letters to the editor on the subject of whipping one's maidservant were clearly regarded as sufficiently racy by some enterprising entrepreneurs to be copied and reproduced verbatim in contemporaneous pornography.

Women's relations with one another were never subject to the same legal scrutiny as those between men, allowing many women to forge intimate bonds, some of which were expressed sexually. Rather than trying to shine torch beams into the bedrooms of the past, it is perhaps more productive to consider such relationships on their own terms. Take, for example, Ethel Sands (1873-1962) and Nan (Anna Hope) Hudson (1869-1957), who lived together for most of their adult lives in France and England, loved each other and yet remained outside heterosexual norms of marriage. While we do not know whether or not there was a sexual dimension to this relationship, a queer interpretation of their work could simply be one that foregrounds the close bond between them and explores its impact on their paintings (pp.105, 107). Rather than trying to pin down the precise identities of the artists, sitters and collectors who are represented in this book, we have instead tried to describe their lives in all their messy emotional complexity.

This approach has the additional advantage of allowing us to bring into view a greater range of relationships than the clearly sexual. Sex is a powerful bond, and it is appropriate to include some erotic material and objects that connect to sexual relationships. Nonetheless, sex is not the only facet of queer identity. Other forms of community can be equally important, not least by providing a network of personal, professional and emotional support. For example, the network of queer artists who gathered around Peter Watson (1908-56), a leading collector and one of the founders of the Institute of Contemporary Arts, included Francis Bacon (1909-92), John Craxton (1922-2009), Robert Colquhoun (1914-62) and Robert MacBryde (1913-66). Within the Bloomsbury Group, the relationship between Dora Carrington (1893-1932) and Lytton Strachey (1880-1932) was the most important bond in each of their lives, towering in significance in comparison with their love affairs. By looking beyond simply the sexual evidence or erotic motivations, it is possible to enrich our understanding of these artists' work, their influences and achievements (p.106).

Of course, having a direct connection to the sexuality or gender identity of the artist is only one possible way in which works of art can be queer. 'When correctly viewed / everything is lewd' sang Tom Lehrer (b.1928) in his 1965 song 'Smut', and the same might be said of the potential queerness of individual works of art, which can snap into focus at certain times for certain viewers and then fall from view again before a different audience. There is little reason to think, for example, that Walter Crane (1845-1915) intended *The Renaissance of Venus* 1877 (p.43) to be a queer work. However, Crane's use of the male model Alessandro di Marco for Venus caused the artist's contemporary, W. Graham Robertson (1866-1948), to offer what looks to modern eyes remarkably like a queer reading of the painting: 'Crane's goddess showed a blending of the sexes which was mystically correct but anatomically surprising. Still she was a fine, upstanding slip of a boy, and... she passed for Venus pleasantly enough.'[3] As in this example, queer interpretations of works sometimes draw on specific contextual knowledge or depend on particular cultural contexts. It may, for example, be difficult for us to recapture exactly why Claude Phillips responded with such confusion to Laura Knight's (1877-1970) 'Self-portrait' of 1913 (pp.122-23), depicting Knight painting a nude model, or why *The National Review* thought that Duncan Grant's (1885-1978) *Bathing* 1911 (p.99) would have such a 'degenerative' effect on the students at the Borough Polytechnic, London. Conversely, we may wonder why Evelyn De Morgan's

(1855–1919) repeated paintings of Jane Hales (1851–1926), whom she often depicted nude and bound, did not arouse more comment at the time (p.37). Queerness is an unstable category and can be rooted in particular contextual frameworks. As those frameworks change or knowledge of them is lost, artworks can acquire or lose a queer significance that was not part of their original conception.

Alongside queer readings that draw on particular social or biographical contexts, scholars such as the American writer and political activist Susan Sontag (1933–2004) have suggested ways in which it might be possible to explore the concept of queer aesthetics. Sontag's *Notes on Camp* (1964) sets out some of the features of camp, which is perhaps the best-known form of this queer sensibility: 'texture, sensuous surface, and style at the expense of content'.[4] Her definition offers a possible way of interpreting, for example, the complex fantasies of Cecil Beaton's (1904–80) photographs, such as *Stephen Tennant as Prince Charming* 1927 (p.66), which invites interpretation as a study in gender non-conformity. The playfully subversive possibilities of such images are perhaps all the more striking given that Beaton operated at the heart of the establishment, photographing high society for publications such as *Vogue*. Yet camp style was not the sole preserve of the social elite: another example might be found in the intricate collaged covers created by working-class playwright Joe Orton (1933–67) and his partner, artist Kenneth Halliwell (1926–67), for books that they borrowed from Islington libraries and, in the eyes of Islington Council, defaced (pp.156–7). Orton and Halliwell explicitly delighted in the transgressive – and illegal – nature of their project and waited to watch the reactions of the library patrons who unwittingly picked up one of their altered books. While both Beaton's photographs and Orton and Halliwell's collages can also be interpreted contextually, perhaps through the sitters' biographies in the case of Beaton, or by tracing specific references to queer culture in Halliwell and Orton's choice of images, the whole in each case can be regarded as queerer than the sum of its parts.

Camp is not, of course, the only possible signifier of a queer aesthetic. While some of Edward Burra's (1905–76) depictions of the seedy underbelly of urban life verge on campness, others have a somewhat different emotional impact. Excess and performance can be found in the exaggerated masked figures in *Soldiers at Rye* 1941 (pp.140–1), for example, yet the military mood of the painting is more one of suppressed menace than playful humour. Equally, it is possible to view John Craxton's lithe Arcadian fantasy in *Pastoral for P.W.* 1948 (p.142) or the sense of melancholy and vulnerability that seems to pervade Keith Vaughan's (1912–77) *Kouros* 1960 (pp.132, 145) as queer in altogether quieter ways. The emotional register of a painting is to some extent subjective. Nonetheless, these images are open to queer interpretations that depend as much on sensibility as on subject matter.

Given the flexibility of queer, it is perhaps unsurprising that it has been difficult to decide what to leave out. Just as art objects can be open to queer interpretations without having been made by a queer artist, so too there are artists who lived queer lives but whose artworks and artistic practices do not readily seem to connect to queer cultures, identities or experiences. Queer readings of such artworks may yet emerge. However, for now, given the limitations of space, it is hard to justify including such works at the expense of other material, the queerness of which is more easily identified.

There are also many identities that we would have liked to represent but for which little if any visual material appears to still exist. The history of queer culture is punctuated by dustbins and bonfires – much has been deliberately destroyed or simply unpreserved. Over the course of our research, we have come across numerous objects that have survived due to a remarkable series of coincidences or chance encounters: photograph albums rescued from junk shops by eagle-eyed collectors, drawings and negatives that have been smuggled out of the house of a dying lover before a family can arrive to scour away any evidence of a life that was less than fully heterosexual. Yet despite such extraordinary successes, we have been constantly frustrated by the comparative scarcity of material relating to intersectional identities: working-class queer lives, queer people of colour, trans and genderqueer identities, even queer women artists. It is not clear in many cases whether such sources never existed, have ceased to exist or whether, tantalisingly, they may yet be out there, hidden from view, perhaps lying uncatalogued and awaiting rediscovery. Wherever possible we have tried to seek out and include material that connects to some of these experiences, however partial or, as Kobena Mercer's piece (pp.102–103) discusses, problematic it may be. It remains our profound hope that more objects and information will emerge in the future as further research is carried out in this area.

Despite such caveats, this book offers an extraordinary breadth of perspectives, as artists, designers, sitters and collectors across the century began to explore their identities in new and exciting ways. Sometimes, this process was painful: Keith Vaughan agonised over his desires and their possible legibility in his paintings. Sometimes it was complicated: the designer Charles Ashbee (1863–1942) revealed to his future wife that he had hitherto only loved men but reassured her that 'there may be many comrade friends' (his term for his male lovers) 'but there can be only one comrade wife'.[5] Yet at other times it was liberating. Michael Field gained public recognition as partners and as poets. The artist Gluck (1895–1978) rejected the name 'Hannah Gluckstein' to adopt an identity with 'no prefix, [no] suffix' and held exhibitions at the Fine Art Society that were attended by members of the royal family.[6] Together, these examples hint at the remarkable range not only of identities but also of experiences and outcomes in this period. The old trope of queer people in the past leading tragic and isolated lives can no longer be sustained. Instead, the objects in this book point to a past that is richer, stranger and more diverse than we could have possibly imagined.

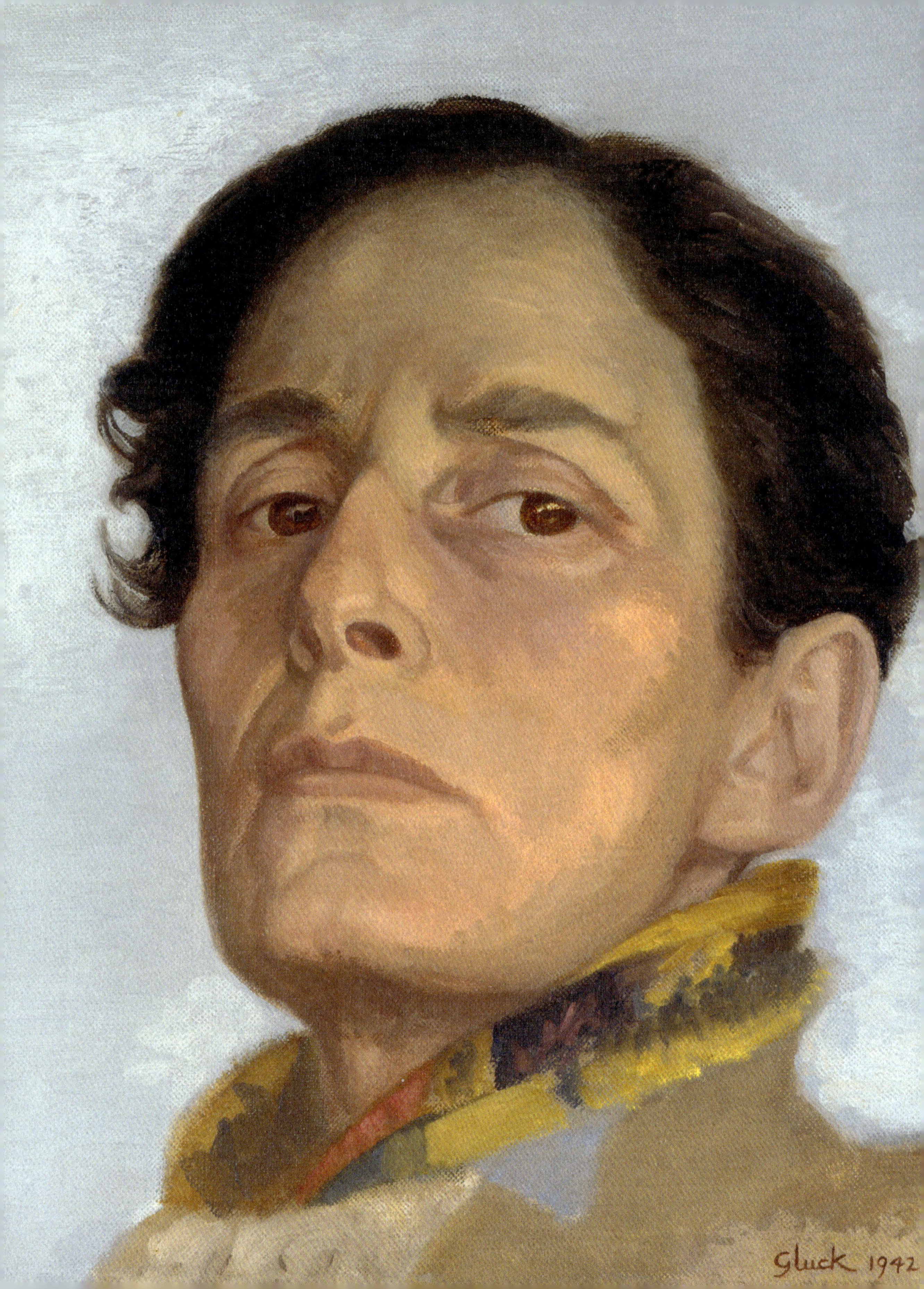

Gluck 1942

FRAMING QUEER BRITISH ART

JACK HALBERSTAM

Gluck 1895–1978

Self-portrait 1942

Oil on canvas

30.6 x 25.4

National Portrait Gallery,

London

IN AN ESSAY on the role of women in picture framing in England from the 1620s onwards, Jacob Simon, a Research Fellow at the National Portrait Gallery in London, presents an overview of the interventions of women into the otherwise mostly male activity of handcrafting frames.[1] While many of the women who were involved with picture framing played the predictable role of helpmate to their artist husbands, some seemed to use it as a springboard to other activities that were also uncommon for women at the time. For example, Hilda Herbert (later Hilda Hewlett, 1864–1943), who built a frame for William Holman Hunt's (1827–1910) *The Light of the World* c.1900–4, became the first British woman aviator to win a pilot's licence and, after separating from her husband in 1914, went on to found a 'successful aircraft manufacturing business'.

Once a queer frame on framing has come into view, many other secret histories embedded in Simon's account can be glimpsed. A story about Katharine Furse (1875–1952) (daughter of the famously gay John Addington Symonds, 1840–1893), also a talented framer, quickly gives way to a narrative about Furse as an explicitly masculine woman who, after her husband died, became the director of the Women's Royal Naval Service.

By the time of the Bloomsbury period, the art of framing has become decisively and explicitly queer and this queer orientation culminates in the work of British artist Gluck (1895–1978), who used framing so prominently that a mode of framing has been named after her (opposite). The Gluck frame, as it is now known, was painted and constructed not to hold and emphasise the art as much as to situate it uniquely in relation to the architecture of the room within which it appeared. Gluck frequently painted her frames to match the walls upon which they hung and to accentuate the continuities between frames and walls. Simon does not mention that Gluck was a masculine woman who never used her female name, and who conducted her relationships with other women openly and without shame or embarrassment throughout the early twentieth century. We can use his history of female framers to offer a queer frame for a longer, queerer history of British art.

This queer history of framing reminds us of the multiple histories of queer art making that have gone unannounced and untold within various accounts of nineteenth- and twentieth-century art. *Queer British Art 1861–1967* neatly wraps a temporal frame of 100 years around the production of art by lesbians, gay men and transgender artists and, in the process, it offers a glimpse into a set of visual themes, codes, motifs and formal strategies with which queer artists painted themselves into history. While some of the nineteenth-century pieces launch their homoerotic imagery using classical figures like Sappho, other work merges its queer content, as Gluck does later on, with the creation of new materials. The sculptor Harriet Hosmer (1830-1908), for example, pioneered innovative methods for producing sculptural moulds and worked out how to turn sandstone into marble. Other artists, such as Keith Vaughan (1912-1977) and Edward Burra (1905-1976), used gouache or opaque painting to capture the layered quality of queer life in the middle of the twentieth century (pp.138-41).

As one might expect, much of the early work by gay men in the book involves the male nude. Henry Scott Tuke's (1858-1929) gorgeous oil paintings of male bathers (opposite, pp.46-7) provide a homoerotic take on impressionist classics such as Georges Seurat's (1859-1891) *Bathers at Asnières* 1884, but they sit more uneasily alongside the male nudes figured in photographs by Wilhelm von Gloeden (1856-1931), which have an orientalist feel to them (pp.29, 42). The male nude appears repeatedly: in Duncan Grant's (1885-1978) *Bathers by the Pond* 1920 (p.98) and in Edward Wolfe's (1897-1982) portraits (p.103); in the work of Christoper Wood (opposite) and of Burra; in Eadweard Muybridge's (1830-1904) *Two Wrestlers* c.1887 (p.161); and in Francis Bacon's (1909-92) blurry studies (pp.158, 164-5).

Other portraits by gay men and lesbians focus on famous figures such as Oscar Wilde (1854-1900), Havelock Ellis (1859-1939), Radclyffe Hall (1880-1943) and members of the Bloomsbury Group (pp.48, 54, 61). This gay history of painting well-known figures or else naked and semi-naked same-sex groups gives way later in the century, in the work of Vaughan most remarkably, to more abstract representations of some of the same topics. For example, Vaughan has a painting titled *Bather: August 4th 1961* (p.145), but the rippling bodies of young men bathed in sunlight and watching each other across water, which also featured in Tuke's work, appear in Vaughan's astonishing paintings, such as *Three Figures* 1960 (p.145), as blocks of colour, fragmented by contact with each other's bodies and shrouded from view by the dark clothing that turns the two figures in the background into silhouetted forms. The one figure in the light has his back to us and, while we see his naked form from behind, the painting does not give the impression of an artist glorying in the male body as much as of a model trying to hide from our gaze. Vaughan later became known for the diaries he kept from the age of twenty-seven in 1939 to the day of his death by suicide on 4 November 1977. These diaries record a bleak vision of life and death, a vision we find in the paintings, alongside lengthy descriptions of the elaborate sado-masochistic practices in which he engaged.

An intriguing queer aesthetic that runs throughout the book concerns studies of interiors, still life, flowers and landscapes. The covert glances at bodies constitute an obvious and manifest thread but the casting of queerness as a relation to furniture, flower arranging, dance, night, journeying, war and solitude offers a more nuanced account of queer looking, queer presence and absence,

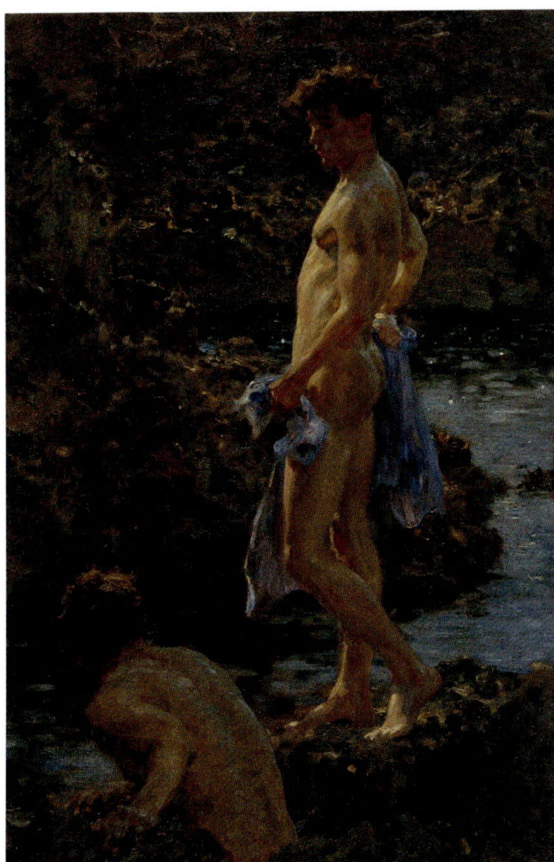

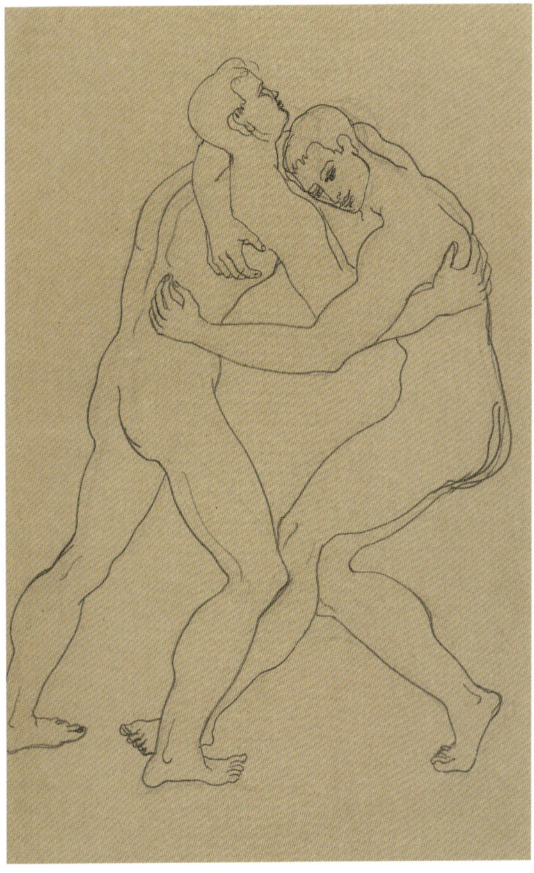

Henry Scott Tuke

1858–1929

A Bathing Group 1914

Oil on canvas

90.2 x 59.7

Royal Academy of Arts,

London

Christopher Wood

1901–30

The Wrestlers c.1920–30

Graphite on paper

43.2 x 27.3

Private collection

and queer relations to nature and culture. For example, the mottled masterpiece *The Chintz Couch* c.1910–11 (p.22) by Ethel Sands (1873–1962) seems at first sight to be a quiet image of interior design, perhaps a metaphor for the domestic realm, or an index of what we are surrounded by everyday without seeing. However, when it is placed in a queer genealogy the painting comes to life in a very different way.

Like many of the women featured here from the first half of the twentieth century, Sands was born into a wealthy family and used that wealth to travel, study art and paint. She lived for most of her life with another woman, Anna Hope Hudson (1869–1957), also a painter, and both women were good friends with Virginia Woolf (1882–1941). The work of Sands is particularly striking. Focusing mainly on interiors (Hudson tended to paint exteriors, p.107), Sands manages to capture an odd quality of light in the rooms she depicts. In *The Chintz Couch* light from an unseen window creates a jagged scar across the domestic façade and offers a reminder of what is missing, namely the female figure itself. The painting evokes both a dusty past and the dawning of a new day as the light filters into the shuttered room and inscribes itself upon the patterned fabric. Vanessa Bell (1879–1961), however, was critical of Sands's work and when Sands and Hudson were nominated to be part of the Omega Workshops, founded by Roger Fry

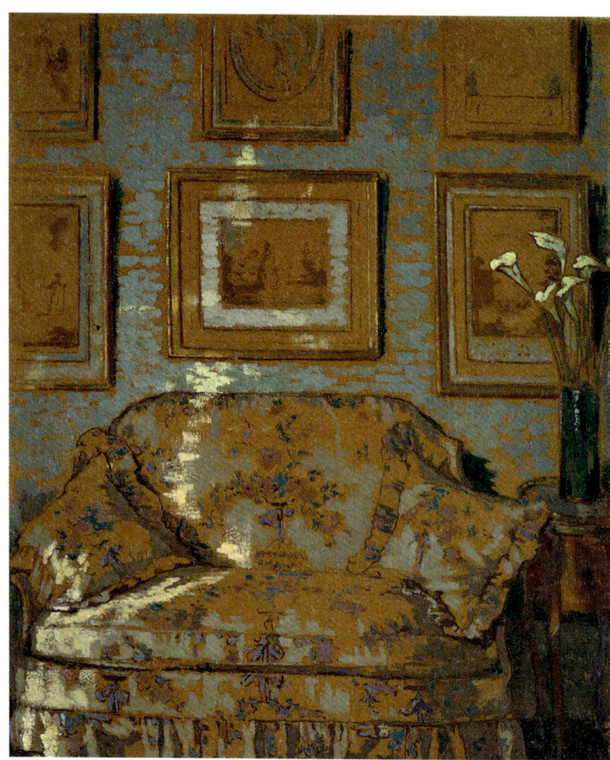

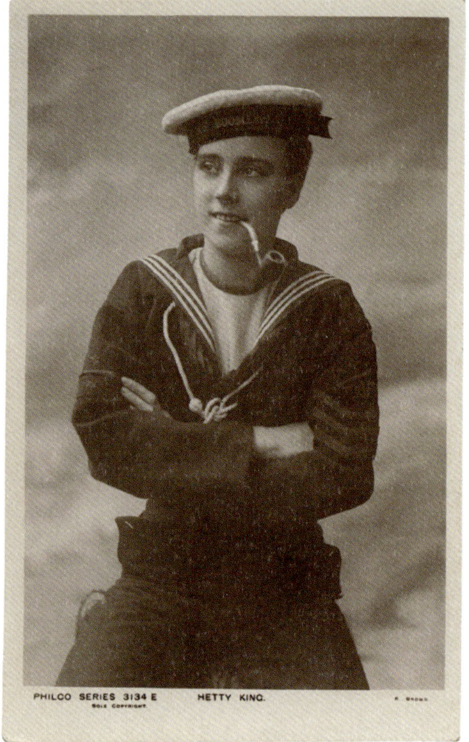

(1866–1934) to challenge the separation of fine arts from crafts, Bell accused Sands in particular of indulging in 'fatal prettiness'. The rooms that Sands painted, though, are far more than a celebration of the decorative: they are rather, like Gluck's work – her frames and her paintings of flowers (p.117) – a kind of deconstruction of the domestic sphere. The chintz sofa in question sits against a wall and next to a table all painted using the same colour scheme so that the sofa almost fades into the wallpaper. The artwork on the back wall, moreover, is underemphasised, forcing the viewer to see everything in the frame as 'art' – the flowers, the table, the chintz fabric, the play of light and the absence of the artist.

It is this play with outside and inside, frame and contents, the explicit and the implicit that really forms the backbone for understanding this book of queer British art. For example, the Omega Workshops sought to de-emphasise the relations between art and craft, interior design and aesthetics, and to force a much broader understanding of art upon us. This book therefore explores the queer aesthetics in jewellery making, photography, set design and theatrical props alongside the fine artwork and sculpture. A pink, hair-netted wig that once belonged to a female impersonator from the 1920s, Jimmy Slater (1898–1998) (p.90), offers a glimpse into the music hall shows given by male and female impersonators from the 1900s. A photograph of Hetty King (1883–1972) as a jaunty sailor (above) remains as evidence of King's long career in the Broadhead Circuit. Photographs of Danny La Rue (1927–2009) among others, also remind us of how central the theatre was to the emergence of queer life and art in the nineteenth and twentieth centuries (p.93).

Most of the images in *Queer British Art 1861–1967* involve white and middle- or upper-class artists or subjects. A few artists, however, depart from the stereotype of the eccentric aristocrat and try to capture impressions of the worlds that lay beyond the rarefied salons of wealthy Londoners. Burra, for example, who, like Vaughan, worked often in gouache, painted scenes from clubs in Harlem and from the Spanish Civil War; he was a frequent traveller and was drawn to night worlds and outsiders (pp.139, 140–1). Cast as reticent and elusive in a 2011 BBC documentary, 'I Never Tell Anybody Anything: The Life and Art of Edward Burra', Burra stands as a paradigmatic figure of closetedness. The documentary represents Burra as secretive and strange and therefore cannot explain the sense of nihilism, sterility, darkness and silence that animates the work. Burra was also disabled by chronic arthritis, which affected him from early childhood, and the film allows his condition to stand in for his sexuality. Rather than finding the queer vein that runs throughout Burra's imagery, the BBC documentary instead depicts his angular art as part of a congenital asexuality. The narrator goes as far as to claim that Burra once said he had only ever had one erection in his life.

This desperate desire to cast Burra as asexual despite the tremendous erotic energy that runs through his paintings allows the art critic in the documentary, Andrew Graham-Dixon, as well as Burra's biographer, Jane Stevenson, to ignore the clear homoerotic themes in all of Burra's work – whether the naked men in the war paintings or the mannish women in the nightclub and flamenco scenes. Ultimately, the programme presents Burra as just a lonely, isolated and enigmatic figure, who refused to speak about or offer interpretations of his art, and never went to his own exhibition openings.

The later work by Burra, gorgeous exploding bouquets of flowers and dynamic, boldly coloured landscapes, could easily be folded in a genealogy of queer art that focused on vegetation and the (un)natural. Situating Burra's flowers against Gluck's for example, or Andy Warhol's (1928–87) for that matter, and not to mention Ithell Colquhoun's (1906–88) extraordinary *Tree Anatomy* 1942, allows us to look beyond the figure, the nude, the portraits of famous queers. Here we begin to discern the contours of a queer aesthetic, one designed to challenge discourses of nature, to refuse easy divisions between domestic and foreign, interior and exterior, homo and hetero, and an aesthetic, moreover, as in the work of Vaughan, Bacon and Burra in particular, that is dark and critical of the human altogether.

The collecting of these artists under the heading of 'queer art' requires us to look closely at the frame – both the framing of British art that has often excluded these artists or at least omitted the fuller stories of who they are and were, but also the framing of queer art itself that can only be limited by its focus upon identifiably homosexual or perverse bodies. As Gluck showed us, the frame, like the camera lens, both holds and rejects, includes and excludes, names and damns to oblivion.

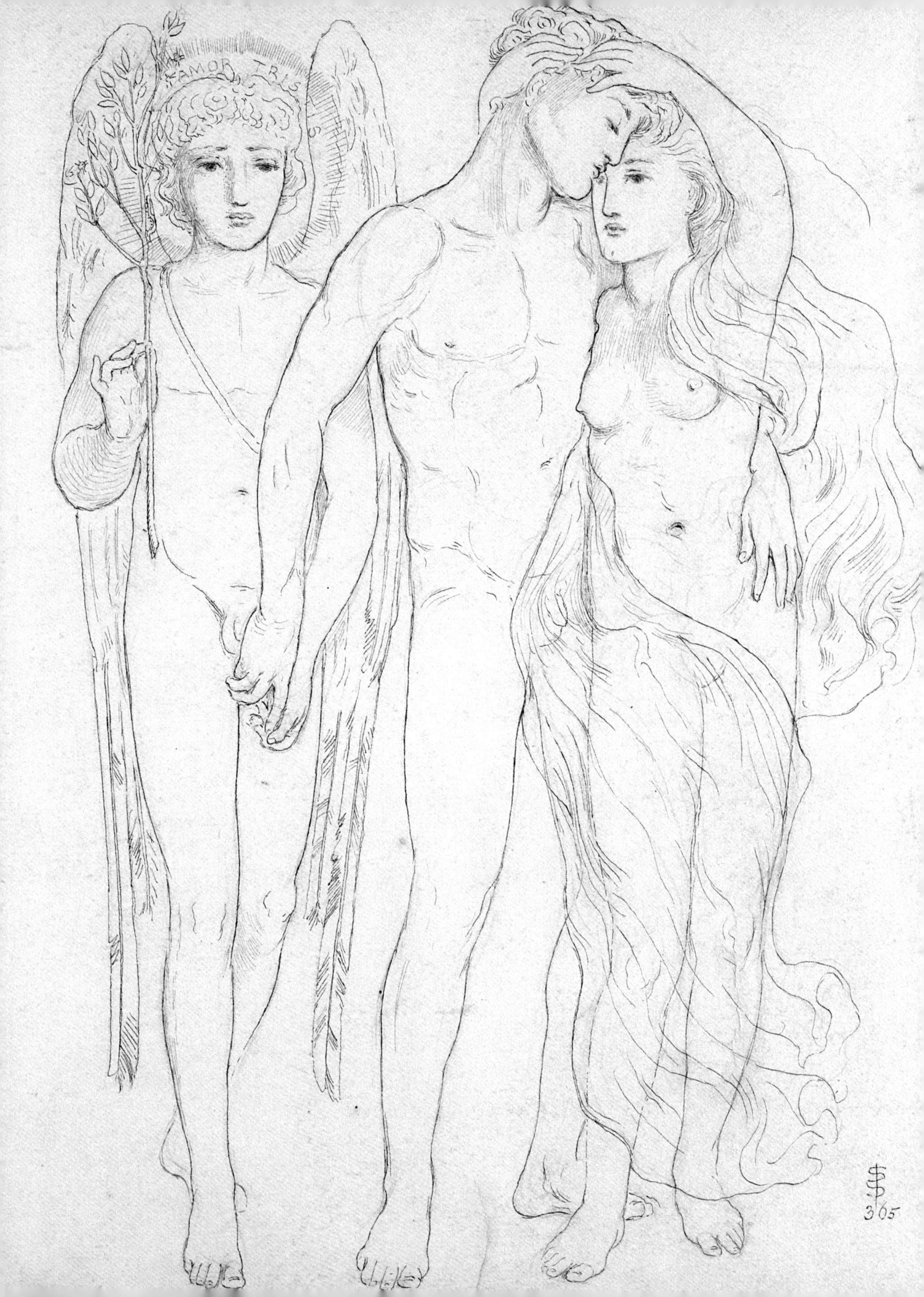

AMOR TRIS
365

CODED DESIRES
COLIN CRUISE

Simeon Solomon

1840–1905

*The Bride, Bridegroom
and Sad Love* 1865

Ink on paper

25 x 19.4

Victoria and Albert
Museum, London

RECENT HISTORIES EXAMINING the emergence of a gay identity in the nineteenth century have focused on landmark legal cases or medical discourses, tracing terminologies and questioning definitions. Yet a more informal, self-defining tendency is identifiable; it reflects a new sensibility in sexual orientation, inspired by images, derived from painting and sculpture, print and photography. Playful and serious at the same time, a heightened engagement with visual culture, art criticism and collecting helped in the construction of a shared identity for 'gay' men and women, for a kind of 'coming out' long before either of those terms was coined. Pictorial and sculptural depictions ranging from Eros to St Sebastian, from Hermes to the telegraph boy, from Sappho to Socrates, acted both as objects of desire and allegories of forbidden feelings. Beneath these images lies a discourse of 'Greek love', a defence of feeling through a display of the naked body, posed in a variety of moods.

CHALLENGING ORTHODOXIES

Following on from the Pre-Raphaelites a decade before, a new generation of painters abandoned the conventions of history and genre painting. From 1865 these younger artists found a venue in the Dudley Gallery, London where watercolour was the favoured medium. The leading exponents of the new style, Edward Burne-Jones (1833–98), Simeon Solomon (1840–1905) and Walter Crane (1845–1915), reintroduced themes derived from ancient Greek and Roman culture, adding a complex dash of Renaissance style. The result was a curious mixture of modes – classicism and medievalism – previously thought oppositional, which suggested a breakdown of categories, a decadent intermingling of styles, the 'new'. Critical reception, rarely approving, veered from puzzlement to mockery, often expressing a variety of anxieties around physical and mental health. The *Pall Mall Gazette* summed up Burne-Jones's work when shown at the Dudley in 1865: 'In style there is something seductive but it is not masculine.'[1] We can detect a more urgent fear of homosexuality in these critiques. The critic of the *Spectator* went as far as noting 'that repulsive sentiment which too frequently marks Mr. Solomon's compositions' but did not elaborate further.[2]

Solomon exhibited some of his more obviously transgressive subjects at the Dudley. *The Bride, the Bridegroom and Sad Love* 1865 (opposite) is an example of particularly difficult imagery, challenging, at once, normative masculinity, the institution of marriage and Christian morality. The gesture of the 'bridegroom' in stretching out his hand towards a winged youth – labelled *Amor Tristis*, 'Sad Love'

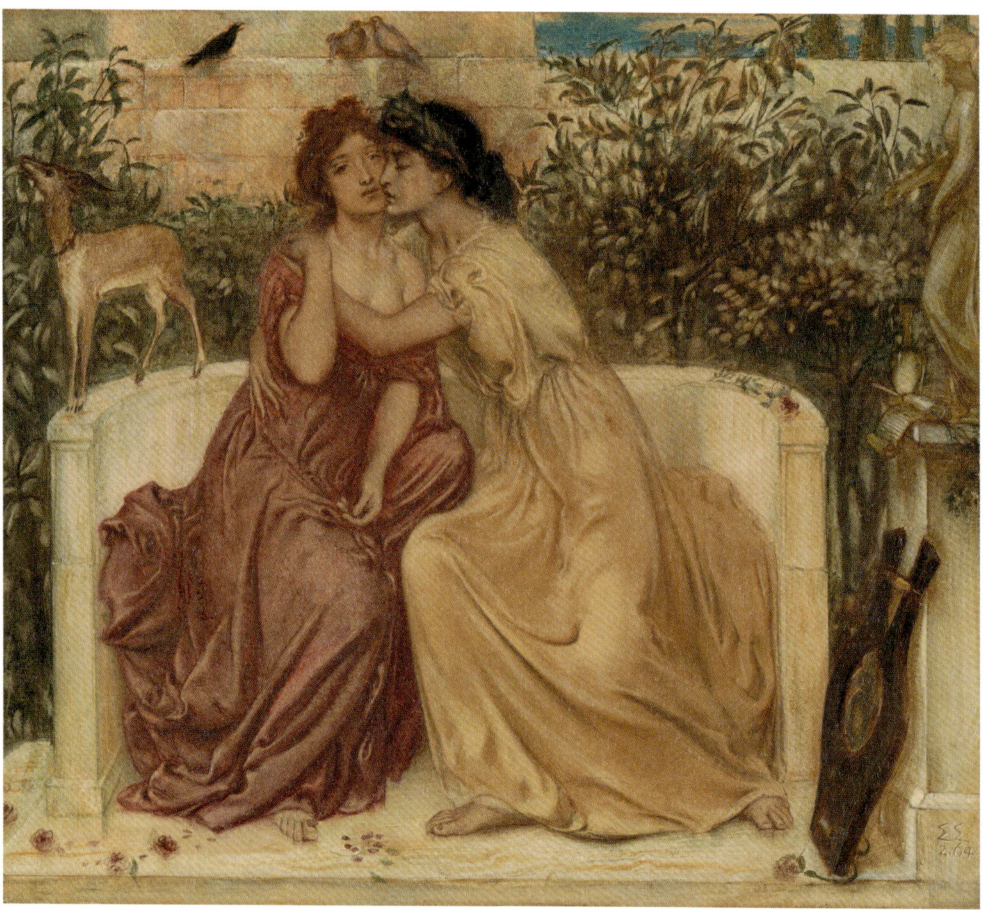

– could be read as one of dismissal, an attempt to 'push aside' a former love. It also looks as if the groom is re-engaging with an old desire, using a vulgar gesture of sexual interest – the scratching of the palm – to indicate arousal.

Narratives featuring winged figures became fashionable at this time. Frederic Leighton's (1830–96) *Daedalus and Icarus* c.1868, shown at the Royal Academy of Arts, London, in 1869, is a good example (p.38). Loosely 'classical' in style, the beauty of the young male figure is more sensual than the usual academic type. Daedalus steps aside in the process of completing his doomed engineering work, revealing his son's beauty in the process. Leighton's picture is one of the sources incorporated into *Dawn* by Solomon, shown at the Dudley in 1872 (not illustrated). The dark cloak, a striking feature of Leighton's Daedalus, becomes, for Solomon, an allegory of night falling away to reveal the morning. Solomon included a description of Dawn in his prose-poem *A Vision of Love Revealed in Sleep* (1871): '…his eyes were yet soft with the balm of Sleep, but his lips were parted with desire; …with one hand he cast away his dim and dewy mantel from him, and with the other he put aside the poppies that had clustered about him…'[3] Here, Dawn is part of a polemic defending love in all its varieties and complexities, particularly same-sex desire.

Simeon Solomon
1840–1905
Sappho and Erinna in a Garden at Mytilene 1864
Watercolour on paper
33 x 38.1
Tate. Purchased 1980

AESTHETICS AND THE HOMOEROTIC

A book of cultural history by Walter Pater (1839–94), *Studies in the History of the Renaissance* (1873), became the central text of the aesthetic movement. In essays on Michelangelo Buonarroti and Leonardo da Vinci, among other artists, it traces a tradition of European art and poetry while, at the same time, detecting a persistent inflection of same-sex desire. On Michelangelo, for example, Pater writes: 'He who spoke so decisively of the supremacy in the imaginative world of the unveiled human form had not been always, we may think, a mere Platonic lover.'[4] On Leonardo: 'Out of the secret places of a unique temperament he brought strange blossoms and fruits hitherto unknown...'[5] In beautifully modulated prose, Pater establishes a new canon, based on close reading and scrutiny, and revealing a gay sensibility in European culture. In the correspondence of the art historian Johann Joachim Winckelmann (1717–68) with his fellow scholars Pater discerns not only a love for the beauty of the sculpted human form but also the 'subtler threads of temperament'. This is a code, although not a very veiled one, for same-sex desire.

Although Pater tells us that the beauty of Greek statues is 'a sexless beauty' he claims that we find there 'a moral sexlessness, a kind of ineffectual wholeness of nature, yet with a true beauty and significance of its own.' In introducing an idea of 'moral sexlessness', Pater posits a comparative morality. The term suggests that the conditions for the realisation of the sexual morals of the past might be regained. The 'pagan' culture of the Renaissance, Pater implies, passes down into the present age through art. In an era vexed with the Christian idea of 'apostolic succession', Pater proposes a distinctively different kind of cultural continuity.

EXAMINING THE NUDE

For Pater, the experience of looking at sculpture through Winckelmann's eyes was transformative. However, there was another source for the revival of interest in both making and looking at sculpture. Leighton's practice of modelling in clay figures to assist the realisation of the painting *The Daphnephoria* c.1874 stimulated new developments in sculpture. His *Athlete Wrestling with a Python* 1877 was one of the first intimations of a renaissance in British sculpture. Hamo Thornycroft (1850–1925) responded to Leighton's teaching at the Academy schools along with his contemporaries, Alfred Gilbert (1854–1934) and Harry Bates (1850–99); they formed a distinctive group in British art, working in what became known as 'the New Sculpture', a term coined by the critic Edmund Gosse (1849–1928). Their sculptures demonstrated the potential of the male nude to represent abstract, allegorical ideas. In Thornycroft's *The Mower* c.1888–90 (p.44) a young man, pausing from work, is lost in thought. The elegant yet self-forgetting pose, strongly recalling Donatello's (1386–1466) bronze *David* c.1445, illustrates the type of internalisation of the female model characteristic of the Pre-Raphaelite painting of the 1850s. Leighton's *The Sluggard* 1886 (p.39), supposedly based on a momentary and informal pose taken up by his model, Gaetano Valvona, abandons the civic or public qualities of figurative sculpture to portray the nude both naturalistically and intimately. In the prevailing Hellenistic mood of same-sex discourse in Victorian Britain the sculpted male figure was most often envisioned as existing in a mythic past, timeless and unchanging. In presenting new and different ideas of interiority and informality, both *The Mower* and *The Sluggard* imagine a modern way of engaging with the male nude, as both erotic yet everyday. The reproduction of these sculptures as statuettes allowed collectors to develop a closer and more intimate relationship with the figures and the ideas they embodied.

One way of regaining the 'impossible love' of pagan cultures in modern times was to travel to foreign countries where different, more liberal, sexual codes were in practice. Improvements in travel and transport helped those who could afford them find forbidden love in other cultures. In the photographs of Wilhelm von Gloeden the youthful subjects are depicted as nostalgic figures from the past (opposite, p.42). Although they are souvenirs they do not remind the purchaser of locations but of encounters, actual or wished for. The togas and lyres suggest the historic through a spurious continuity; they reveal, as well as conceal, the bodies of the peasant youths, adorning their tanned bodies in a kind of charade of high culture.

The continued appeal to the classical, however, was challenged in the last decade of the nineteenth century by the growth of a less reassuring neo-paganism that embraced the pantheism of Greek culture and set itself against Christianity in the process. It incorporated 'Uranian' writers who appropriated some of the ideas of 'Greek love' into a more general, non-specific Hellenism, stressing an idealised, non-physical love of youth. A related tendency can be found in the work of the American poet Walt Whitman (1819–92) that heralded a kind of liberation from social and sexual convention. Where the Uranians championed the 'New Chivalry', Whitman seemed to promise a new democracy that might lead not only to social change but also, by necessity, to a new order of comradely feeling between men. Some of these ideas were implemented in the arts and crafts movement in Britain, particularly in the writings of Edward Carpenter (1844–1929) and in the work of C.R. Ashbee (1863–1942) (p.45). In the canvases of Henry Scott Tuke the spirit of ancient Greece is resited in Cornwall (pp.46–7). Tuke's plein-air paintings are a contemporary reflection upon what were regarded as the essential features of ancient Greek religion. In modern culture he finds continuities with antiquity through nature and the pastoral, as well as in depictions of the male body. In the assemblies of naked youths at the edge of the sea he discovers a fresh vision that allows him to free his models from the dark confines of the Antique and Life Rooms into dazzling sunlight.

What we find in the coded same-sex discourse of the nineteenth century is a rich engagement with ideas and aspirations played out through images and their interpretation. An important feature of the appeal to the classical was that it was also an appeal to what were perceived as the foundations of British civil culture: philosophy, law, morality, even aesthetics itself. However, by the end of the century a complex relation between sculpture and a notion of the 'beautiful body' is evident. Michael Hatt detects a 'connection between nudes like Leighton's and the

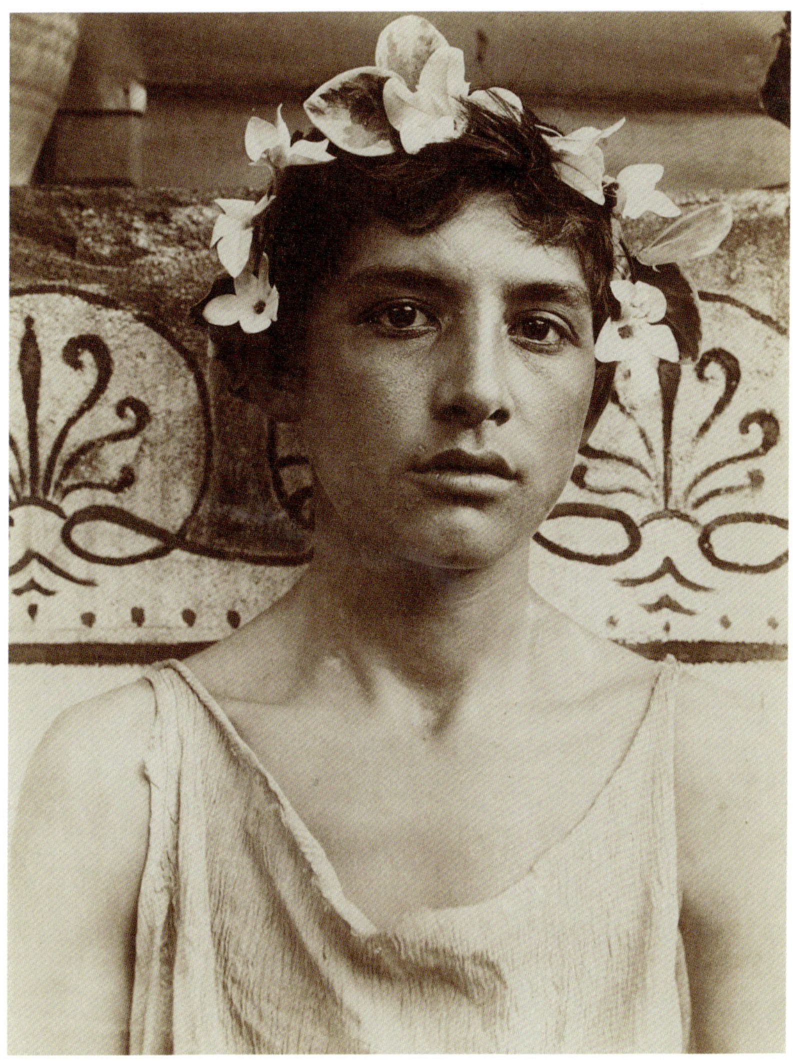

Wilhelm von Gloeden
1856–1931
Head of Sicilian Boy 1890s
Photograph, gelatin silver
print on paper
21.1 x 16.8
Victoria and Albert
Museum, London

living statue of physical culture', finding it personified in the figure of Eugene Sandow (1867–1925) at the turn of the century. Sandow was 'the great guru of health and bodily control [who] effectively turned himself into a sculpture...'[6] Sandow's exploitation of photography accords with the uses made by commercial photographers from the 1860s onwards. Their work multiplied works of fine art, as well as transcriptions of the bodies of models in various kinds of display, and was distributed to wider audiences with passions and tastes, both orthodox and unorthodox. The canon was challenged and expanded by admission of personal desire as an aid to aesthetic appreciation with some help from modern technology.

SIMEON SOLOMON

COLIN CRUISE

Simeon Solomon (1840–1905) was born in London into a well-off, assimilated Jewish business family. His early works were influenced by paintings by the Pre-Raphaelites although there was always a striking originality to his compositions. In his juvenilia, his choice of the story of David and Jonathan showed his early interest in same-sex desire. The hectic erotic atmosphere of *Babylon hath been a golden cup* 1859 (opposite) and the sexual ambiguity of the figures seem deliberately designed to puzzle and shock audiences.

Throughout the 1860s, Solomon exhibited a series of works using experimental watercolour techniques depicting youths engaged in a variety of religious rituals. They demonstrate a fascination with beauty, colour and mystery. His male figures are far removed from the academic models studied by generations of artists as the basis of their training. His pallid young men represent an inner state of longing and alienation; they are allegories of forbidden feelings. Despite critical disapproval his pictures had a cult following. Photographs of his drawings and paintings were made by Frederic Hollyer (1838–1933) and sold to discerning collectors, among them Walter Pater, John Addington Symonds and Oscar Wilde. Many appeared to have responded to Solomon's androgynous types, finding a representation of their own frustrated desires in the sadness of their faces. One of the recurring motifs of Solomon's later drawings is a tormented Medusa-like head, the face displaying emotions that suggest a disruption of the placid beauty of his other subjects, presented publicly (opposite).

At the very height of his success, in February 1873, Solomon was arrested in a public lavatory and charged with the crime of 'attempted buggery'.[7] The *Manchester Guardian* reported that 'poor Solomon' was suffering from an 'illness' and that his public career was over.[8]

The following year he was arrested and charged in Paris for 'indecent touching' in a lavatory.[9] These scandals were to prove disastrous for his reputation. In the years that followed Solomon continued to draw and paint, usually representing intensified, expressionless heads; in them, it is easy to see a trope for a sexual conundrum still being worked through into a new century. As Arthur Symons observed, 'they have the sorrow of those who have no cause for sorrow except that they are as they are in a world not made after their pattern'.[10]

Solomon is now regarded as a Victorian pioneer of gay visual art for the modern period. His bravery in depicting his own desires and his invention of a synthetic visual language in order to portray them have been acknowledged in more recent times. His disastrous fall from fame, followed by his inability to return to the security of the semi-bohemianism of the London art world, have been suggestive for modern gay liberationists. Solomon provided a model for the lawless gay misfit in eternal exile. Legal penalties against the active expression of his sexuality forced him to become an outcast living a life that rejected bourgeois norms.

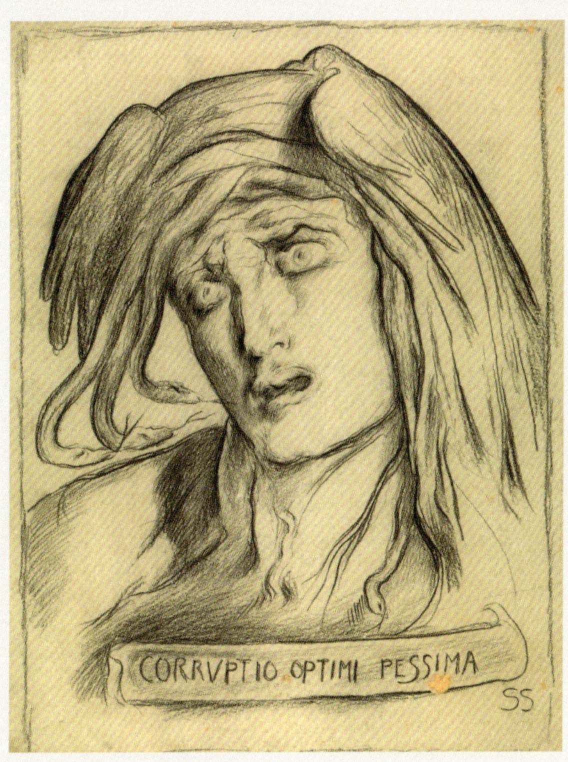

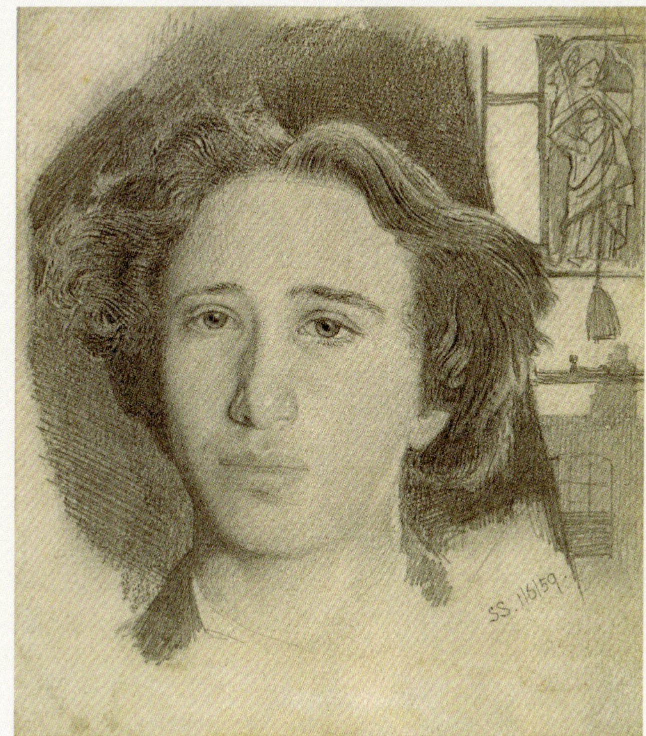

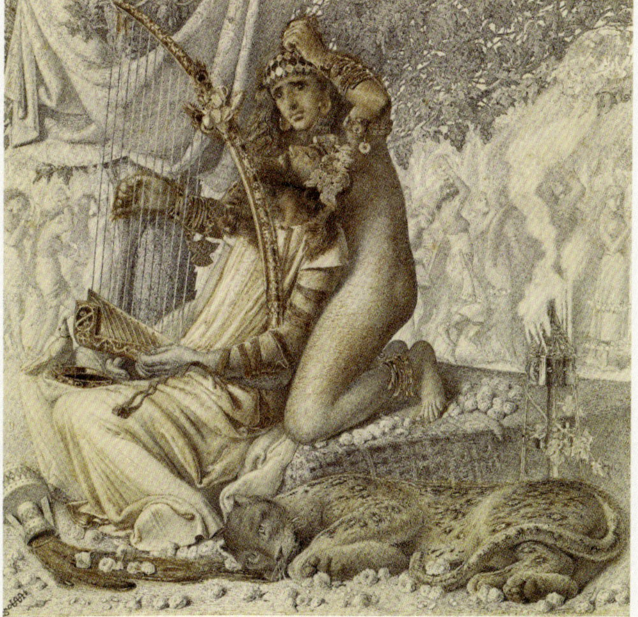

*Corruptio Optimi Pessima:
Medusa c.*1890s
Chalk on paper
40 x 31.5
Neil Bartlett and James
Gardiner Collection

Self-Portrait 1859
Graphite on paper
26.7 x 20.9
Tate. Presented
anonymously 1919

*Babylon hath been a golden
cup* 1859
Ink and graphite on paper
26.6 x 28.3
Birmingham Museums
and Art Gallery

Simeon Solomon 1840–1905

Bacchus 1867

Oil on paper on canvas

50.3 x 37.5

Birmingham Museums and Art Gallery

When Simeon Solomon's oil painting *Bacchus* was exhibited at the Royal Academy in the summer of 1867 there was surprisingly little critical reaction, either positive or negative. However, a watercolour on the same subject (private collection), shown at the Dudley Gallery the following year, was greeted with puzzlement. The *Morning Post* noted an 'expression of ineffable sadness' on the face of the god, adding 'there is nothing about him in the slightest degree suggestive of the jovial god of wine'.[11] In both works, Solomon stresses the ambiguous gender identity of Bacchus/Dionysus, and his refined sensuality rather than his earthiness. The critic of the *Art Journal* suggested that 'Bacchus is a sentimentalist of rather weak constitution; he drinks mead, possibly sugar and water, certainly not wine. The idea is that the young fellow is the inspirer of Art and Poetry, the beloved of the Muses; and the painter, it must be confessed, has thrown over his work a certain aroma of poetry and colour.'[12]

In this painting Solomon anticipates Walter Pater's interest in the myths of Bacchus in the essay 'A Study of Dionysus', first published in 1876. Pater notes Solomon's work and discusses 'the darker side of the double god of nature'. He describes the painter's vision of Bacchus as 'a complete and very fascinating realisation [of] the god of the bitterness of wine, "of things too sweet"; the sea-water of the Lesbian grape become somewhat brackish in the cup'.[13] Here, Pater recognises the suggestive subtlty of Solomon's depiction of the god's sexuality, its elusiveness and playfulness and, at the same time, its sadness.

Bacchus heralds the obsessive use of a motif in Solomon's later works: the representation of the head and face to suggest the entire body and its desires. In this they are similar to Dante Gabriel Rossetti's (1828–82) paintings of the female head and shoulders, such as *Bocca Baciata* 1859 or *Fair Rosamund* 1861, in which slight changes of expression and differences in accessory are made to bear larger messages about the fate of the sitter, usually a historic character. The viewer must engage with the nearly expressionless face and read other signs to understand the picture fully. In this case, the more the viewer knows of the bisexuality of Bacchus/Dionysus and his 'double nature' the more meanings the picture yields. [CC]

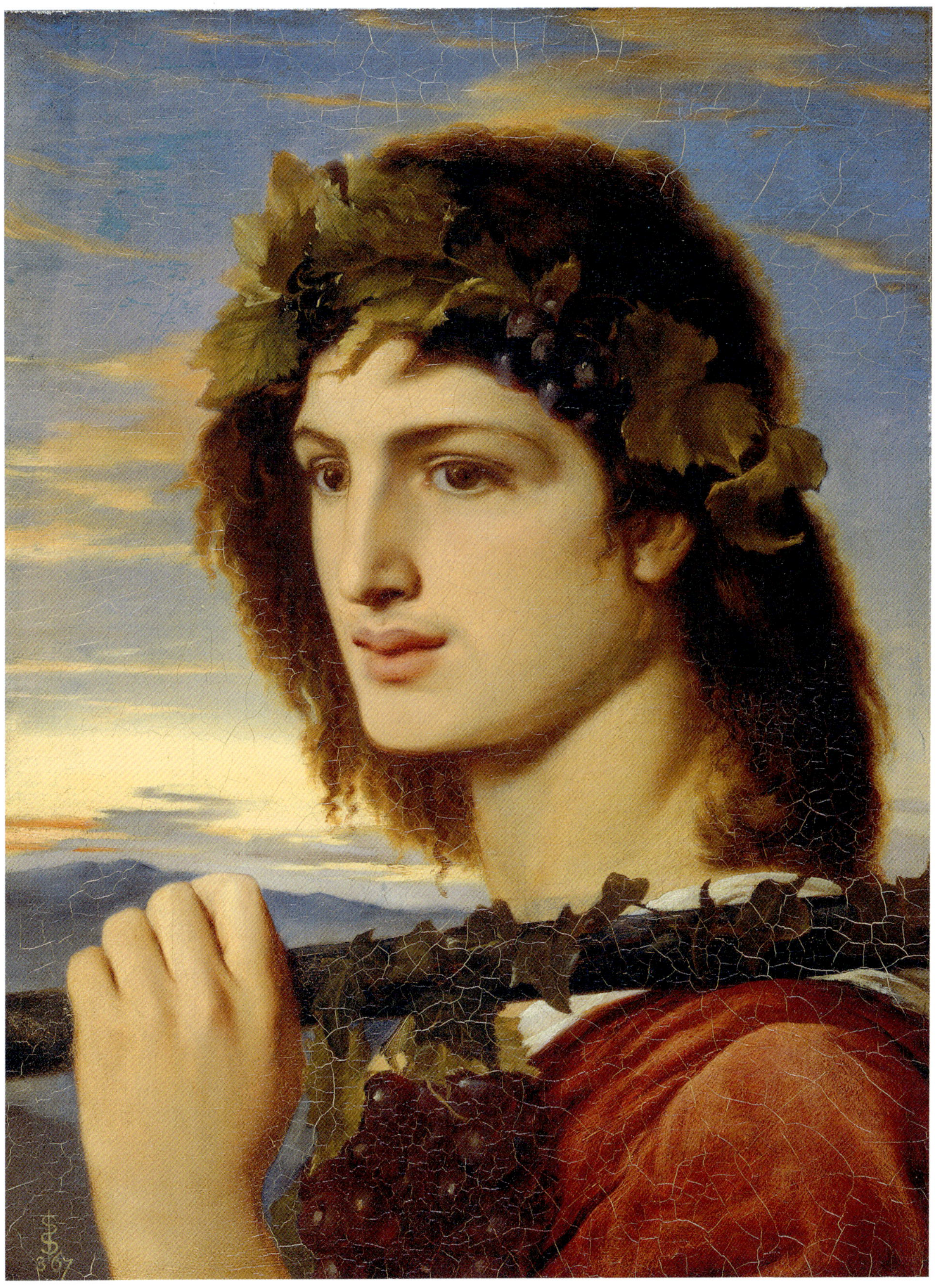

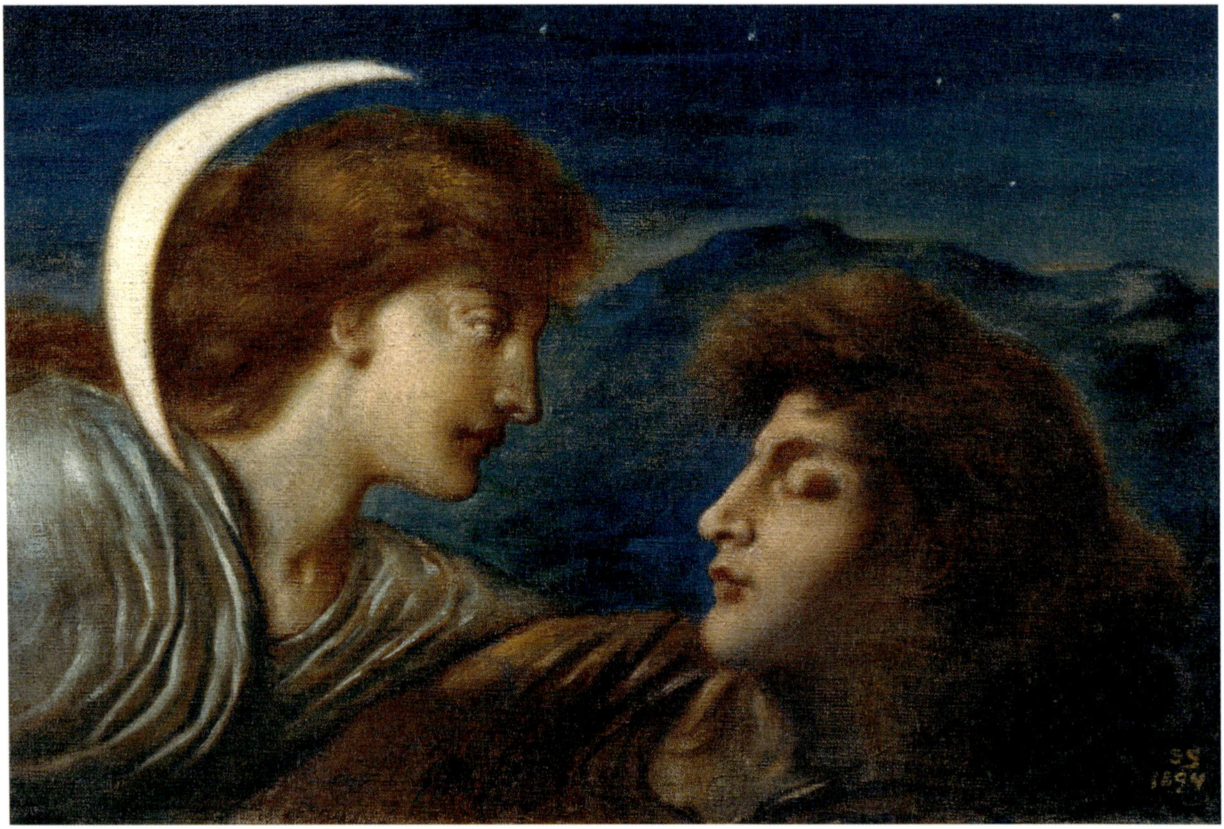

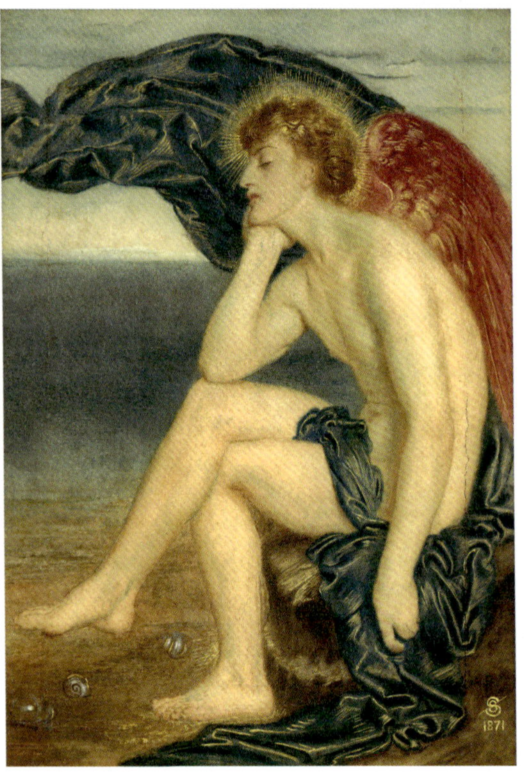

LEFT

Simeon Solomon
1840–1905
Love Dreaming by the Sea
1871
Watercolour on paper
36 x 26.5
Aberystwyth School of
Art Museum and
Galleries, George E.J.
Powell Bequest

Simeon Solomon 1840–1905
The Moon and Sleep 1894
Oil on canvas
51.4 x 76.2
Tate. Presented by Miss Margery Abrahams in memory of Dr Bertram L. Abrahams and Jane Abrahams 1973

The Moon and Sleep is a rare example of an oil painting from Simeon Solomon's later career. The subject – the obsession of the goddess of the moon, Selene, with a beautiful young shepherd – was one that he might have encountered in several classical literary sources. However, given Solomon's interest in poetry of the Romantic period, it may have been John Keats's poem *Endymion* (1818), that was the immediate inspiration. Keats was enjoying a vogue in Pre-Raphaelite and aesthetic movement circles, partly through the advocacy of Dante Gabriel Rossetti (1828–82). However, Percy Bysshe Shelley (1792–1822) was Solomon's favourite poet; the opening lines to *Queen Mab* (1813), addressing the 'brothers' Death and Sleep, might well have stimulated the artist to invent allegorical or mythical figures in conjunction with ideas about love and desire. (For the title page of the 1821 edition, Charles Landseer designed a similar scene depicting the Queen of the Fairies watching a sleeping maiden.)[14]

Solomon would have been aware of the more flagrantly erotic version of the subject by the French neoclassicist painter, Anne-Louis Girodet (1761–1825), whose *Endymion* 1791 (Musée du Louvre, Paris) depicts the nude body of the sleeping youth in striking detail. Solomon's composition, in which only the heads are depicted, has its origins in his experiments of his earlier career, in watercolours such as *The Sleepers and the One who Watches* 1870 (Leamington Art Gallery). In *The Moon and Sleep* the curious gaze of the goddess, bestowed upon the captive object of desire, is contrasted with the passive facial features of the shepherd. These details are enough to convey a story of sexual obsession, specifically about the

potential of the male to arouse the kind of fervour usually bestowed on the female subject in Victorian painting. Endymion's flared nostrils belie the calm of his facial features, suggesting a responsive sensuality rather than impassivity. It is extraordinary how much erotic charge Solomon achieves by simply placing the two heads opposite each other.

A work that realises the homoerotic potential of the story is the watercolour *Love Dreaming by the Sea* 1871 (below left). There the viewer is put in the position of Selene gazing on a naked youth. Along with *The Moon and Sleep*, it has a motif repeated in many of Solomon's other works: closed eyes, conveying ideas of spirituality, interiority and imagination. *The Athenaeum* described the figure as a 'young person, of uncertain sex...seated on a stone by a mysterious sea' and complained that 'this emasculated personage is neither articulated nor even moderately well proportioned...'.[15] *The Times* commented upon 'the heavy and intoxicating atmosphere' of the work.[16] Both reviews expressed unease with Solomon's depictions of the male figure.[17]

By 1894 a return to more conventional poetic subjects might have signalled Solomon's need for money. *The Moon and Sleep* belonged to the physiologist Dr Bertram Abrahams, author of *The Elements of Neurology* (1897). It was, presumably, bought directly from the artist, who begged at the service door in the Abrahams's family home in Mayfair. By then the artist was a social outcast. Abrahams's purchase might have originated as an act of charity by a young, yet successful and well-connected Jewish doctor. Nonetheless, by this time, critics and collectors defied conventional morality to praise and purchase Solomon's works, if only covertly. By 1877, for example, Oscar Wilde, at the very start of his career as a critic, in his review of the Grosvenor Gallery summer exhibition, complained that 'the name of that strange genius who wrote the *Vision of Love revealed in Sleep* cannot be found in the catalogue'.[18] [CC]

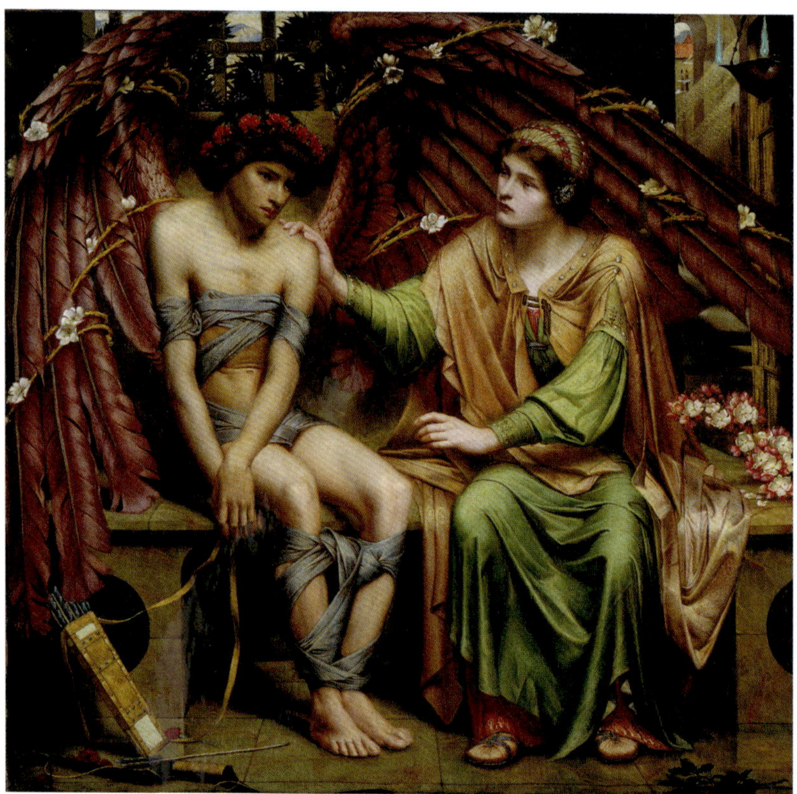

Sidney Harold Meteyard 1868–1947
Hope Comforting Love in Bondage exh.1901
Oil on canvas
104.2 x 109.2
Birmingham Museums and Art Gallery

This allegorical painting was exhibited at the Royal
Academy, London in 1901. While the sufferings of
love were an established theme in art, Sidney
Meteyard's composition does not appear to refer
to any specific literary source and the theme was
probably his own invention. Hope is depicted as a
respectably fully-clothed matron, whereas Love is
portrayed nude and elaborately bound with cloth
and with rose briars that are delicately threaded
through the feathers of his wings. The flowers and
thorns of the roses hint at pleasures and pains
combined. His pensive expression and androgynous
beauty is reminiscent of the work of Simeon Solomon
and, while Hope stretches out her hand to comfort
him, his gaze is fixed elsewhere, leaving the object
of his affections undefined. Little is known about
Meteyard's sexuality, other than the fact that he was
married, but the sensuous and ambiguous nature of
this painting allows for queer readings. [CB]

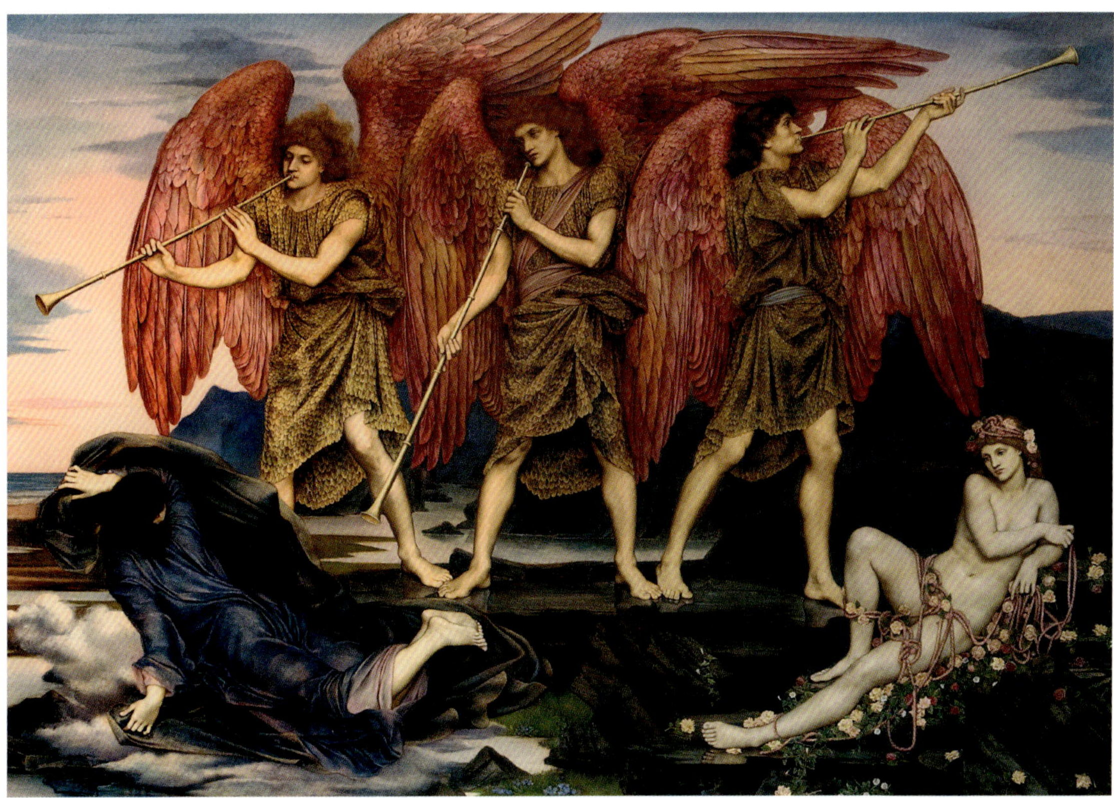

Evelyn Pickering De Morgan 1855–1919
Aurora Triumphans 1877–8
Oil on canvas
114.5 x 187.8
Russell-Cotes Art Gallery and Museum,
Bournemouth

This visually striking allegorical painting by Evelyn De Morgan depicts Aurora, goddess of the dawn, gently disentangling herself from the bonds of night, shown as a woman departing in a swirl of dark drapery. De Morgan was a keen spiritualist and the dichotomy between light and dark is a recurrent theme in her work. Edward Burne-Jones's initials, 'EBJ', were added at a later date by an unscrupulous art dealer yet the painting is perhaps closer to the work of Simeon Solomon, an artist admired by De Morgan.

De Morgan's model for Aurora was Jane Hales (1851–1926), who was appointed nursemaid in 1866, to care for Evelyn's sister Wilhelmina (1865–1965).

De Morgan's repeated images of Hales – often depicted nude – have encouraged some scholars to speculate on the nature of their relationship. In this painting Aurora's nudity and slack bonds in conjunction with night's covert departure might be taken as giving the painting a homoerotic charge. No definitive evidence survives about the nature of the relationship between Hales and De Morgan. Recent research into female same-sex desire in this period, however, suggests that a sexual relationship of this kind might not have been regarded as incompatible with heterosexual marriage, such as De Morgan's marriage to the ceramicist William De Morgan. Other women, including Mary Benson (1841–1918), wife of the Archbishop of Canterbury (1829–96), had relationships with women that were tolerated or condoned by their families. Whatever the truth, Hales was a much-loved member of the household and was buried next to Evelyn and William. [CB]

Frederic Leighton 1830–96
Daedalus and Icarus c.1869
Oil on canvas
138.2 x 106.5
Private collection

In a story from the ancient Roman poet Ovid's *Metamorphoses*, Daedalus made wings for his son Icarus to escape from Rhodes. When the boy flew too close to the sun, the heat melted the wax that attached the wings' feathers and Icarus plunged to his death. Frederic Leighton's painting presents the moment before the fateful ascent. Icarus's pose is taken from the Apollo Belvedere, a famous statue of Apollo, Roman god of the sun, perhaps an ironic reference to Icarus's fate. His golden beauty is contrasted with Daedalus, who is weather-beaten, and posed to appear diminutive and contorted. The image was generally well received at the Royal Academy Summer Exhibition in 1869 but it also raised questions for some of Leighton's audience. *The Times* anxiously remarked that Icarus had the air of 'a maiden rather than a youth' and discovered 'the soft rounded contour of a feminine breast' in his chest.

The femininity that *The Times* saw in Icarus corresponded to growing anxieties about the male relationships in classical texts such as Plato's *Phaedrus and Symposium* (both c.385–370 BC). British scholarship on Plato was undergoing a revival led by Benjamin Jowett (1817–93), who was appointed Regius Professor of Greek at Oxford in 1855. The mentoring relationship that Plato championed between an older man and beardless youth was celebrated as a model for male friendship but the original texts also contained many passages discussing this relationship in terms of desire. This led some, such as the scholar and critic John Addington Symonds, who first read the *Symposium* in 1858, to view Plato as offering a possible precedent for their own same-sex attraction. In his translation of the *Symposium* (1871), Jowett conversely tried to argue that some of the phrases referring to desire were 'mainly a figure of speech'. However, Symonds was unconvinced and gave his own interpretation of these phrases in *A Problem in Greek Ethics*, written in 1873, which he later reworked for inclusion in Havelock Ellis's *Sexual Inversion* (1897).

It is difficult to know exactly how to position Leighton's painting in relation to these debates, although his inclusion of pairings of an older man and younger boy in other works, such as *Jonathan's Token to David* 1868, suggest that he was aware of the Platonic model of male–male relationships. Leighton's sexuality has been the subject of much speculation from his own times to the present, but he guarded his privacy closely. Nonetheless, as *The Times* review suggests, these debates were current in the minds of some of Leighton's audience. [CB]

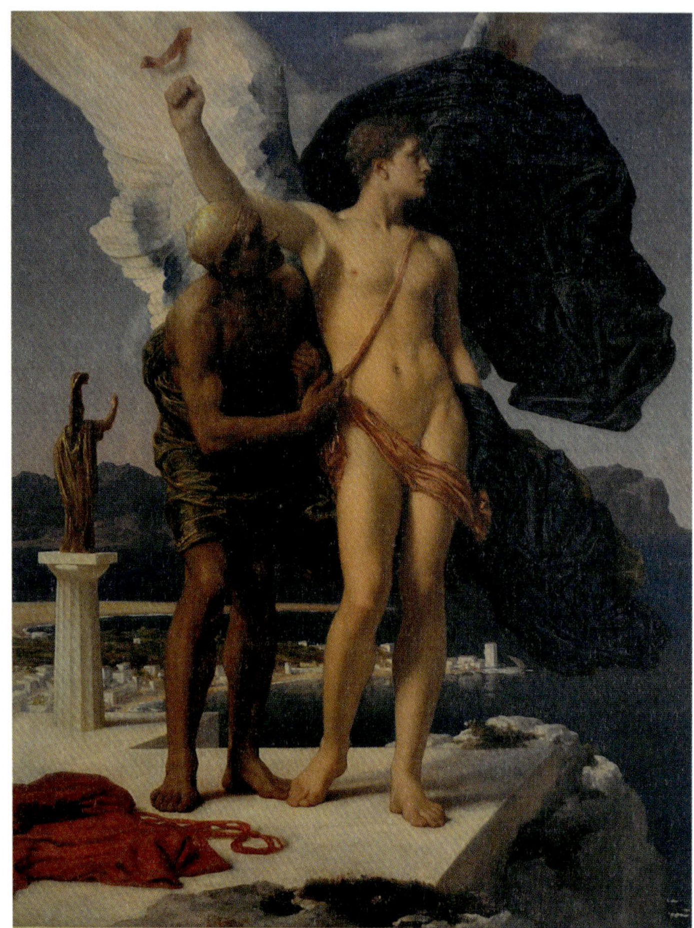

Frederic Leighton 1830–96
The Sluggard 1885
Bronze
191.1 x 90.2 x 59.7
Tate. Presented by Sir Henry Tate 1894

Frederic Leighton's *The Sluggard* seems to epitomise
the dangerous beauty of aestheticism. While his body
is well-toned, his actions are involuntary and he is
shown trampling his laurel crown as he throws off
the last vestiges of sleep. Leighton changed the
sculpture's title from *An Athlete Awakening From Sleep*
to *The Sluggard*, the title by which it has always been
known, explicitly associating the work with idleness.

Nonetheless, the inescapable beauty of Leighton's
figure, its refined musculature and fluid pose that
moves, as Edmund Gosse put it, 'from hardness into
suppleness and flexibility' undercuts any simplistic
moral. Several of the reviews pointed out this
incongruity. The *Western Daily Press* argued that 'a
sluggard is usually understood to be a fat person
and the symmetrical and sinewy form designed by
Sir F Leighton scarcely conforms to that tradition'.[19]
Instead, Leighton's 'sluggard' seems to embody
the values associated by Walter Pater with the
Renaissance: man's 'reassertion of himself' in
opposition to what Pater viewed as the medieval
tendency 'to depreciate man's nature... to make it
ashamed of itself'.[20] *The Sluggard* is a work in which
the subject's pleasure in his body – and the viewer's
pleasure – is such that not even the note of danger
sounded by the trampled laurel crown can give the
viewer pause for thought. One of the sources for
Leighton's figure was Michelangelo's dying slave –
a work that explicitly connected the sluggard with
one of the Renaissance's greatest artists. Given the
homoerotic pleasures of viewing Leighton's figure,
it is perhaps telling that it was executed at the very
moment when Michelangelo's own sexuality was
beginning to be re-evaluated. [CB]

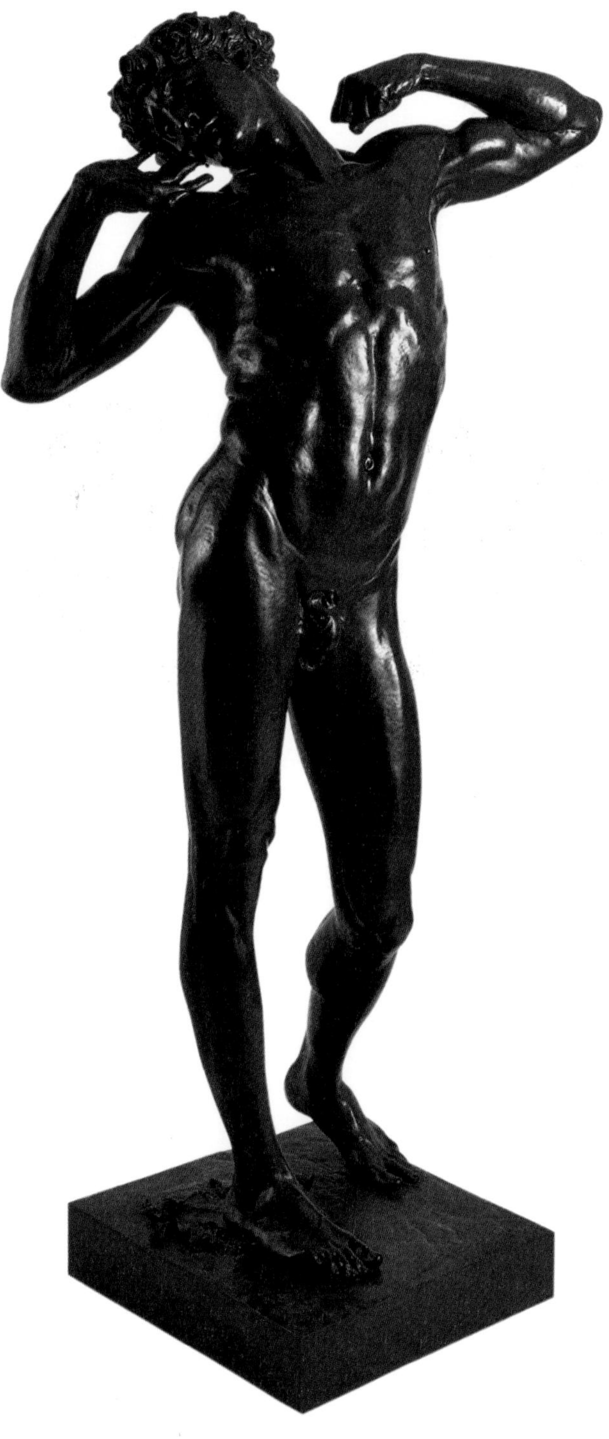

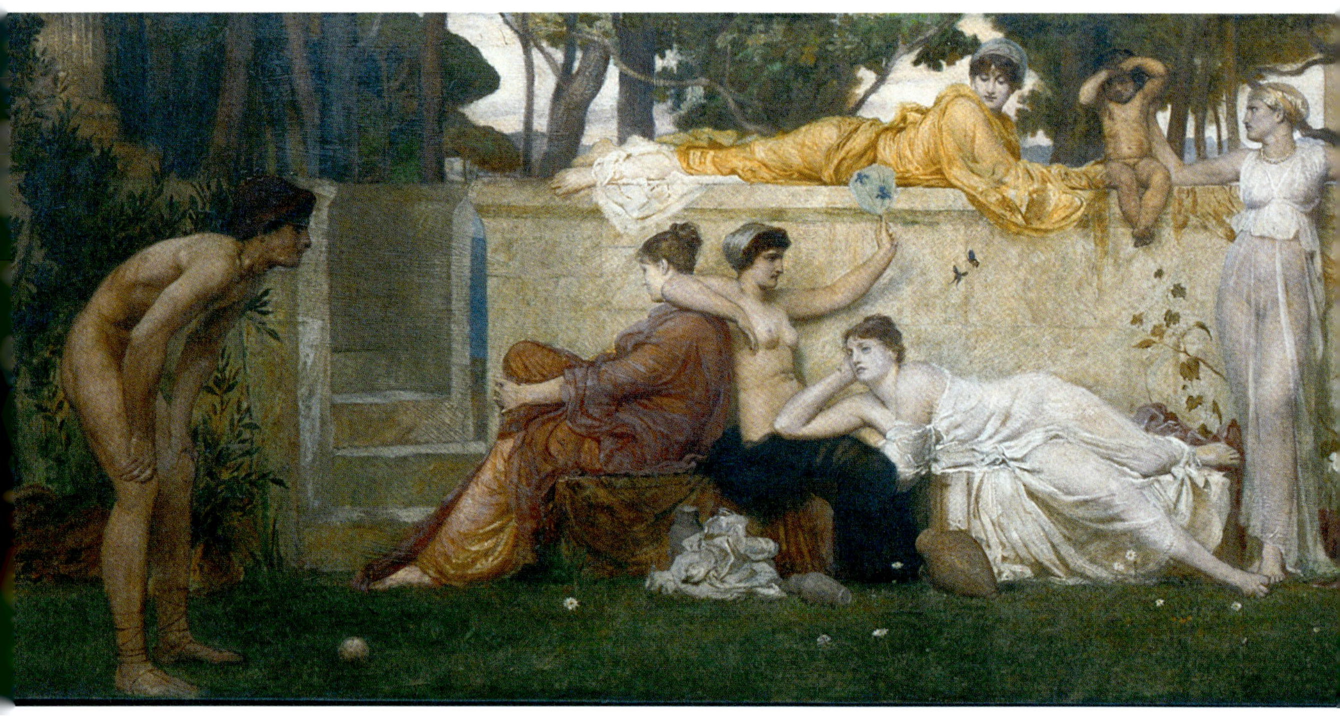

William Blake Richmond 1842–1921

The Bowlers 1870

Oil on canvas

64.1 x 269.9

The Master, Fellows, and Scholars of Downing
College in the University of Cambridge

William Blake Richmond's painting shocked viewers
when it was first displayed at the Royal Academy in
1871. Lady Frederick Cavendish (1841–1925) described
the painting in a diary entry for 6 May 1871 as depicting
'ancients playing at bowls with nothing on, which I can
not appreciate', while *The Times* dryly remarked
'The presence of maidens at the exercises of perfectly
nude young men is as inconsistent with Greek as
with English usage'. Significantly, these commentators
reacted to the heterosexual possibilities of the painting
rather than any homoerotic potential. Only the *Art
Journal's* description of it as showing 'a certain *dolce
far niente* [sweet idleness] style with a general Sybarite
[self-indulgent] state of mind' seems to reference

nineteenth-century associations of aestheticism with
supposedly unmanly devotion to pleasure.

The painting abounds with allusions to classical
statues: the easy embrace of the two standing men is
taken from the ancient figure group *Castor and Pollux*
and the bending pose of the bowler is evocative of the
iconic ancient sculpture of *Discobolus*. Nonetheless,
some modern scholars have noted that these poses
combine in ways that are open to homoerotic
interpretation. This effect is perhaps amplified by
Richmond's compositional confinement of each
gender to different zones, divided by the wisteria tree.
In their separate worlds, the sexes seem indifferent to
each other's presence, which is in keeping with the
nineteenth-century belief that the artistic nude should
transcend desire. *The Bowlers* was painted before the
1895 trials of Oscar Wilde put aesthetic masculinity
in the dock. In this context, the homoerotic possibilities
of the composition may not have been viewed as such
by the artist or original audience. [CB]

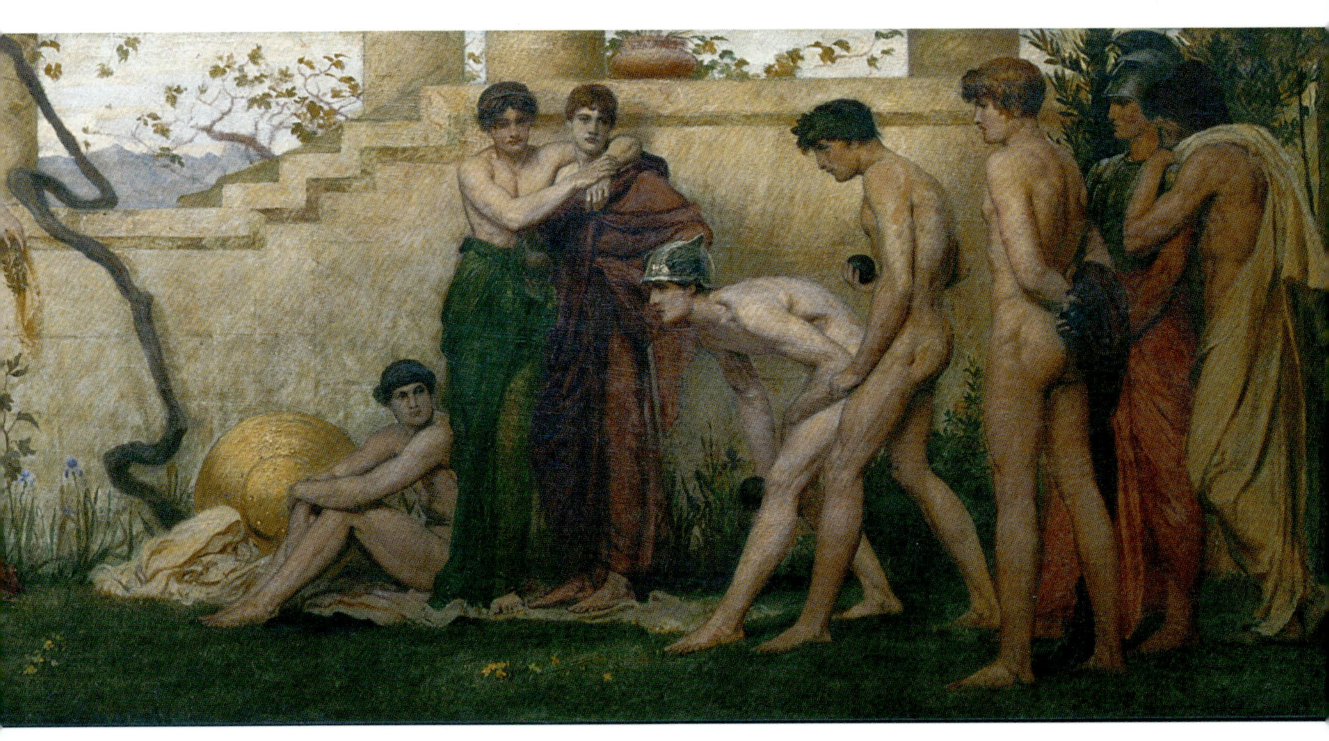

Wilhelm von Gloeden 1856–1931
Three Nude Youths c.1900
Photograph, gelatin silver print on paper
33 x 26
Victoria and Albert Museum, London

Images of attractive Sicilian youths by the German
photographer Wilhelm von Gloeden were widely
admired in Britain. In 1889 Edmund Gosse wrote
to thank John Addington Symonds for a packet of
photographs that he had taken with him to the funeral
of Robert Browning (1812–89). 'As I sat in the Choir,
with George Meredith at my side, I peeped at it again
and again.'

Von Gloeden took up photography professionally
in 1888, after his family fortunes declined, and exhibited
the less sexualised of his images around the world to
great acclaim. He wrote of his work: 'I tried to resurrect
ancient Greek life in these images... Fortunately, I did
not choose professional models so I did not have to
fight against academic poses and practiced positions.'[21]
These twin aspirations of classicism and naturalism
run through the images. While the models are
carefully posed, sometimes to suggest scenes from
classical literature, they are often presented as if the
viewer stumbled across them in the landscape or
ruins of Taormina, where Von Gloeden settled in 1878,
receiving visitors including Oscar Wilde. To modern
eyes, there is a troubling power dynamic between Von
Gloeden and the impoverished Sicilian community,
and his presence there can be viewed as sex tourism.
Some of his contemporaries were aware of the
'bacchanalian revels' that took place at Von Gloeden's
villa, but his wealth ensured that there was no scandal:
he paid for dowries, funded businesses and employed
many of his models as servants. This image, and that
on p.29 are among the less explicit of Von Gloeden's
oeuvre. The context of sexual exploitation, however,
and the uncertain age of some of his models gives a
disturbing undercurrent to his work. [CB]

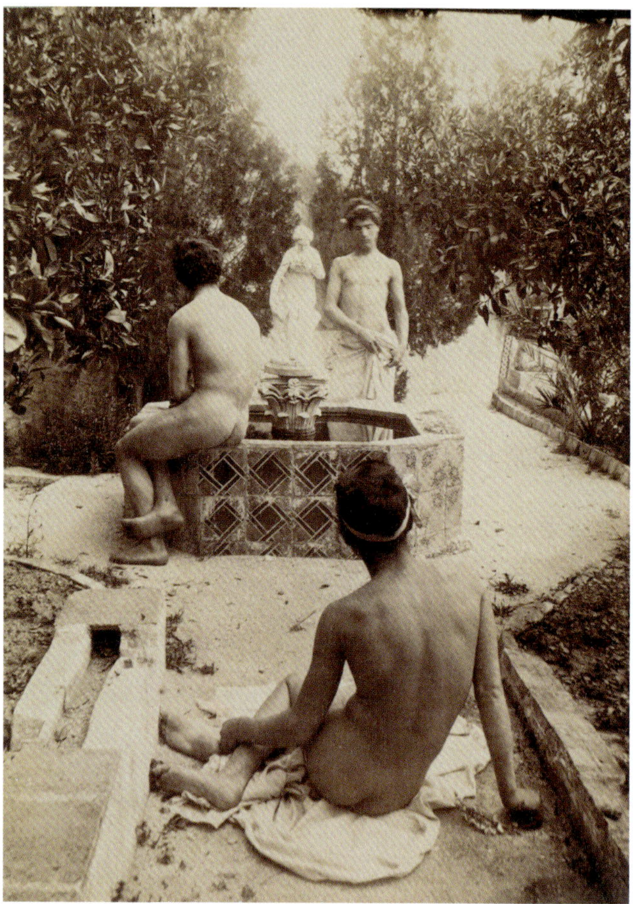

Walter Crane 1845–1915

The Renaissance of Venus 1877

Tempera on canvas

138.4 x 184.1

Tate. Presented by Mrs Watts by the wish of the late George Frederic Watts 1913

The goddess of love's flowing hair and prominence in Walter Crane's composition call to mind Botticelli's *The Birth of Venus* c.1485, while her pose emulates the classical *Venus Esquilina* statue, which had been rediscovered in 1874. The goddess's identity is confirmed by Crane's inclusion of doves and myrtle bushes – Venus's attributes.

According to the author and painter W. Graham Robertson (1866–1948), the artist Frederic Leighton remarked on seeing the painting, 'But my dear fellow, that is not Aphrodite – that is Alessandro.'[22] Leighton was referring to Alessandro de Marco, one of the most successful male artists' models. According to Robertson, Crane turned to Alessandro because his wife would not let him use female models.[23] Yet the title of Crane's painting, calling to mind Walter Pater's *Studies in the History of the Renaissance* (1873), suggests another possibility. Pater's essay on the seminal eighteenth-century writer on classical sculpture, Johann Joachim Winckelmann, told how 'The Hermaphrodite was a favourite subject from ancient times. It was wrought over again and again with passionate care.'[24] This echoed Winckelmann's description of the 'hermaphrodite' as the ideal form. Robertson seems to have enjoyed the gender fluid aspects of the painting, which he described as 'mystically correct but anatomically surprising', continuing, 'Still, she was a fine, upstanding slip of a boy, and in the clear sunlit atmosphere and charming colour scheme of ivory, blue and almond she passed for Venus pleasantly enough'.[25] This painting was admired at the inaugural exhibition of the Grosvenor Gallery in London in 1877, and an image of it was selected by the artist Aubrey Beardsley (1872–98) for inclusion in *The Yellow Book* (volume 2, 1894). [CB]

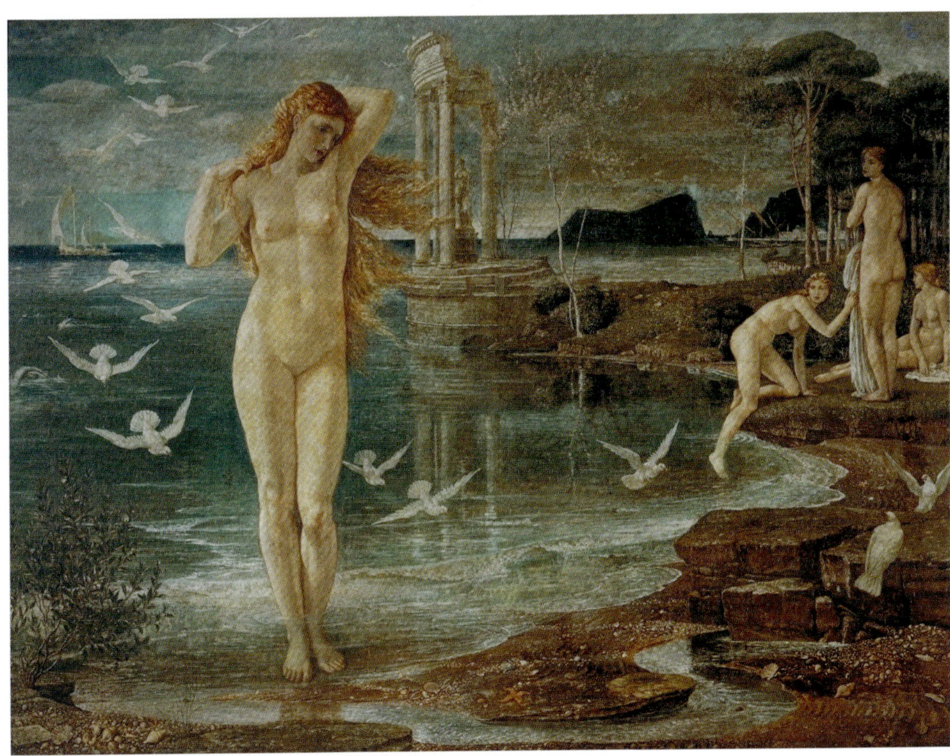

Hamo Thornycroft 1850–1925
The Mower 1888–90
Bronze
58.5 x 33 x 18.5
Tate. Presented by Arthur Grogan 1985

Hamo Thornycroft exhibited a life-size version of this
sculpture at the Royal Academy in 1884 with lines
from Mathew Arnold's (1822–88) poem 'Thyrsis':

> ...A mower, who, as the tiny swell
> Of our boat passing, heaved the river-grass,
> Stood with suspended scythe to see us pass.

It was based on a sketch made during a summer boat
trip along the Thames with a group of friends in 1882.
The party included Edmund Gosse who, as Michael
Hatt has argued, was deeply in love with Thornycroft
and sent him passionate letters and poems that went
'beyond conventions of the expression of friendship,
even by Victorian standards'.[26] Gosse's 'The Shepherd
of the Thames', published after Thornycroft's marriage,
can be interpreted as a homoerotic reworking of
Arnold's 'Thyrsis' in which the Thames is repeatedly
evoked as a site of nostalgia and desire. Gosse reviewed
the sculpture when it was exhibited at the Royal
Academy, writing that 'The modelling was never
more learned or beautiful in any previous work of
Mr. Thornycroft's, nor the flesh more finely contrasted
against the various textures'.

We do not know if Thornycroft reciprocated
Gosse's passion, although he apparently did not take
offence. Nonetheless, it is hard to avoid the erotic
potential of the muscular bare-chested mower, an
evolution from the fully-clothed figure in Thornycroft's
original drawing and from his original nude concept
for the sculpture. It appears to be the first major
British sculpture to depict a worker in labouring dress,
a decision that may have been political but may also
reflect Victorian fascination with the eroticised
working-class body. The body of a mower is evoked
to similar effect in Uranian poet John Gambril
Nicholson's (1866–1931) poem 'In Working Dress',
which he published in his suggestively titled volume
A Garland of Ladslove (1911).[27] Nicholson explicitly
fetishises the 'working dress' of the title and was
possibly inspired by seeing Thornycroft's sculpture.
[CB]

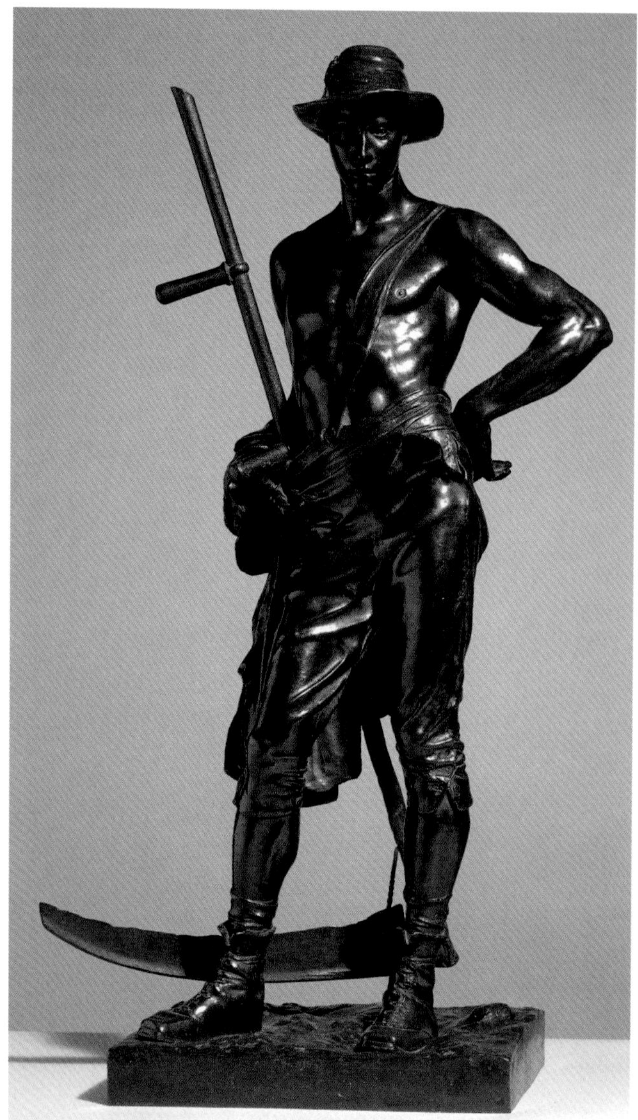

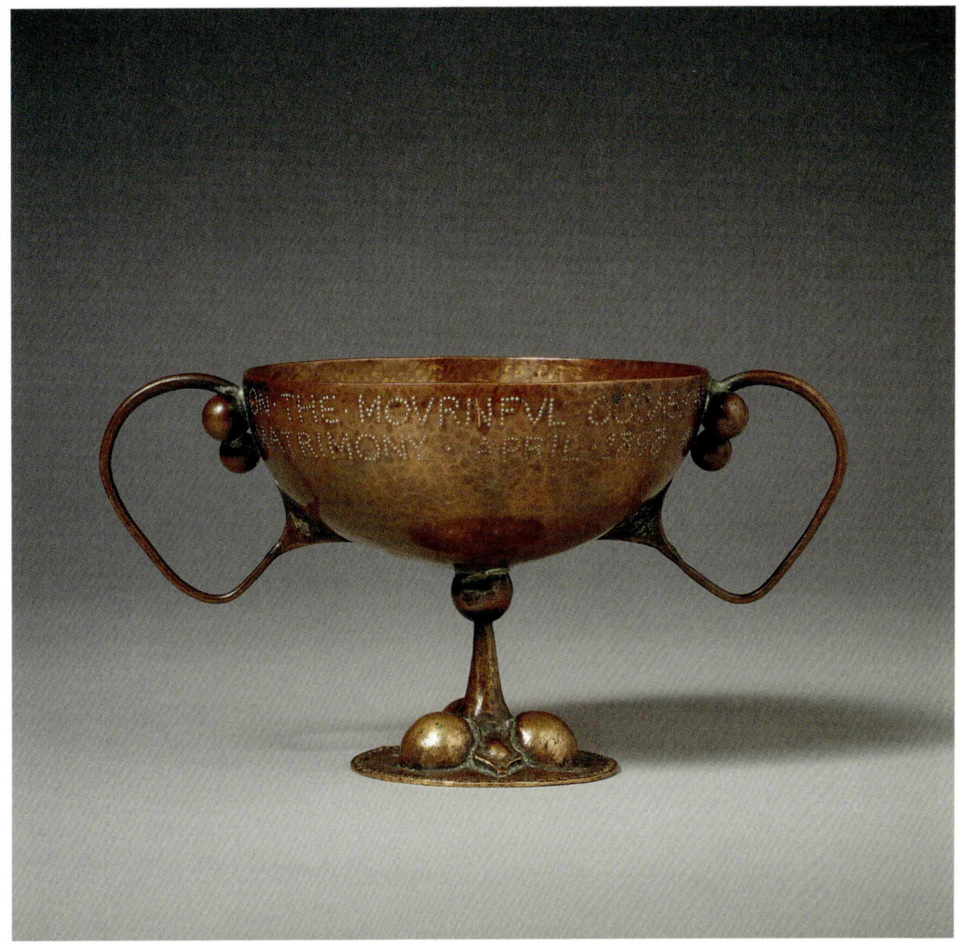

Charles Robert Ashbee 1863–1942

Twin-handled Cup 1893

Metal

8.2 x 16.1

Private collection

The designer Charles Ashbee made this cup for his friend James Headlam (1863–1929), styled 'the ancient' in the surprising inscription: '*To the ancient, from CRA, on the mournful occasion of his transition into matrimony, April 1893*'. This could be a joke about Headlam's loss of bachelor freedoms but within the queer camaraderie of Ashbee's circle it could also signal Headlam's presumed regret on abandoning same-sex passions for a respectable heterosexual union. Ashbee's choice of decorative motif is suggestive in this context: the balls at the bases of the central stem and beneath the top of each of the drooping handles give them the air respectively of an erect and flaccid penis. Ashbee exhibited a similar cup in the arts and crafts exhibition of 1893 but with differences of design that caused the phallic effects to be lost.

Ashbee married Janet Forbes in 1898 although he continued to have sexual liaisons with men throughout his life. Shortly after proposing, he told her of his attraction to men, acknowledging that 'Some women …would shrink from a man who revealed himself thus.' However, he reassured her that 'There may be many comrade friends, there can be only one comrade wife.'[28] Janet accepted his proposal. [CB]

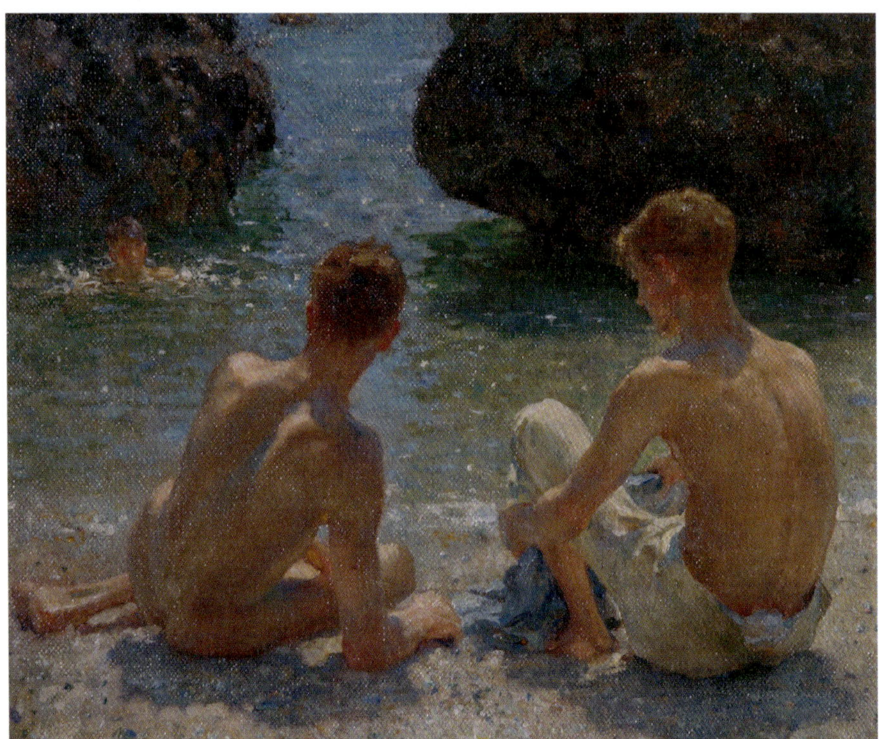

Henry Scott Tuke 1858–1929
The Critics 1927
Oil on board
41.2 x 51.4
Leamington Spa Art Gallery and Museum
(Warwick District Council)

The Critics is one of Henry Scott Tuke's (1858–1929)
last paintings, finished just two years before his death.
It is typical of a group of works depicting reclining
figures by the sea, sometimes sunbathing. ('Sun
worshipping' and nudism were just coming into
fashion as offshoots of neo-paganism, untainted by
later associations with Nazism.) Tuke had returned
to Cornwall from London and, after 1885, much of
his work depicts the coast around Falmouth. He worked
with models he met in the town, forming lasting
friendships with them.[29] Some writers have suggested
that these relationships were sexual in nature but
there is no evidence to support this contention.

The scenes described in many of Tuke's paintings
– as in *The Critics* – avoid overt mythological or
religious content. One exception is *Hermes by the Pool*
1900, in which Johnny Jackett (1878–1935), later an
English rugby team member, is posed in winged helmet,
holding the caduceus, the snake-entwined staff.[30]
Tuke's Hermes is a slim, nude athlete. The *Glasgow
Herald* reviewer was one who thought it not 'one of his
successes': 'An ordinary bather would have been more
appropriate to Mr Tuke's mind and method.[31]

In *The Critics* Tuke seems more concerned with the
everyday than the classical. Drawing upon theories
of beauty and its appreciation, however, it reflects
upon Pater's 'Conclusion' to *The Renaissance*: 'Not to
discriminate every moment some passionate attitude
in those about us, and in the very brilliancy of their
gifts some tragic dividing of forces on their ways, is,
on this short day of frost and sun, to sleep before
evening.'[32] One of the 'passions' that Pater lists is 'the
face of one's friend'. Perhaps here, the two 'ordinary
bathers' are assessing their friend's physical qualities,
rather than his swimming style, as he approaches
them through the turquoise water. [CC]

Henry Scott Tuke 1858–1929
A Bathing Group 1914
Oil on canvas
90.2 x 59.7
Royal Academy of Arts, London

The recurring subject matter of Henry Scott Tuke –
naked youths swimming or resting by the sea
or working on boats – was familiar to approving
audiences at the annual Summer Exhibition at the
Royal Academy for decades. Tuke's interest in colour
harmonies and painting en plein air link him to French
and British Impressionist painting as well as the
advanced aesthetic painting practices of artists such
as James Abbott McNeill Whistler (1834–1903).
The combination of the male nude figure depicted
in a modern style, combining realism with idealism,
was appreciated. For example, the reviewer of *The
Speaker* found another of Tuke's canvases, *Ruby, Gold
and Malachite* 1902, 'admirable in form, colour and
arrangement … a poetic harmony of crystalled rock,
transparent emerald waters, and idealized boyhood…'[33]

In *A Bathing Group* the standing figure is posed as
if his body, seen in profile, is a cameo, his pallor set
against serpentine stone. It is a visual conceit that
links painting to the art of the ancient world, to Greek
and Roman sculpture, engraved gems and the athletic
bodies of gods. The painting celebrates the beautiful
physique of an Italian model, Nicola Lucciani, whose
torso is illuminated by a shaft of sunlight. A second
figure, at the bottom left of the canvas, crouches as
if in awe of his godly appearance. The revelation is
ambiguous and the viewer is forced to reassess the
relation of the divine to the human, mortal male.

A Bathing Group is the artist's Royal Academy
Diploma Work, accepted when he was elected as
Member of the RA in 1914. It represents something of
the confidence Tuke must have felt with his handling
of his characteristic subjects. [CC]

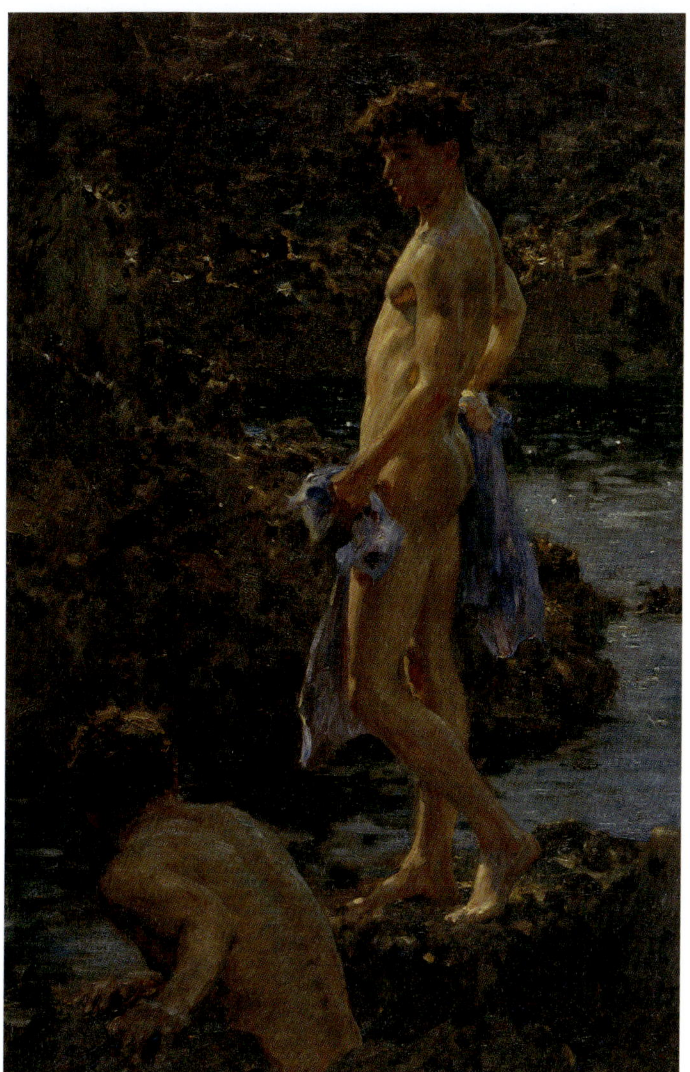

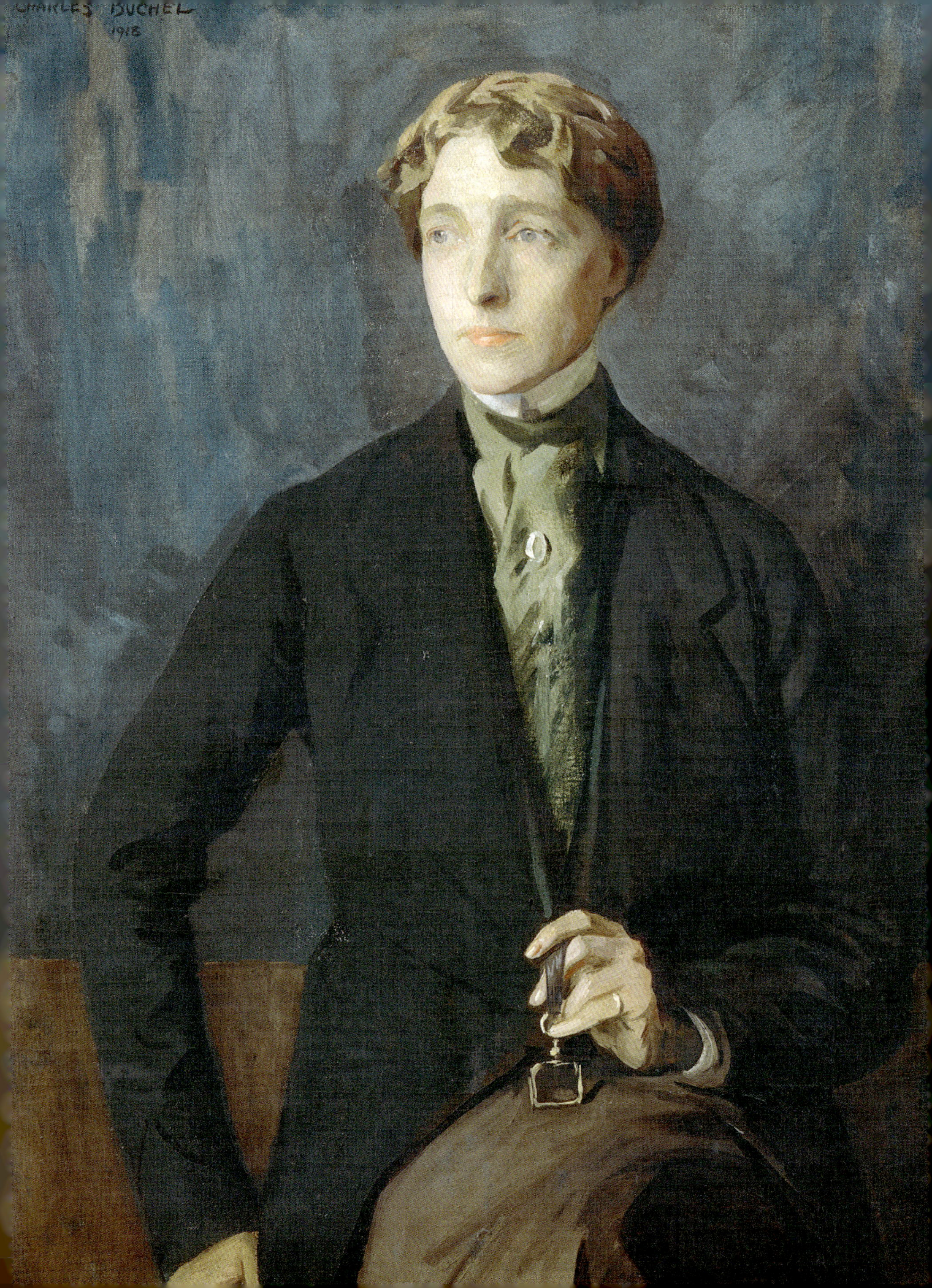

CHARLES BUCHEL
1918

PUBLIC INDECENCY: PORTRAIT OF AN X

LAURA DOAN

Charles Buchel 1872–1950

Radclyffe Hall 1918

Oil on canvas

91.4 x 71.1

National Portrait Gallery,

London

SPOTTING AN X in *Queer British Art 1861–1967* should not be difficult. Signs of queerness – lesbian or gay, trans or bi – abound in the portraits of historical figures such as Oscar Wilde or Radclyffe Hall (opposite), two writers now widely associated with X-ness (here insert any social category based on sexuality or gender that comes to mind). For contemporary viewers, assigning labels – say, effeminate gay man or butch lesbian – feels almost second nature. Yet, as historians of sexuality explain, we acquired the habit of defining people based on their looks relatively recently.

In Britain this inclination to read the sitter in a portrait as gay or straight can be traced back to the late nineteenth and early twentieth centuries when sex radicals and sexologists began to investigate bodies and desires. Edward Carpenter, whose mystical writings championed feminism and encouraged sex reform through free love, believed the anatomy of certain individuals – Urnings, or intermediate types – did not match their mental or emotional make-up (p.55). Psychologist Havelock Ellis, along with colleagues largely from the German-speaking world, used more 'scientific' methods (p.54). This entailed investigating sexual acts, desires, fantasies, love interests, erotic pleasures, bodily attributes or gender expression to determine specimen types. Influenced by medical practitioners, sexologists devised terms to capture the essence of one type or another.

In gathering and analyzing their data sex researchers did not discover the 'truth' of sexual nature, as if a heterosexual or homosexual already existed in the psyche or body. Mapping sexual desire or behaviour was not like mapping terra incognita or unearthing a long-buried artefact, even though this is what they thought they were doing. The achievement of this great classificatory project was to invent a new way of thinking about sexuality. The science of sex transformed people into objects of study by examining their bodies, working out their gender, and soliciting intimate information about their romantic entanglements or sexual desires, preferences or inclinations.

Often branded a science, sexological methods were hardly objective. Sexual scientists were conditioned by the values and beliefs of their age: masculinity and femininity were understood as natural rather than cultural; the purpose of the normal 'sexual instinct' was to make babies; and sexual acts not leading to reproduction were judged as abnormal. For better or worse, the immense erotic diversity of humankind was shoehorned into categories so that X-ness came to represent not what someone did but who they were. Sexologists paid little attention to normal folk – more interesting to them were the physical traits or outward signs of anomalies or aberrations from an assumed norm.

The idea that sexual proclivities bestowed an identity did not catch on overnight – this way of thinking would drift gradually and haphazardly into the public sphere in the first half of the twentieth century through the print media, marital advice literature and sex education. The Victorians talked about an individual's 'character'; only in the twentieth century did we come to talk about someone's 'identity'. The historical record indicates that just before the outbreak of the First World War a small group of sex radicals, including Carpenter, gathered in London to found the British Society for the Study of Sex Psychology, their meetings and lectures attracting a handful of progressives, bohemians, intellectuals, artists and writers. For those in the know, the codes of X-ness could be deciphered in dress or demeanour, but the circulation of such modern sexual knowledge was limited.

Numerous examples in the archive point to the risks we take in assuming people in the early twentieth century understood the meaning of the sexual and of sexual identities as we do now. In 1920, for instance, a landlady's testimony that her husband had given her permission to sleep with the female plaintiff was accepted as proof of virtue beyond all doubt. Equally strange, a 1922 letter sent to the sex guru Marie Stopes (1880–1958) by a woman physician acknowledges her homosexuality while also expressing a concern that she might have impregnated her female partner through a kiss. This is the bizarre world on view in *Queer British Art*, but it is a world that is exceptionally difficult to enter from the vantage point of the sexological age. Our categories are so powerful – so hardwired in our brains– it is unimaginable that Wilde's green carnation or Hall's short hair did not automatically signal X-ness. Yet I wonder if we shortchange ourselves if we do not approach queerness in visual representation as an opportunity to enter another sexual universe.

A good place to begin coming to terms with a sexual past before X-ness – the past as *unlike* the present, strange and alien – is the sensational Allan vs Billing case of 1918. In the final months of the First World War the Canadian dancer Maud Allan (1873–1956) sued the radical right-wing Member of Parliament Noel Pemberton Billing (1881–1948) for claiming she belonged to the 'cult of the clitoris' in her 1906 performance as Salome in the *Vision of Salome* (based loosely on Oscar Wilde's play) (opposite). The *News of the World* described Allan as having 'an obscene and indecent character, so designed as to foster and encourage unnatural practices upon women'.[1] References to obscenity and indecency were catch-all terms for any act deemed nasty, filthy, corrupt, depraved, disgusting, polluting, licentious, wicked, debauched or immoral. Missing in these descriptions of lewd behaviour is a crystallised understanding of an X.

Decades later we would dispense with all the messy ambiguities of 1918 and state simply that membership in the 'cult of the clitoris' denoted lesbianism, pure and simple. However, nailing down the meaning of this spectacular phrase to signify an X represents an act of translation. The power of Billing's expression resided in its potential to mean anything or nothing, something unpleasant, vague,

Unknown photographer, published by J Beagles & Co.
Maud Allan as Salome in 'The Vision of Salome' c.1908
Bromide postcard print
13.9 x 8.9
National Portrait Gallery, London

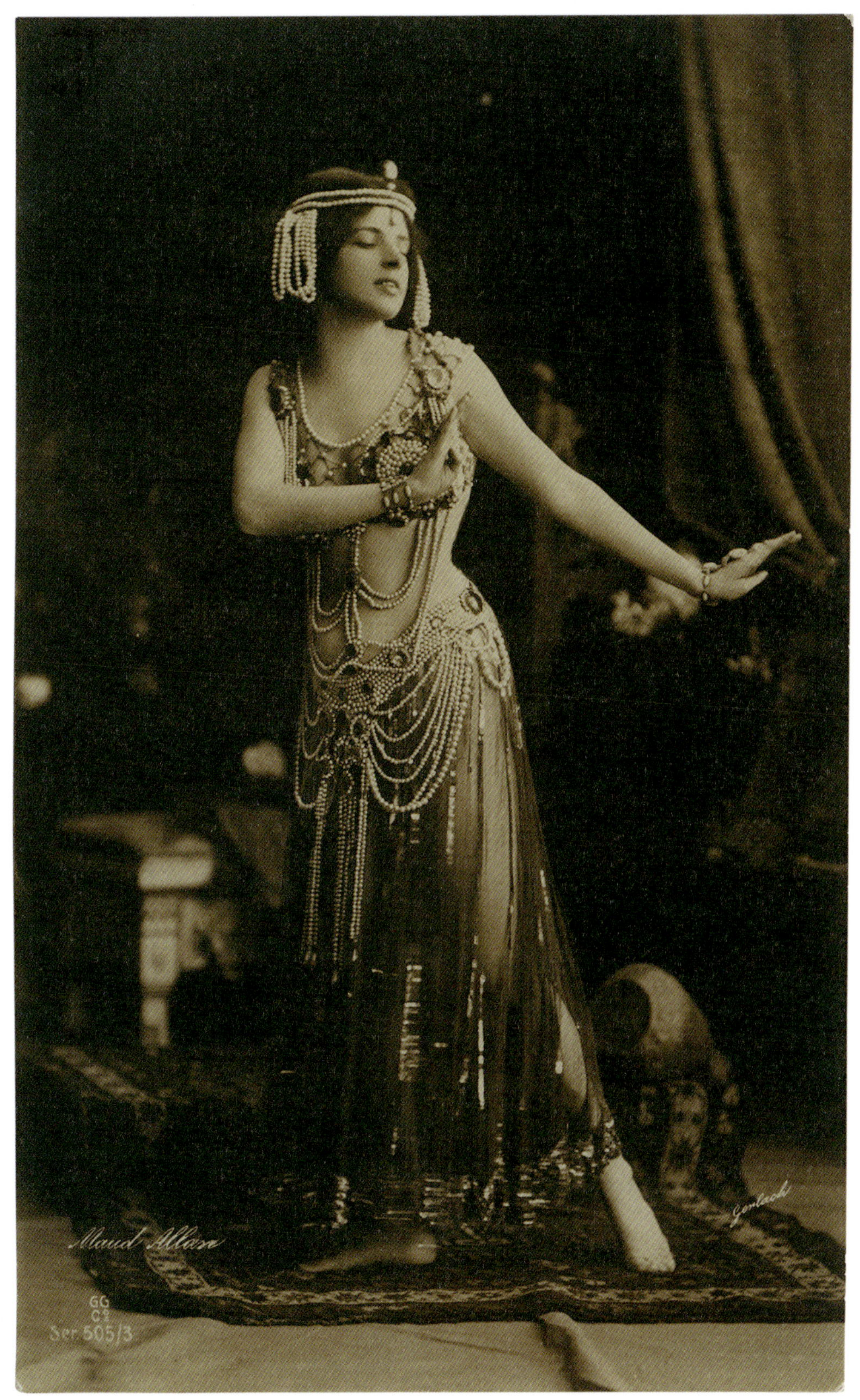
Maud Allan
Gerlach
GG
Cᵒ
Ser. 505/3

unclean or degenerate – the very attributes ascribed to Wilde. During the trial, the judge interrupted the proceedings time and again to ask the meaning of terms such as sadism, masochism and fetishism. When the word orgasm was used the prosecution counsel inquired if it referred to an unnatural vice. Allan's admission of her familiarity with this bodily function sealed her fate: sex ignorance was de rigueur for any respectable woman of the middle or upper classes. She lost both the case and her career.

A decade later another extraordinary trial would tarnish a woman's reputation when the British government banned Hall's *The Well of Loneliness* (1928) as obscene. Today Hall's sympathetic portrayal of a 'congenital sexual invert' is understood as lesbianism. Turning to the 1918 portrait by Charles Buchel (1872–1950) we now see the X as a sexual outlaw who cross-dressed as an act of rebellion (p.48). The sartorial detail secures not only the writer's X-ness but also reveals her influence on the fashion sensibilities of an emergent sapphic subculture that apparently flourished in the interwar era: short-cropped hair, monocle, tailored black jacket, high stiff collar, cravat and white starched shirt.
Our scrutiny of Hall's bodily posture and facial expression suggests a defiant stance against compulsory heterosexuality. Another equally plausible interpretive framework is to see the portrait in terms of gender variance. Reading the work as an X, however – whether lesbian or trans – obscures rather than illuminates what Hall was up to in promoting herself as a professional writer.

How and when Hall's name became a byword for lesbianism is a matter for historians to consider. Evidence from the archive suggests Hall understood inversion as pertaining to gender variance rather than same-sex desire. In a 1926 short story 'Miss Ogilvy Finds Herself' about the bleak post-war existence of the leader of an all-female ambulance unit, the eponymous hero dreams of becoming a man – and, in a weird flashback fantasy, on transitioning to a man rapes his female partner; hardly the imaginings of most lesbians then or now.

Buchel's portrait shows the seated figure of a thirty-eight-year-old, upper-middle-class woman gazing pensively into the distance. At the time of the sitting Hall had published several volumes of poetry but had not yet produced any of the novels that would later establish her literary reputation. On display is a writer on the verge of fame, her engagement with the world of letters signalled by the gold-framed eyeglass suspended on a black ribbon delicately entwined in her fingers. She does not seek to pass as a man but instead exploits the austerity of formal dress to present herself as a serious writer and aesthete, anticipating the popular 1920s fashion style called the severely 'masculine mode'. We glimpse in the portrait the salient codes of an aspiring dandy: high white collar and dark velvet tailored jacket, austere in its fastening with a button or two. Viewed this way the portrait is a site in which Hall stages her literary aspirations by appropriating the distinctive style of the leading artistic figures of her day. Hall's get-up strikes us now as the epitome of lesbian chic, but what people saw then was a style of dandyism invented by the writer Sir Henry Maximilian Beerbohm (1872–1956).

Hall's portrait, produced by an artist best known for his paintings and sketches of actors on the London stage, often costumed and sometimes ambiguously gendered, redefines masculinity and femininity in ways that would only later be associated with a particular category of sexual identity.

Perceived resemblances between past and present shed little light on the past to look forward. Reading the portrait solely in terms of its depiction of X-ness confirms what we think we know already, a transaction vital to feeling connected to the past. Yet another way to look at art as 'queer' is to enter the queerness of a past where people did not yet name themselves or others as an X. Stepping outside the framework of modern sexual knowledge opens up alternative perspectives on how people in the past understood or talked about sex, perhaps in terms of morality and respectability rather than normality and deviance.

A new generation of students in gender and sexuality studies looks askance at the fixity of labels, favouring instead the fluidity of an LGBTQ+ spectrum. I take this as a sign we have come full circle in our growing awareness of the inadequacies of organising sexual knowledge in terms of types. There is nothing wrong in yielding to the urge of reading the queer portrait as an X, but queering British art points in equally captivating ways to a visual encounter with the unknown, a world at once familiar and radically unlike our own.

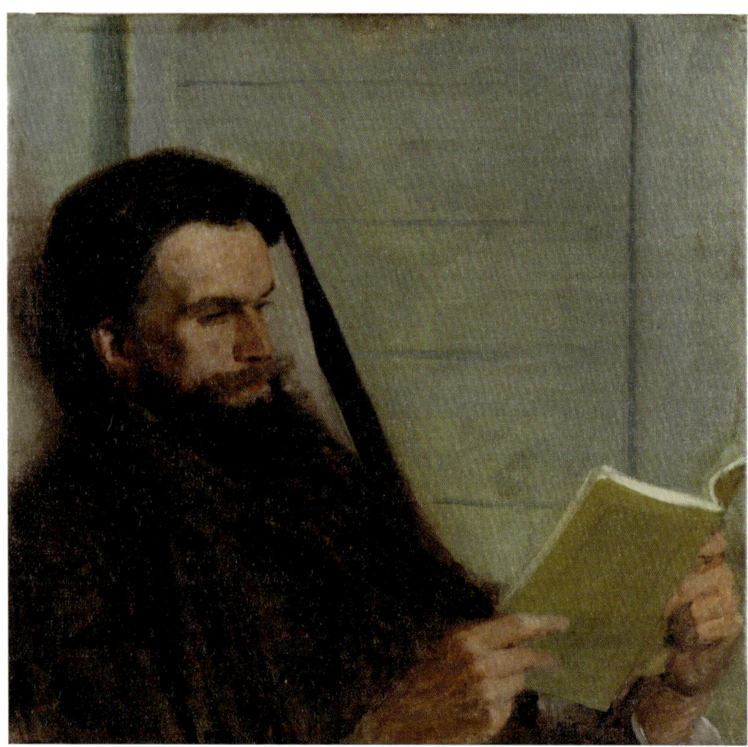

Henry Bishop 1868–1939
Henry Havelock Ellis 1890s
Oil on canvas
58.3 x 61
National Portrait Gallery, London

The sexologist Henry Havelock Ellis defined queer
sexualities in Britain for a generation. Ellis was the
first to set aside the prevailing judgemental attitudes
to categorise a wide variety of sexual practices in his
book *Sexual Inversion* (German edition 1896, first English
edition 1897), sexualities and gender identities, including
same-sex desire, gender variance, cross-dressing and
fetishism. He co-authored this book with the writer
John Addington Symonds, who was himself attracted
to men and whose contributions situated same-sex
desire in a historical context stretching back to Plato.
The campaigner Edward Carpenter, who knew Symonds,
offered his own same-sex relationship as a case study
and persuaded some of his friends to do the same,
ensuring that the book drew on lived experience. Ellis
was aware that the text would be highly controversial
and first published his book in Germany to test the

ground for an English edition. However, the 1897
English edition was effectively banned after the
bookseller George Bedborough was successfully
prosecuted for 'obscene libel' for selling a copy.
Ellis circumvented British censorship by moving
publication of his works to the United States.

Henry Bishop's portrait of Ellis was probably
painted around the time of the Bedborough trial,
yet there is little sign of these turbulent times in
this informal image. Here, Ellis is depicted sitting
in a deckchair in Bishop's studio in St Ives, absorbed
in a soft-backed book. There is some evidence that
Bishop was attracted to men and Ellis's non-judgemental
attitudes may have encouraged Bishop to make his
acquaintance. He became a lifelong friend. [CB]

Roger Fry 1866–1934
Edward Carpenter 1894
Oil on canvas
74.9 x 43.8
National Portrait Gallery, London

In defiance of his times, Edward Carpenter was a
socialist, a vegetarian and a passionate advocate for
same-sex desire (which he termed 'homogenic love'),
open relationships, asexual relationships and women's
sexual autonomy. The radical freedom that Carpenter
preached in works such as *Towards Democracy*
(1883–1902), *England's Ideal* (1885), *Civilisation: Its
Cause and Cure* (1889) and *Homogenic Love* (1895)
amounted to a broadside attack on what he summed
up as 'cant in religion, pure materialism in science,
futility in social conventions, the worship of stock and
shares, the starving of the human heart'.[2] This wholesale
assault on Victorian middle-class values is perhaps
the more surprising as Carpenter was borne into
relative affluence and had been elected to a clerical
Fellowship in Mathematics at Trinity Hall, Cambridge.
He was profoundly influenced by the poetry of Walt
Whitman, which he first read in 1868, and later told
how, in Whitman, with 'a great leap of joy…I met
with the treatment of sex which accorded with my
own sentiments'.[3] Carpenter resigned his Fellowship
and left Holy Orders to go on a lecture circuit of the
industrial cities of the Midlands and the north before
settling at Millthorpe, near Sheffield. Here he lived
openly with his lover, George Merrill,
a labourer whom Carpenter met in 1881.

Roger Fry met Carpenter in 1886, when Carpenter
came to Cambridge to lecture at the invitation of Fry's
friends, Charles Ashbee and Goldsworthy Lowes
Dickinson (1862–1932). Fry and Ashbee subsequently
went to visit Carpenter at Millthorpe and they forged
a lasting friendship. Fry painted this work in 1894
and described it in a letter to his mother as depicting
Carpenter in his 'very anarchist overcoat'.[4] The
painting was exhibited at the New English Art Club,
London in 1894 and was shown again by invitation
at the Liverpool autumn exhibition, causing Fry to

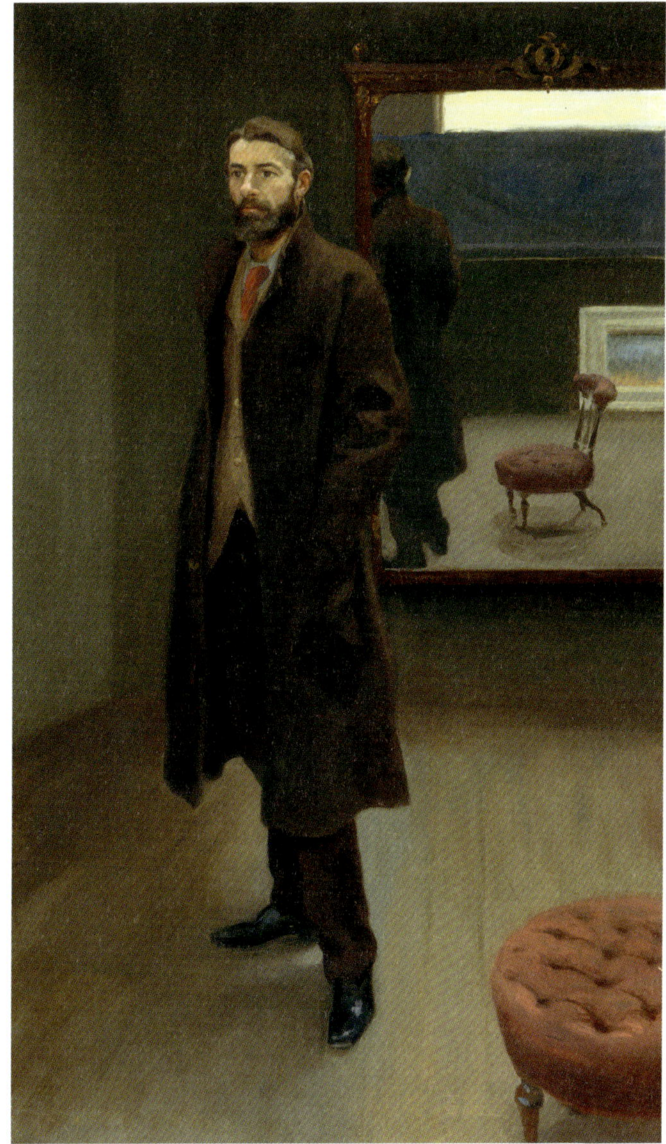

comment 'that painting has certainly done me a lot
of good'.[5] The inclusion of the chair half-seen in the
foreground and the reflection in the mirror behind
Carpenter establishes the setting as a distinct space,
possibly Fry's studio or a room in Carpenter's home.
[CB]

Jacques-Émile Blanche 1861–1942
Aubrey Vincent Beardsley 1895
Oil on canvas
92.6 x 73.7
National Portrait Gallery, London

Aubrey Beardsley was the foremost artist of the decadent movement in Britain. His career lasted only seven years but he gained an international following. He first came to public attention through his illustrations for J.M. Dent & Co.'s *Le Morte d'Arthur* (1892) and for *The Studio* magazine. It was, however, his extraordinary images for the English edition of Oscar Wilde's play *Salome* (1894) that forged his reputation, attracting praise and abuse in equal measure.

Beardsley's association with Wilde damaged his status after Wilde's arrest in April 1895. Beardsley was sacked from his position as art editor of *The Yellow Book* and was accused in an article in *St Paul's* magazine of being 'sexless' and 'unclean'. Little is known about Beardsley's desires and there is no evidence that he was attracted to men, but he moved in queer circles and his sensuous macabre images challenged norms of gender and sexuality.

This portrait was painted in August 1895, in the wake of the Wilde scandal, when Beardsley was visiting Dieppe. He became friends with Jacques-Émile Blanche, who enjoyed his conversation and stories, which were 'so daring it would have been better had he told them in Greek'.[6] The portrait matches Blanche's description of Beardsley as always dressing in 'a light grey suit, a flower in his buttonhole, gloved, he held vertically in the middle a big cane with which he struck the ground chanting his sentences and accompanying his words'.[7]

Beardsley found work again with the somewhat disreputable publisher Leonard Smithers (1861–1909), illustrating editions of Alexander Pope's (1688–1744) *The Rape of the Lock* and Aristophanes's (445–385 BC) *Lysistrata* (both 1896), and was appointed art editor for *The Savoy*, which ran for eight issues. Yet by the middle of 1896 he was showing signs of advanced tuberculosis and died in 1898. [CB]

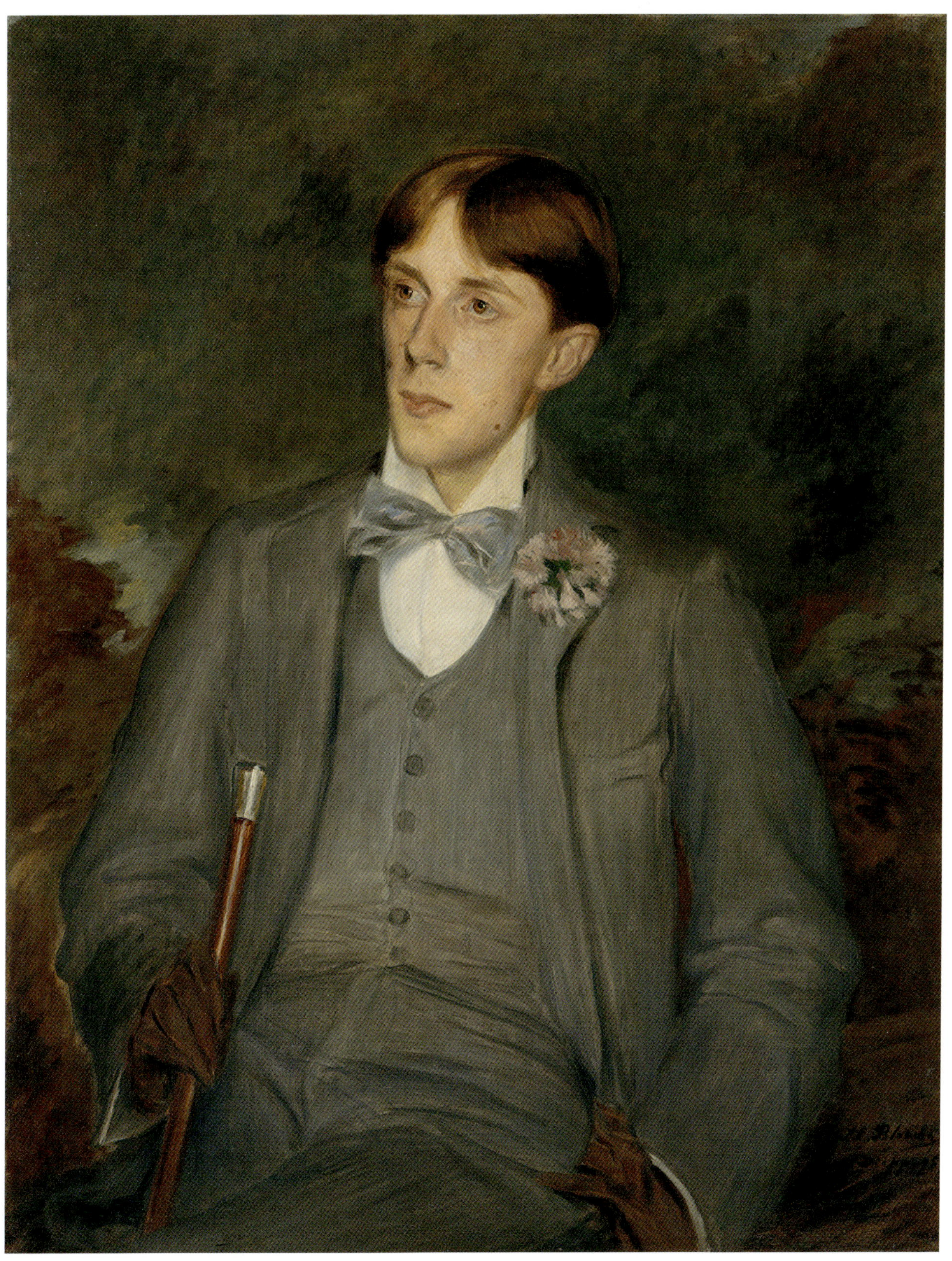

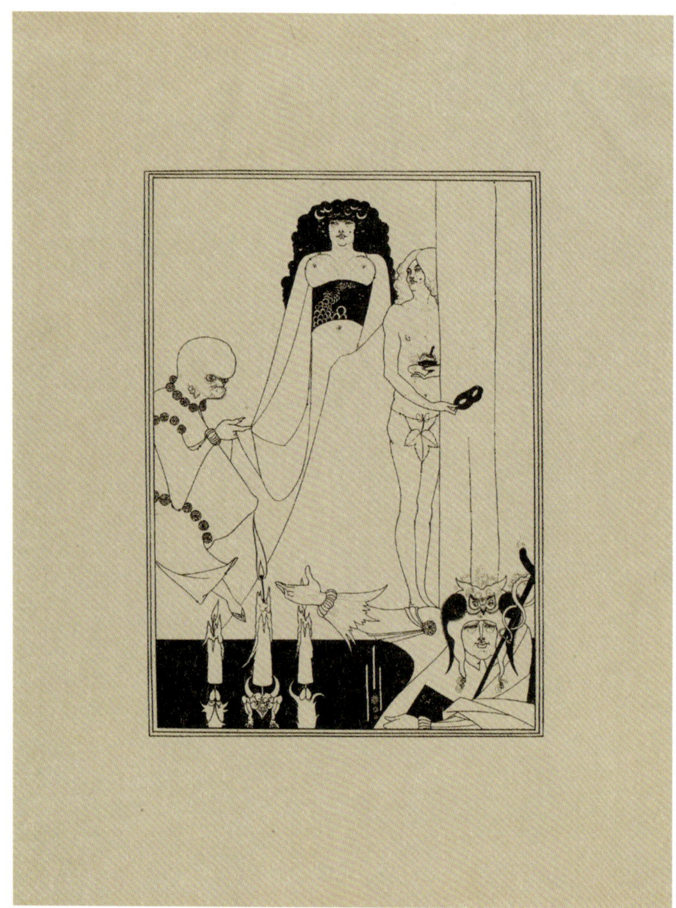

Aubrey Beardsley 1872–98
Enter Herodias from 'Salome' c.1890s
Photo process print on paper
28.6 x 22.4 (sheet)
Victoria and Albert Museum, London

Oscar Wilde is portrayed in the foreground of this image as the showman-like Jester, identified by his book, titled *Salome*. The crossed snakes on his crutch identify it as the caduceus of Mercury, god of orators and messengers, which Susan Owens suggests may be a veiled reference to Wilde's affairs with telegraph boys.[8]

The title of Aubrey Beardsley's illustration comes from a stage direction for the entrance of Herodias, wife of Herod and mother of Salome. Herodias's bare breasts make her an irrefutably feminine presence, while her position at the centre of the composition invites the viewer to make a comparison between the radically different male figures that flank her. The grotesque figure on the left fingers her cloak, his own robe barely concealing the form of his giant phallus, while the slender page on the right appears detached from the scene, his fig-leaved genitals notably unmoved by her presence. As Allison Pease puts it, 'He is in every sense a sexual other, denying not only a heteronormative response to Herodias's presence but also sexual classification itself.'[9] The viewer is therefore presented with two forms of masculinity – the absurdly heterosexual and the elegantly ambiguous. Wilde's gesture towards the scene behind him suggests his complicity in creating this contrast.

The page's fig leaf was a concession to modesty added at the insistence of John Lane, Beardsley's publisher, although, as Linda Zatlin notes, the phallic candlesticks in the foreground seem to have escaped Lane's censorious gaze.[10] Beardsley responded in verse:

> Because one figure was undressed
> This little drawing was suppressed
> It was unkind
> But never mind
> Perhaps it was all for the best. [CB]

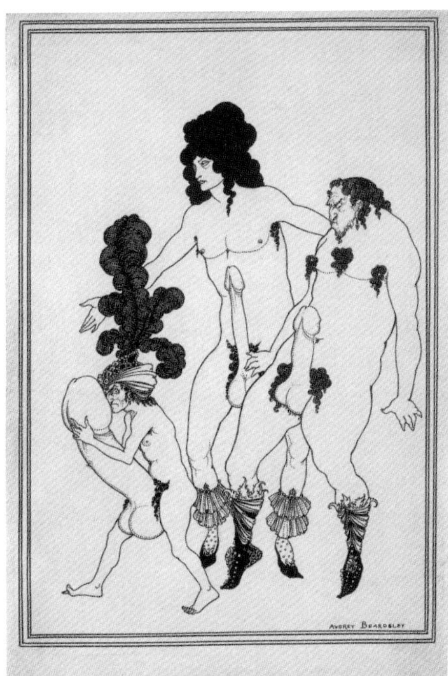

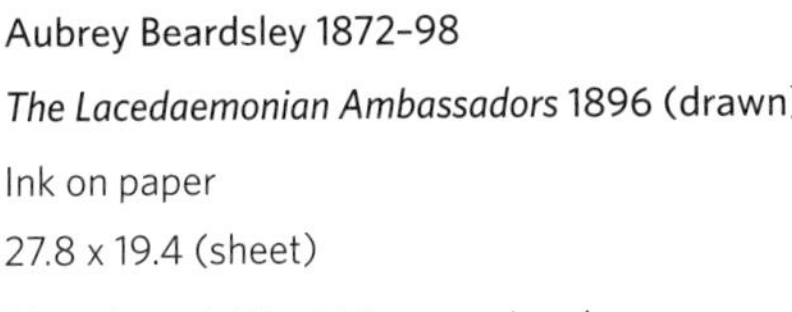

Aubrey Beardsley 1872–98
The Lacedaemonian Ambassadors 1896 (drawn)
Ink on paper
27.8 x 19.4 (sheet)
Victoria and Albert Museum, London

Refused sex by their women, Aubrey Beardsley
portrays the Lacedaemonian ambassadors arriving
in an obvious state of priapism. Beardsley individualises
each man's predicament – the short man at the front
clutches his own enormous phallus, a gesture that
may imply masturbation, while the man at the rear
stretches his hand out towards the central man's
penis, their intertwined feet suggesting entangled
bodies. This is a very different encounter, however,
to the easy lesbianism of the Athenian women (right):
the instigator here looks away furtively, signalling the
illicit nature of this attraction. His chest hair and beard
contrast with the central figure's clean shaven androgyny.

There is little suggestion of pleasure in these
furtive fumblings. As Linda Zatlin puts it, 'All three
men are more burdened with their erections than
proud of them.'[11] [CB]

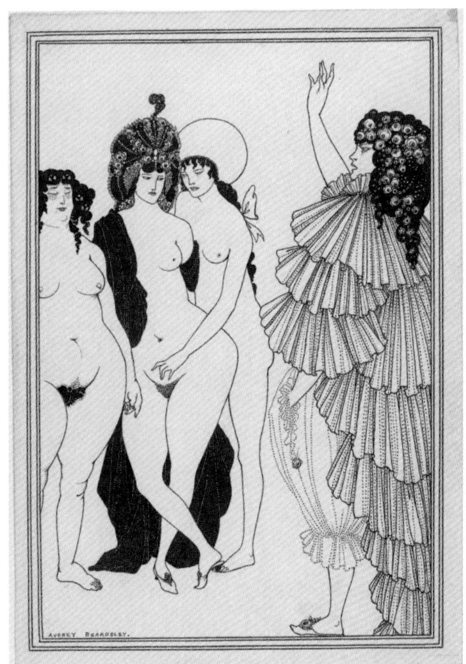

Aubrey Beardsley 1872–98
Lysistrata Haranguing the Athenian Women 1896
Ink on paper
27.8 x 19.4 (sheet)
Victoria and Albert Museum, London

This illustration for the 1886 edition of Aristophanes's
bawdy play *Lysistrata* (411 BC) published by Leonard
Smithers, shows the titular heroine telling the
Athenian women that they can put 'an end to war'
if they will 'Abstain from – Penis' (1896 translation).
The comfortable nudity of the women contrasts with
Lysistrata's elaborately ruffled cloak and bloomers,
suggesting, perhaps, a contrast between natural
sexuality and artificial abstinence. Agreeing to go along
with Lysistrata's plan does not seem to be constraining
the women to a life of chastity. The heavy-lidded
figure on the right of the trio is already reaching
towards the central woman's pudenda, her delicately
outstretched figures emphasising the means by which
she can offer sexual gratification, and her advances do
not appear to be unwelcome. [CB]

OSCAR WILDE: THE PENNINGTON PORTRAIT

JOSEPH BRISTOW

Robert Goodloe Harper Pennington's (c.1854–1920) full-length portrait of Oscar Wilde is the finest likeness of the Irish author made during his lifetime. The American artist gave the portrait as a wedding present to Wilde in 1884 when he married Constance Lloyd (1859–98). It took pride of place in Wilde's beautifully decorated home in Tite Street, Chelsea.

Wilde probably became acquainted with Pennington sometime in 1883 when he travelled to London to join the band of James Abbott McNeill Whistler's (1834–1903) young male 'Followers': a cosmopolitan group of artists who gathered at Whistler's studio, also on Tite Street. Pennington recalled in 1908 how Wilde 'dropped in every day almost, to loll, to smoke, and talk his best, while I worked away at my easel in the big room'. In the portrait Wilde is nicely attired, and he cuts a figure that is much more graceful than the portly one he later developed. Critics such as Ben Harvey have noted that the poised stance Wilde adopts – with his legs confidently apart, his left hand holding his gloves above his hip, the other planting an elegant cane on the ground – resembles Anthony van Dyck's (1599–1641) famous depiction of King Charles I at the hunt (c.1635).

Pennington's portrait is very different from the Wilde we see in the famous photographs sold to the audiences that flocked to hear him talk during his lecture tour of North America in 1882. These iconic images feature Wilde in a trimmed velvet jacket, sumptuous knee breeches, silken hose and opera pumps. In America, Wilde became something of a figure of fun. By contrast, Pennington presents Wilde as a self-possessed young gentleman, one who looks stylish but not sensational.

By the early 1890s Wilde was a well-connected celebrity, having made his name with the plays, *Lady Windermere's Fan* (1892) and *A Woman of No Importance* (1893), and the dazzling essays he brought together in *Intentions* (1891). Yet an abrupt downfall followed.

In April 1895, Wilde took out a hazardous lawsuit against John Sholto Douglas, 9th Marquess of Queensberry, and father of his young lover, Lord Alfred Douglas, after Queensberry sent a notoriously misspelled visiting card on which he had scrawled that Wilde was 'posing as a Somdomite'. As Wilde's case unfolded, Queensberry's defence revealed that Wilde had been sexually involved with several young men, some of whom had engaged in prostitution. Faced with such damaging evidence, Wilde had no choice but to withdraw the suit. He was arrested for 'gross indecency', and bankrupt.

On 24 April 1895 Pennington's portrait went up for sale – along with all of Wilde's household belongings – at an auction at his home. Wilde's life was in tatters: his marriage was broken, he had lost contact with his two young sons, and his finances were ruined. Wilde's friends retrieved many of his manuscripts before the auction, but other items disappeared for good. Pennington's portrait, however, was rescued and Ernest Leverson (the husband of Wilde's friend Ada Leverson) acquired the painting. Leverson stored the painting in his family home, into which Wilde was welcomed soon after he was finally granted bail on 7 May 1895. Pennington's portrait, though, became a bone of contention. Ernest did not share Ada's enthusiasm for such art. Several weeks after he completed his two-year prison sentence in May 1897, Wilde told a friend that Ernest believed he 'could not have [the Pennington portrait] in his drawing-room as it was obviously, on account of its *subject*, demoralising to young men, and possibly to young women of advanced views'. To prevent any further embarrassment, Wilde arranged for Pennington's painting to be entrusted to his friend More Adey from whom it passed to Adey's friend and Wilde's former lover, Robert Ross (1869–1918).

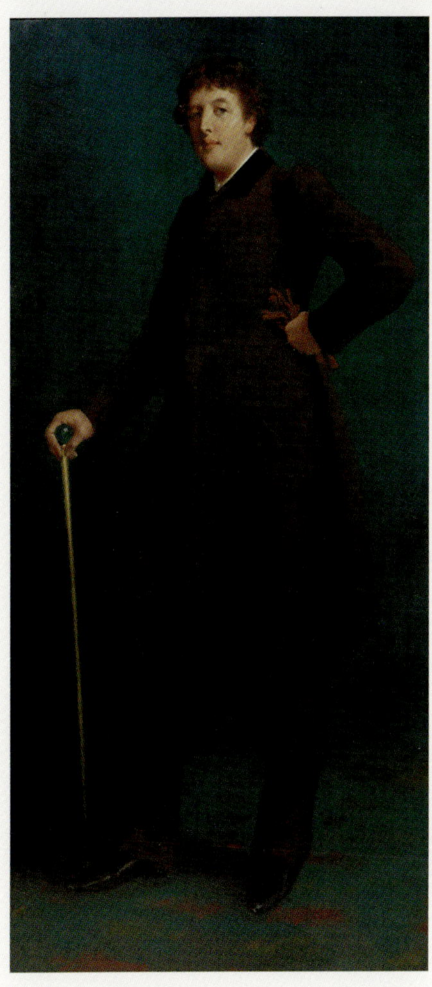

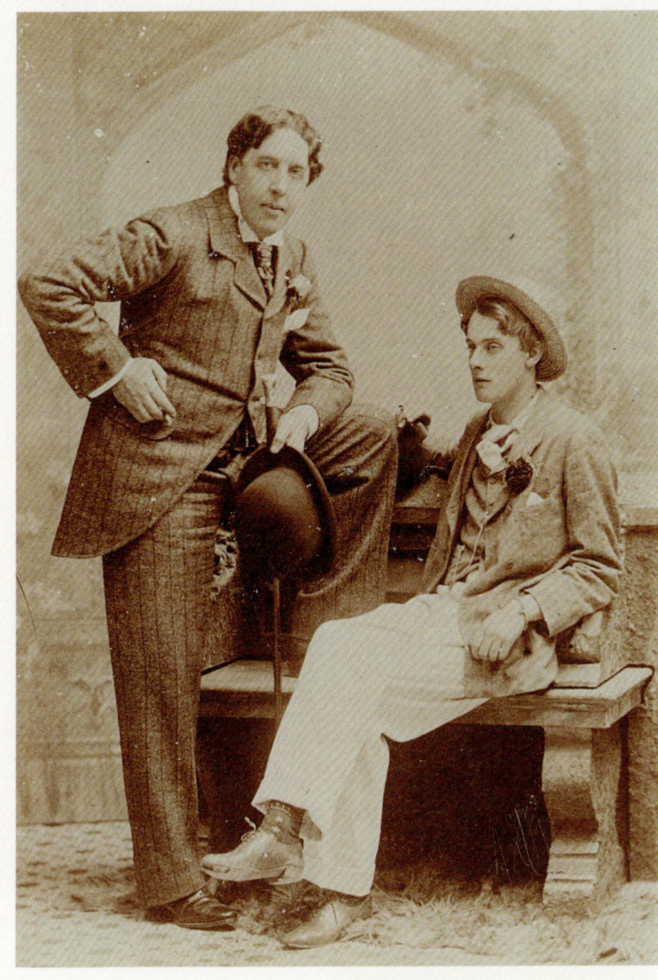

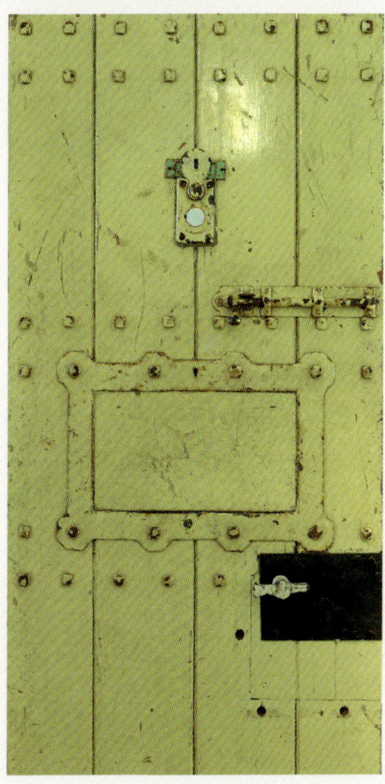

Robert Goodloe Harper
Pennington
Oscar Wilde c.1884
Oil on canvas
177.8 x 91.4
William Andrews Clark
Memorial Library, Los
Angeles

*Prison door from Reading
Gaol, believed to be from
Oscar Wilde's cell*
182.5 x 67. 5
The National Justice
Museum, Nottingham

Gillman & Co
*Oscar Wilde and Lord
Alfred Bruce Douglas* 1893
Photograph, gelatin silver
print
13.6 x 9.7
National Portrait Gallery,
London

Edmund Dulac 1822–1953

Charles Ricketts and Charles Shannon as Medieval Saints 1920

Tempera on fine linen over board

38.7 x 30.5

The Fitzwilliam Museum, Cambridge

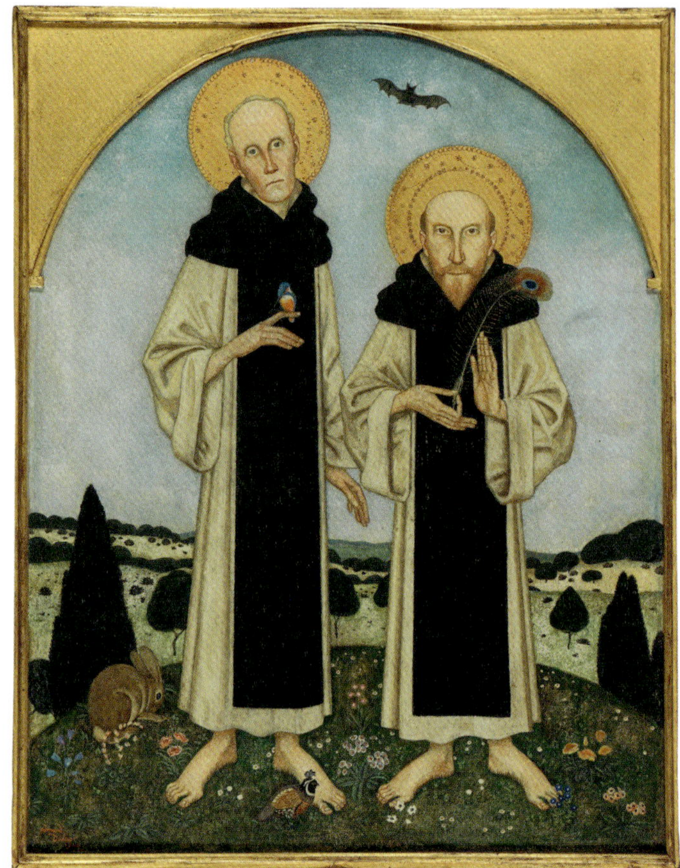

This painting is one of a number of double portraits of the artist and designer Charles Ricketts (1866–1931) and his lifelong partner the painter Charles Shannon (1863–1937). They were friends of Oscar Wilde, who described their home at the Vale to the artist Sir William Rothenstein (1872–1945) as 'the one house in London where you will never be bored'.[12] Their bond was much commented on in their lifetimes: as their friend, art critic Lewis Hind (1862–1927) put it 'They live together; they collect together; they work in adjoining studios.'[13] Ricketts nursed Shannon devotedly in old age after he suffered severe brain damage in a near-fatal accident. According to a story passed on to Ricketts's late twentieth-century biographer J.G.P. Delaney, John Addington Symonds tried to probe the nature of their relationship, eventually causing Ricketts to throw him out of the house. Turning at the bottom of the stairs, Symonds exclaimed 'But you are, aren't you? You do, don't you?', but Ricketts made no reply.[14] Modern scholarship has read much into this silence; however, as Matt Cook has argued, some of these attempts at fixing their sexualities do 'scant justice to the intensity of their bond, or to how they and others perceived it'.[15]

This joint portrait by Ricketts's and Shannon's friend Edmund Dulac playfully hints at their closeness. They are depicted in the matching robes of Cistercian friars, possibly intended as a reference to the chaste ideal of their union but perhaps also alluding to the permanence of their bond: monastic vows were, after all, intended to mark entry for life into an all-male community. Their costumes do not signify religiosity: in a letter to Cecil Lewis (1898–1997) dated 24 December 1920, Ricketts described the Gospels as being something 'I no longer read nor believe in'.[16] Instead, their devotion is to aestheticism, pointed to

by the peacock feather in Ricketts's hand – by the 1920s, an emblem of a previous era. Ricketts and Shannon were uninterested in modernism and the medievalism of Dulac's painting may be light-heartedly signalling their archaic tastes. They admired the arts and crafts movement, and the birds, animals and flowers that surround Shannon in the image are reminiscent of the medieval tapestries that inspired William Morris (1834–96). [CB]

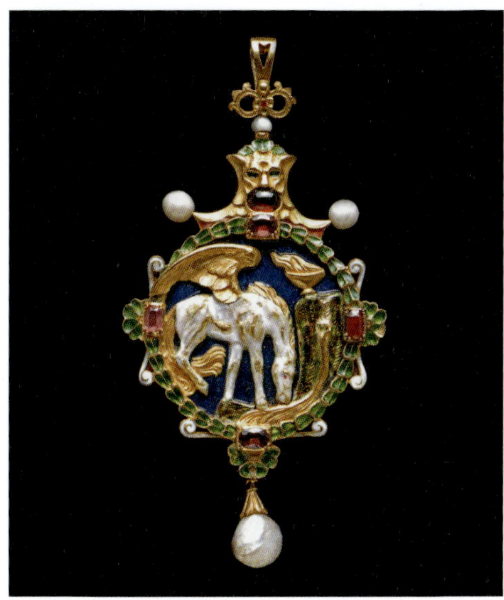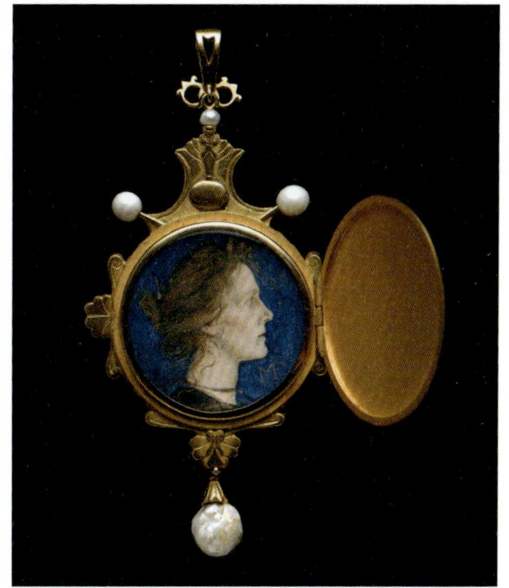

Charles de Sousy Ricketts 1866–1931
Pegasus Drinking from the Fountain of Hippocrene 1901
Locket designed for Edith Cooper – Michael Field
Made by Carlo & Arthur Giuliano, jeweller, London
Pendant
10.1 x 5.1 x 3.4
The Fitzwilliam Museum, Cambridge

This locket was designed by Charles Ricketts for his close friend Edith Cooper (1862–1913) and contains the portrait of Katherine Bradley (1846–1914), Cooper's lover and, shockingly, her aunt. In their joint diary, Cooper and Bradley recorded how Ricketts had trouble with the face until he settled on the idea of depicting it as seen under a flash of lightning: 'Then he discovered the infinite greyness of gold used as shadow & that gave the pallor and sensitiveness to the face, specially the nose.'[17]

Cooper and Bradley were life partners and published poets, whose poems contained passionate declarations of love addressed to female protagonists. The monogram 'MF' on the locket refers to their collective identity as 'Michael Field'. While they initially adopted the name as a nom de plume for their poetry, it rapidly became an identity that they lived out in their lives and letters alongside their original identities. They shunned the emerging vocabulary of 'inversion' and preferred to dress in a traditionally feminine manner but often (although not exclusively) used male names ('Michael' for Bradley, 'Henry' or 'Field' for Cooper) and pronouns. The sexologist Havelock Ellis enquired about their literary collaboration and Katherine/Michael replied: 'We cross and interlace like a company of dancing summer flies; if one begins a character, his companion seizes and possesses it... Let no man think he can put asunder what God has joined'.[18] This final sentence, referring to the Anglican marriage service, makes an explicit link between their intertwined lives and authorial identities. When comparing their relationship to that of the poets Robert Browning (1812–89) and Elizabeth Barrett Browning (1806–61), Katherine/Michael wrote 'we are closer married'.[19] [CB]

CECIL BEATON

Anybody who was anybody in London's high society was photographed by Cecil Beaton. Having left Cambridge University without a degree in 1925, Beaton learnt photography at the studio of Paul Tanqueray (1905–91) and quickly gravitated to the world of *Vogue*. His career, which included work in fashion, theatre and as a war photographer, was launched by his definitive images of the Bright Young Things in the 1920s. Many in this circle had same-sex relationships, including Beaton, who had affairs with both men and women. While Beaton's approach to photography was not the inevitable result of his sexuality, some scholars have discerned a queer aesthetic in the fantastical plethora of surfaces, fabrics, costume and elements of masquerade that fill his images.

Nowhere is this clearer than in Beaton's image of Stephen Tennant as Prince Charming (p.66). Beaton first met Tennant (1906–87) at a house party in 1926. Tennant was flamboyantly queer and had been raised by his mother to be a genius, qualities that later made him Evelyn Waugh's (1906–66) inspiration for Sebastian Flyte in *Brideshead Revisited* (1945). His elaborate quasi-Elizabethan costume in the photograph was designed by Beaton for Tennant's appearance as Prince Charming in a charity matinée, *A Pageant of Great Lovers*, at the New Theatre, London. Tennant lies as if asleep on shimmering silks, his lips glossy, his hair perfectly curled, his eyes demurely closed and his hands joined as if in prayer. While he is Prince Charming, the pose is more reminiscent of Snow White, resting chastely for his prince to come and wake him.

Beaton's photograph of Madge Garland (p.67) was taken in the year that he signed his first contract with *Vogue*. Garland, who had been initially employed as a receptionist before rising to become an influential fashion journalist, attributed her success to her stylish wardrobe. Beaton captures her elegant presence, depicting her with smartly shingled hair against a modernist background. Garland was the lover of Dorothy Todd, British *Vogue*'s second editor, who had turned the magazine into a bastion of avant-garde style. The two women lived together, causing one of their circle to quip, 'A Garland is a lovesome thing, Todd wot.'[20] Yet their relationship made them vulnerable: the year before this photograph was taken, they were both sacked when Condé Nast, *Vogue*'s publisher, became alarmed at the growing rumours and threatened Garland and Todd with public exposure.

British *Vogue* continued to champion British modernism even after Todd's departure: the image of the poet and novelist Sylvia Townsend Warner (1893–1978) (opposite) was taken for a group of images of literary subjects which were published in the magazine in July 1927. Warner had achieved literary success with *Lolly Willows* (1926). In 1930, she met Valentine Ackland (1906–69), the woman who became her lover and lifelong partner. She regularly explored themes of female sexuality in her work and included a lesbian relationship in her 1936 novel, *Summer Will Show*. Beaton and Warner were friends, often attending the same parties. Beaton depicts Sylvia in soft focus against one of his characteristic shimmering satin backgrounds. [CB]

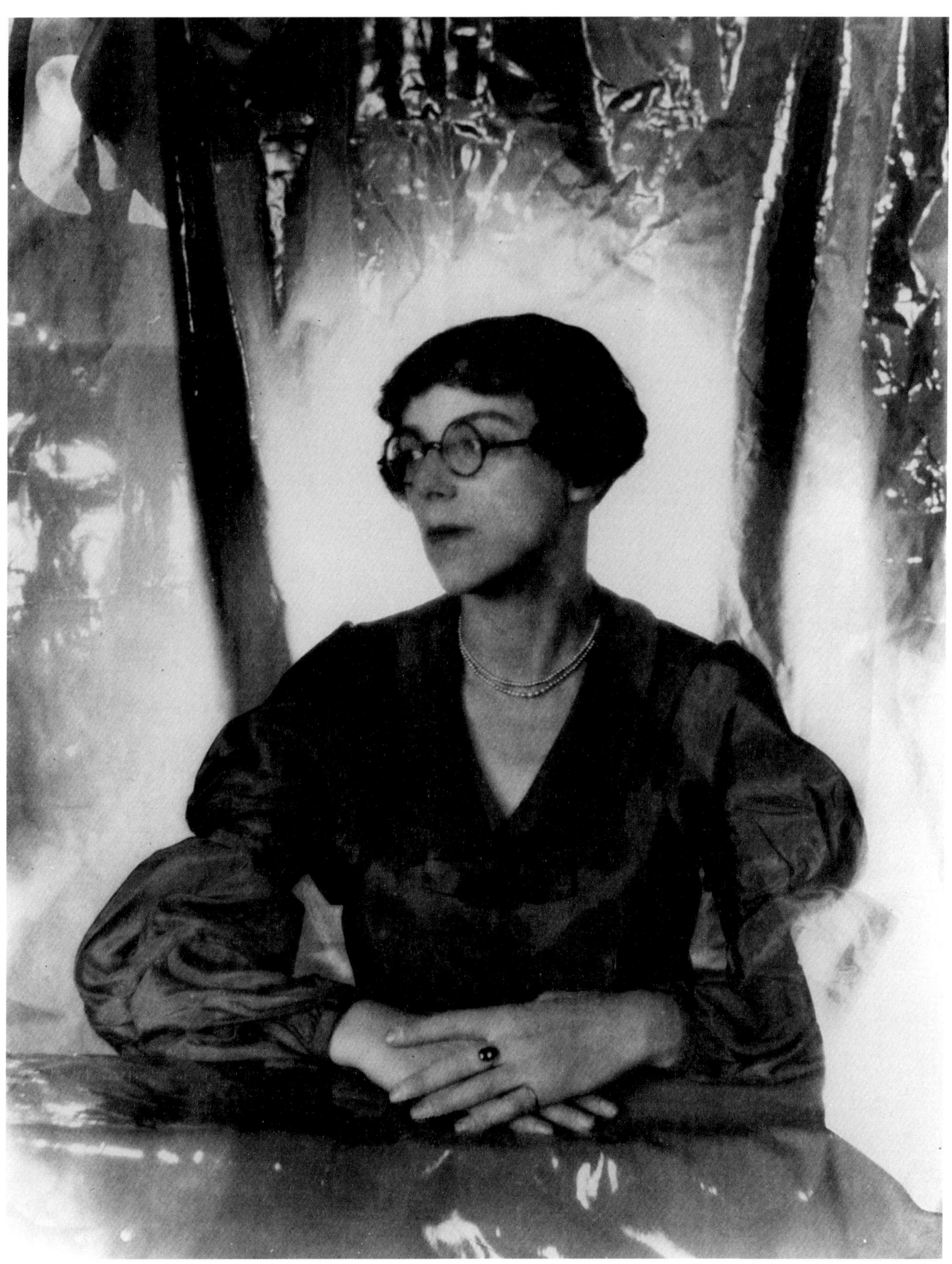

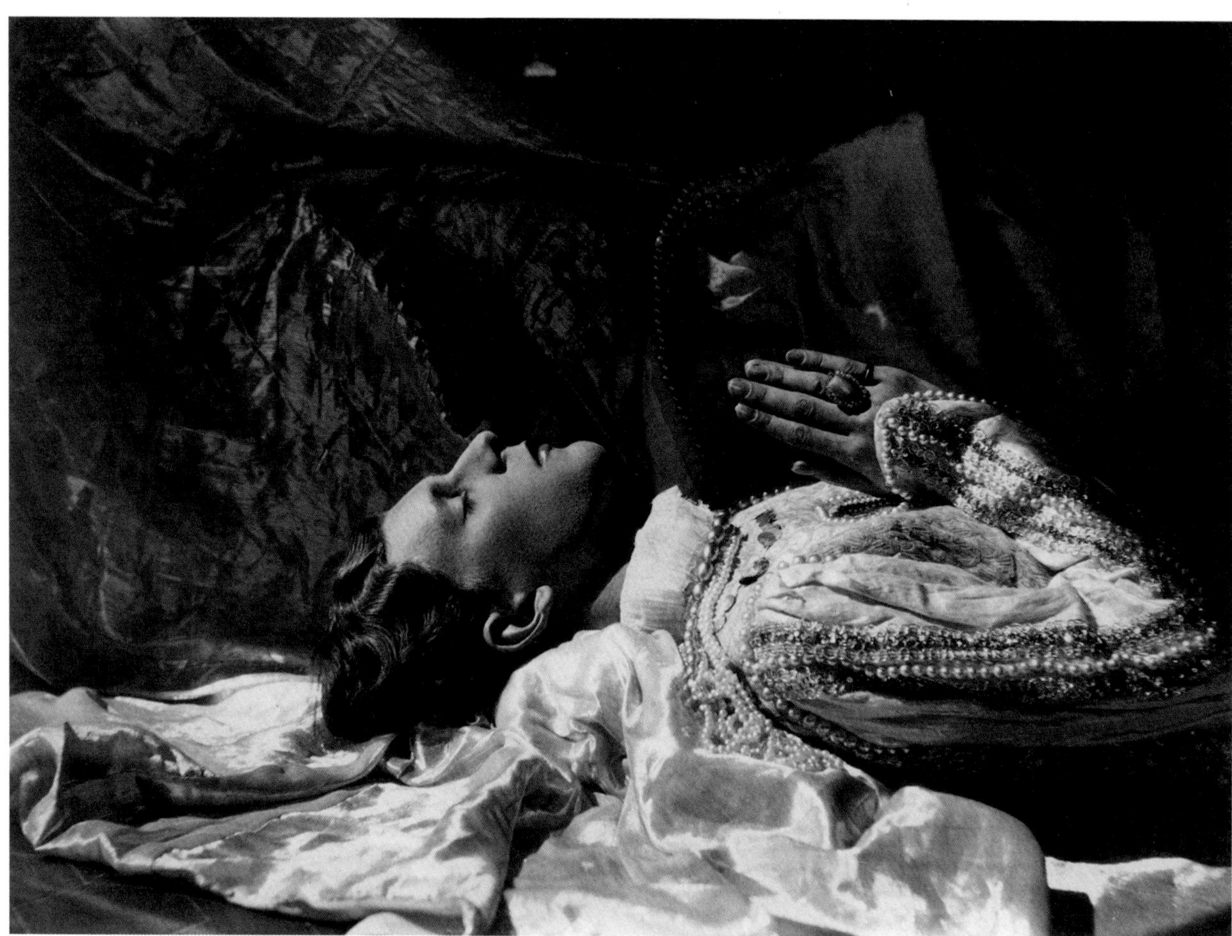

ABOVE

Cecil Beaton 1904–80

Stephen Tennant as Prince Charming 1927

Photograph, bromide print on paper

19 x 26.4

National Portrait Gallery, London

OPPOSITE

Cecil Beaton 1904–80

Madge Garland 1927

Photograph, bromide print on paper

20.3 x 20.3

National Portrait Gallery, London

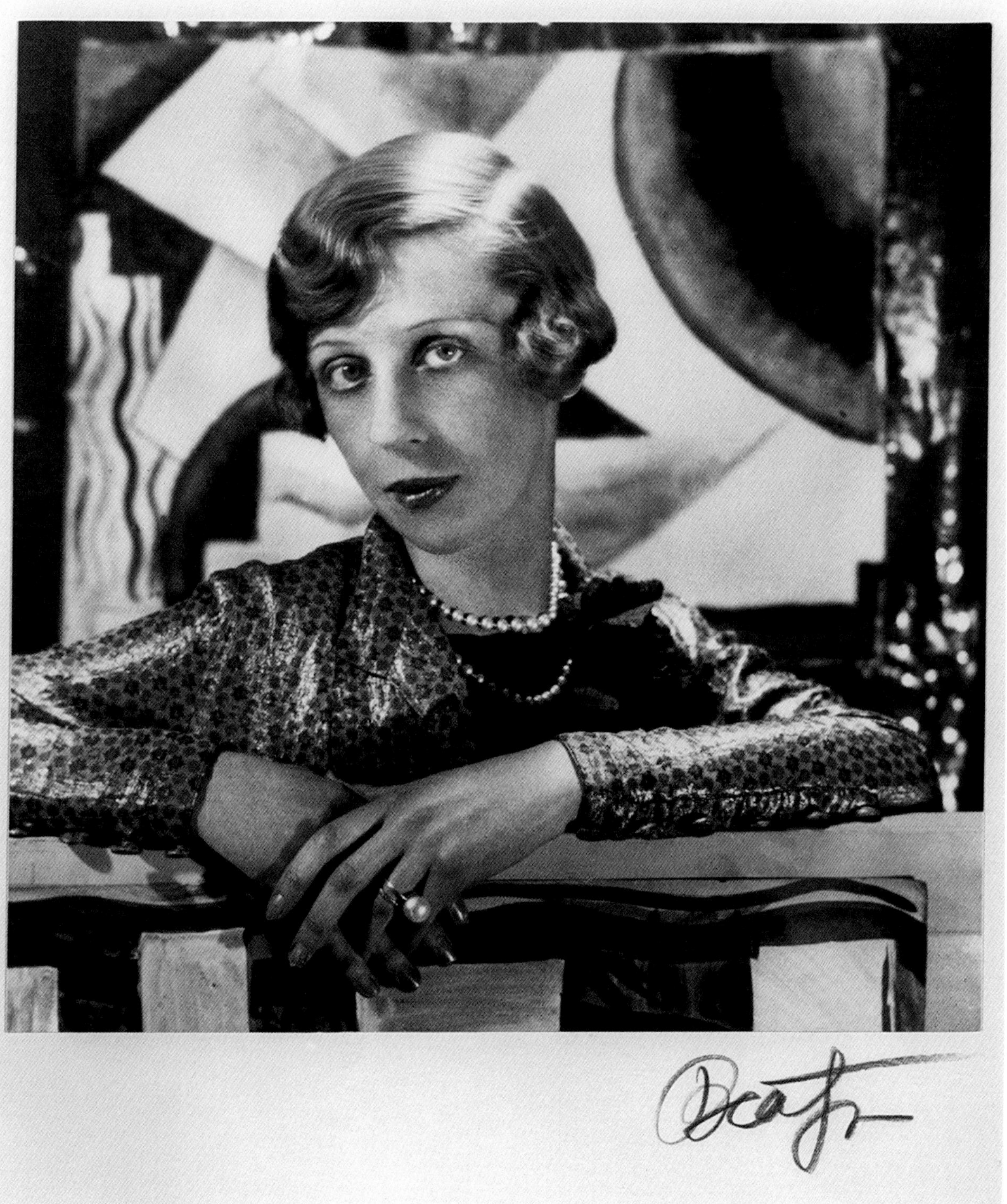

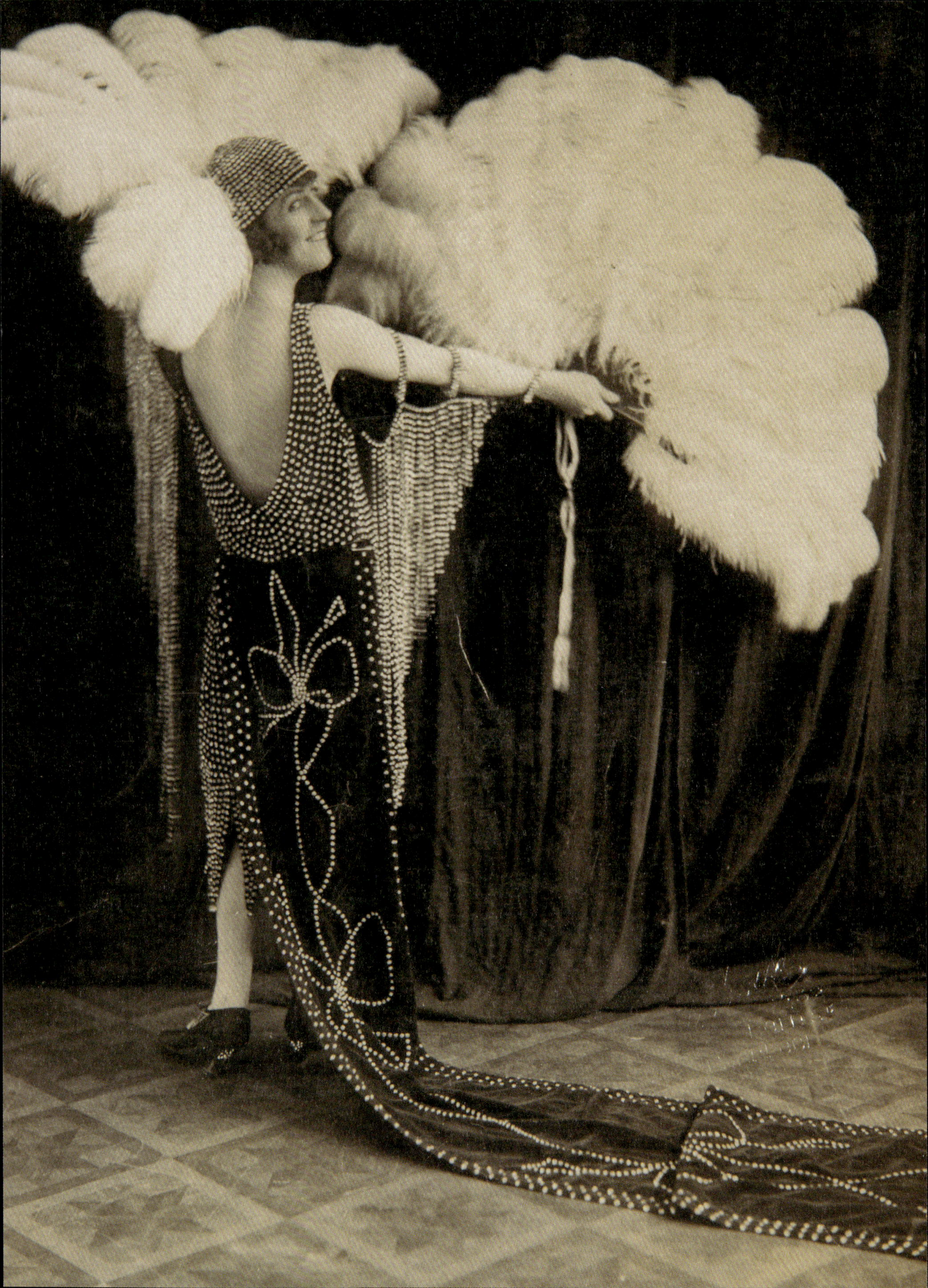

THEATRICAL TYPES

NEIL BARTLETT

'Me, I've always been the theatrical type'
(Vince the barman, in Neil Bartlett and Nicolas
Bloomfield's *Night after Night* 1993)

YOU MIGHT THINK the word 'theatrical' as a euphemism for queer is a term that has had its day; surely, after all the advances of the last few decades, we are what we are. However, the word still has a curious traction, and I think this is because two powerful mirror-image myths loom up out of recent popular culture whenever it is used to describe either a queer person or a queer work of art. One of these myths is the lingering suspicion that some, most or even possibly all queer people are at least one or more of the following: colourful, self-dramatising, amusing, artificial, melodramatic, camp, over-emotional, over-dressed, over-sexed, stylish, role-playing, histrionic, great with accessories, attention-seeking or (under pressure) borderline hysterical. The second myth – an equally enduring one – is that theatre and performance have always been our natural professional homes. Shuttling between these two myths, and using each one as the alibi to reinforce the other, the word remains potently double-edged; even when it is apparently being used to praise, it is necessarily – if sometimes subtly – pejorative, suggesting as it does that the work or person in question is somehow less authentic, less fully matured, and above all, less real than the other works or people from which it, she, he or they are being distinguished.

Well, if we are talking history as opposed to mythology, we may as well cut to the chase. There is absolutely no evidence that the performing arts were any more associated with or practised by or welcoming to homosexual people in the hundred years or so between 1861 and 1967 than (say) ambulance-driving, trade unionism, embroidery or motherhood; nor do we know whether theatrical types have been any more legion among our number than non-theatrical types. This landmark anniversary of the partial decriminalisation of male homosexuality in 1967 might be the perfect opportunity to relegate the idea that we as queer people have an innate predisposition towards one profession or personality-type or indeed anything else at all to the dustbin of history – or, more exactly, to the annals of oppressive and divisive categorisation. However, the question of whether theatrical queers and queer theatres of many different kinds have been conspicuously present in all levels of British society during those hundred years is another matter entirely. As this book so richly attests, our queer pioneers and ancestors – the

practitioners of our extraordinarily resilient and distinctive queer cultural traditions
– were absolutely everywhere.

It is crucial to realise when looking back that all of these practitioners operated
under quite extraordinary pressure; the fact that our sexual lives were illegal for the
whole of the hundred years in question was merely the tip of the iceberg. Being queer
was something that was not supposed to be talked about, and which certainly could
not be shown in public – or not in theory, at least. How, then, could it possibly be
made manifest in the theatre, a business that consists entirely of showing and telling?

Broadly (and provocatively) speaking, queer people have chosen to live and
work within two very different traditions of theatre.

The first is a theatre that is self-proclaimedly serious. At the end of the
nineteenth century, the heavyweight genre of 'the problem play' took on all
the social and political issues of the day – and the 'problem' of homosexuality
soon featured. John Gray (1866–1934) and Marc-André Raffalovich's (1864–
1934) gloriously over-the-top and deliciously sympathetic depiction of queer
villainy in their 1894 play *The Blackmailers* (opposite) may well be the first time
we took centre stage in this particular genre, and as subject matter for serious
discussion we have never really gone out of fashion in London's West End since.
Notable box-office hits pre-1967 featuring us and our 'problems' include Mordaunt
Shairp's (1887–1939) *The Green Bay Tree* (1933) and Shelagh Delaney's *A Taste
of Honey* (1958 – a breath of fresh, frank and for once female air). John Osborne
(1929–94) gave the genre a new and rather odd twist with his 1965 costume
drama *A Patriot For Me* at the Royal Court Theatre. Osborne was an often homophobic
playwright and the Court a frequently homophobic management, so their use of
a lavishly staged drag ball as the centrepiece of the play was problematic in more
ways than one. Like Raffalovich before him, Osborne had to have the piece presented
as a club performance so as to avoid having cuts imposed by the Lord Chamberlain.
The Lord Chamberlain's office was responsible for formally censoring every
professionally produced theatre script in advance of production, and it had a very
sharp eye for all things queer. Once that office was abolished in 1968, things could
get a little more explicit, and 1968 and 1969 saw an explosion of commercial
queer-themed plays in London, led by Colin Spencer's (b.1933) *Spitting Image* (1968)
at the Hampstead Theatre Club. Half a century later, the genre is still firmly with
us; plays as successful and as different as Kevin Elyot's (1951–2014) *My Night
With Reg* (1994) and Alan Bennett's (b.1934) *The History Boys* (2004) still rely
on its basic mechanism of disclosing queerness as a fascinating problem, then
tracing that problem as a revealing fault line in contemporary society .

The second tradition assumes that to be queer is not a problem, but a pleasure
– and it places queerness not in the words of a script, but in the body of the performer,
often outrageous, and always the focus of attention. Significantly, this second
tradition (of which the many and diverse strands are traditionally collected under
the single and not especially helpful heading of Camp) operated pre-1967 at all
cultural levels – low, middle and high. Indeed, it often specifically delighted in

PRINCE OF WALES THEATRE.

Mr. CHARLES THURSBY'S MATINEE,

ON THURSDAY, JUNE 7th, AT 2.30,

THE BLACKMAILERS,

A New and Original Play of Modern Life,

By JOHN GRAY and ANDRE RAFFALOVICH.

Admiral Sir Felbert Dangar	Mr. JULIAN CROSS
Mr. Dangar Felbert	Mr. C. COLNAGHI
Edward Bond-Hinton	Mr. A. BROMLEY DAVENPORT
Guy Joscelyn	Mr. HARRY EVERSFIELD
Claud Price	Mr. W. L. ABINGDON
Servant to Hal Dangar	Mr. FRANK WEATHERSBY
Servant to the Bond-Hintons	Mr. E. BELLENDEN

AND

Hyacinth Halford Dangar	Mr. CHARLES THURSBY
Lady Felbert	Miss EMILY MILLER
The Hon. Miss Alcyra Felbert	Miss MARY CALLAN
Mrs. Dangar	Mrs. THEODORE WRIGHT
Violet Bond-Hinton	Miss M. T. BRUNTON
Susan (Mrs. Dangar's Parlourmaid)	Miss HENRIETTA CROSS

AND

Camilla Bond-Hinton	Miss OLGA BRANDON

ACT I.

Scene ... SMOKING ROOM AT THE BOND-HINTON'S HOUSE. "Camilla."

ACT II.

Scene ... HALFORD DANGAR'S CHAMBERS. "Master and Pupil."

ACT III.

Scene ... Mrs. BOND-HINTON'S DRAWING ROOM. "A House of Cards."

ACT IV.

Scene ... Mrs. DANGAR'S DRAWING ROOM IN CHESTER SQUARE. "A Perfect Scoundrel."

Produced under the direction of **Mr. JULIAN CROSS.**

The above Artistes appear by kind permission of their respective Managers.

Furniture by W. F. LYONS. Wigs by Fox.

Business Manager (for CHARLES THURSBY) Mr. HARRINGTON BAILY.

THE RIVIERA OF ENGLAND, VENTNOR, ISLE OF WIGHT.

THE ROYAL HOTEL, VENTNOR.

Patronized by the Queen and Royal Family, also by distinguished English, American, and Continental Families. This old-established high-class Hotel stands in its own charming grounds of four acres commanding magnificent Sea View. Cuisine a Special Feature. Table d'Hote (Separate Tables) at 7 p.m. Tariff and all particulars upon application to the Manager.

Support Home Industries.

Bryant & May's MATCHES.

Are used in the Bars of this Theatre.

Programme for
The Blackmailers 1894
Victoria and Albert
Museum, London

confounding and confusing these categories. Cross-dressed comediennes Fanny (1846–81) and Stella (1847–1904) (aka Frederick Park and Ernest Boulton – working thirty years before *The Blackmailers*) might have attained some respectability before their arrest in 1869, but they rose unapologetically from London's queer sex-trade subculture, and took that culture's manners and frocks with them when they went on the road with their polite comic one-acters (pp.84–5). Designers Edward Burra and Oliver Messel (1904–78) took the highest of High Culture – working for the Sadler's Wells Ballet and the Royal Ballet respectively – and made it the vehicle for their own deliciously queer (and in Burra's case, distinctively rough-trade) visions (pp.82–3). Angus McBean (1904–90) earned his living documenting the stars of the commercial West End, but made his studio portraits a unique marriage of surreal technique and queer insight (pp.74–7).

This second tradition is normally thought of as being an art that delights in not speaking its name, preferring to play around with it instead. In contrast to the first tradition, it works by making queer a verb, not a subject, and by transferring or transforming the forbidden rather than spelling it out. However, while it is the first tradition that always claims to be the liberal and confrontational one, it is in fact

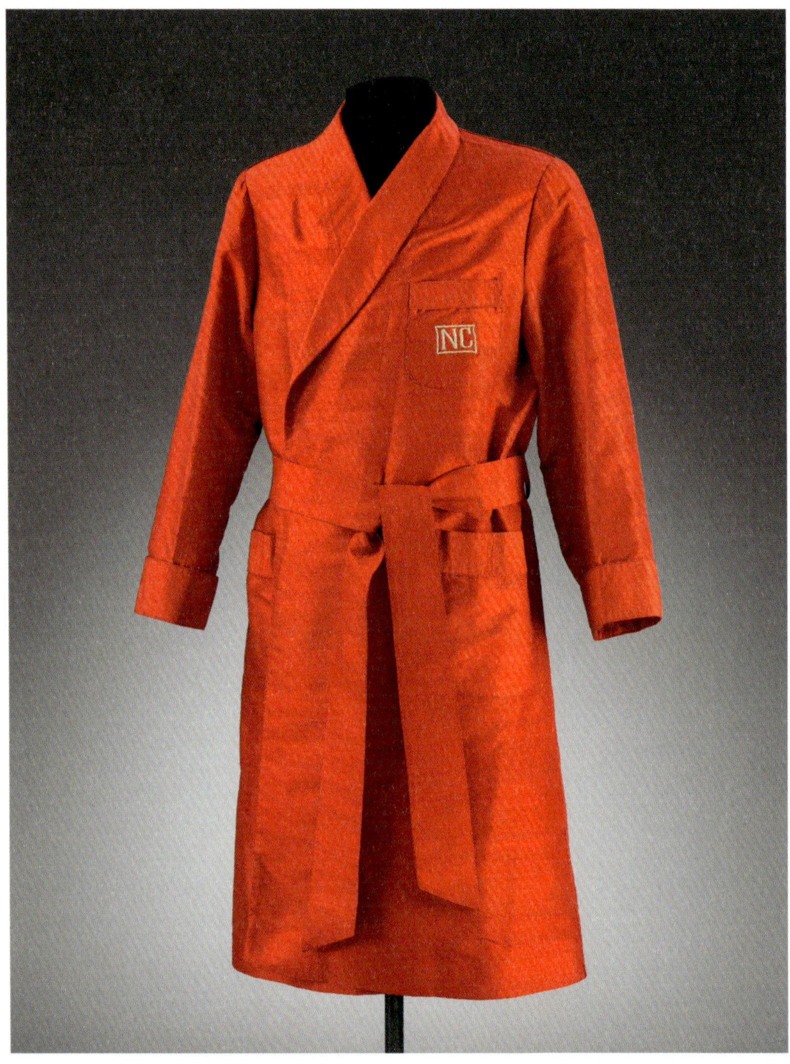

this second tradition that has done much of the heavy lifting in the fight for queer cultural freedom. Many of the artists working within this tradition employed what is arguably the best tactic of all for confronting prohibition: they got the audience on their side and their names at the top of the bill. Comedians Fred Barnes (1885–1938), Hetty King, Malcolm Scott (1872–1929), Douglas Byng (1893–1987) and Danny La Rue (to name just some of those who feature in this book) were queer artists of very different times and decades, but they were all big stars. Once on stage, their sheer popularity gave them extraordinary licence. Their performances made mincemeat of the idea that the owner of a queer body ought to feel obliged to pretend that it was anything other than just exactly that – queer.

There is – of course – one more tradition of queer theatre running through the second half of the hundred years, which is only touched on here. The commercial London theatre of that particular half-century was dominated by a series of hugely

Noël Coward's dressing gown c.1920–60 (made)
Silk dupion, machine stitched, detailing added with appliqué and machine embroidery in white cotton
Victoria and Albert Museum, London

successful and influential male authors and author-performers in same-sex relationships, who policed both their private lives and any direct expression of queerness in their work with extraordinary thoroughness once they achieved their success – Somerset Maugham (1874–1965), Ivor Novello (1893–1951), Noël Coward (1899–1973) and Terence Rattigan (1911–77). The reason for their reticence is not hard to locate. Like the rest of the British theatrical establishment, they were working in the long shadow of the arrest and subsequent disgrace and death of Oscar Wilde (pp.60-1). Maugham was already twenty when Wilde was arrested; Novello, Coward and Rattigan all had their first hits within living memory of his death. The swift and brutal silencing by the law of the most fashionable and successful playwright of the preceding generation provided the immediate context for Maugham's bitter delineations of sexual dissidence, Rattigan's extraordinary empathy for the disgraced and wounded, and even, perhaps, for Novello's lurid frivolity and the carefully calculated outrage of both Coward's machine-gun wit and his trademark dressing-gowned public persona (opposite). What *Queer British Art* cannot document is the myriad absences and silences that the destruction of Wilde gave rise to – but the distorting pressure exerted on even those major names should remind us of all the things that were never said or shown on stage in the century following Wilde's arrest for gross indecency; all the theatre careers, for instance, that were frustrated or curtailed. The artists who are included here were the brilliant , brave exceptions, not the dismal, homophobic rule.

Our sex lives were partially decriminalised in 1967; the Lord Chamberlain's Office was abolished in 1968 – and queer theatres of all kinds proliferated. On the radical end of the spectrum, Lindsay Kemp (b.1938) was about to scandalise the Edinburgh Festival; Philip Prowse (b.1937) and Giles Havergal (b.1938) were about to take over the Glasgow Citz; Bette Bourne (b.1939) was about to play opposite Ian McKellen (b.1939) in Christopher Marlowe's (bap.1564–93) *Edward II* (1594); and (three years down the line) the Almost Free Theatre would provide the meeting place for the future founders of Gay Sweatshop. Meanwhile, pantomime, ballet, a thousand West End choruses and drag queens of every denomination from Rogers and Starr to Frederick Ashton (1904–88) and Robert Helpmann (1906–86) kept mainstream queer performance traditions vibrantly alive. However, it would be a huge mistake to divide our history into the bad old days before 1967 and a new age afterwards. Our history is complex and continuous, and the faces and bodies in *Queer British Art* bear witness to that. The magnificent self-possession of Hetty King and Beatrix Lehmann (1903–79) (pp.74–5); the strange wedding of vulgarity and hilarity presided over by Malcolm Scott (p.89), and all the other pioneers of queer solo performance art; the flaming scarlet of Mr Coward's absent-yet-present self – these are the materials out of which we are still all working to dramatise and create our queer selves.

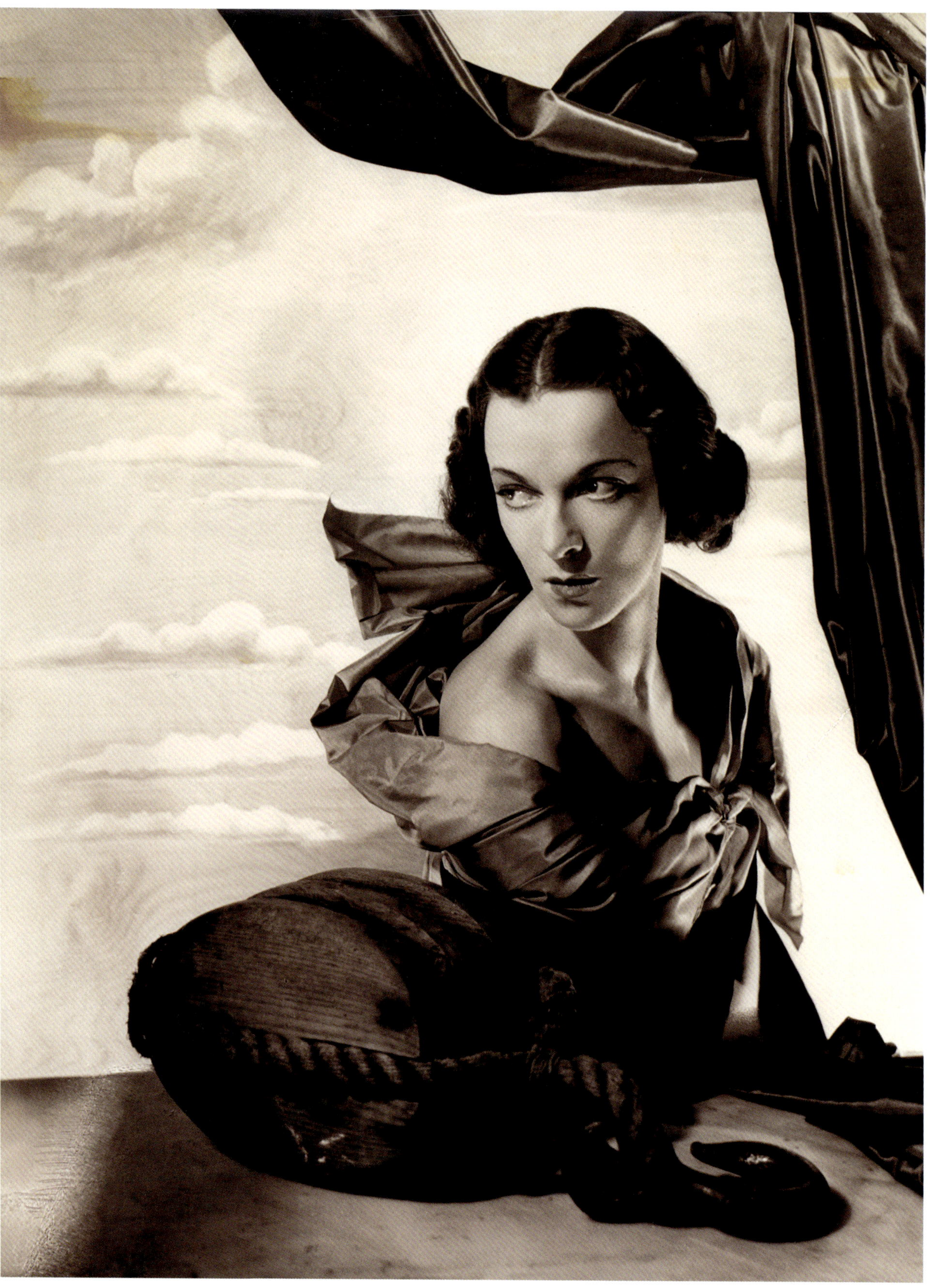

Angus McBean 1904–90

Beatrix Lehmann 1937

Photograph, bromide print

on paper

29.2 x 23.1

National Portrait Gallery,

London

ANGUS MCBEAN

Angus McBean's career was forged in the theatre. Success came in 1936 with his work for Ivor Novello in Max Beerbohm's *The Happy Hypocrite* (1896). McBean not only made masks for Novello but was also invited to take close-up portraits for the production, which were published in the leading papers. In a break with convention, McBean's images were staged as intimate tableaux that captured the psychological drama of the characters. Inspired by the International Surrealist exhibitions of 1936 and 1937, he began to make playful 'surrealised portraits', which were initially published in *The Sketch*. These used complex props and staging to create fantastical scenes and to give the illusion of distorted scale.

The images here depict sitters who were in same-sex relationships. McBean's own relationships with men led to a police raid on his house and his arrest in 1942 for criminal acts of homosexuality. He was convicted and sentenced to four years in jail but was released in 1944 and re-established himself as a photographer.

Beatrix Lehmann was one of McBean's first surrealised portraits, published in *The Sketch* on 29 December 1937 (opposite). It was made to publicise Eugene O'Neill's (1888–1953) 1931 play, *Mourning Becomes Electra*, in which Lehmann had the starring role of Lavinia. The composition was influenced by paintings of William Acton, and McBean later told how 'I simply decided it would be fun to produce a photograph that looked like one of his self-portraits.'[1] He described it as 'the most simply achieved of all my surreal efforts and certainly one of the best'.[2]

The dancer and choreographer Berto Pasuka (1904–63) had known McBean since 1944 and had modelled for him (p.76). Together with his friend Richie Riley (1910–97), Pasuka started *Les Ballets Nègres* in 1946. This was not only the first company in Britain to be composed of black dancers but was also the first to offer what Riley later described as 'in every shape and form, ballet in a black idiom.'[3] McBean took a number of portrait and publicity shots for them, including this image. *Les Ballets Nègres* was immensely successful, attracting large audiences and gaining substantial critical acclaim.

Published in the *Tatler and Bystander* on 6 August 1947, McBean's portrait of the theatrical producer Binkie Beaumont (1908–73) was one of the most celebrated in McBean's 'Play Personalities' series. It depicts Beaumont apparently manipulating puppets of the actors Emlyn Williams (1905–87) and Angela Baddeley (1904–76), in their roles in the first production of Terence Rattigan's *The Winslow Boy* (1946) (p.77). The surreal effect of this image could have been achieved through montage but McBean staged it using a toy theatre and cut-out images of the actors.

McBean's portrait of Robert Helpmann (p.76), published in the *Tatler and Bystander* on 28 April 1948, shows him in the role of Hamlet. The backdrop was created from a blown-up photograph of text from the First Folio of Shakespeare's play. The production was designed to be Victorian gothic: an Elsinore of guttering candles and chiaroscuro lighting effects. There is perhaps some suggestion of this in the heavy shadows of McBean's photograph, while Helpmann's dramatic make-up emphasises his melancholic expression. [CB]

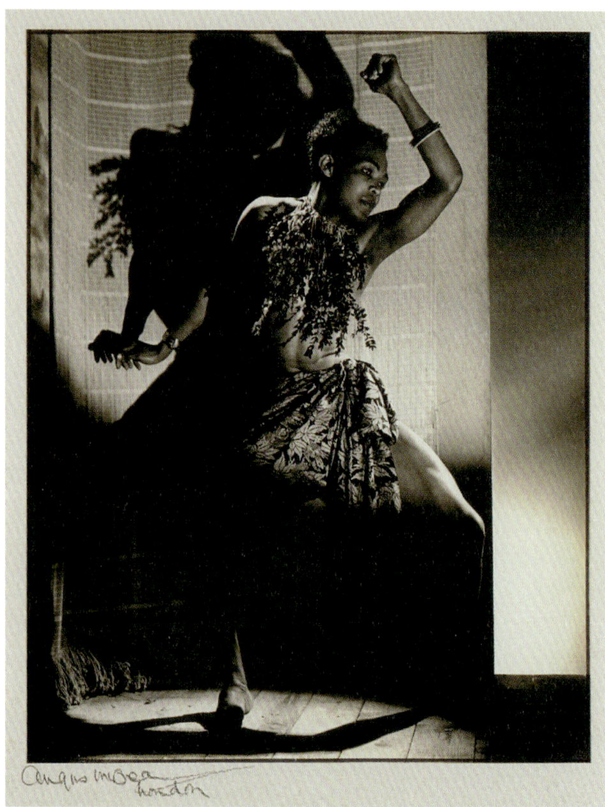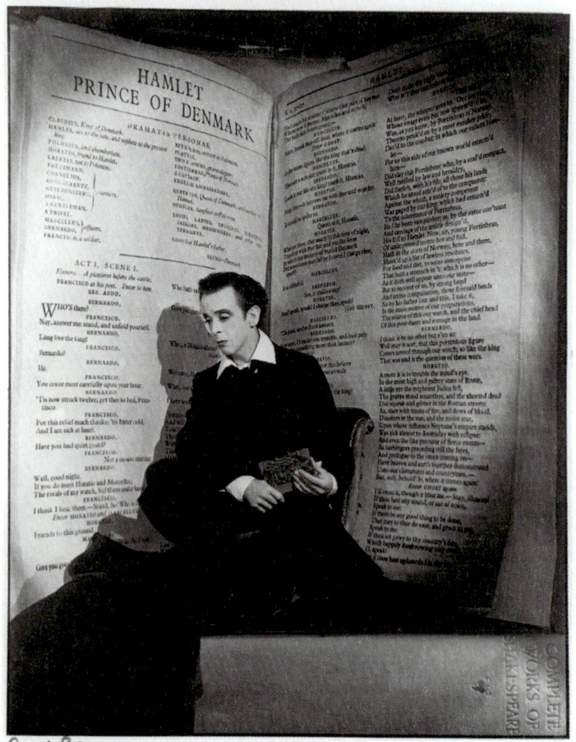

Angus McBean 1904–90

Berto Pasuka

Published in *Ballet*, January 1946

Photograph, bromide print on paper

37.4 x 29.9

National Portrait Gallery, London

Angus McBean 1904–90

Sir Robert Murray Helpmann 1950

Photograph, bromide print on paper

50.8 x 40.3

National Portrait Gallery, London

Angus McBean 1904–90

Binkie Beaumont, Angela Baddeley and

(George) Emlyn Williams 1947

Photograph, bromide print on paper

38 x 29.7

National Portrait Gallery, London

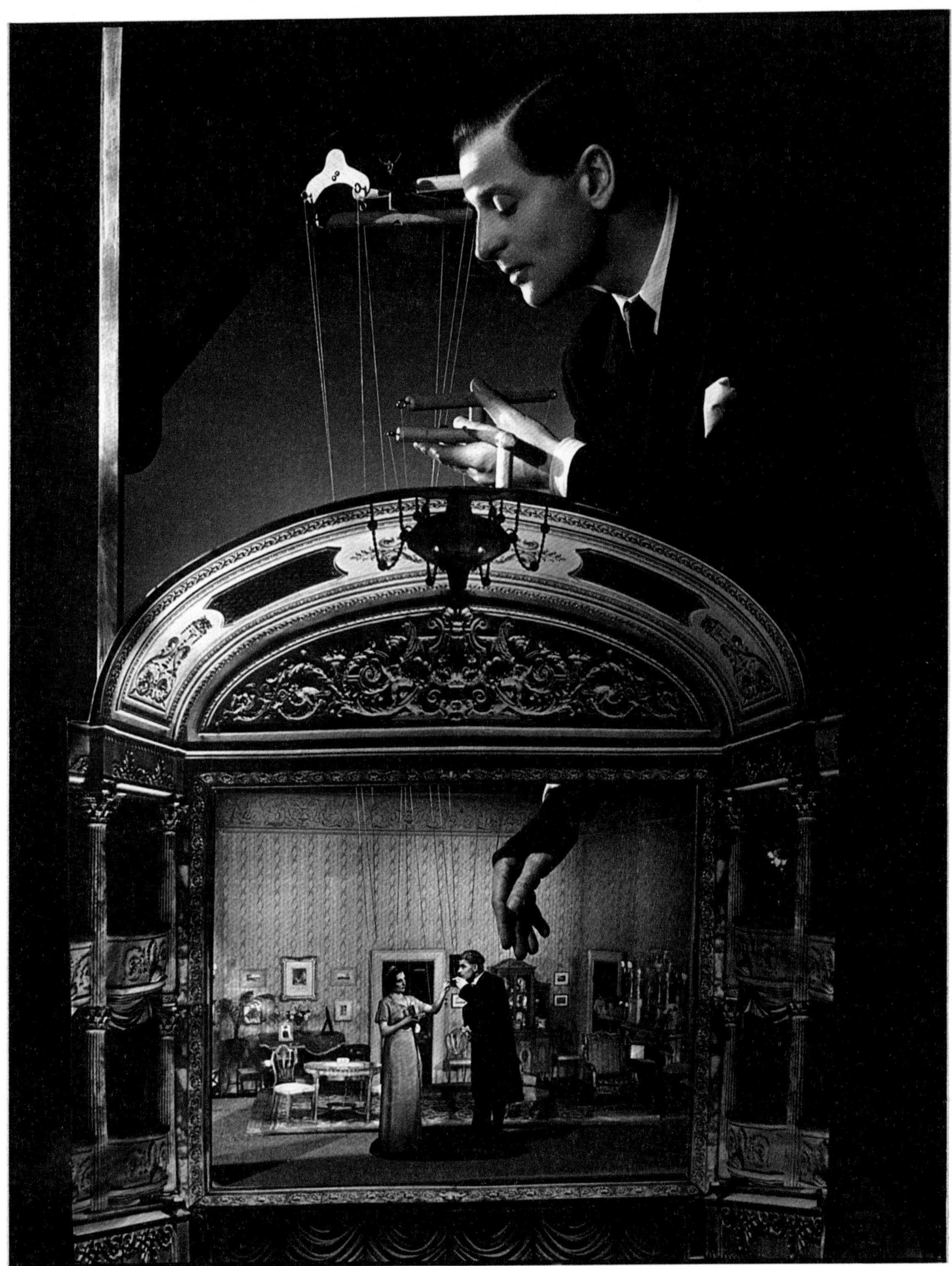

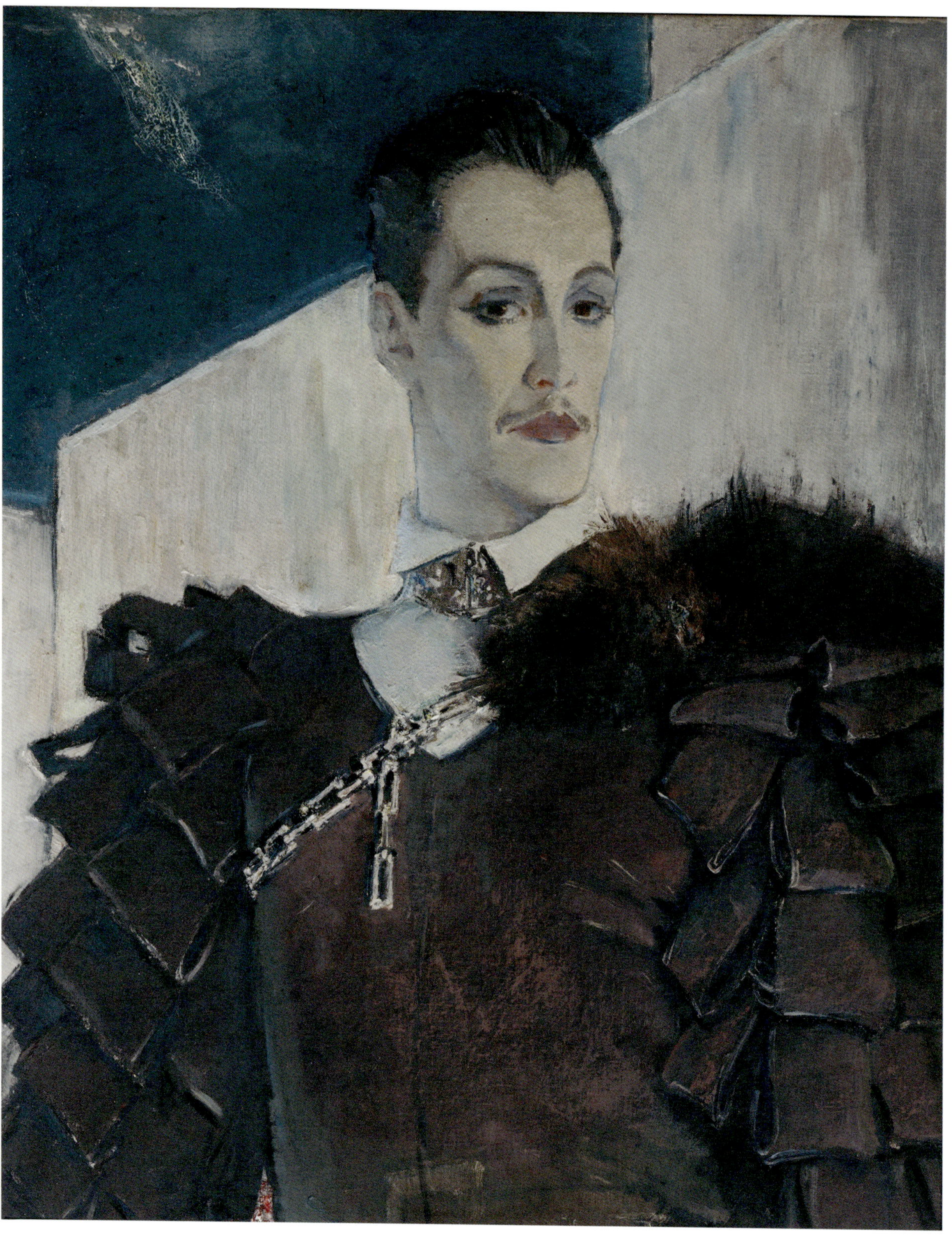

Glyn Warren Philpot 1884–1937
Glen Byam Shaw as 'Laertes' 1934–5
Oil on canvas
75 x 62.2
Private collection

Glyn Philpot probably knew the actor and director
Glen Byam Shaw (1884–1937) socially: before his
marriage to the actor Angela Baddeley in 1929,
Byam Shaw had almost certainly been the lover of
the poet Siegfried Sassoon (1886–1967), a friend
of Philpot and the subject of one of Philpot's most
acclaimed portraits, executed in 1917.

Philpot's image of Byam Shaw shows him in full
theatrical dress for the role of Laertes in John Gielgud's
(1904–2000) critically-acclaimed 1934 production of
Hamlet, at the New Theatre. His elaborate costume
was designed by Motley, the collective working name
of Elizabeth Montgomery (1902–93), Margaret Percy
(1904–2000) and Percy's sister, Sophie Harris
(1900–66). Harris later told how the bearskin cloak
slung across Byam Shaw's shoulders was intended 'to
suggest the cold, damp, northern climate' of Denmark,
while the ruched jerkin and heavy chain were features
used in other costumes for the production. The original
portrait was three-quarter-length and showed Byam
Shaw loosely holding a white handkerchief. It was cut
down by Philpot sometime after the work was exhibited
at the Royal Academy, London in 1935: the full version
was reproduced in *R.A. Illustrated* (1935). This reduction
puts even greater focus on Byam Shaw's face with
its heavy stage make-up. While this was typical of
productions of the period and would have been less
noticeable under stage lighting, the medium of the
portrait sets it at remove from its original theatrical
context. Coupled with Byam Shaw's arch expression,
the overriding impression is one of high camp. [CB]

Una Troubridge 1887–1963
Vaslav Nijinsky as the faun from
L' après-midi d'un faune 1912
Plaster
48 (incl. base) x 23
Victoria and Albert Museum, London

Una Troubridge's plaster bust of the Ballets Russes
dancer and choreographer, Vaslav Nijinsky, is depicted
here in the role of the faun from the one-act ballet
L' après-midi d'un faune, first performed on 29 May
1912 at the Théâtre du Châtelet in Paris with music
by Claude Debussy (1862–1918). It was exhibited
with four studies at an exhibition of portraits of
Nijinsky at the Fine Art Society in London in March
1914. The British sculptor Troubridge, who trained at
the Royal College of Art, was the partner of the writer
Radclyffe Hall, whom she met in 1905. The bust was
derived from sketches which Troubridge made at
the Ballets Russes rehearsals. It was originally in the
possession of Nijinsky, after being cast in a series of
four bronze versions. It was then lost and found later
in 1954 by the English ballerina Lydia Sokolova
(1896–1974), who had danced in the Ballets Russes
company under its director and Nijinsky's lover, Sergei
Diaghilev (1872–1929). Men who desired men were
among the leading figures in the development of ballet
dancing, after its reintroduction by the Ballets Russes
in 1909, and many enjoyed great international prestige.
Nijinsky's reputation as probably the most athletic
and highly skilled male ballet dancer of the twentieth
century was based upon his physical prowess, which
exploited the homoerotic spectacle of his agility on
stage. Troubridge's bust of Nijinsky as a promiscuous
faun accentuates the dancer's Tartar features: his high
cheekbones, oriental eyes and muscular forehead and
neck, which were seen as exotic and much admired
by the star's many queer fans. [AS]

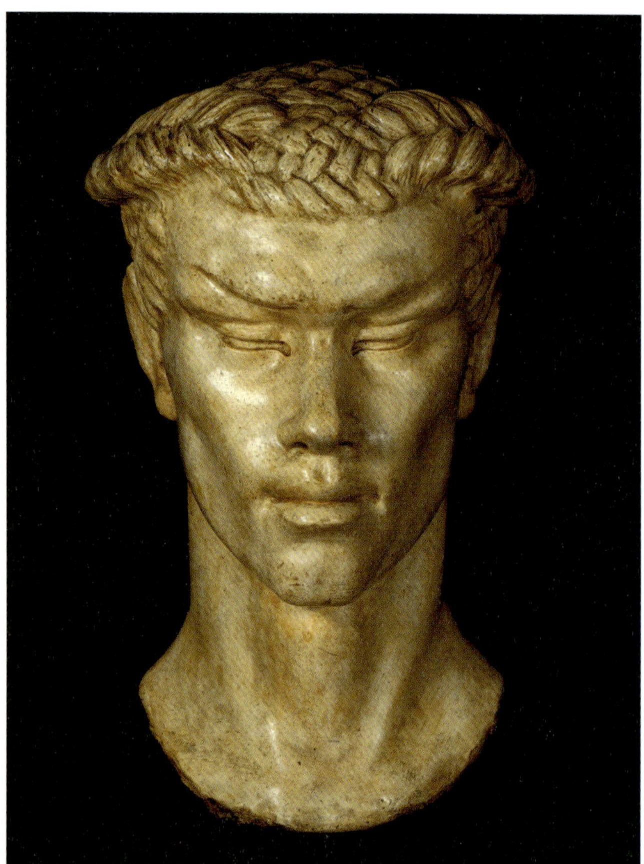

Francis Goodman 1913–89
Oliver Messel 1945
Photographic print from negative
56.6 x 56.6
National Portrait Gallery, London

Oliver Messel was the foremost British stage designer
from the 1920s until the 1950s, when his ethereal
creations fell out of fashion. After studying painting at
the Slade, he started out in theatre designing masks for
Sergei Diaghilev's Ballets Russes and for Noël Coward's
Cochran Revues, named after their producer, Sir Charles
Blake Cochran (1872–1951). Messel established
himself as the master of artifice and surface texture,
combining materials in surprising ways. Cochran
recalled how 'Every time I saw him, he would pull
something new out of his pocket – usually something
used for domestic work – which he proposed to
employ to give the illusion of some other fabric.'[4]
Goodman's photograph of Messel in his studio,
surrounded by props and bits of costume, gives
some indication of the importance of Messel's practical
grasp of theatrical illusion to his identity as a stage
designer. Messel is shown seated on the floor in the
act of cutting, foregrounding his skills as a fabricator,
while the palette at his feet alludes to his status as
an artist. The eclectic pieces around him – a pair of
painted legs, a Roman helmet, artificial flowers – give
the impression that the studio is a treasure trove in
which the designer creates wonders.

Messel was attracted to men and the fascination
with surface texture, dandyish excess, pastiche and
artifice in his work has been interprerted as a queer
aesthetic. Together with his arch-rival Cecil Beaton
(1904–80), Messel placed this aesthetic at the heart
of British theatre. [CB]

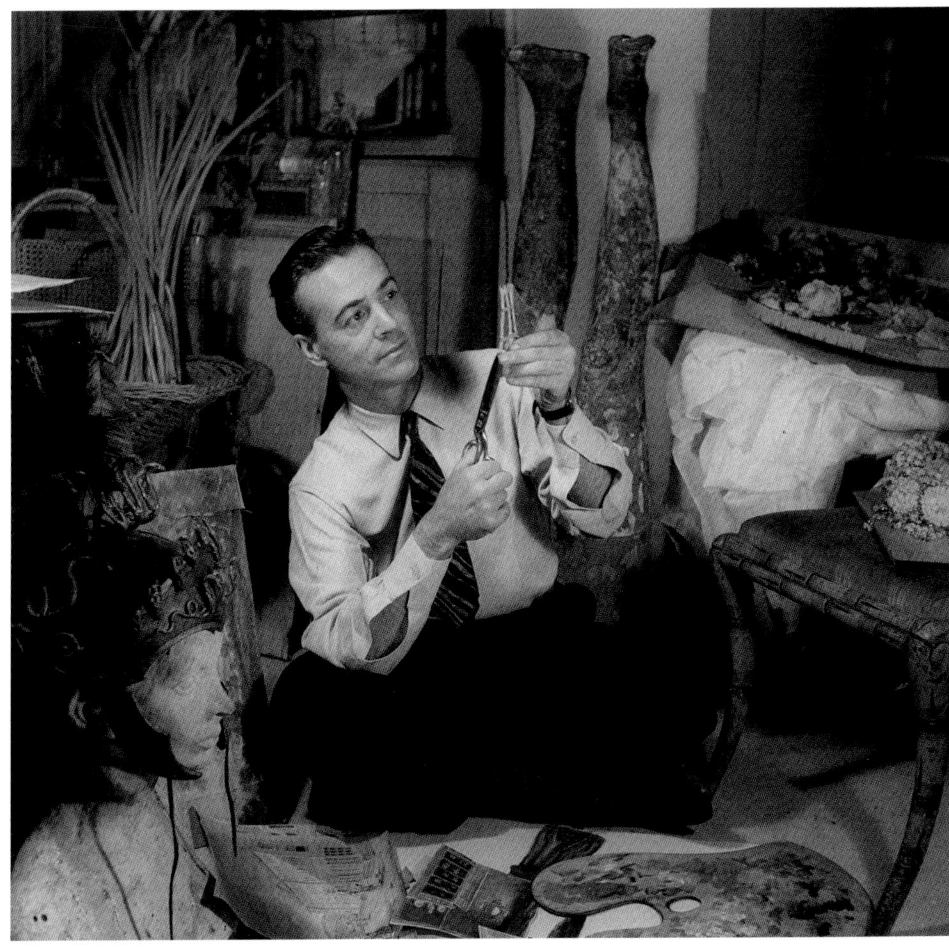

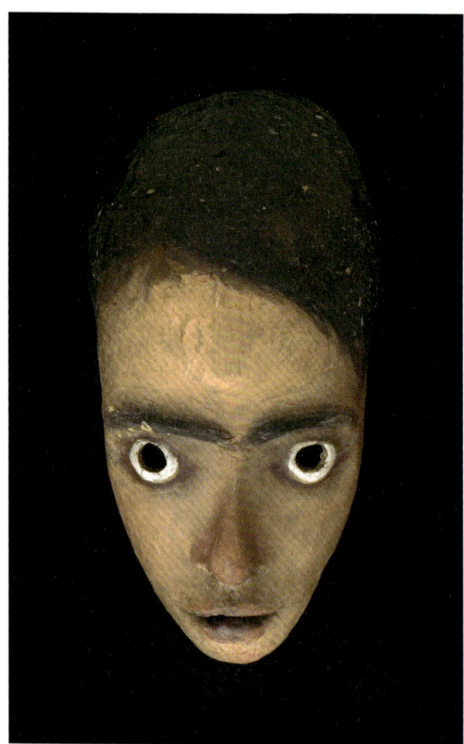

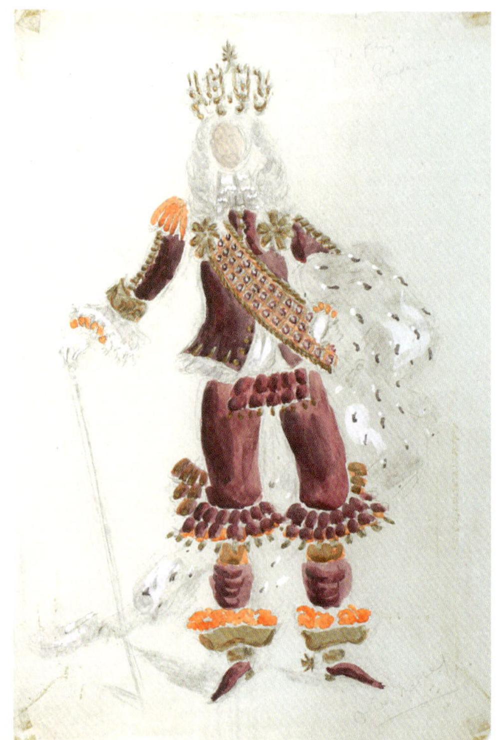

Oliver Messel 1904–78
*Mask c.*1927
Paper, paint, glaze, glue and
synthetic hair
24 x 17 x 31
Victoria and Albert Museum, London

An inscription in Oliver Messel's hand inside this
mask tells how 'this was the mask that Noël Coward
saw that gave him the idea for "Dance, Little Lady".
This song and dance number was one of the star
turns in *This Year of Grace*, Cochran's 1928 revue for
which Coward wrote the book, music and lyrics.
Combining sketches with songs and dances, the revue
was highly successful, running for 319 performances
and earning Coward £1000. 'Dance, Little Lady' satirised
the Bright Young Things in which Lauri Devine was
surrounded by Messel's pop-eyed, open-mouthed
masks. According to Cochran, it 'faithfully reproduced
the mirthless vacuous expressions that could be seen
any night in smart restaurants and bars'.[5] [CB]

Oliver Messel 1904–78
*Design for the King in 'Sleeping Beauty' c.*1946
Charcoal, graphite, gouache and watercolour on paper
56.5 x 37.9
Victoria and Albert Museum, London

Produced for the 1946 reopening of Sadler's Wells
Ballet (now the Royal Ballet) after the Second World
War, Messel's designs for Tchaikovsky's (1840–93)
Sleeping Beauty are widely recognised to be his
masterpiece. Messel's work contained references
to seventeenth- and eighteenth-century art – Antoine
Watteau, Inigo Jones, Diego Velázquez – which were
brought together to create a sumptuous pastoral fairy
tale. Choreographed by Frederick Ashton and starring
Robert Helpmann, the spectacular production was all the
more striking for having been realised at a time of
post-war austerity. This design for the King is typically
flamboyant: a tasselled vision of burgundy and gold,
topped with a seemingly solid gold crown, made from
papier mâché. Messel's designs continue to be used
today as part of the Royal Ballet's repertoire. [CB]

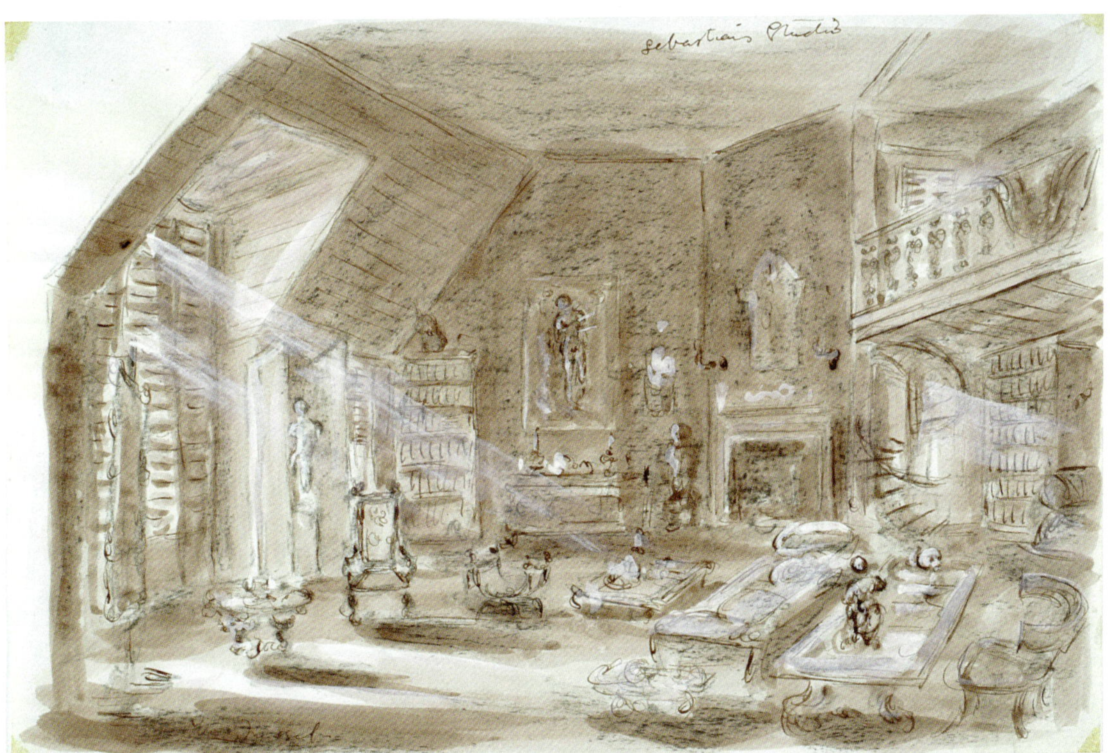

Oliver Messel 1904–78
Design for Suddenly Last Summer 1959
Charcoal, graphite, ink and wash on paper
25.1 x 37.9
Victoria and Albert Museum, London

Messel's last film *Suddenly, Last Summer* (1959) was based on a 1958 play of the same name by the American playwright Tennessee Williams (1911–83), who had relationships with men and regularly explored gay themes in his work. Filmed at the Shepperton Studios near London, it was a queer gothic fantasy with an all-star cast including Katharine Hepburn (1907–2003), Montgomery Clift (1920–66) and Elizabeth Taylor (1932–2011). Messel was nominated for two Oscars, for scenery and stage designs. Set in New Orleans, the plot focuses on Catherine Holly, who has apparently lost her mind after her cousin Sebastian Venerable died on holiday in Rome. It slowly transpires that Sebastian, who is not seen on screen, used Holly as bait to attract young men and has been torn apart and eaten by a group of begging youths. In America, the Legion of Decency together with the Motion Picture Production Code Administration gave special permission for the film's inclusion of a gay character on the grounds that 'Since the film illustrates the horrors of such a lifestyle, it can be considered moral in theme even though it deals with sexual perversion' – a bleak reminder of the restrictions on depicting explicitly queer lives on screen.[6] Messel decorated Sebastian's studio, the scene shown in this design, with some of his masks. [CB]

FANNY AND STELLA

NEIL MCKENNA

28 April 1870: The beautiful Miss Stella Boulton and the decidedly plain Mrs Fanny Graham are leaving the Strand Theatre after an evening performance. As they get into their carriage a plain-clothes detective suddenly appears.

'I'm a police officer from Bow Street,' he declares, 'and I have every reason to believe that you are men in female attire and you will come to Bow Street with me now.'
There is a shocked silence from the two women.
'How *dare* you address a Lady in that manner, Sir,' Mrs Fanny Graham demands with frigid hauteur. For a moment it almost seems as if she might slap his face as a reward for such impudence.[7]

And so began the Victorian sensation of 'the Funny He-She Ladies'.[8] Fanny and Stella were taken to Bow Street Police Station, forced to strip themselves of their female finery only to reveal that they were two young men. Frederick Park, or Fanny, was twenty-three and a trainee solicitor. Stella was Ernest Boulton, aged twenty-two, a sometime music hall artiste and part-time male prostitute.

What had started as an arrest for dressing up in women's clothes quickly turned into something more serious and more sinister. It emerged that the Metropolitan Police had been watching Fanny and Stella night and day for nearly a year. They had names of many witnesses who would testify to seeing Fanny and Stella in drag, parading in the streets and theatres, winking and smiling at gentlemen like common prostitutes.

They had a list of maids and landladies who would swear to seeing Stella living as the wife of Lord Arthur Clinton MP (1840–70). And they had letters between Fanny and Stella and various gentleman admirers, including Mr John Safford Fiske (1837–1907), the handsome young American Consul in Edinburgh who was besotted with Stella. They even had a doctor ready to testify that he had treated Fanny for a sexually-transmitted 'affliction of the rectum'.[9] The police also had some photographs of Fanny and Stella in drag, sometimes alone, sometimes together and sometimes with Stella's 'husband', Lord Arthur.

But Fanny and Stella preferred dressing up – or drag as they termed it. They were drawn to the lures and easy morals of the world of theatre and make-believe. They chose to live in the underworld of men who wanted to have sex with other men, of male prostitutes, of bars and theatres, like the famous Alhambra, where like-minded young men, sometimes wearing make-up and dressed in drag, would congregate and flirt outrageously with the mostly male clientele. Indeed, Mr John Reeve, the manager of the Alhambra, had made half-a-dozen complaints to the police about the lewd behaviour of these gangs of effeminate young men.

Fanny and Stella, and six other young men, including Lord Arthur, were charged with conspiracy to commit the 'Abominable Crime of Buggery' and with 'conspiring and confederating' to induce others to commit buggery.[10] In Victorian Britain sex between men was seen not just as a perversion or as an abominable crime – a crime in many people's eyes worse than murder – but, more worryingly, as an infection or contagion, which, if left unchecked and untreated, would spread and become epidemic, like cholera or scarlet fever (which had supposedly killed Lord Arthur before he could be captured or put on trial). The only way to deal with the threat of this 'pestiferous and pestilential' epidemic of sex between men was to identify, isolate and punish the carriers of the contagion.[11]

Fanny and Stella, together with their lovers and friends, were seen as the most visible, obvious and defiant manifestation of this male-to-male sexual contagion. And Fanny and Stella's effeminacy, the fact that they

dressed and acted as women, served only to compound
their crimes. They had to be stopped and, more importantly
for Victorian Britain, they had to be seen to be stopped
and made an example of.

The full weight of the Victorian Establishment bore
down on Fanny and Stella. The case ended up in the
highest court in the land, in Westminster Hall in the
Houses of Parliament, before the Lord Chief Justice.
The prosecution was led by the Attorney-General, assisted
by the Solicitor-General.

And yet, despite this judicial onslaught, much to
everyone's surprise, a jury found Fanny and Stella
innocent of all charges. They were released and the
extraordinary case of the 'the Funny He-She Ladies'
was over. Fanny died soon after in the United States,
probably of syphilis. Stella revived her theatrical career
and lived until 1904.

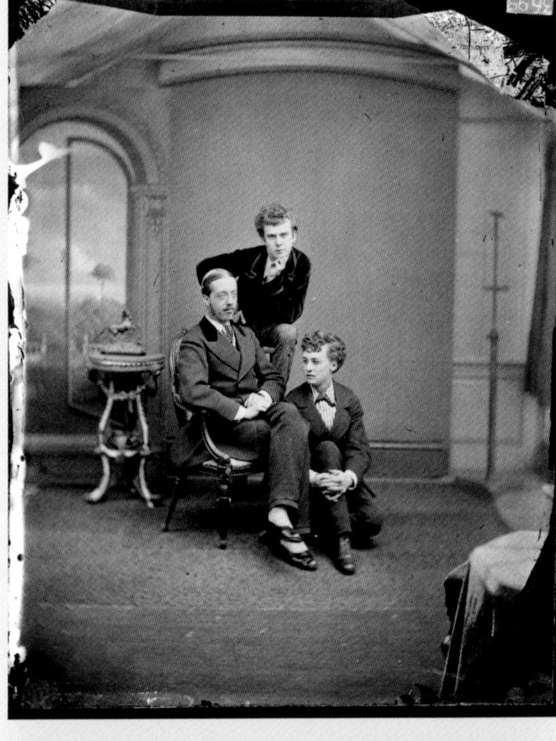

Frederick Spalding
*Lord Arthur Pelham-
Clinton, Stella (standing)
and Fanny c.1870*
Essex Record Office

Frederick Spalding
*Stella (left) and Fanny
(right) c.1870*
Essex Record Office

GENDER SWAPS ON STAGE

Whether as a plot device, a marketing ploy or an illusion to delight an audience, gender-swapping acting roles, female and male impersonators and drag acts all have long histories on the British stage. Men played all female roles in professional productions until the arrival of women on the stage in the early 1660s, 'breeches parts' for women became popular in the late eighteenth century, while the pantomime traditions of the male dame and female principal boy were well established by late 1880s.

Male and female impersonation acts flourished from the 1890s until the 1950s, spurred by the rise of vaudeville shows and revues. Comics such as Dan Leno, Malcolm Scott and Douglas Byng also worked as pantomime dames and drew on this tradition. Alongside such comic acts, a glamorous tradition developed, popularised by American stars like Julian Eltinge and the Swedish artist John Lind (1877–1940). All of these acts played on the audience's sense of wonderment and curiosity at the perfect nature of the transformation and were popular across the country.

The Second World War provided a fresh training ground for female impersonators in concert parties entertaining the troops. Revues starring ex-servicemen became popular across Britain in the post-war period, touring under such titles as *We Were in the Forces* (the first, formed in 1944), *Soldiers in Skirts*, *Forces in Petticoats* and *This Was the Army*. These launched the careers of a number of star performers, including Tommie Rose, Ronnie Stewart and Danny Carroll, later Danny La Rue (pp.91, 93). As the popularity of female impersonation declined in the 1950s, some of these acts endured, with performers like Rose and La Rue moving from female impersonation into drag, a field in which new performers such as Chris Shaw also made their names (p.92).

There is no simple connection between theatrical gender swaps and the lives or tastes of people with queer sexualities or variant gender identities. While drag is now predominantly associated with queer culture, its forerunners appealed to (and, in some cases, continue to appeal to) large, diverse audiences. This diversity was also true of the performers: Charlotte Cushman, Jimmy Slater, Douglas Byng and Danny La Rue had same-sex relationships, but Hetty King and Vesta Tilley did not, and there were other performers, such as Malcolm Scott, whose sexuality is not known. These performances could, however, offer something extra to their queer audiences: a fantasy of gender fluidity, a chance to openly admire someone of the same sex or, at the very least, the possibility of signalling alternatives to the status quo through jokes and innuendoes. [CB]

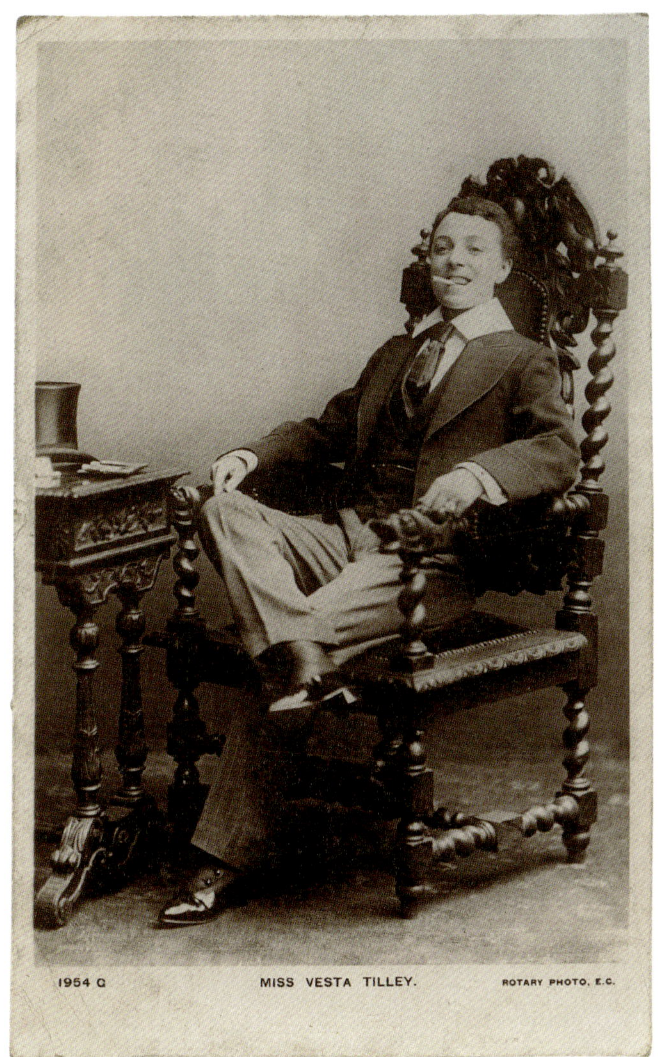

Unknown photographer, published by Rotary
Photographic Co. Ltd
Vesta Tilley 1900s
Bromide postcard print
13.8 x 8.7
National Portrait Gallery, London

Born Matilda Alice Powles, Vesta Tilley (1864–1952)
gained international success as a male impersonator.
First appearing on the stage in male attire at the age
of five in 1869, she made her London debut in 1874
and was first billed as Vesta Tilley in 1878. She took a
range of comic male characters in this early phase of
her career, saying later of her act, 'I felt that I could
express myself better if I were dressed as a boy.'[12] She
was best known for perfoming 'Burlington Bertie'
(1900), a song written from the perspective of an idle
aristocratic 'swell'. She also took roles in pantomime,
becoming a sought-after principal boy.

Tilley played to sell-out audiences in Britain and
America and performed in the first Royal Variety
Performance, in 1912. She continued to be popular
during the First World War, singing songs such as
'Jolly Good Luck to the Girl who Loves a Soldier'.
Off stage, she cut a glamorous figure, often dressing
in the latest fashions. When she retired from the
profession, on the grounds that her husband wanted
to become an MP, she donated the proceeds of her
farewell tour to local children's charities. [CB]

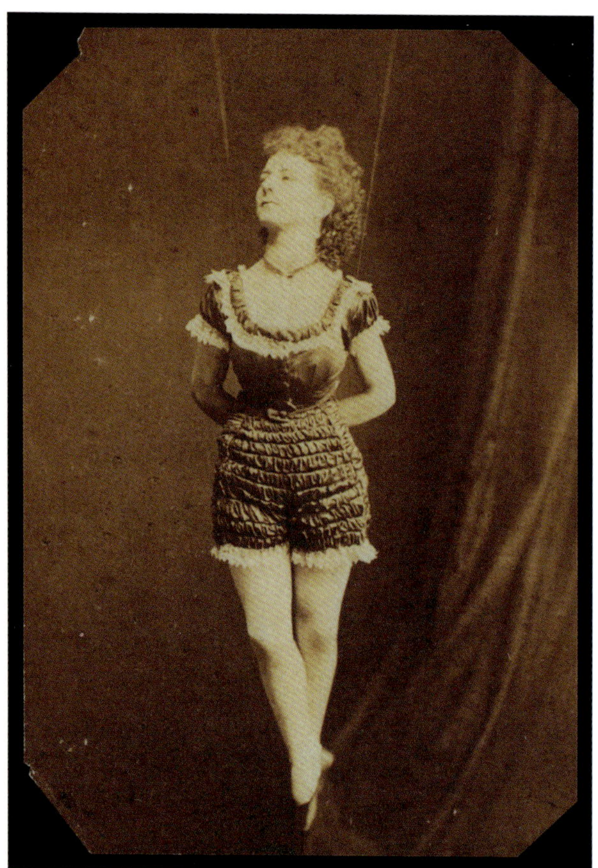

'Lulu' was born Samuel Wasgate (1855–1939) and originally performed in England as El Niño Farini, appearing for the first time at Chelsea Pleasure Gardens in 1866. The decision to adopt a female stage gender seems to have been pragmatic. His death-defying feats on the trapeze were, however, considered to be all the more impressive when performed as 'Lulu – the eighth wonder of the world', a professional identity that he adopted for the first time in Paris, in 1870. The revelation of Lulu's gender after a stage accident in 1878 caused some consternation to Wasgate's many fans. Once the secret was out, he cut his hair and adopted male dress again. [CB]

As 'The Woman Who Knows', Scott made his name in Britain and America with his characterisations that ranged from Nell Gwyn (1650–1687) to fashion plates. He even did his own version of the popular 'Salome dance', replacing the head of John the Baptist with a quart bottle of whisky. The *New York Dramatic Mirror* described his act: 'Creeping upon it stealthily as the usual Salome approaches the head of John the Baptist, Scott makes sure of its identity and then breaks forth into a madwhirling dance of joy, throwing himself upon the object of his affection and hopping ecstatically about. Nothing funnier than this moment has been seen in a New York vaudeville theatre.'[13] [CB]

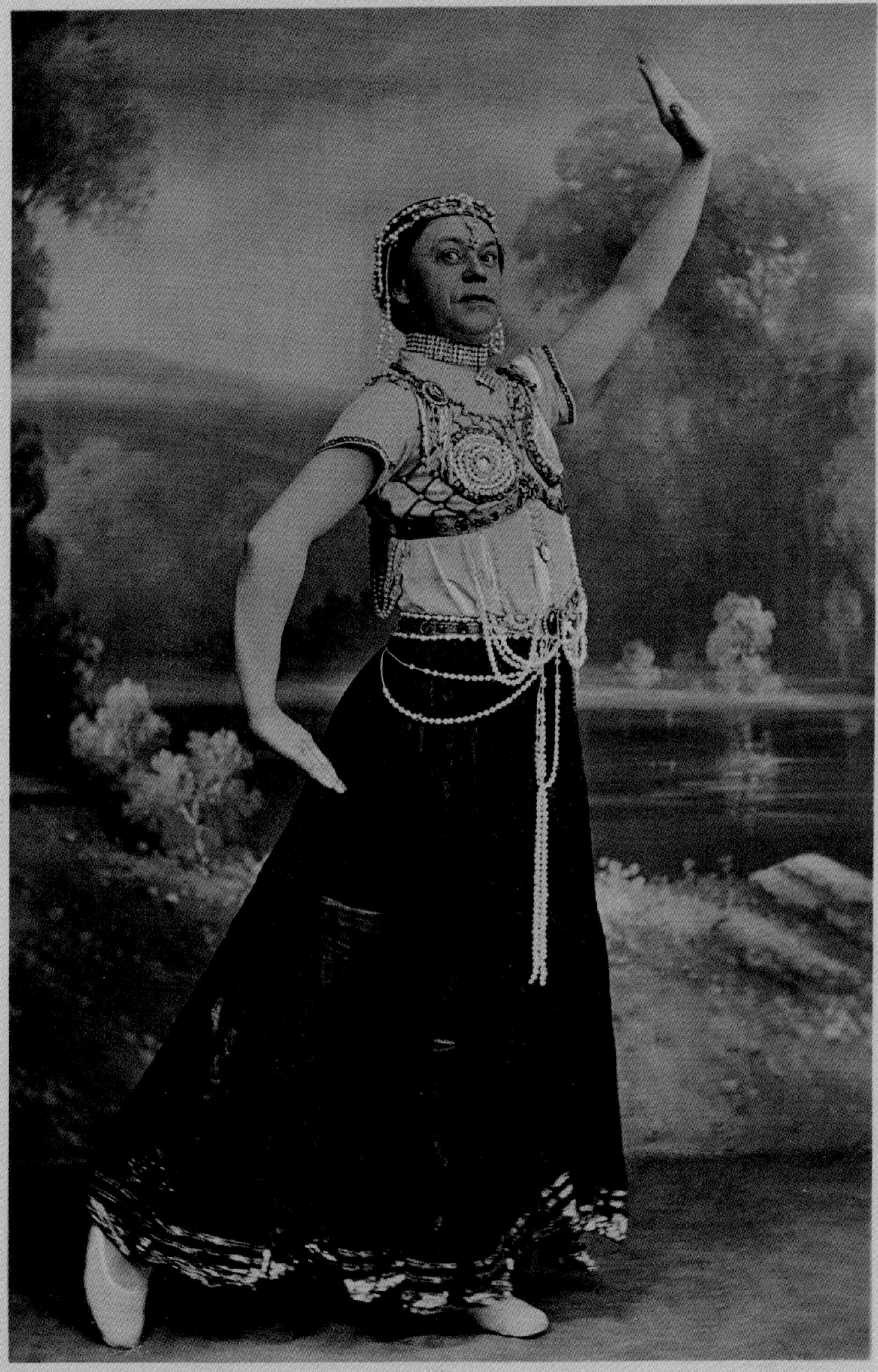

PHILCO SERIES 3480E.   MR. MALCOLM SCOTT
IN HIS "SALOME" DRESS

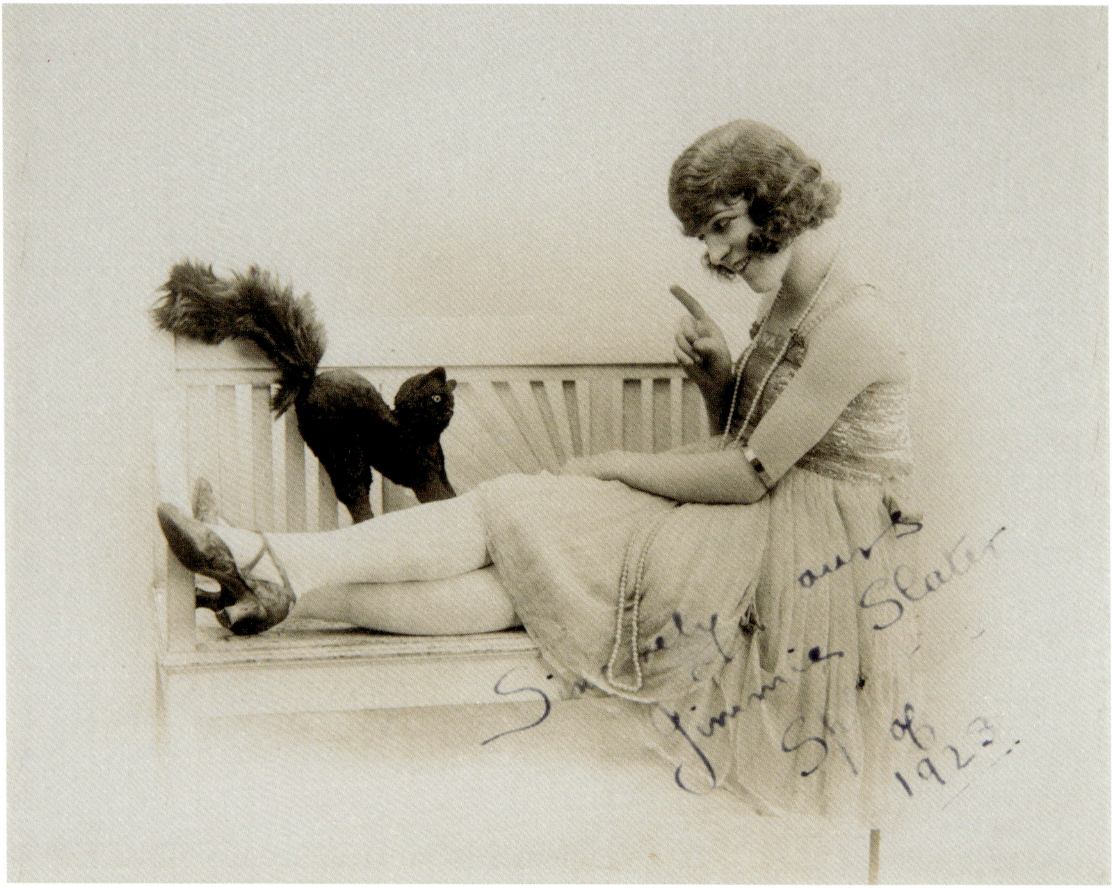

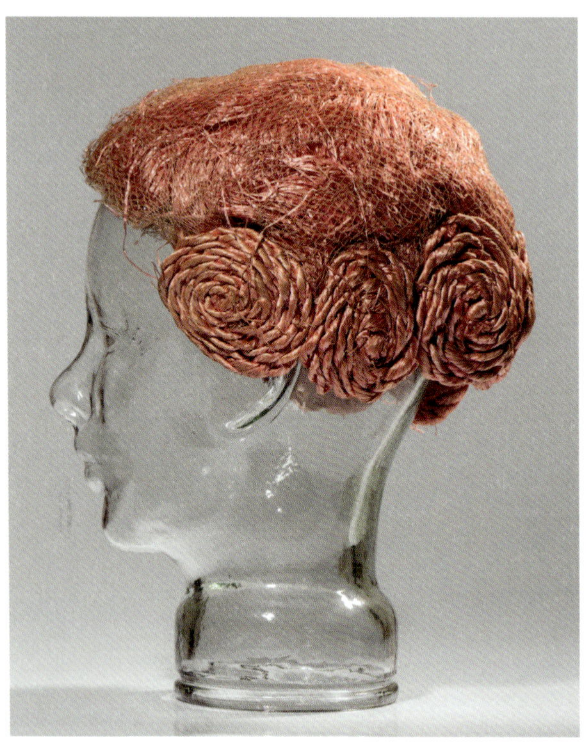

Unknown photographer

Jimmy Slater with a Kitten 1923

Photograph, silver gelatin print

on paper

15 x 18.6

Private collection

Unknown photographer

*Pink wig worn by Jimmy Slater c.*1930s

Private collection

Jimmy Slater began his career in 1914 and developed his skills as a female impersonator at concert parties in the military during the First World War. After the war he joined other ex-servicemen in the revue *Splinters* before striking out on his own in the 1920s touring seaside towns. Slater wore the latest styles in his act:

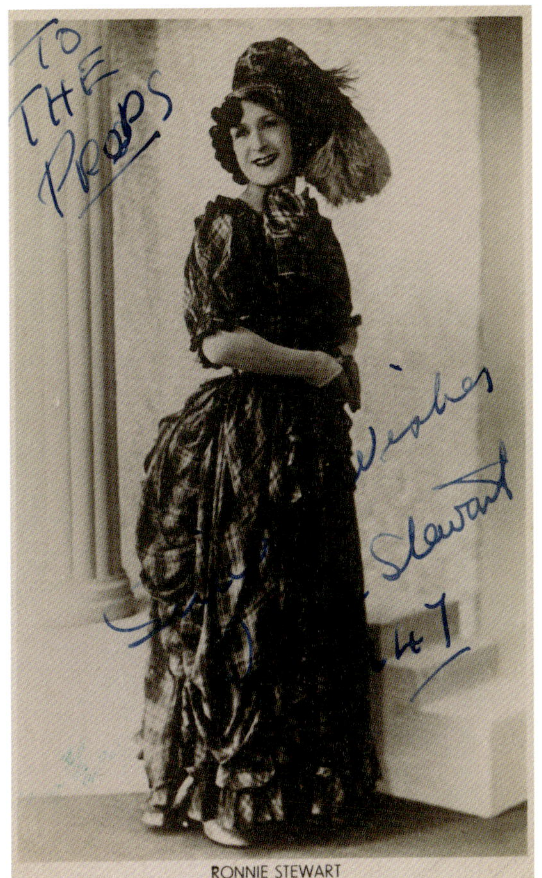

RONNIE STEWART

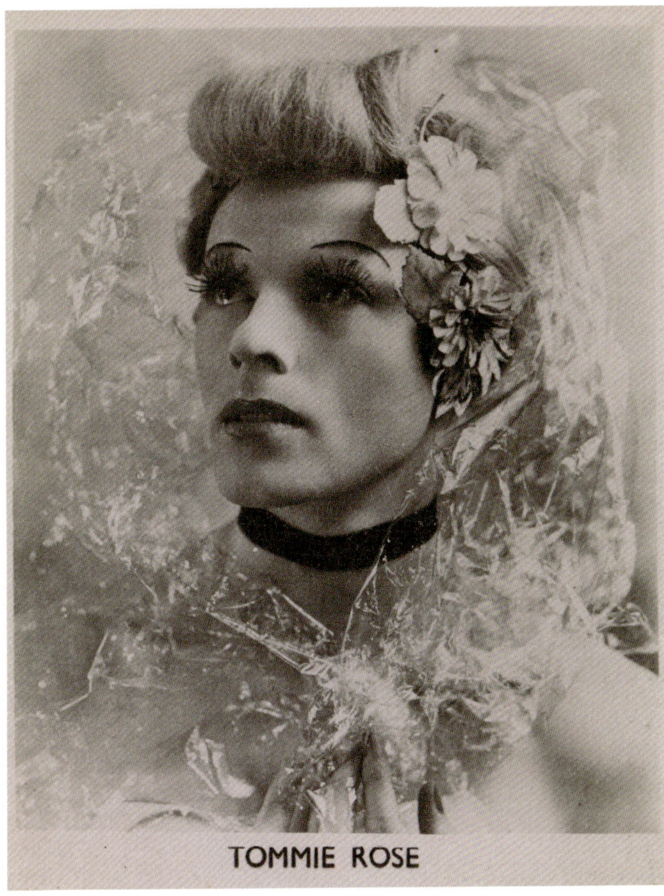

TOMMIE ROSE

ABOVE LEFT

Unknown photographer

Ronnie Stewart in 'Soldiers in Skirts' 1947

Photograph, silver gelatin print

on paper

13.8 x 8.8

Wellcome Library, London

ABOVE RIGHT

Unknown photographer

Tommie Rose 1948

Photograph, silver gelatin print

on paper

8.6 x 7.2

Wellcome Library, London

the wig shown here probably dates from the 1930s, when there was a brief fashion for pink hair. Slater's act dazzled: a review in the *Illustrated Leicester Chronicle* from April 1927 described his costumes as 'the envy of all the West End Mannequins' and told how 'his slim figure and perfectly modelled face has so often "taken in" old gentlemen in the stalls'. When asked in later years if he ever wore his costumes on the street as a joke, Slater replied, 'we would never cheapen ourselves like that'. When he grew too old for the glamour parts, he moved into comic female roles and became a notable pantomime dame. [CB]

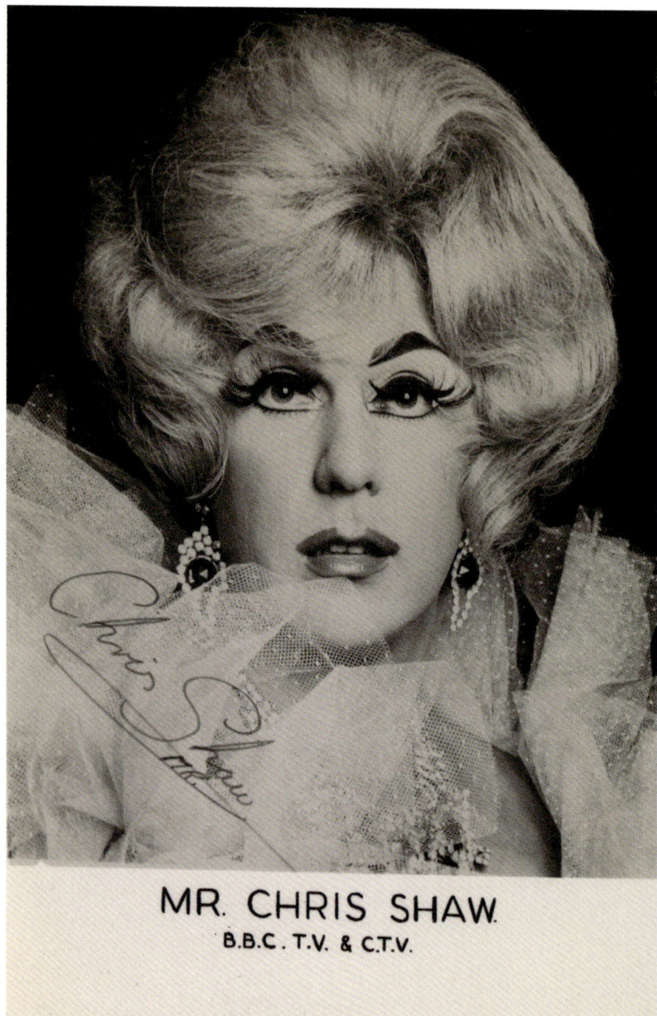

Unknown photographer
Chris Shaw c.1960s
Photograph, silver gelatin print
on paper
14 x 9
Wellcome Library, London

Angus McBean 1904–90
Danny La Rue 1968
Photograph, bromide print on paper
40 x 29.3
National Portrait Gallery, London

Born Danny Carroll, Danny La Rue was one of the greatest stars of the drag scene and one of the first of the new generation of performers to break through into mainstream entertainment. He made his first stage appearance while in the navy during the Second World War, taking the role of a girl in a comic send-up of Leon Gordon's 1923 play, *White Cargo*. John Gielgud saw his performance and told him 'I don't like men who dress up as women but you make me laugh.'[14] On his return, La Rue took a couple of straight roles before touring with the all-male revues, *Forces Showboat*, *Misleading Ladies* and *Forces in Petticoats*. The producer Ted Gatty came up with his stage name, telling Danny 'You are also long and lean, like a lovely French street. So I thought I would call you "Danny the Street" – Danny La Rue.'[15] La Rue swiftly became a hit on the cabaret scene, first appearing at the Mayfair club Churchill's in 1952 and opening his own club, 'Danny's', in 1964. He also performed in pantomime, teaming up with Alan Haynes in 1958 to play the Ugly Sisters in a long-running partnership.

The year of this portrait by Angus McBean, 1968, was a career highpoint: La Rue was playing the Palace Theatre and starred in a television special, *An Evening with Danny La Rue*. Preferring the term 'comic in a frock' to female impersonator, his glamorous appearance on stage was undercut by the gruff 'wotcher mates', with which he opened his set. This approach distinguished La Rue from the previous generation of female impersonators. His description of his act as 'playing a woman knowing that everybody knows it's a fella' sums up the essence of drag.[16] [CB]

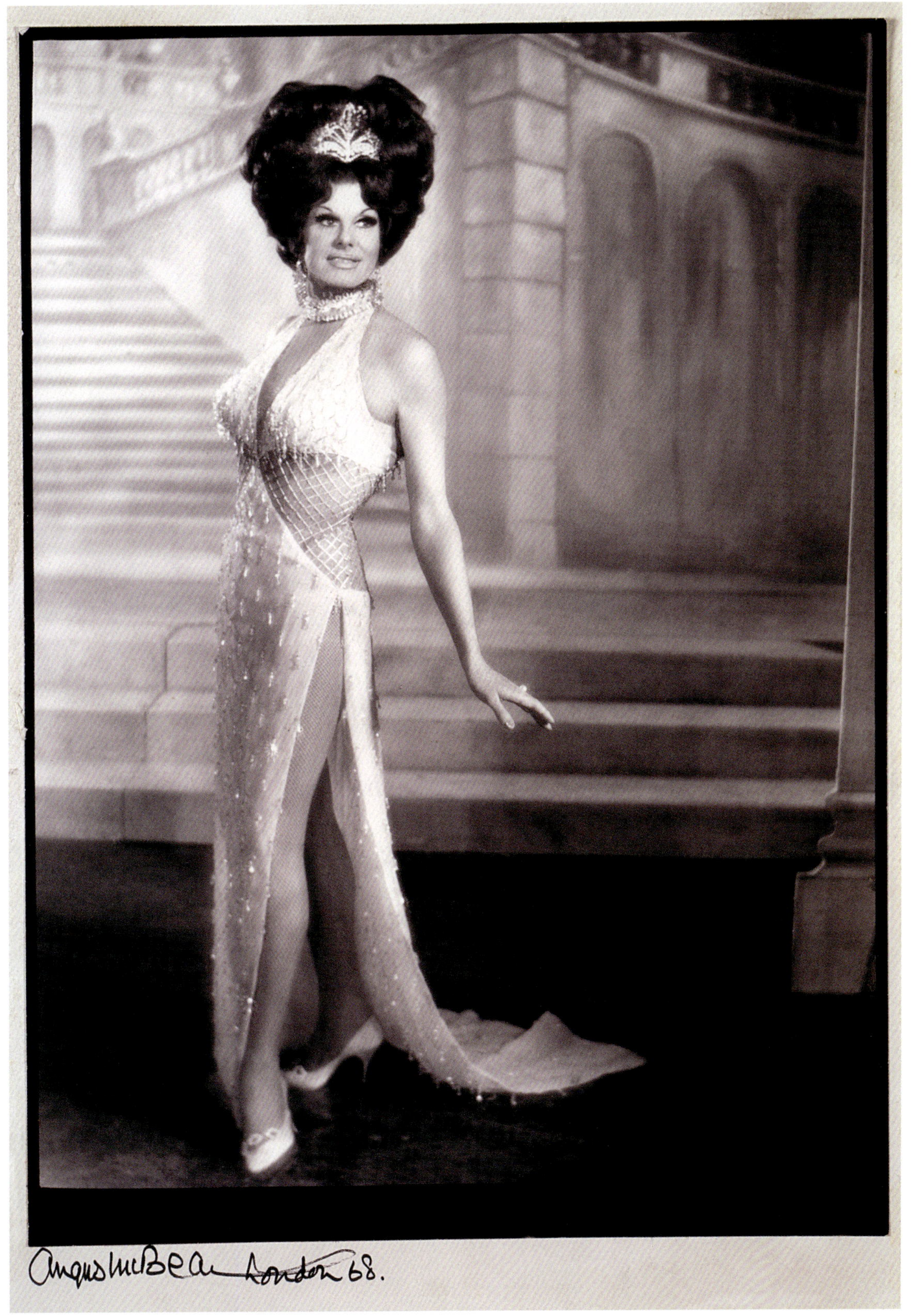

Angus McBean London 68.

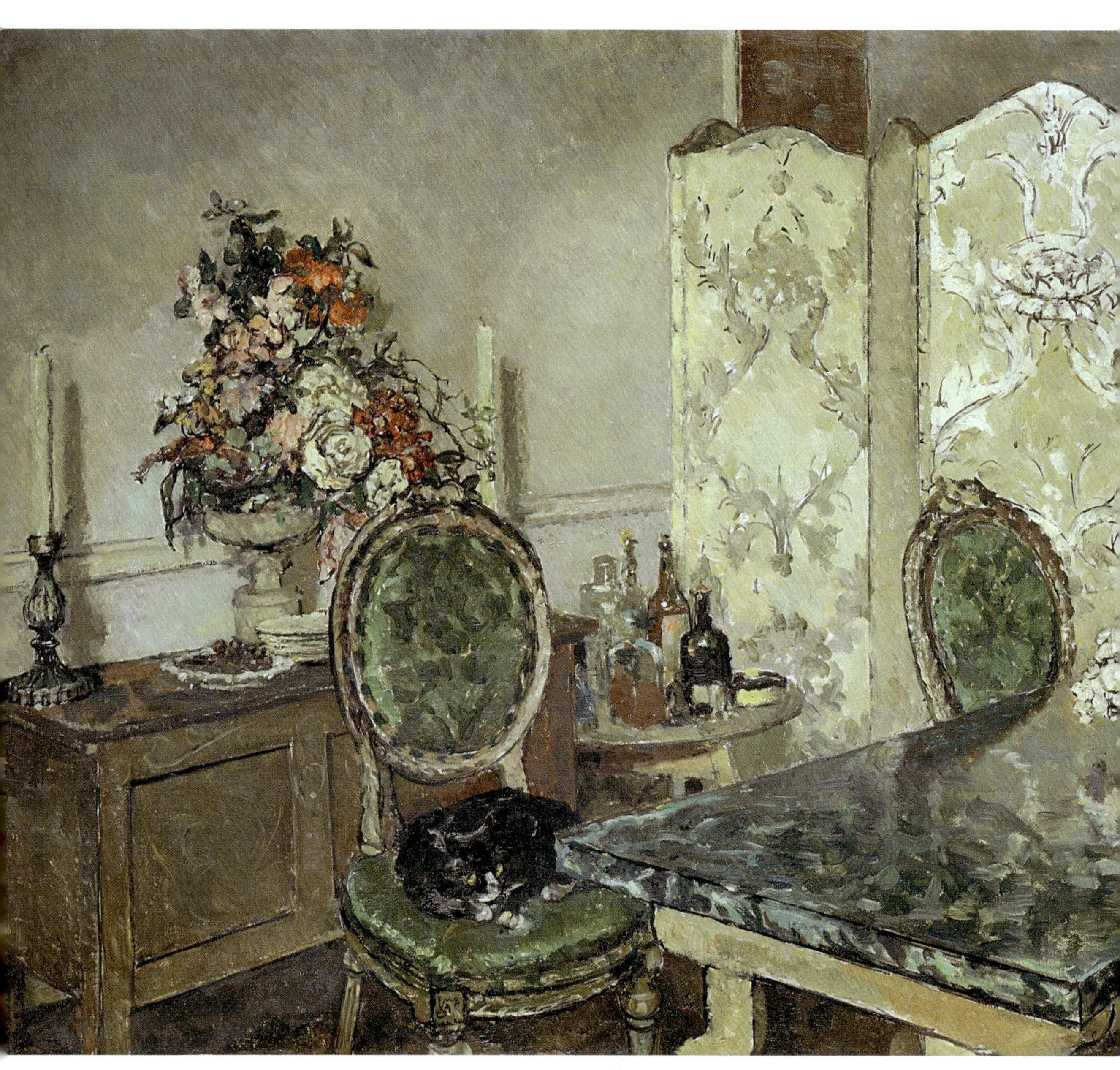

BLOOMSBURY AND BEYOND

ELEANOR JONES

Clare Atwood 1866–1962

John Gielgud's Room 1933

Oil on canvas

63.5 x 76.4

Tate. Presented by Mrs
E.L. Shute 1937

CLARE 'TONY' ATWOOD'S (1866–1962) picture, *John Gielgud's Room* 1933 (opposite), was painted in Sir John Gielgud's flat at 7 Upper St Martin's Lane, London, at the time when he was playing Richard II in Gordon Daviot's (1896–1952) highly successful *Richard of Bordeaux* at the New Theatre. In 1953, Gielgud was arrested for 'importuning for immoral purposes' a man in a public lavatory. He was fined and released. Despite the *Evening Standard* reporting the case, his celebrity was not diminished and audiences continued to cheer him.

The painting presents an unpeopled interior, animated only by a small cat curled up on a chair. Nonetheless, the collection of objects in the room is redolent of human presence: the table topped with bottles and an ashtray is suggestive of solitary nightcaps, gossipy conversations or boisterous parties, while the theatrical bouquet of flowers, perhaps a gift, indicates an investment in beauty. The cat is someone's companion, cared for and loved. These remnants of the everyday are an index of Gielgud's daily existence, hinting at moments of both solitude and community. Through its emphasis on absence, Atwood's observational work draws our attention to how places, things and social interactions shape our identities, and how we become legible to others.

Atwood would have encountered Gielgud through his second cousin, Edith (Edy) Craig (1869–1947). Craig, the illegitimate child of the revered actress Ellen Terry (1847–1928) and architect Edward Godwin (1833–1886), was a designer, a director and an early exponent of feminist theatre. In 1896, she met Christopher St John (1871–1960, born Christabel Marshall), a feminist playwright whose work dramatised women's suffrage, as in her 1909 play, *How the Vote Was Won*. Craig and St John were overwhelmingly attracted to one another, and by 1899 they were living together.

The couple met Atwood in 1916. Atwood had trained at the Slade, and was a member of the Friday Club, an artists' group founded by Vanessa Bell. St John later stated that 'the bond between Edy and me was strengthened not weakened by Tony's association with us'.[1] The painter moved into their home in Covent Garden soon after their first meeting, and the three women continued to live in a *ménage à trois* for the rest of their lives.

The artists in this section are alike in their impulse to record the subtleties of intimate experience. Personalities and desires are distilled into both figurative and non-figurative works. Through gesture, posture and clothing, the nuances of attitudes and relationships are revealed to the viewer. In these small traces, queer lives become perceptible, and such moments pierce through a history that has long neglected them.

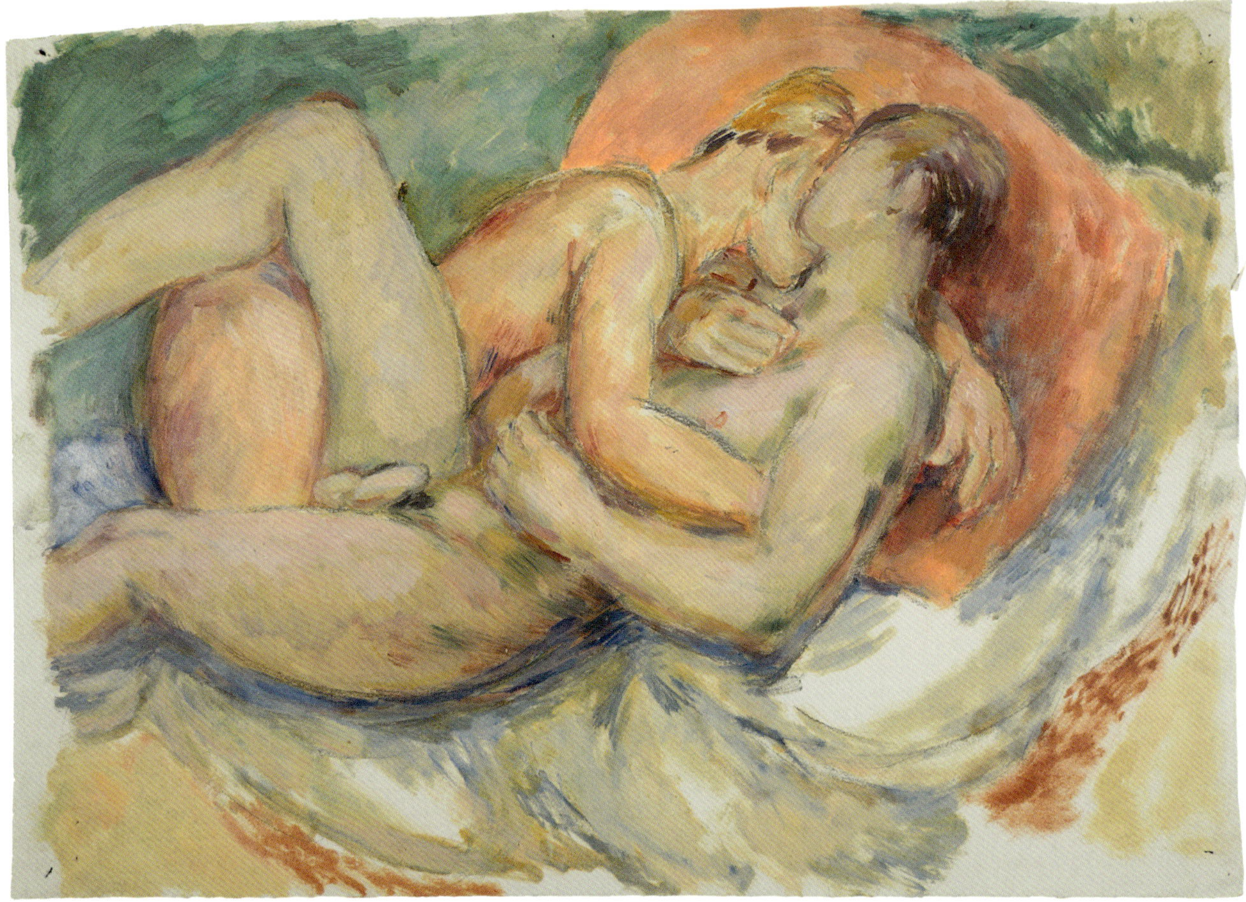

From the sensual proximity of bodies in Ethel Walker's (1861–1951) *Decoration: The Excursion of Nausicaa* 1920 (pp.108–9) to Patrick Nelson's (1916–63) indirect gaze in his 1930 portrait by Edward Wolfe (1897–1982) (p.103), these artworks communicate how our private worlds are connected to issues of deep social significance.

Though many of the intimacies conveyed in these works were probably sparked by physical attraction – for instance, Paul Roche (1916–2007) and Duncan Grant (p.100), Ethel Sands and Nan Hudson (pp.104–5, 107), as well as Clare Atwood, Edy Craig and Christopher St John – the range of representation moves beyond the sexual encounter. The types of relationships portrayed here are not limited to pure romance or eroticism. Instead, these works insist on the importance of friendship and kinship, alongside sexual desire and fantasy. Depictions of urgent lust are matched with mellow companionship. Friendships within queer communities and subcultures can provide love and support where heteronormative society does not. The artworks are an exploration into the ways organic connections are formed, outside of the socially sanctioned arenas of sexual legitimacy.

The Bloomsbury Group was one such close-knit community. In the thorough dissection of its legacy that ensued in the latter half of the twentieth century, a tendency emerged among critics to perceive Bloomsbury as a rigid and exclusive cultural entity: a snobbish coterie of privileged artists unwilling to collaborate

Duncan Grant 1885–1978
*Erotic Embrace c.*1950
Oil on paper
44.7 x 66.7
The Charleston Trust,
Lewes

outside of their Bloomsburian squares in central London. The artworks included here, however, demonstrate rich cultural exchange across diverse artistic networks and creative groups, whereby artists' homes, studios and salons are coordinates on a broader map of queer British art history.

Works by Duncan Grant and Dora Carrington (1893–1932) reflect a queering of both domestic and public spheres. Carrington's *Lytton Strachey* 1916 (p.106), for instance, is an intimate testimony to the life Carrington and Strachey (1880–1932) created at Tidmarsh Mill House, and latterly Ham Spray House in Wiltshire, where they lived with Carrington's husband and Strachey's object of desire, Ralph Partridge (1894–1960). In Grant's practice, social, artistic and sexual experimentation converge, and the variety of formal techniques he uses – inspired by modern Continental art and an interest in geometric abstraction – are emblematic of Bloomsbury's creative open-mindedness. Such varied interpretations of their surroundings reflect an era coming to grips with what British modernity might mean, and how these experiences of modernity, sexual or otherwise, might be expressed.

Of course, relationships and social groups do not exist in a perpetual state of harmony, serenely isolated from the world. Relationality, by its nature, breeds moments of anxiety. The openness of both Paul Roche's and Patrick Nelson's bodies with their torsos bare and limbs extended, painted by Grant and Wolfe respectively, is evocative of the inherent vulnerability attached to exposing yourself to a lover, and even to a friend. Moreover, our relationships to ourselves and each other are not insulated from pre-existing norms and structures of oppression. Glyn Philpot's (1884–1937) profile of Henry Thomas (d. c.1957) of 1934–5 (p.103), as well as Wolfe's portrait of Patrick Nelson, draws our attention to the tendency towards exoticism – a form of racist stereotyping that was prevalent in British art at this time, in which black subjects are fetishised as 'Other'. The visual strategies of this process went hand in hand with Britain's history of imperialism: both exoticisation and colonialism are exercises in control over bodies, spaces and cultures. As white gay men, Wolfe and Philpot were stigmatised and sexually oppressed, yet simultaneously racially privileged: both forms of identity inform these paintings.

Nonetheless, while we as viewers may have queries or concerns over particular objects, it is hard to deny that the queer artistic networks of this section interacted to produce complex, innovative and quietly revolutionary art. As artists came to terms with modernity, living through the changing social, political and cultural landscape of the early twentieth century, their practices reveal art as a force for forming identities and exploring desires, as well as consolidating difference and framing anxiety. Most significantly, these objects speak to how queer art creates the space to understand the self and forge connections with each other, in ways not commonly expressed or indeed condoned in the mainstream.

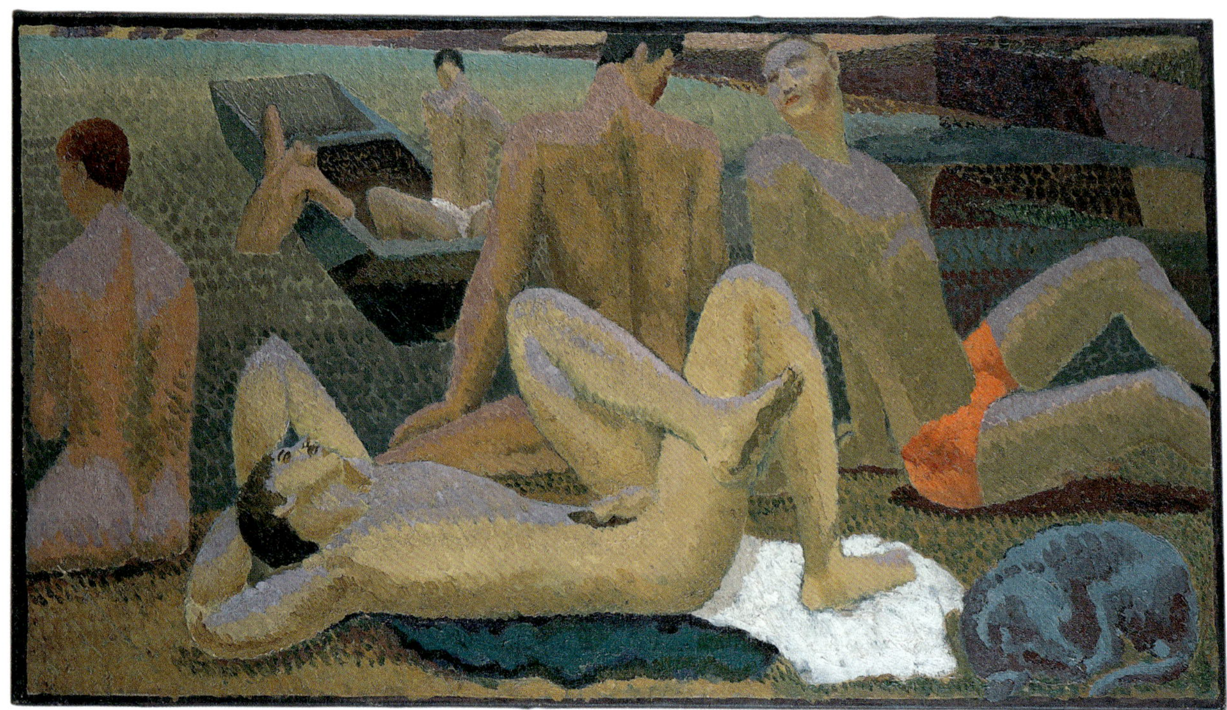

Duncan Grant 1885–1978
Bathers by the Pond 1920–1
Oil on canvas
49 x 90
Pallant House Gallery, Chichester

As in *Bathing* 1911 (opposite), this painting depicts an open-air pond as a site suffused with erotic possibilities. However, the frank nudity of the central figure, the appraising glances between the two seated figures, as well as the flash of red bathing trunks, ensure an overall more provocative atmosphere than in the earlier work.

The setting of the painting is Charleston Farmhouse in East Sussex, which Duncan Grant moved to in October 1916 with Vanessa Bell, her two sons, and David (Bunny) Garnett (1892–1981). It had long been one of Grant's fantasies to populate the pond with nude men, and this unsatisfied desire informs the dreamlike, languorous quality of the work.

The stippled paint surface demonstrates Grant's interest in modern Continental art, and the pointillist technique of Georges Seurat (1859–91) is a clear influence on Grant's practice. In 1919, Grant convinced his friend the economist John Maynard Keynes (1883–1946) to purchase an oil study of Seurat's famous work *A Sunday Afternoon on the Island of La Grande Jatte* 1884. Additionally, the nude figure seated at the edge of the water quotes from Seurat's *Les Poseuses* 1884–6. The work is therefore a reflection of Grant's cosmopolitan outlook – a sentiment common to the Bloomsbury Group as a whole – and it is an exploration into both artistic and sexual experimentation. [EJ]

Duncan Grant 1885–1978

Bathing 1911

Oil on canvas

228.6 x 306.1

Tate. Purchased 1931

Bathing was conceived as part of a decorative scheme
for the dining room at Borough Polytechnic, and it was
Duncan Grant's first painting to receive widespread
public attention. Art critic and fellow Bloomsbury
Group member Roger Fry had been invited to organise
the decorations on the theme 'London on Holiday'.

Grant's two designs for the room, *Bathing* and
Football, take inspiration from summers spent in Hyde
Park. In *Bathing*, the progression of diving and swimming
figures across the canvas evokes the continuous
movement of a single figure, and the painting revels in
the strength and beauty of the nude male form.

Earlier in 1911, Grant had travelled to Sicily and
Rome, where he saw the mosaics in the cathedral at
Monreale, as well as Michelangelo's Sistine Chapel.
These visits had a strong impact on Grant's practice,
clearly influencing his use of line and contour when
depicting the male body. These Italian references
were noticed by the press, and *The Times* remarked
that the figures 'seem, rather than Cockney bathers
in the Serpentine, to be primitive Mediterraneans in
the morning of the world'.[2]

The Serpentine was one of a number of sites
associated with London's queer culture, offering the
opportunity for men to see and be seen as they bathed
in the nude. These implications were not lost on Grant's
contemporaries: the *National Review* described the
dining room as a 'nightmare', which would have a
'degenerative' effect on the polytechnic's working-
class students.[3] *Bathing* not only marks a transitional
moment in Grant's career; it also marks a queer
intervention in a public space. [EJ]

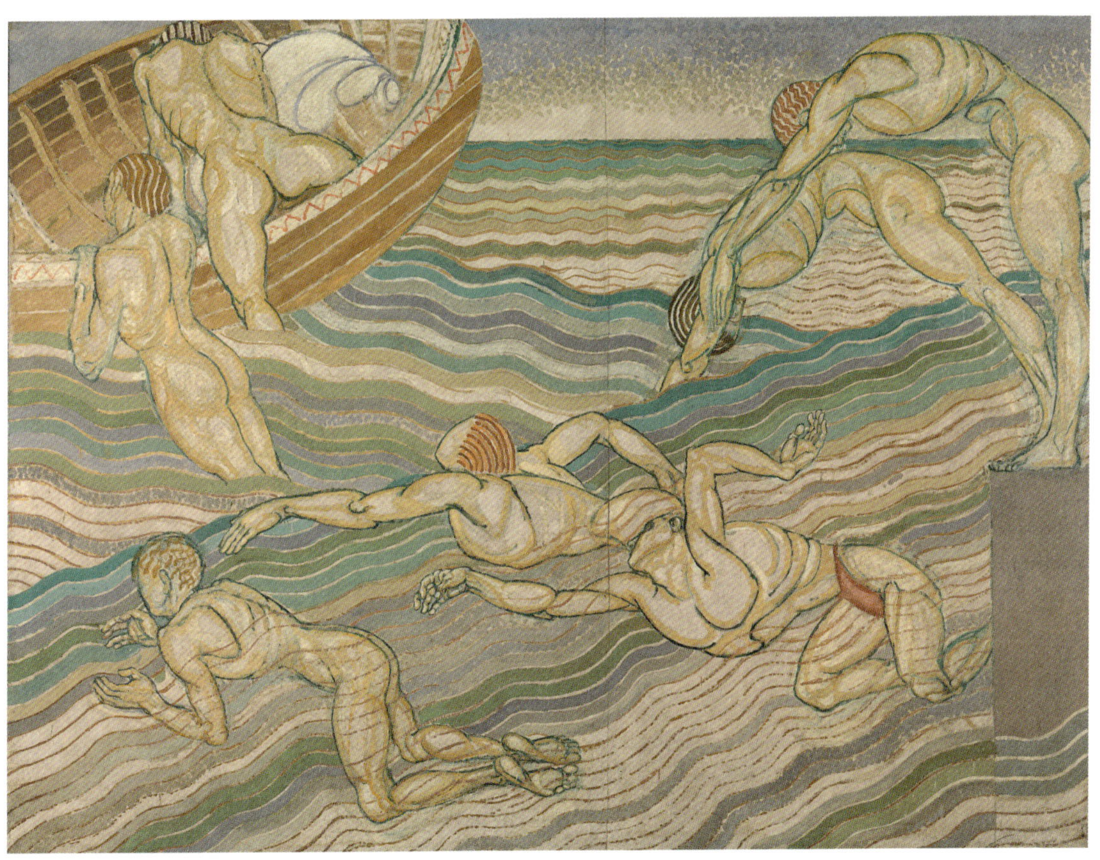

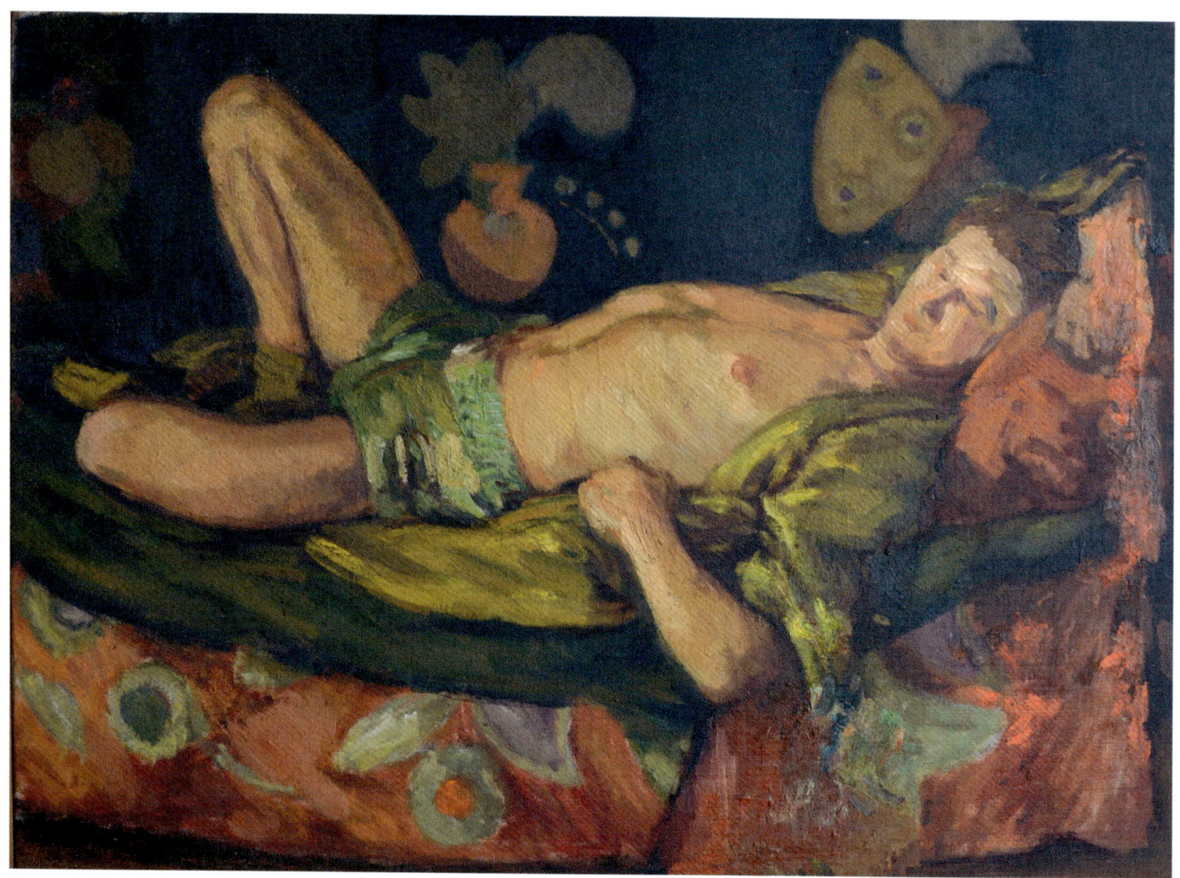

Duncan Grant 1885–1978
*Paul Roche Reclining c.*1946
Oil on canvas
57.2 x 78
The Charleston Trust, Lewes

Grant's painting depicts his lover and friend Paul
Roche. They met by chance in July 1946: after making
eye contact crossing the road at Piccadilly Circus, the
two struck up a conversation, commencing a deep
friendship that would last until Grant's death in 1978.

The deaths of Julian Bell in 1937, Virginia Woolf in
1941 and John Maynard Keynes in 1946 had a profound
effect on the idyllic domesticity Grant and Vanessa
Bell had created at Charleston, in East Sussex.
Grant described this period in his life as tinged with
'resigned melancholy'.[4] Meeting Roche at this pivotal
moment therefore galvanised Grant, and provided him
with a much-needed sense of vitality and freshness
outside of the strained atmosphere of Bloomsbury.
Grant's painting, composed of flurried brushstrokes,
is imbued with the thrill of a new attachment. The
relaxed openness of Roche's pose is suggestive of
the ease with which he assumed the role of artist's
model, and the tranquil intimacy he had with Grant.

Grant's sexual attraction to Roche, thirty years
his junior, was never fully reciprocated, and Roche's
heterosexual preferences were a frequent source of
frustration to Grant. In 1953, Roche married and moved
to America with his wife and their child. Before leaving,
he wrote to Grant: 'My love for you has never been
deeper or more enduring. If only you could see this.
My relationship with Clarissa cannot interfere with
my feelings for you, for it is something quite different.'[5]
[EJ]

Glyn Warren Philpot 1884–1937

Man with a Gun 1933

Oil on canvas

114.5 x 92

The Ashmolean Museum, Oxford

Glyn Warren Philpot studied at the Lambeth School
of Art before developing a strong reputation as a society
painter and traditional portraitist. He was elected to
the Royal Academy in 1923.

In 1931, Philpot travelled to Berlin and experienced
the decadent queer culture of the Weimar Republic.
As he noted, this trip provided a 'complete break with
everything I am accustomed to which has put everything
into focus for me & with such intensity that I feel the
paint will *explode* onto the canvas'.[6] Berlin's atmosphere
of sexual liberation, combined with the impact of
German expressionism, inspired a dramatic stylistic
change in Philpot. Upon returning to London in 1932,
his newly modernist approach attracted harsh criticism
from the British press, with *The Scotsman* reporting:
'Glyn Philpot Goes Picasso'.[7]

This painting, then, belongs to Philpot's period of
artistic experimentation, as evidenced by the lighter
colour palette and the broken daubs of paint. It captures
the striking good looks of Philpot's friend Jan Erland
(1913-2009), who was the subject of a series of
paintings on the theme of sports and leisure. Erland is
depicted cradling a gun in the crook of his arm, which,
he later recalled, had been specifically borrowed for
the occasion. In this context, Erland's firm grip on the
gun's phallic barrel is possibly suggestive. Erland
credited Philpot with introducing him to a 'gentlemanly,
civilised attitude to life', and the painting is a testament
to their close friendship near the end of Philpot's life.[8]
[EJ]

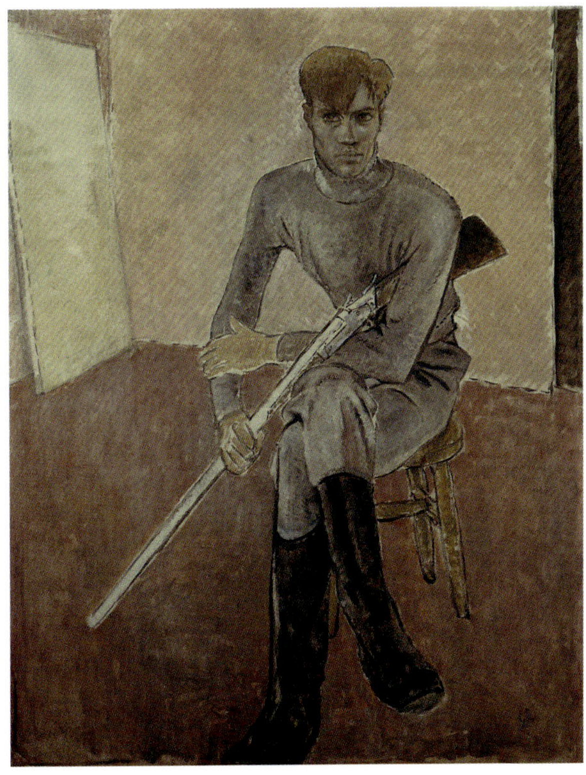

BLACKNESS IN BLOOMSBURY

KOBENA MERCER

With his slender frame, high cheekbones and hair brushed up at a diagonal slant, the Jamaican-born model, Henry Thomas, had looks that fitted well with Glyn Philpot's angular modernism. But knowing the artist's model was also his servant presents us with a challenge. On the one hand, Philpot brought an intimate attentiveness to his portrayal of Thomas that completely went against the grain of the master/servant relationship in the colonial era. But on the other hand, to notice that Thomas never looks back, for his eyes are always averted, is to recognise that we are surely not among equals. Philpot was undoubtedly attracted to Thomas's blackness, yet the way in which he, as artist, repeatedly returned to his favoured model suggests that Thomas's beauty gave him, as servant, a degree of power too. Was there something in this interplay across racial lines that eluded capture, thus sparking off the artist's quest to depict him time and again? What Thomas felt about his years with Philpot from 1929 to the artist's death in 1937 is unknown, but the words he wrote on his benefactor's funeral wreath – 'For memory to my dear master as well as my father and brother to me' – suggest many overlapping layers.[9]

London became increasingly cosmopolitan during the interwar years as a result of two-way traffic from colonial periphery to metropolitan centre. When Edward Wolfe came from Johannesburg to the Slade School of Fine Art, London, his journey intersected with Patrick Nelson's, who travelled from Jamaica to study law. Living in Bloomsbury, Nelson also met Duncan Grant in 1938, becoming one of his many lovers.[10] While Grant's watercolours of interracial couplings have little to do with observable reality and everything to do with unbridled erotic fantasy, Wolfe's portrait of Nelson is based on life-drawing skills, which pose the model with arms upturned, thus rendering his black body submissive to our gaze and inviting us to take pleasure

in looking. Nelson and Grant wrote letters throughout the 1940s and 1950s, and a poignant late portrait of Patrick (not illustrated here) is imbued with affection, showing an older man, comfortably seated, wearing a scarf made in the Omega Workshop that Grant had run with critic Roger Fry.

When Edward Burra travelled to Harlem in 1933–4 he left the confines of his studio for outward-looking interactions in African-American street life, departing from Britain's colonial context to one where black gay artists, such as sculptor Richmond Barthé (1901–1989), had contributed to the creative upsurge of the Harlem Renaissance. Exploring cross-cultural contacts that emerged in this fertile moment, contemporary artist and film-maker Isaac Julien (b.1960) took Philpot's portrait of Antillean dancer Julien Zaire (aka 'Tom Whiskey') as a source of inspiration for his poetic film *Looking for Langston* (1989), which, in revealing the dynamic energies set into play when gay artists crossed racial and national boundaries in the 1920s and 1930s, also showed that queer desire was a vital catalyst in the genesis of modernism as a whole.

Glyn Warren Philpot
1884–1937
Henry Thomas 1934–5
Oil on canvas
52.5 x 36.4
Pallant House Gallery,
Chichester

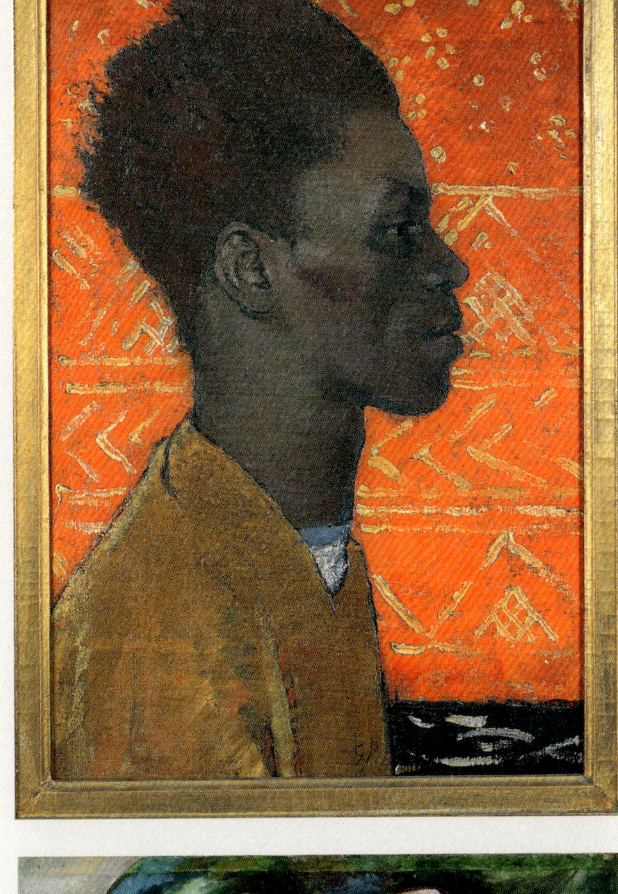

Edward Wolfe 1897–1982
Portrait of Patrick Nelson
1930s
Oil on canvas
94 x 73.1
Private collection

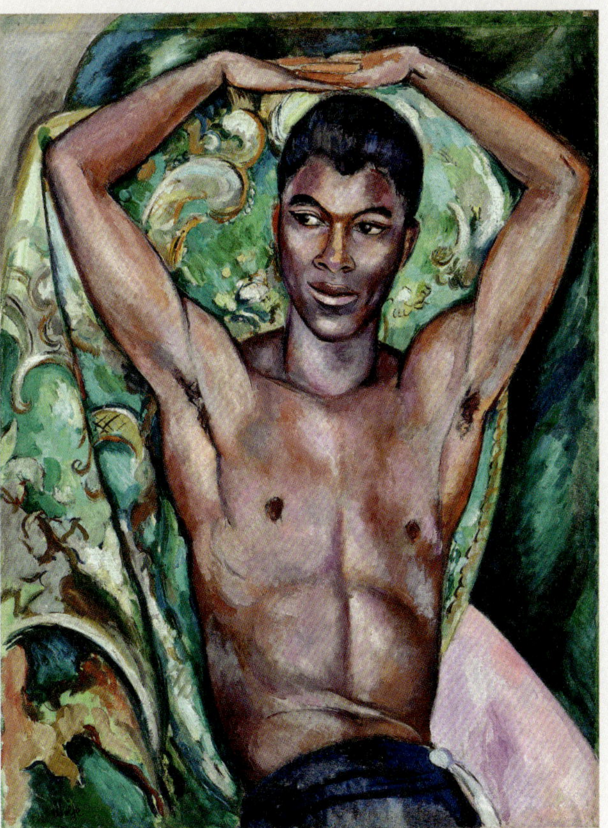

Ethel Sands 1873–1962

Tea with Sickert c.1911-12

Oil on canvas

61 x 51

Tate. Bequeathed by Colonel Christopher Sands
2000, accessioned 2001

This painting features Walter Sickert (1860–1942),
a prominent figure in both nineteenth- and twentieth-
century art, and a great friend and mentor to both
Ethel Sands and her lifelong partner and fellow artist,
Nan (Anna Hope) Hudson. The two women met
Sickert in Paris in 1906, with Sickert later describing
Hudson as 'refreshing' and Sands as 'amazing'.[11]
He seems to have seen himself in a mentoring role
towards the two artists, writing to Hudson: 'I particularly
believe that I am sent from heaven to finish all your
educations!! And, by ricochet, to receive a certain
amount of instruction from the younger generation.'[12]
He welcomed them to his weekly Saturday 'At Homes',
organised around afternoon tea, at his studio on
Fitzroy Street. These meetings formed the basis of
the Fitzroy Group, later known as the London Group.
Sands and Hudson became closely associated with
the all-male group, whose members, along with Sickert,
included Harold Gilman (1876–1919) and Spencer Gore
(1878–1914). As women, Ethel and Nan were precluded
from exhibiting with their male contemporaries.
Although Sands's work frequently engaged with similar
issues, such as representations of women, domestic
interiors and modern urban living, her gender placed
her in a somewhat different relationship to her subject
matter, which arguably opened up her work to
alternative interpretations. In her own time, Vanessa
Bell accused Sands and Hudson's work of 'fatal
prettiness', while Roger Fry dismissed Sands and
Hudson's 1912 show at the Carfax Gallery as 'frankly
feminine'.[13] However, once these gendered value
judgements are set aside, Sands's unashamed interest
in the domestic and feminine is open to reinterpretation
as a celebration of the domestic space as a site
of female experience and creativity, as well as her
unapologetic identity as a woman artist.

In 1912, *Tea with Sickert* drew mixed reactions:
The Westminster Gazette called it 'a daring picture' but
'a somewhat overwhelming indulgence in pure orange
vermilion'.[14] In this exhibition, the painting was simply
titled *A Tea-table*, and while it has often been interpreted
solely in terms of Sickert's presence, the female figure,
probably Nan, is given equal emphasis. Although
Sickert's relaxed pose suggests he is at ease in this
space – almost certainly Hudson and Sands's home at
42 Lowndes Street – he does not dominate it. Sands
painted from life, and the composition is arranged as if
she were standing behind Nan's sofa, positioning the
couple together in the image. As in the *Chintz Couch*
(p.22) – a piece of furniture and fabric pattern particularly
associated with femininity – Sands's *Tea with Sickert*
is open to interpretation as a quietly subversive
image, in which there are queer undercurrents to
the ostensibly traditional domestic image. [EJ]

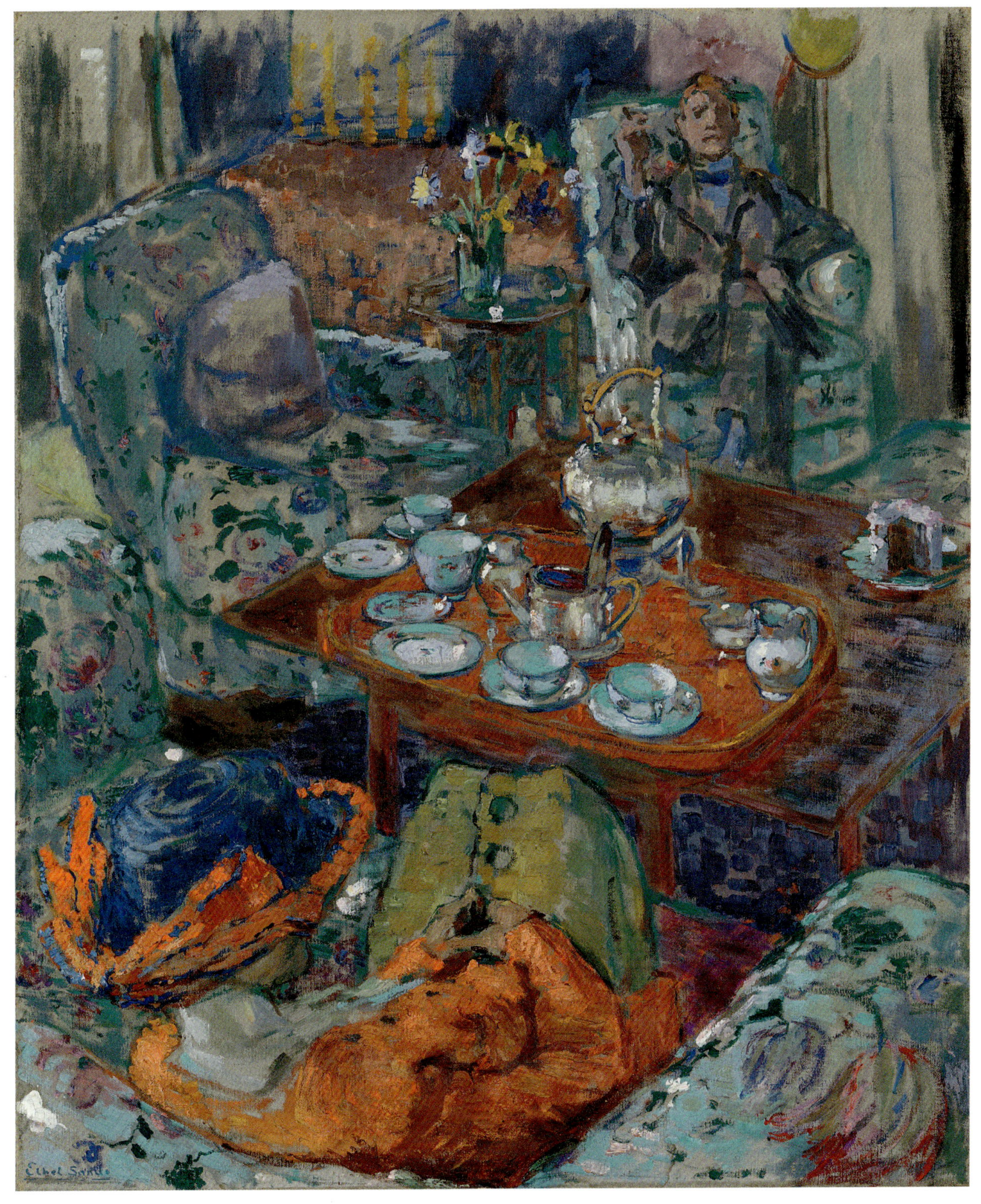

Dora Carrington 1893–1932
Lytton Strachey 1916
Oil on panel
50.8 x 60.9
National Portrait Gallery, London

Dora Carrington met Strachey in December 1915. She had been invited to stay with Strachey and his friends, including Duncan Grant and Clive Bell (1881–1964), at Asheham House in Sussex. Strachey was taken by Carrington's androgynous appearance, and one day, while walking on the downs, kissed her. Outraged, Carrington sought revenge that evening, and crept into Strachey's bedroom as he slept with the intention of cutting off his beard. As she leaned over him, Strachey opened his eyes, captivating Carrington.

Their relationship is hard to characterise, yet while Strachey was attracted to men and Carrington had relationships with both men and women, they continued to love each other very deeply. There are 'a great deal of a great many kinds of love', as Strachey put it in one of his letters to her.[15] Carrington was sometimes playfully nicknamed 'boy', an identity that is perhaps suggestive in the light of Carrington's androgyny and Strachey's exclusive attraction to his own sex. Strachey continued to live with Carrington after her marriage to Ralph Partridge, with whom Strachey was in love. Strachey's death in 1932 contributed to Carrington's suicide in the same year: when she shot herself, she was wearing his dressing gown.

This portrait, completed just over a year after they met, is strikingly intimate. Strachey is depicted reading in bed, the focus of the image falling on his long slender fingers. Writing in her diary after painting the portrait, Carrington addresses Strachey: 'I would love to explore your mind behind your finely skinned forehead. You seem so wise and so coldly old. Yet in spite of this what a peace to be with you, and how happy I was today'.[16] [EJ]

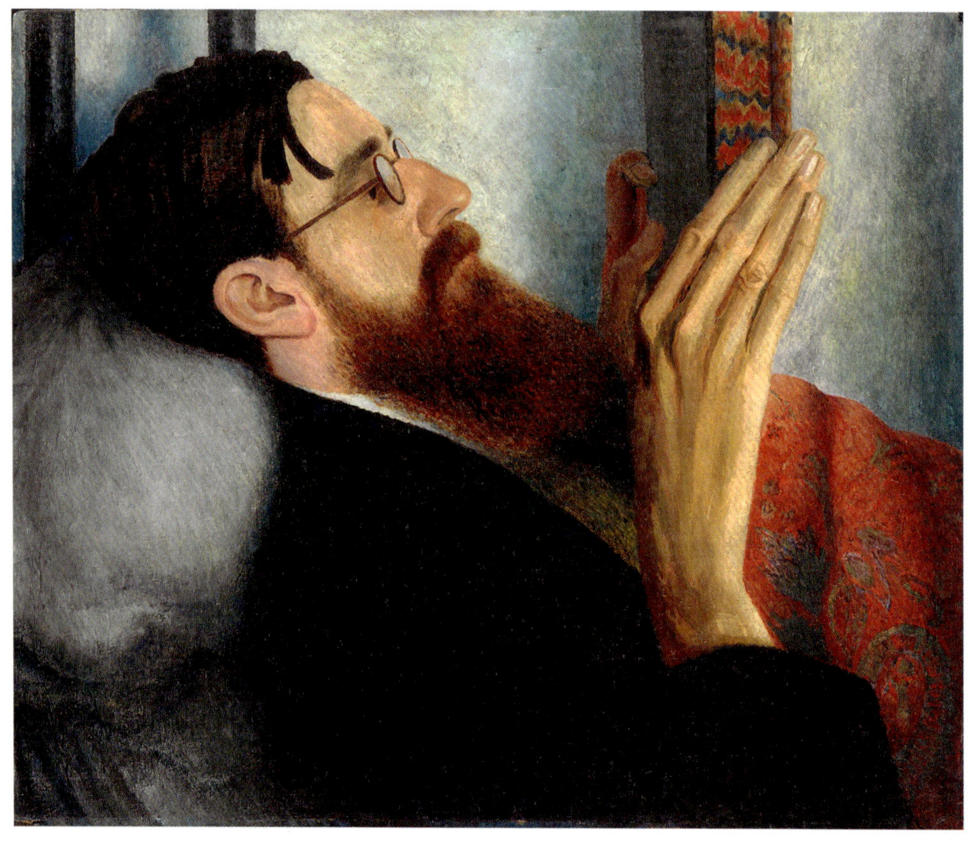

Anna Hope Hudson 1869–1957
Château d'Auppegard after 1927
Oil on board
46.2 x 38.2
Tate. Bequeathed by Colonel Christopher Sands
2000, accessioned 2001

This painting features Château d'Auppegard, a large
seventeenth-century house 16 km from Dieppe,
where Nan Hudson (Anna Hope) and Ethel Sands
spent summers together. The two American women
met in Paris in 1894 while they were both art students,
and maintained a deeply loving relationship for over
sixty years. While they were extraordinarily close,
they enjoyed different lifestyles, and this difference in
tastes necessitated periods of separation. As Sands
described it, 'although we love each other so dear, we
don't like the same places, or the same things, or the
same people'.[17] After summering together Sands, an
Anglophile, would return to London while Hudson
remained in France.

Surviving letters from these winter months apart
testify to their unhappiness at being separated.
Chateau d'Auppegard is inscribed on the back of the
canvas, 'Darling Ethel, from Nan'. The painting was
perhaps intended as a gift to Sands, to hang in her
London house, and remind her of her partner and the
home they shared together.

As in the work of Sands, this painting is evidence
of the pride they both took in their domestic space.
The house was in a state of dilapidation when first
acquired, and the couple's letters are revealing of their
passion for interior design. In 1923, the house was
featured in *Vogue*, and in 1927 Vanessa Bell and
Duncan Grant were commissioned by the artists to
decorate the walls of the building with murals. During
the Second World War, their homes in both London
and France were badly damaged, and for this reason
very little of Nan's work survives. This painting is
therefore a rare example of her work. [EJ]

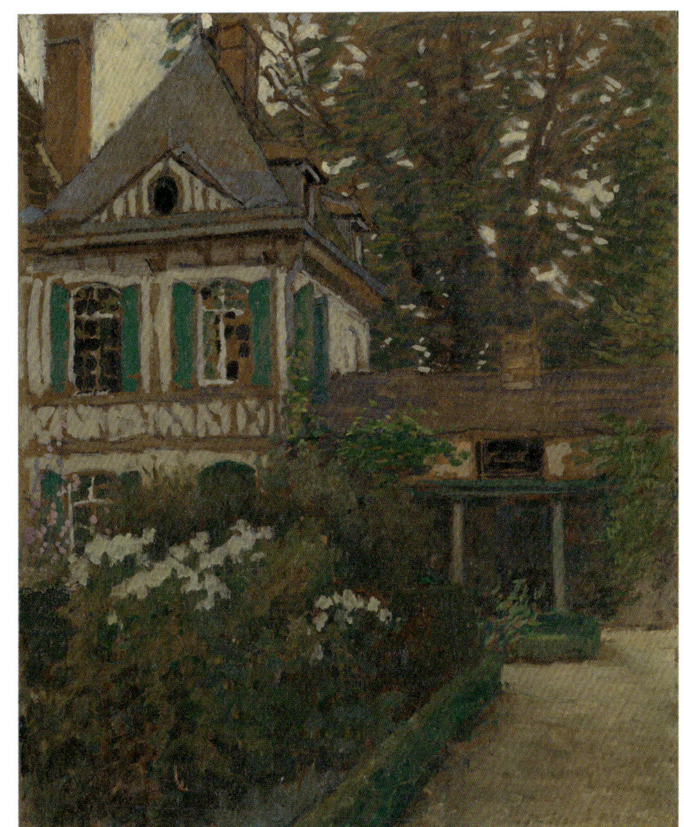

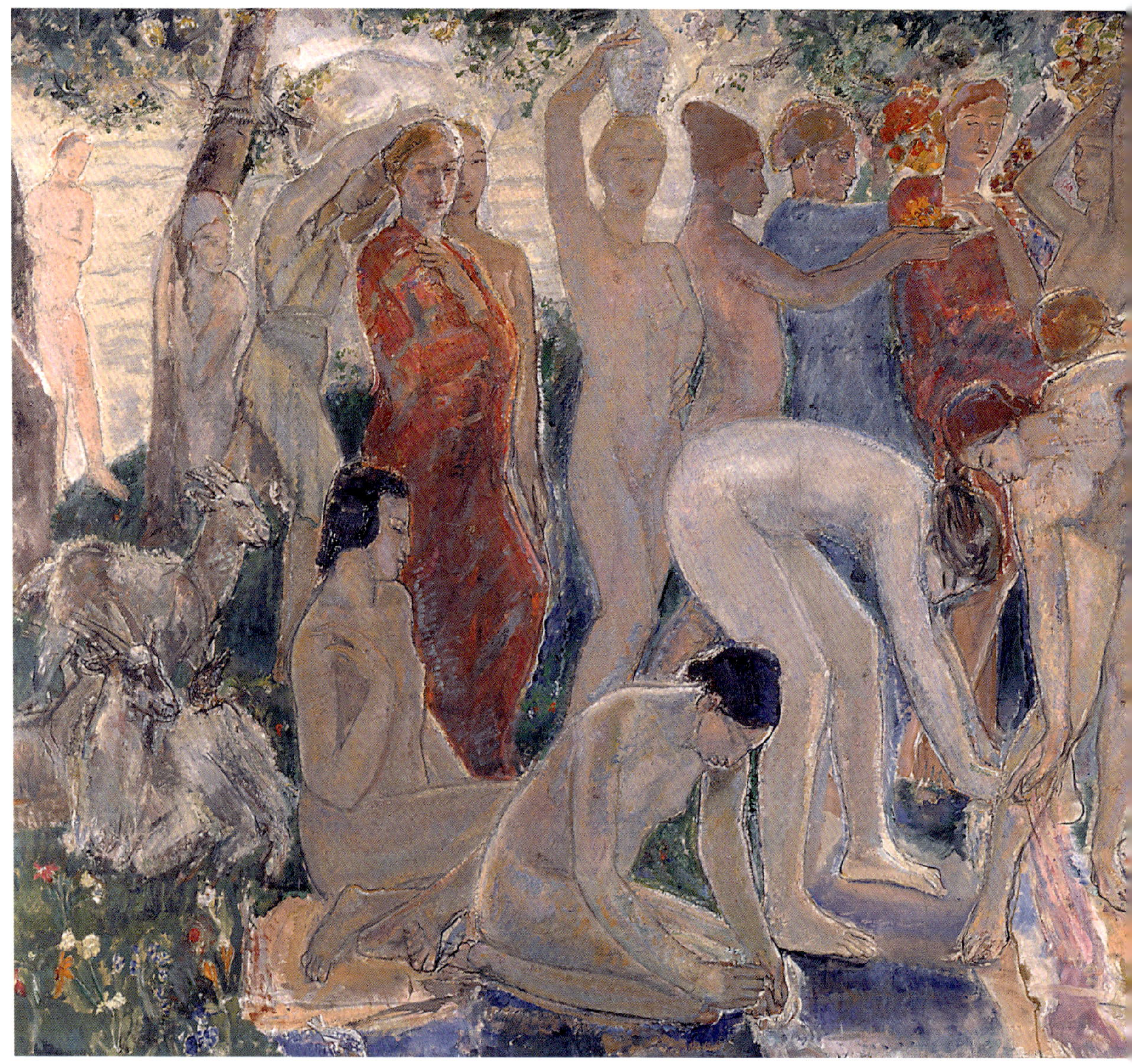

Dame Ethel Walker 1861–1951

Decoration: The Excursion of Nausicaa 1920

Oil on canvas

183.5 x 367

Tate. Purchased 1924

Ethel Walker was born in Edinburgh, though she spent most of her long life in London after her family settled in the English capital when she was nine. She received little formal training as an artist before attending the Putney School of Art and Design at the unusually mature age of thirty-eight. From here she went on to be taught by Walter Sickert at the Slade, who became a vocal supporter of her work.

Since her death, her art has fallen into relative obscurity. However, her work was widely exhibited during her lifetime, and she was elected to exhibiting societies such as the Royal Academy. In 1938, she was appointed Commander of the British Empire. According to a report from a party celebrating her appointment, Walker was introduced as 'England's leading woman artist', to which she retorted: 'There is no such thing as a woman artist. There are only two kinds of artist – bad and good. You can call me a good artist if you like.'[18]

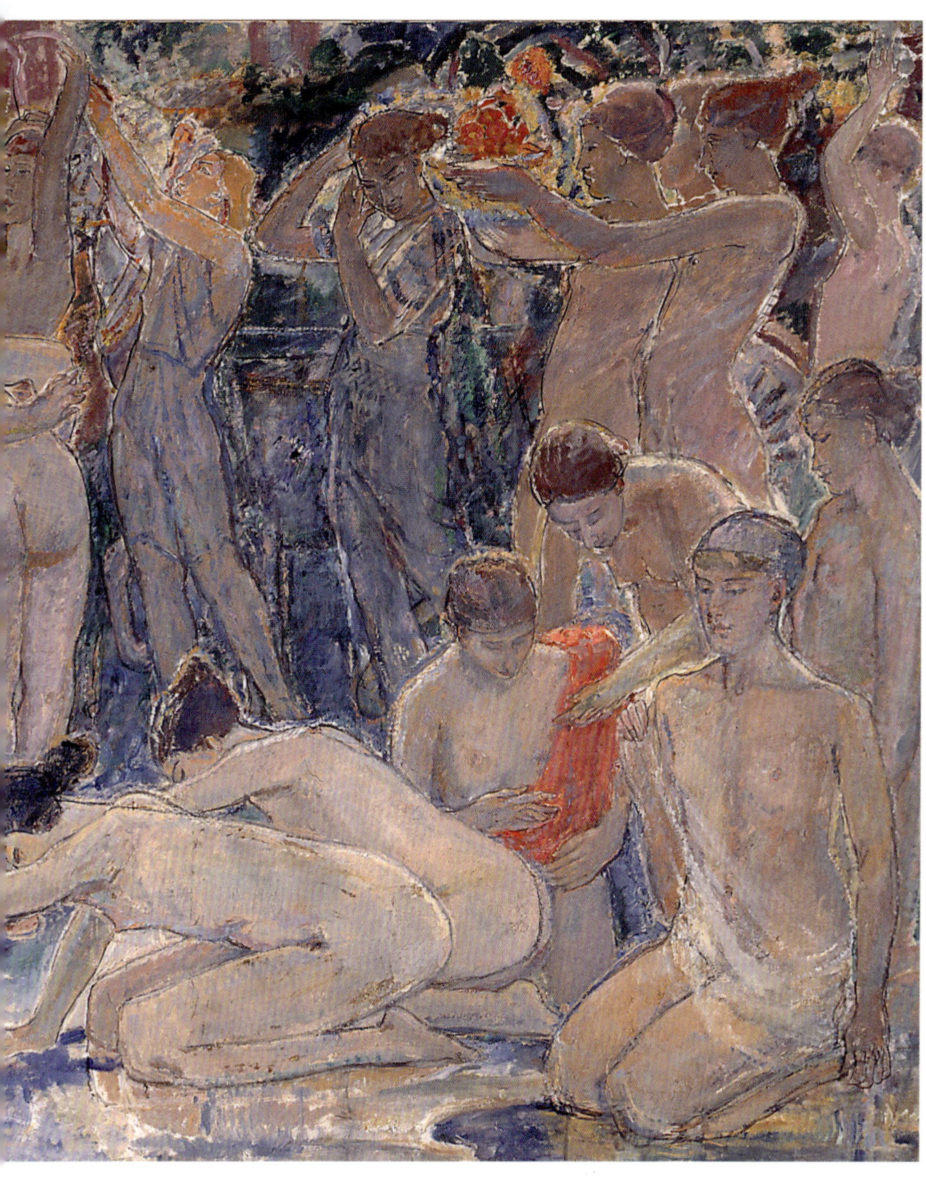

When *Nausicaa* was placed in front of the New English Arts Club select committee, it was received with 'spontaneous and enthusiastic applause'.[19] The painting is inspired by Book VI of Homer's *Odyssey*, which sees the Phaeacian princess Nausicaa going to a river, along with her maidens, to bathe herself and her clothes: 'they spread / The raiment orderly along the beach / Where dashing tides ... /... leaving the garments, stretch'd / In noon-day fervour of the sun, to dry'. As the women wash, they are discovered by Odysseus, and Nausicaa guides him through the next stage of his journey.

The composition of the work, featuring a cluster of nude female figures in a variety of poses, demonstrates Walker's fascination with both Greco-Roman friezes and the artistic possibilities of the nude female body, a regular theme in her paintings. There has been some scholarly speculation about the nature of Walker's relationship with Clara Christian (1868–1906), with whom she lived and worked in the 1880s, although little evidence survives. In any case this work, like many of Walker's paintings, offers a utopic vision of an all-female community as the foundation for peaceful creativity and artistic innovation. [EJ]

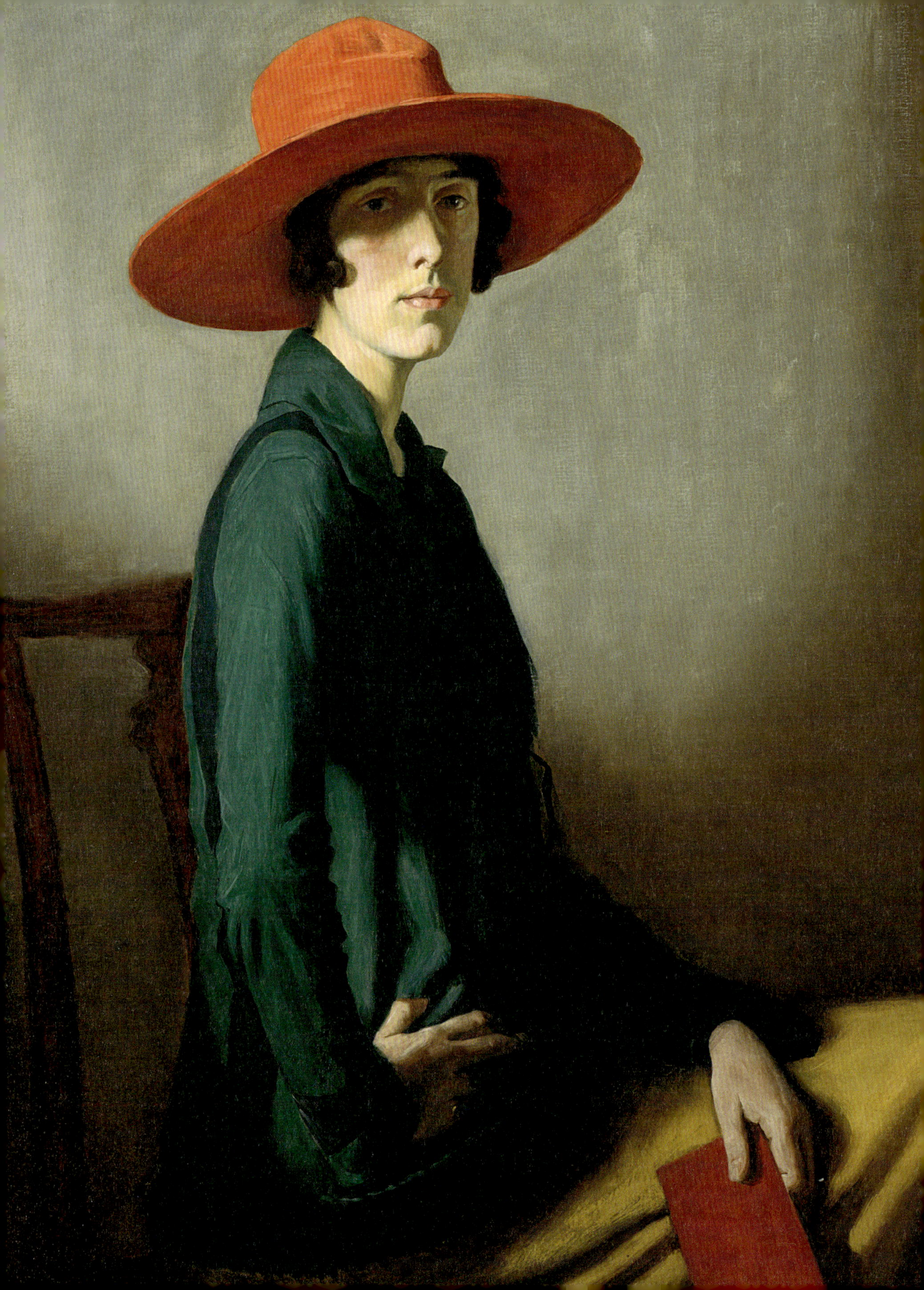

DEFYING CONVENTION

CAROLINE GONDA

William Strang 1859–1921

Lady with a Red Hat 1918

Oil on canvas

129 x 103.4

Glasgow Museums and
Libraries Collection

ALMOST TOO GOOD to be true, this story: a love poem from one woman to another, undiscovered for close to a century, falls out of a book during the cataloguing of the author's library and into the hands of a scholar. Written in French, the poem contrasts the open landscape of the women's friendship with their fevered coupling 'in the heavy fragrance of intoxicating night'; it speaks of searching for 'a madder caress', of 'tear[ing] secrets from your yielding flesh'. The poet was Vita Sackville-West (1892–1962) and the woman she addresses as 'my mistress' was Violet Keppel (1894–1972), soon to be Violet Trefusis.

The works in this section abound with a sense of the hidden, the possible and the just-out-of-sight, whether in the realm of the visible/hidden body or the more distant realm of unseen desires, identities and relationships. *Lady with a Red Hat* (opposite), the androgynous portrait of Sackville-West painted by William Strang (1859–1921) in 1918, the year of the poem's composition, epitomises this nexus of possibilities. The book she holds, which matches the red of her hat, could be her most recent volume of verse, *Poems of West and East*, published to favourable reviews in 1917. But it is tempting to read it as also standing in for other books: for *Challenge*, the novel she was writing about her affair with Keppel, and which because of family pressure and censorship would not be published in Britain until 1974; or for the book with her love poem to Keppel hidden in it, a book that Keppel had given her. That temptation becomes all the stronger when we know that Keppel was present at the portrait sittings, and that Sackville-West here is the object of her lover's gaze as well as that of the artist.

The painting is ghosted, too, by the portrait that Sackville-West's mother originally thought of commissioning, of Vita in her farm-girl's breeches: 'I do want to get her painted like that', Lady Sackville wrote; 'she looks so charming in her corduroy trousers. She ought to have been a boy!'[1] (As a boy, Sackville-West could have inherited Knole, her family's estate; as a woman, she could not.) Wearing breeches gave her the freedom to act on her desires, in ways her mother could not approve. She adopted a male persona, 'Julian', to carry on her affair with Keppel; the two of them posed as a married couple to spend the night at a boarding house, and danced publicly together in Paris.

Adopting masculine or androgynous clothing was not confined to the wealthy and privileged, nor was it always associated with lesbianism. As Alison Oram suggests in *Her Husband Was A Woman!* (2007),[2] the popular press at the time framed stories of working-class women's cross-dressing in terms of the women's ingenuity and resourcefulness rather than as sexual aberration or gender transgression. New styles of clothing and their relation to gender became the subject of a popular song, 'Masculine Women and Feminine Men'. Imported from America, it was recorded in 1926 by Billy Mayerl (1902–1959) and Gwen Farrar (1899–1944), a singer celebrated for her onstage and offstage partnership with Norah Blaney (1893–1983). 'Girls were girls and boys were boys when I was a tot', the song ran, 'Now we don't know who is who or even what's what. / Knickers and trousers baggy and wide, nobody knows who's walking inside. / Those masculine women and feminine men.' Identity itself, the song suggested, could no longer be taken for granted.

This deconstruction of identity and gender could be liberating. For the novelist Bryher (Annie Winifred Ellerman, 1894–1983), conventional femininity was unbearable. After meeting Havelock Ellis for the first time, Bryher reported to her lover, the poet H.D. (Hilda Doolittle, 1886–1961),

> Then we got on to the question of whether I was a boy sort of escaped into the wrong body and he says it is a disputed subject but quite possible and showed me a book about it... We agreed it was most unfair for it to happen but apparently I am quite justified in pleading I ought to be a boy – I am just a girl by accident.[3]

For Bryher, nicknamed 'Boy' by H.D., the idea of being an invert was not confining but freeing, enabling her to write and live as she wished. Like Vernon Lee (1856–1935), Marlow Moss (1889–1958) and Claude Cahun (1894–1954), she chose a name that reflected her gender identity and rejection of the feminine.

Marriage – the right sort of marriage – could also offer a certain freedom. Sackville-West's marriage to Harold Nicolson (1886–1968) provided a measure of camouflage for her affairs with women, as for his affairs with men. 'Bloomsbury' became a kind of shorthand for polyamorous relationships (the painter Cecile Walton (1891–1956) described the complexities of her own amorous network as having a 'Bloomsbury atmosphere'). On one memorable occasion in 1929, Sackville-West and Nicolson took part in a radio discussion on the subject of marriage, in a programme devised by Vita's then lover, Hilda Matheson (1888–1940), Director of Talks at the BBC. The discussion must have had a particular piquancy for those who recognised the fictional version of the Nicolsons' marriage in Virginia Woolf's *Orlando: A Biography* (1928), and even more so for those who knew about Sackville-West's affair with Woolf (opposite), which had inspired the novel.

Orlando's central character, a young Elizabethan nobleman and aspiring poet, lives for 300 years (though ageing only to thirty-six) and changes sex from male to female at some point during the eighteenth century. For Lady Sackville, Woolf's novel, illustrated with family portraits from Knole and with photographs of Sackville-West as Orlando, was an outrage. She wrote furiously to the editor of the *Observer*, James Louis Garvin (1868–1947), in a bid to stop the book being reviewed, listing all the sexually suggestive passages (complete with page

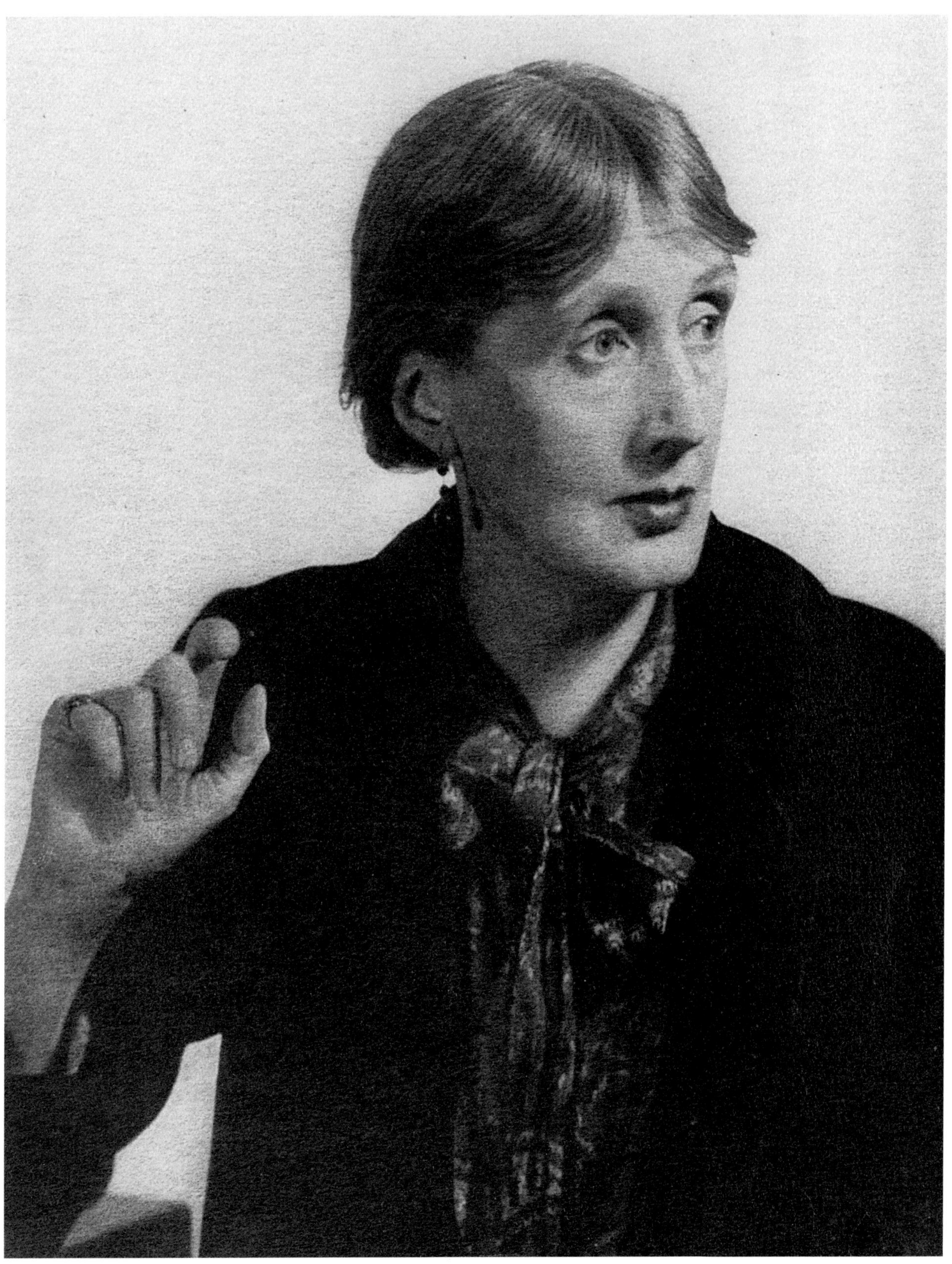

numbers). 'I have spent years, hiding what Harold and Vita really are, I am sorry
to confess it', she told him. 'And it makes it twice as dreadful now and such food
for indecent gossip.'[4] She visited bookshops and hid copies of Orlando under piles
of other books, to no avail. The book was a popular success, selling twice as many
copies in six months as Woolf's previous novel, *To The Lighthouse* (1927), had
done in a year, and the reviews did not fail to point out 'Mrs Harold Nicolson'
as the original of *Orlando*.

Six days before *Orlando*'s publication, Woolf had testified at the obscenity trial
of Radclyffe Hall's *The Well of Loneliness* (1928); the climate for producing a novel
in which, as Woolf put it, 'Sapphism is to be suggested' must have appeared
unfavourable, to say the least. Yet Orlando triumphantly got away with it, in part
through that very suggestiveness. Hall had defied convention by writing a serious
work of realism, pleading for the social acceptance of inverts and their recognition
as part of humanity. *Orlando*'s defiance was deliberately fantastical, a spoof on
biography, playing fast and loose with the very idea of a coherent self as well
as with questions of gender and sexuality. The novel teases the reader with a
shimmering cloud of possibilities that refuses to stay still long enough to be
grasped. It presents sexual difference as both profound and fluid, but also as
possibly only a matter of habit and performance. At one point the narrator even
suggests that 'it is clothes that wear us, and not we them...The man has his hand
free to seize his sword, the woman must use hers to keep the satins from slipping
from her shoulders.' Orlando in the eighteenth century changes sex 'far more
frequently than those who have worn only one set of clothing can conceive...
For the probity of breeches she exchanged the seductiveness of petticoats and
enjoyed the love of both sexes equally.'[5]

In the weeks before and after *Orlando*'s publication, Woolf visited Cambridge to
give talks to the women undergraduates at Newnham and Girton Colleges. These
talks on 'Women and Fiction', published in 1929 as *A Room of One's Own*, see
relations between the sexes as irreparably altered and fractured by the First World
War, but suggest that this makes possible new ways of living and writing. Woolf's
imaginary novelist, Mary Carmichael, ruptures both stylistic and narrative convention:
'First she broke the sentence; now she has broken the sequence.' The modern
woman writer, Woolf suggests, represents relationships between women in a
new light: '"Chloe liked Olivia . . ." Do not start. Do not blush. Let us admit in the
privacy of our own society that these things sometimes happen. Sometimes women
do like women.' Woolf frames this passage with an anxious joke about the *Well*
trial, and reveals that Chloe and Olivia share (not a bed but) a laboratory, and that
Olivia is married with children. Yet this, she says, is 'a sight that has never been
seen since the world began': the affection, which may also shade into desire,
between women who work together.[6]

Something of that world of women together can be seen in Dorothy
Johnstone's (1892–1980) painting, *Rest Time in the Life Class* 1923. The painting is
both tender and matter-of-fact in its view of the tired model's naked body, and

in the exchange of glances between the two young women in the foreground (pp.2, 126-7). This all-female scene is a far cry from the world in which Laura Knight (1877-1970), starting art school in 1890, was not even allowed to attend life classes. Knight's radical 1913 self-portrait painting her friend and fellow artist Ella Naper (1886-1972) challenged this exclusion and, in doing so, overturned the conventional balance of power in life painting (pp.122-3). Perhaps it was this shift that caused the *Telegraph* critic of the day to miss the point so spectacularly in his response to Knight's painting: 'Somehow, woman painting woman hardly ever infuses into her work the higher charms of the "eternal feminine".'[7] The unspoken assumption here is that eroticism depends on sexual difference, and cannot exist without it.

Woolf had an answer to that, in the passage from *Orlando* where sapphism is most clearly suggested:

> And as all Orlando's loves had been women, now, through the culpable laggardry of the human frame to adapt itself to convention, though she herself was a woman, it was still a woman she loved; and if the consciousness of being of the same sex had any effect at all, it was to quicken and deepen the feelings which she had had as a man. For now a thousand hints and mysteries became plain to her that were then dark. Now, the obscurity, which divides the sexes and lets linger innumerable impurities in the gloom, was removed, and if there is anything in what the poet says about truth and beauty, this affection gained in beauty what it lost in falsity.[8]

It is easy to miss how quietly radical this passage is, as Woolf reassigns the gloom and obscurity so often associated with lesbian relationships in fiction to heterosexual ones. Echoing I Corinthians in the New Testament of the Bible, the passage implicitly elevates female same-sex love to the status of the divine.

Many of the artists here seek to challenge and move beyond the constraints of sexual difference, gender identity and normative models of relationships between the sexes, finding fresh approaches to exploring worlds of desire between women, worlds beyond gender, or even worlds beyond the limits of the human. For readers and spectators, too, refusing the obscuring filter of conventional assumptions about sex, gender, identity, sexuality, and about the relation between any or all of these things, can open up new ways of seeing, as we respond to the dazzling array of queer invitations, provocations and possibilities offered by these works.

Gluck 1895–1978

Self-portrait 1942

Oil on canvas

30.6 x 25.4

National Portrait Gallery, London

In this uncompromising self-portrait, Gluck locks gaze
with the viewer, jutting her chin as if daring them to
contradict her. Gluck was unapologetic in her work,
her desires and her many battles with authority. Born
Hannah Gluckstein, she quickly abandoned her birth
name and requested that Gluck be reproduced with
'no prefix, suffix or quotes'.[9] When the Fine Art Society
printed her name as 'Miss Gluck', she threatened to
resign. Gluck continued to use female pronouns, so
we have followed her choice here, while acknowledging
that we do not know how she would have perceived
her gender identity had more possibilities been
recognised at the time.

Her hair was habitually cut in the Eton crop shown
here, and she dressed in androgynous and masculine
clothes long after this had ceased to be fashionably
avant-garde. The photographer Emil Otto Hoppé
(1878–1972), who encouraged her to exhibit her work,
wrote of her in *The Royal Magazine*, December 1926,
'To look at her face is to understand both her success
as an artist and the fact that she dresses as a man.
Originality, determination, strength of character and
artistic insight are expressed in every line.'

Gluck's shows at the 'Gluck Room' of the Fine
Art Society were highly acclaimed and attended by
society figures such as Queen Mary, Cecil Beaton
and C.B. Cochran.

This is an unflinching self-portrait, although there
is perhaps a note of sadness in her creased brow and
weary eyes. It was painted in 1942, in a difficult period
in her relationship with Nesta Obermer, her 'darling
wife'. Gluck and Obermer had met in 1936 and their
relationship was a consuming passion, but Obermer
was frequently away, sometimes with her husband
Seymour Obermer. In 1944, Gluck moved in with
Edith Shackleton Heald (1885–1976), the woman
with whom she would spend the rest of her life. [CB]

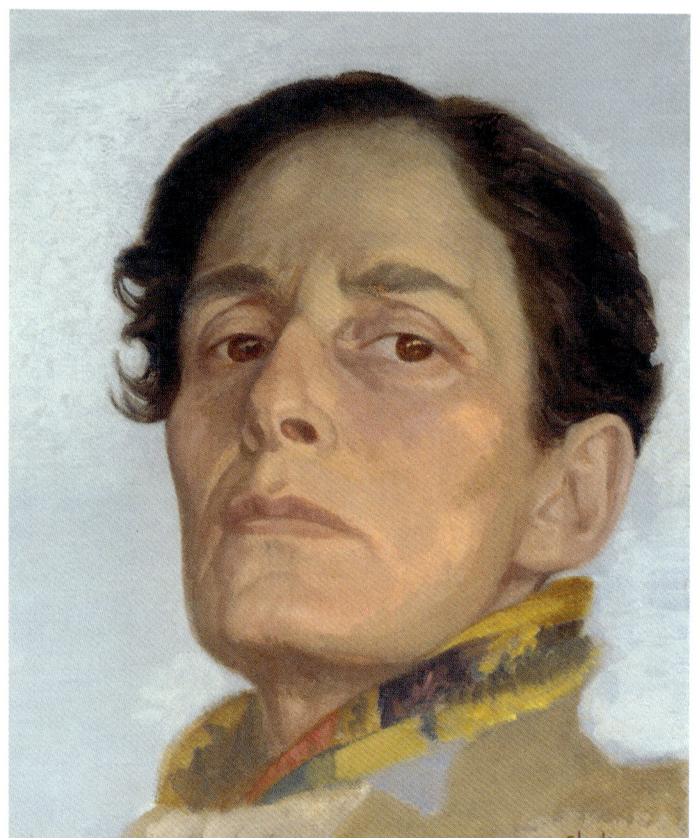

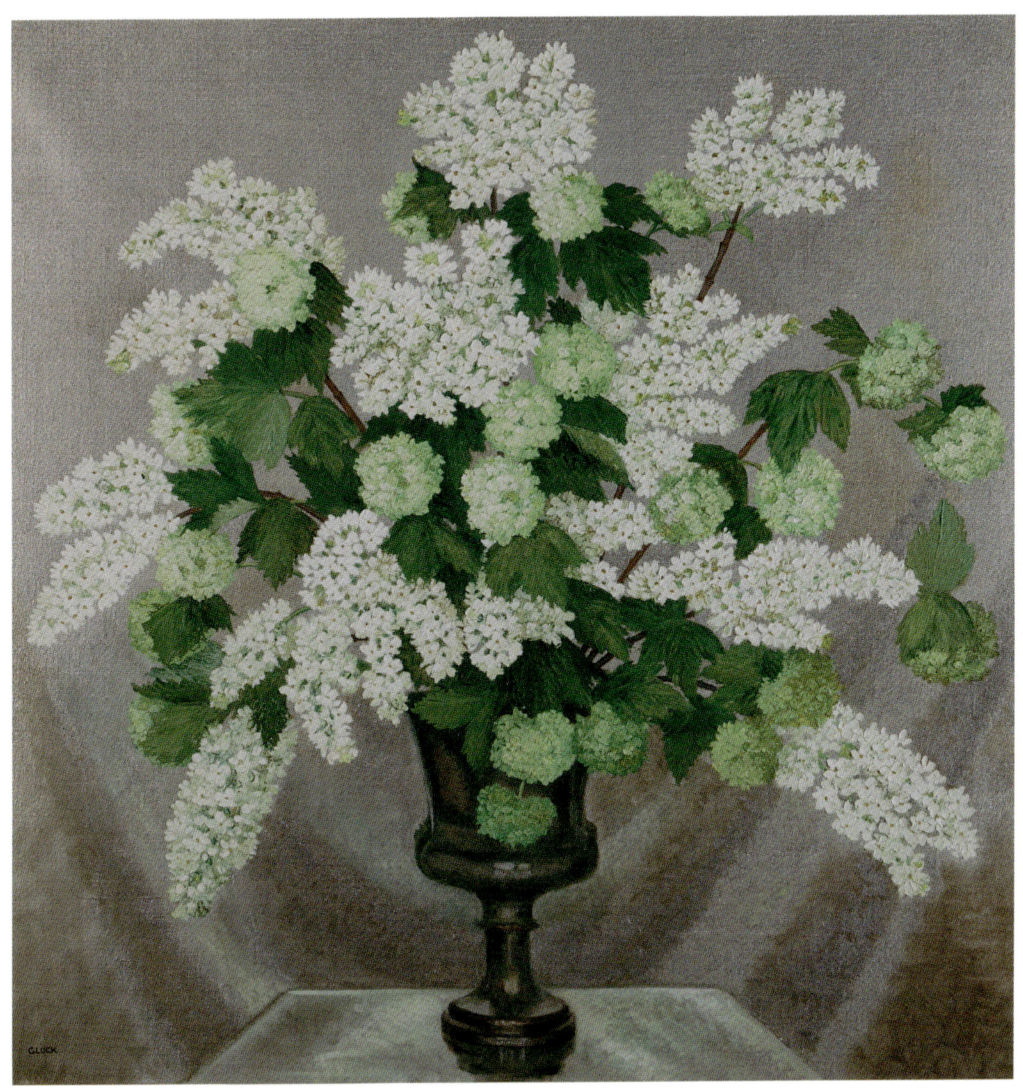

Gluck 1895–1978

Lilac and Guelder Rose 1932–7

Oil on canvas

109.2 x 109. 3

Manchester City Galleries

This was one of a number of flower paintings that Gluck made around the time of her relationship with society flower arranger and decorator Constance Spry (1886–1960). They met in 1932, when designer and interior decorator Prudence Maufe (1882–1976) sent Gluck an arrangement by Spry to paint. Spry was a leading figure in cultivating a fashion for white flowers, and often used Gluck's paintings to illustrate her articles. Many of Spry's customers also commissioned flower paintings from Gluck. When *Lilac and Guelder Rose* was exhibited at Gluck's 1937 exhibition at the Fine Art Society, it was much admired by Lord Villiers, who remarked 'It's gorgeous, I feel I could bury my face in it'.[10] Gluck's mother bought it at the show and presented it to Manchester City Art Gallery under the pretence of acting as an agent for a rich American benefactor. [CB]

John Singer Sargent 1856–1925

Vernon Lee 1881

Oil on canvas

53.7 x 43.2

Tate. Bequeathed by Miss Vernon Lee through
Miss Cooper Willis 1935

Born Violet Paget (1856–1935), Paget took the name
'Vernon Lee' because 'it has the advantage of leaving
it undecided whether the writer be a man or a woman'.
She forged her literary reputation with *Studies of the
Eighteenth Century in Italy* (1880) but worked in a variety
of genres, from aesthetics to supernatural fiction.[11]

Friends from childhood, Lee and John Singer
Sargent called each other 'twin'. Lee described sitting
for this portrait in a letter from 25 June 1881:

> ...about three hours sitting with Mabel [Robinson]
> looking on; I enjoyed it very much; John talking the
> whole time & strumming the piano between
> whiles. I like him. The sketch is, by everyone's
> admission, extraordinarily clever & characteristic;
> it is of course mere dabs & blurs & considerably
> caricatured, but certainly more like me than I
> expected anything could – rather fierce &
> cantankerous.[12]

Lee had a passionate relationship with the writer
Mary F. Robinson (1857–1944), Mabel's (1858–1954)
sister, whose portrait Sargent gave to Lee in 1885 as

a pair to this image. The suffragette Ethel Smyth
(1858–1944), herself attracted to women, wrote that
Lee loved, 'humanely and with passion; but being the
stateliest, chastest of beings she refused to face the
fact, or indulge in the most innocent demonstrations
of affection preferring to create a fiction that these
friends were merely *intellectual* necessities'.[13]

Nonetheless, there is little doubt about the depth
of feeling between Lee and Robinson: in a letter from
31 January 1881, Lee told Robinson that she would have
proposed if she had been a man. Henry Havelock Ellis
considered them as a possible case study on 'female
inversion' and wrote to John Addington Symonds on
the 'curious contrast between the straight-forward
"Vernon Lee" – addressing a meeting as best I
remember her, with her hand on her hip – and
the ultra-feminine kitten-ish little Mary D'
(3 January 1893). There has been some recent
speculation over Lee's apparently androgynous
appearance, yet while Lee's manner was considered
masculine, her clothes were not thought unusual.

In 1887, Robinson married James Darmesteter
(1849–1894), leaving Lee devastated. Lee forged a
relationship with Clementina 'Kit' Anstruther
Thomson (1857–1921), who assisted with Lee's work
on aesthetic experience, which she published in the
Contemporary Review in 1897 under the title 'Beauty
and Ugliness'. [CB]

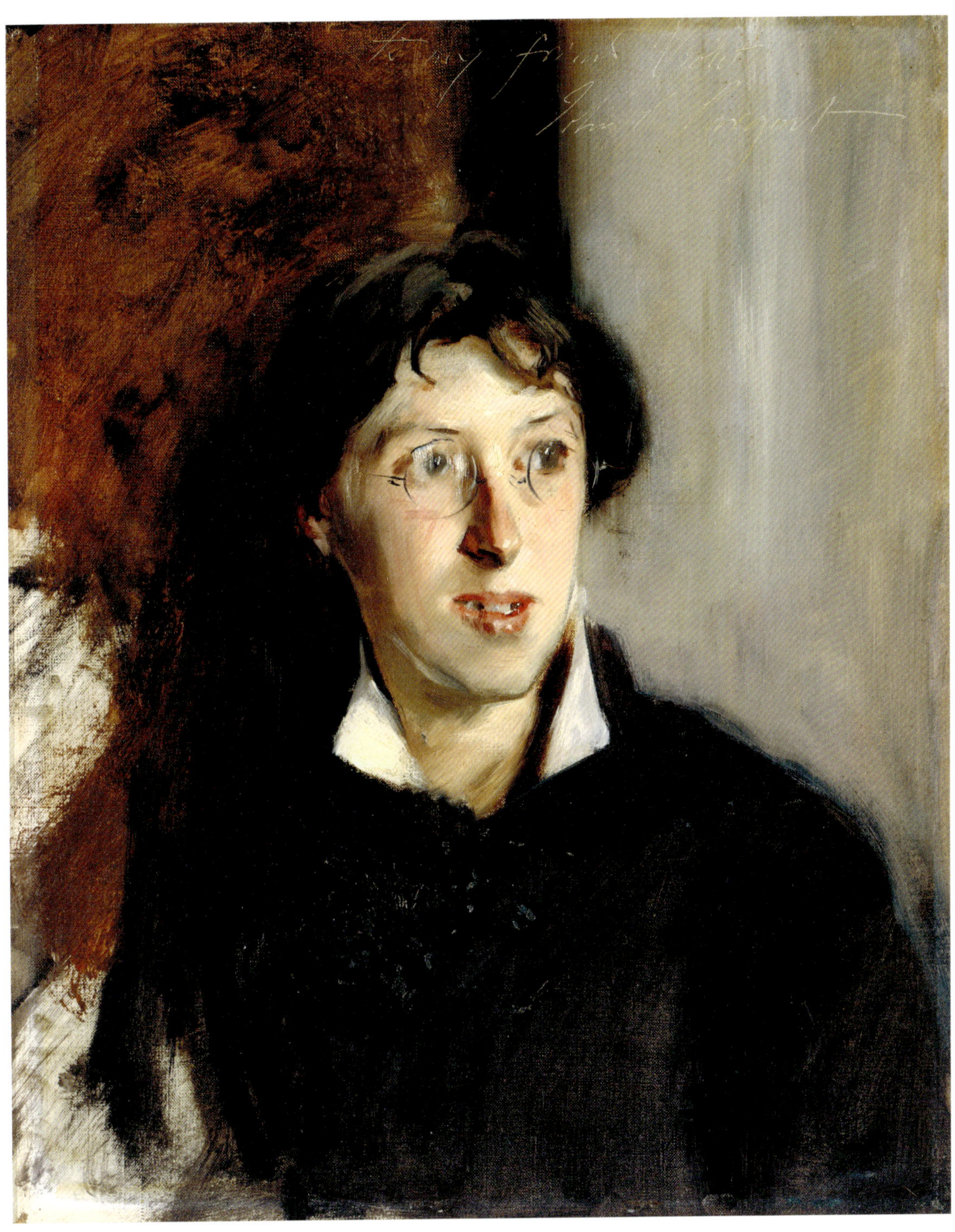

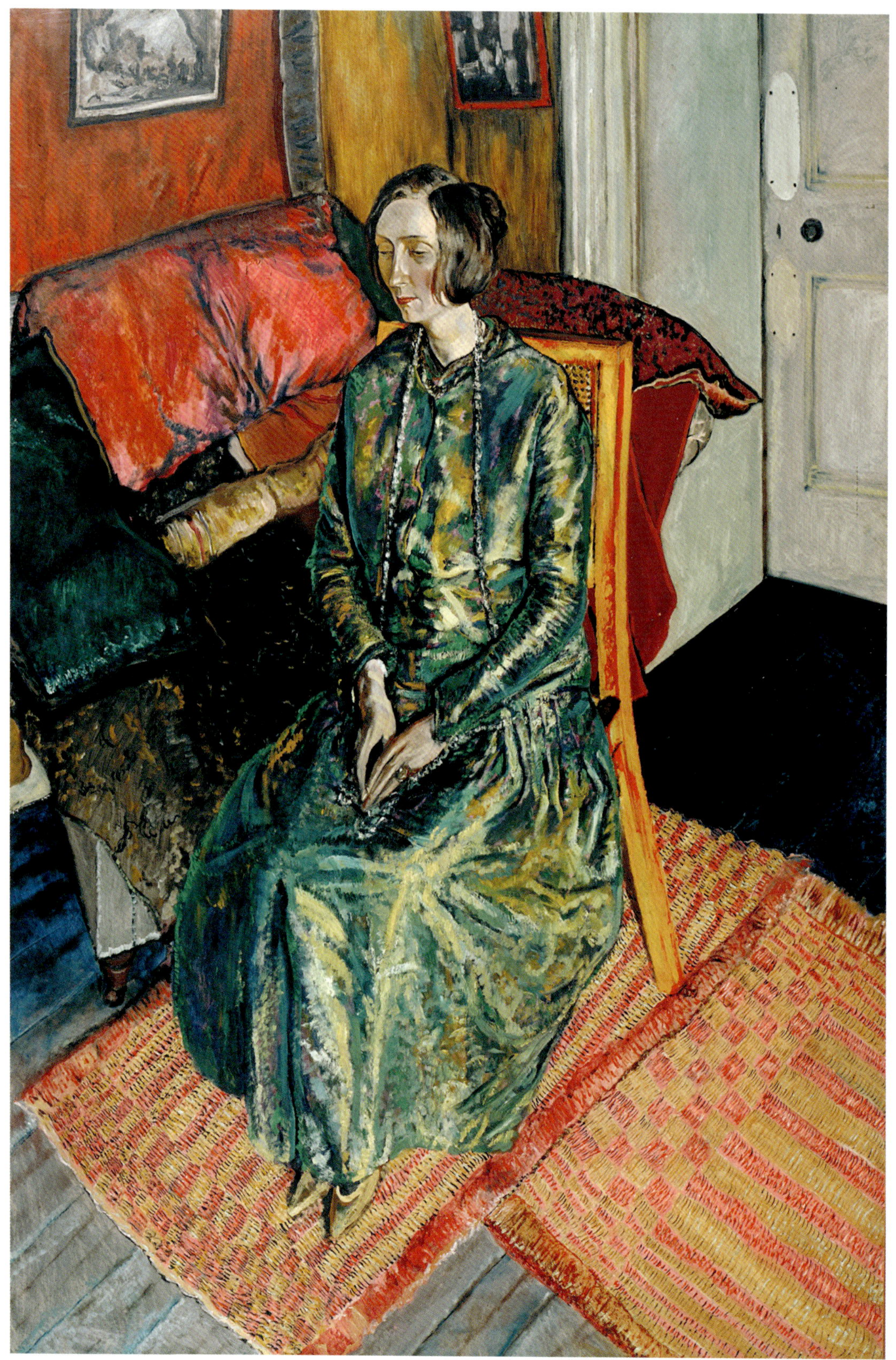

Alvaro Guevara 1894–1951

Dame Edith Sitwell 1916

Oil on canvas

196.2 x 136

Tate. Presented by Lord Duveen, Walter Taylor and
George Eumorfopoulos through the Art Fund 1920

The poet Edith Sitwell (1887–1964) was close friends
with the artist Alvaro Guevara. Guevara was born in
Chile and moved to England with his parents in 1910,
settling in London where he attended the Slade School
of Fine Art from 1913 to 1914 and befriended the
Bloomsbury set. This painting was exhibited at the
International Exhibition at the Grosvenor Gallery in
1919 under the title 'Editor of Wheels' – a reference
to a quarterly publication that Sitwell had founded
to represent those contemporary poets who had not
been included in Edward Marsh's *Anthology of Georgian
Poetry*. Guevara designed the endpapers for the second
edition of Sitwell's journal and also joined the group
of artists associated with Roger Fry and Vanessa Bell's
Omega Workshops. The dining chair on which Sitwell
sits in the painting is an Omega chair designed by Fry,
and the colour scheme of the rugs and cushions is
similar to Omega designs.

Diana Holman-Hunt (1913–1993) in her 1974
biography of Guevara titled *Latin Among Lions*
suggests that Sitwell and Guevara shared a love
that was 'not physical but certainly romantic and
spiritual.'[14] Both were unconventional in their approach
to sexuality: Guevara had relationships with men and
women before eventually marrying Meraud Guinness
(1904–1993), while Sitwell has been referred to by
modern scholars as 'seemingly asexual'. She once
described the life of the artist as being 'very Pauline',
which may suggest (with reference to the letters of St
Paul) that she thought marriage would be an unwelcome
distraction. She was satirised by Wyndham Lewis
(1882–1957) in his novel *The Apes of God* (1930)
conflictingly as both a spinster and as a lesbian,
reflecting perhaps a lack of belief on Lewis's part
that a woman could willingly exist outside the
framework of sexuality. [CB]

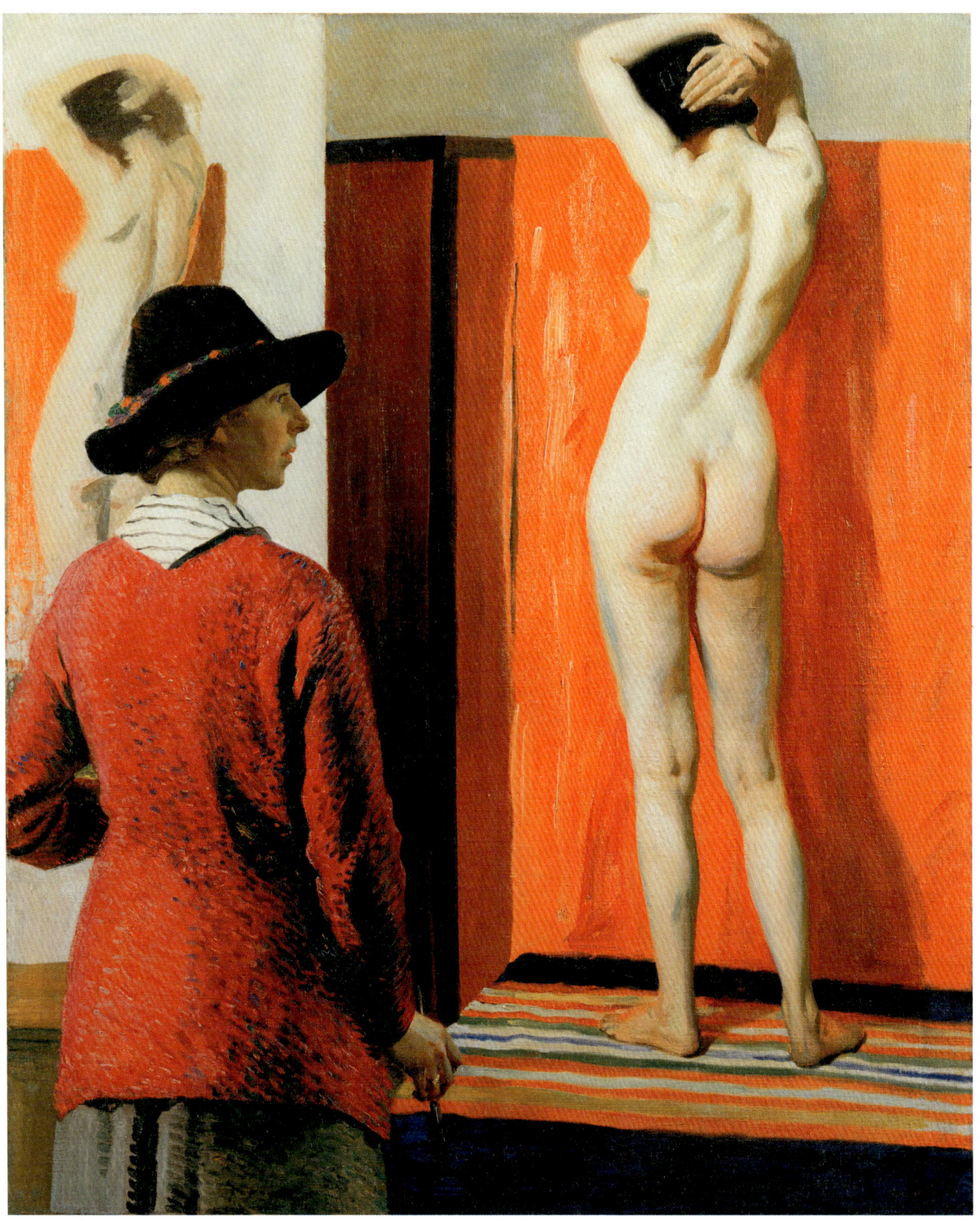

Laura Knight 1877–1970

Self-portrait 1913

Oil on canvas

152.4 x 127.6

National Portrait Gallery, London

When Laura Knight's self-portrait was exhibited at the Grosvenor Gallery's International Society exhibition in April 1913, under the title 'The Model', Claude Phillips of the *Telegraph* reviewed it in the following terms:

> Somehow, woman painting woman hardly ever infuses into her work the higher charm of the 'eternal feminine'. This painting is obviously but an exercise and as such might quite appropriately have stayed in the artist's studio. It repels, not by any special inconvenance [*sic*]– for it is harmless enough and with an element of sensuous attraction – but by dullness and something dangerously close to vulgarity.[15]

This exemplifies the problem that contemporary critics had in responding to women painting the female nude. He oscillates between different positions: the work, for him, manages to be simultaneously dull, seductive, vulgar and harmless.

The erotic potential of details such as the rosy blush on the model Ella Naper's bottom is acknowledged in his reference to 'sensuous attraction', yet it seems that this is the wrong kind of eroticism for Phillips, too unstable in its position outside the conventional heterosexual hierarchy of male artist/female model to be admired.

In dismissing this painting as 'an exercise', Phillips does not recognise the battle that underpinned Knight's access to life drawing – and, consequently, to the status of a professional artist. Knight had originally studied at art school in Nottingham but was unable to attend life classes due to her gender. It was only as part of the artistic community in Newlyn, where Knight moved with her husband Harold Knight (1874–1961) in 1907, that she was able to push the boundaries of her art, hiring professional models from London and painting friends and fellow artists such as Naper. In this context, Knight's decision to depict herself in the act of painting a nude model was a radical gesture, marking her confident assumption of a professional artistic identity. Her achievement would be acknowledged in 1936, when she became the first woman since 1769 to be elected to the Royal Academy. [CB]

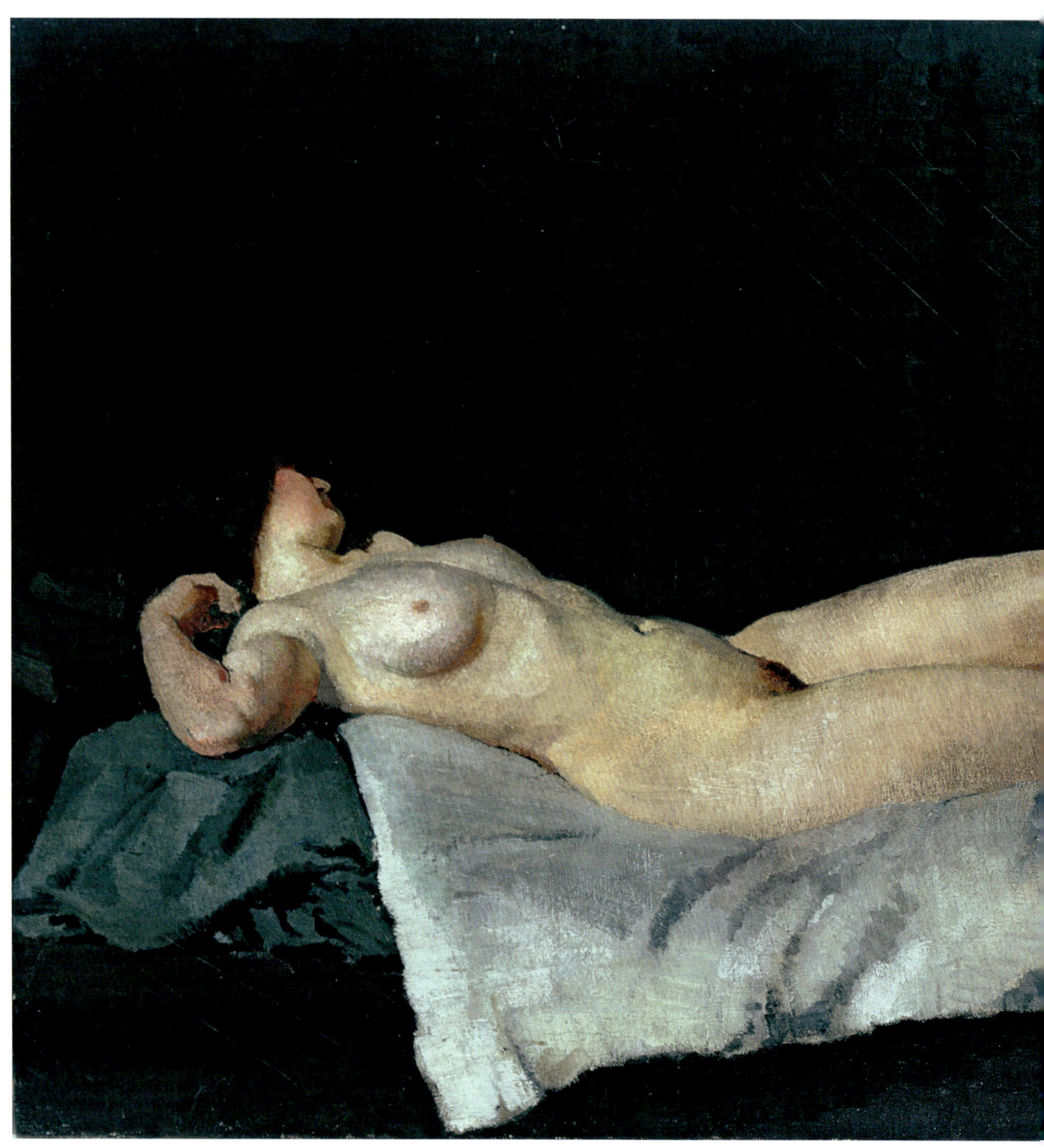

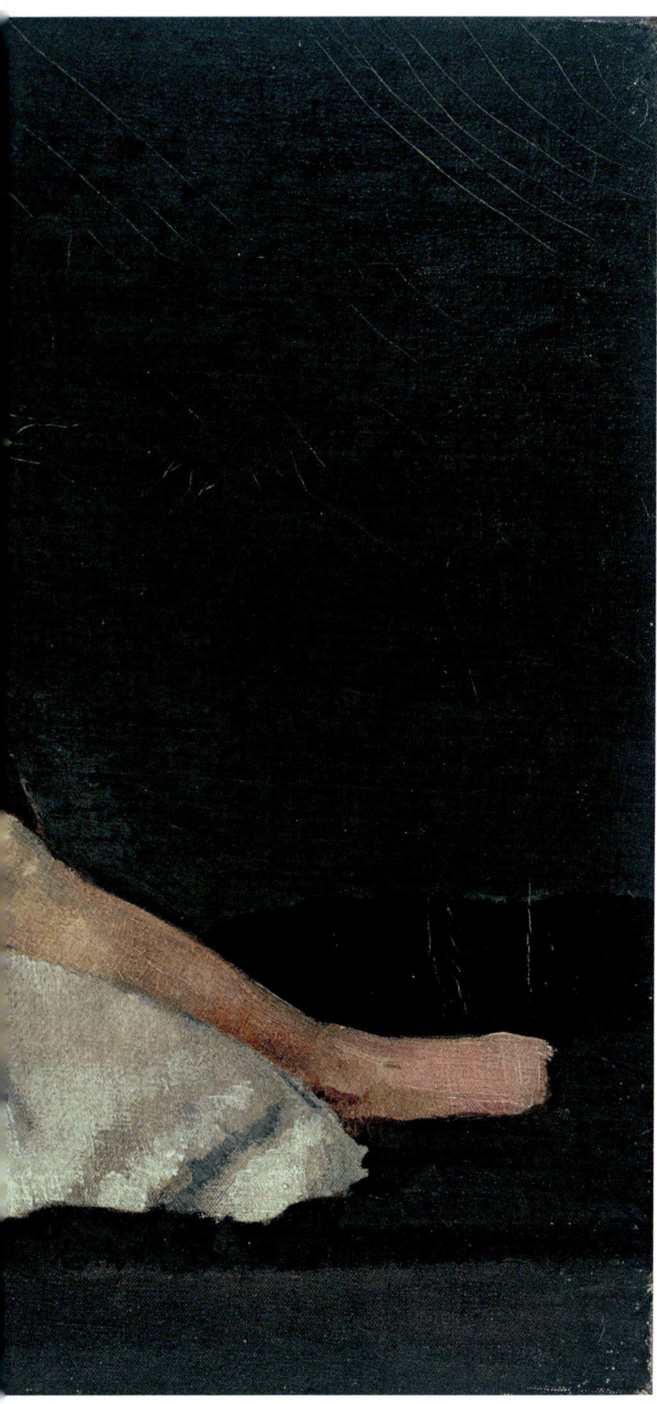

Dora Carrington 1893–1932

Female Figure Lying on her Back 1912

Oil on canvas

50.8 x 76.2

University College London Art Museum

This sensuous life study by Dora Carrington won second prize in a life-drawing competition at the Slade School of Fine Art, where Carrington was a student from 1910 to 1914. Women were allowed access to life-drawing classes at the Slade from its foundation in 1871, although they were taught in separate classes to the men. In 1912, the same year that this was painted, Carrington was awarded the prestigious Slade Scholarship. Fellow student Mark Gertler (1891–1939) was deeply in love with her, but it seems from Carrington's writings that, at this point in her life, desire of any sort made her uncomfortable. In addition to her close relationship with the writer Lytton Strachey and her marriage to Ralph Partridge, Carrington would go on to have affairs with women, most notably Henrietta Bingham (1901–68). In this context it may be tempting to read a lesbian sensibility into this languid image. While it is impossible to say if this work expressed any unacknowledged desires on Carrington's part, it remains striking as a sensual example of the female nude by a woman artist. The dark background focuses the viewer's attention on the model's body and particularly the stark whiteness of her breasts, which contrast with her flushed cheeks and softer flesh tones. [CB]

Dorothy Johnstone 1892–1980
Rest Time in the Life Class 1923
Oil on canvas
121.5 x 106.2
City Art Centre, City of Edinburgh Museums
and Galleries

The life class in this image is based on one that
Dorothy Johnstone taught at Edinburgh College of
Art, and it includes portraits of Johnstone's students.
This college, established in 1908, held life-drawing
classes for women but female students had more
limited access: segregated from the men, they initially
worked from sculptural casts and their models
remained partially clothed, as in this painting.

Johnstone's depiction of her art class casts light
on this exclusively female realm. Her composition is
suggestive of its utopian possibilities, in which women
are connected through friendship and collaboration.
One of the women in the foreground appears to be
commenting on her companion's drawing, while in
the background Johnstone depicted herself gesturing
authoritatively towards the canvas. This is not an erotic
scene, but it is an intimate one that proclaims the value
of female community and the right of women to look
at and depict the nude female body.

Johnstone had an intense relationship with Cecile
Walton (1891–1956) and Walton's husband Eric
Robertson (1887–1941), who were also part of the
Edinburgh Group of artists. In 1923, the year that this
was painted, Robertson and Walton's relationship
eventually broke down. She and Johnstone appear
to have lived together for a while and staged a joint
exhibition in 1924, the same year that Johnstone
married fellow artist David Macbeth Sutherland
(1883–1973). The marriage bar meant that Johnstone
was forced to give up her teaching position, although
she continued to paint and exhibit under her own name.
[CB]

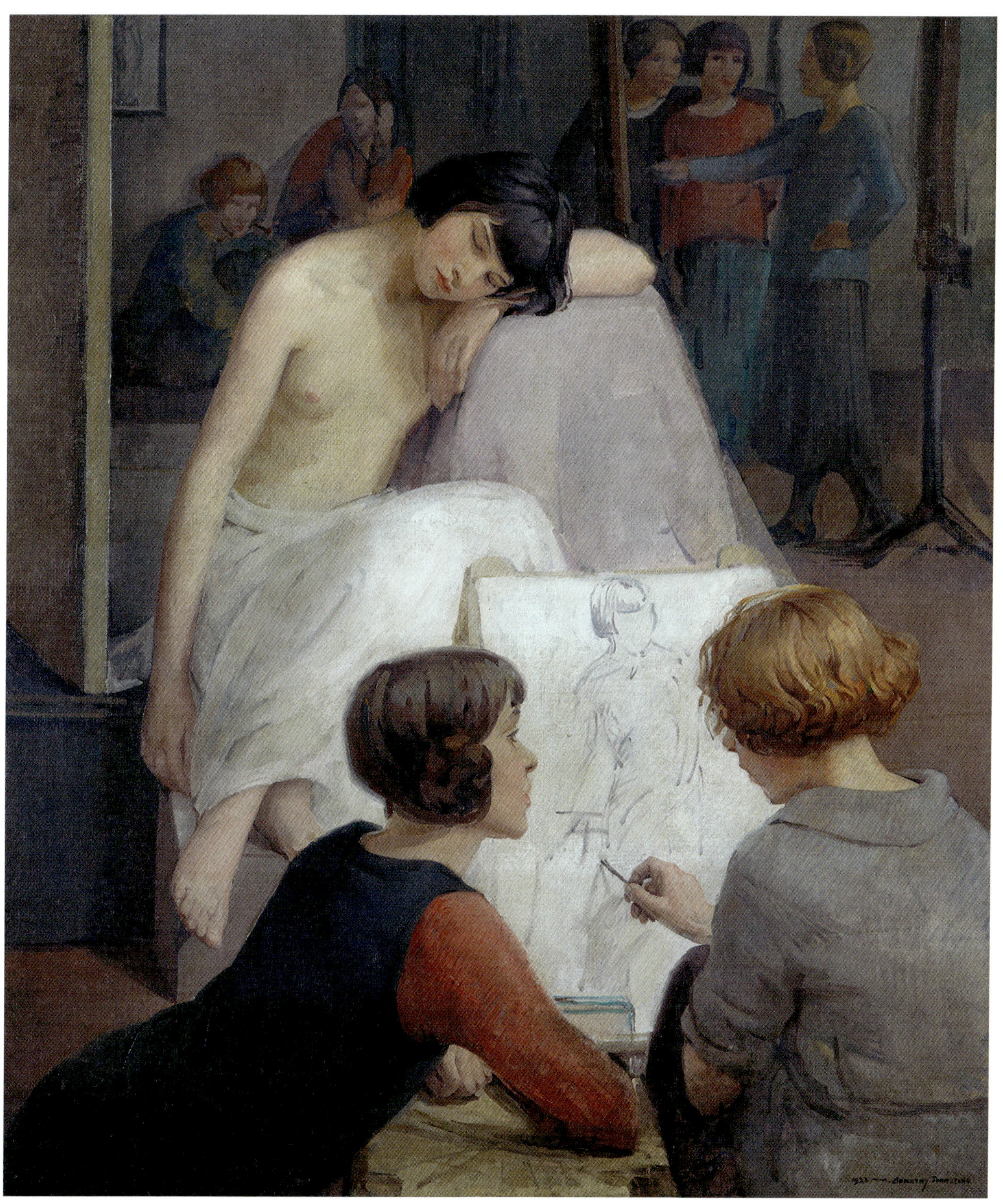

Cecile Walton 1891–1956

Romance 1920

Oil on canvas

100.6 x 150.9

Scottish National Portrait Gallery, Edinburgh

Cecile Walton's unconventional self-portrait depicts herself with her two sons, but the composition and iconography of the image unsettles any attempt to interpret the image solely within a narrative of motherhood. Modern critics have noted that Walton's pose and the relative positions of herself and the nurse in the image references Edouard Manet's (1832–1883) *Olympia* 1863, a painting that caused controversy for its depiction of a nude sex worker and her black servant. Walton is semi-nude: a potentially shocking choice in a painting that was publicly exhibited. Prior to their marriage, she had refused to pose nude for her husband, the artist Eric Robertson, on the grounds that by doing so she would 'lose her independence'.[16] When the image was shown at the second Edinburgh Group show in 1920, the critical response was mixed, one commentator remarking on the painting's 'frank treatment of an intimate subject'.[17]

In contrast to the proposed painting by Robertson, here Walton is fully in control of her representation. The restrained composition seems to hint at the potentially contradictory nature of traditional expectations of women: as lover, mother (implied by the presence of her children) and carer (suggested by the inclusion of the nurse). While Walton alludes to these roles, she depicts herself at a critical distance from them, presenting herself as indifferent to the ministrations of the nurse and the potentially eroticising gaze of the viewer, staring at her infant son – who does not meet her gaze – with cool appraisal. The apple on the table may refer to the Christian tradition of Eve's temptation, which caused original sin, supposedly the reason why childbirth is painful, while the crushed rose petals on the floor offer a reminder of the transient nature of love. In this context, it is hard to read the title of the painting – *Romance* – as anything other than ironic. [CB]

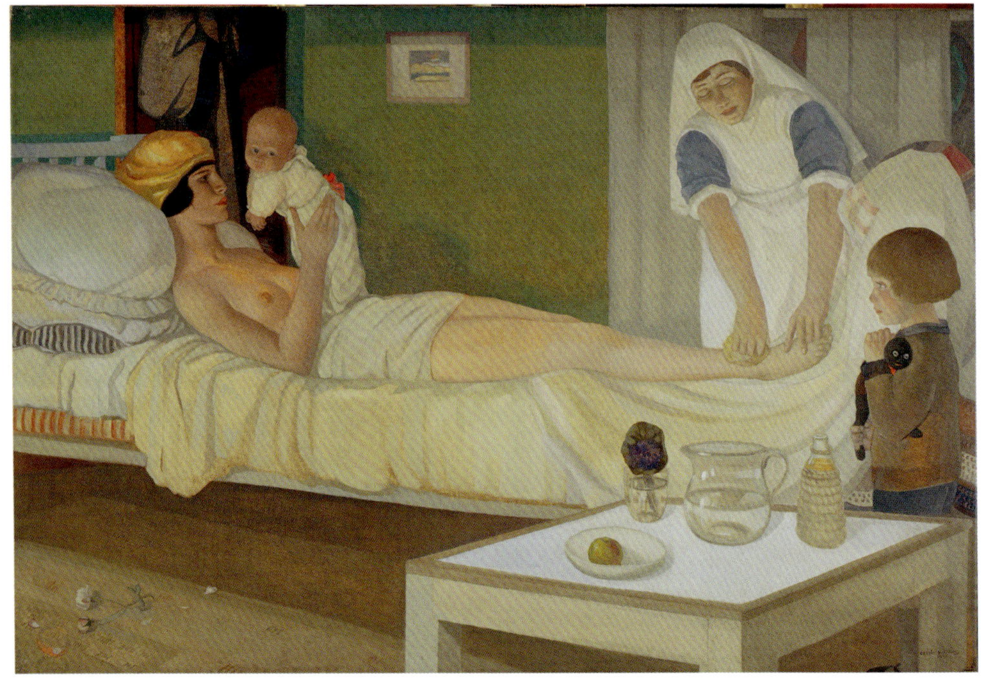

Marlow Moss 1889–1958

Composition in Yellow, Black and White 1949

Oil and wood on canvas

50.8 x 35.6 x 0.6

Tate. Presented by Miss Erica Brausen 1969

Raised as 'Marjorie Moss', Marlow Moss told how in
1923 'I destroyed my old personality and created a
new one'.[18] One manifestation of this transformation
was Moss's cropped hair and masculine wardrobe: a
style that could be interpreted in the 1920s as merely
reflecting an identity as an avant-garde artist.

In 1927, Moss moved to Paris and fell in love with
the writer A.H. 'Netty' Nijhoff (1897–1971). Nijhoff
introduced Moss to Piet Mondrian in 1929 and
Moss began to experiment with constructivism,
using primary colours and straight lines on a white
background. Scholars such as Florette Dijkstra have
traced Moss's original contributions to this movement,
for example the application of mathematical principles
to composition and the innovative use of a double line
in some of her paintings. The outbreak of the Second
World War forced Moss to return to England in 1940,
settling in Cornwall. Here, she continued to experiment,
adding strips of wood to the canvas, which gave form
to the compositions. *Composition White, Black and
Yellow* 1948 is from this series.

Scholars such as Lucy Howarth have explored
potential intersections between Moss's queer identity
and work as a constructivist artist. The erasure of
the self in Mondrian and Moss's rigorous form of
abstraction is arguably open to queer interpretations
as the work is liberated from specificities of gender
and sexuality. Prejudice against women artists did,
however, have a profound effect on Moss's
posthumous reputation: the critic John Russell
responded to the 1958 retrospective of Moss's work
at the Hanover Gallery by arguing that compared
to Mondrian, Moss's work 'was a department of the
housewifely arts'.[19] It is only in the last two decades
that Moss has begun to be re-evaluated as an
important and original artistic voice. [CB]

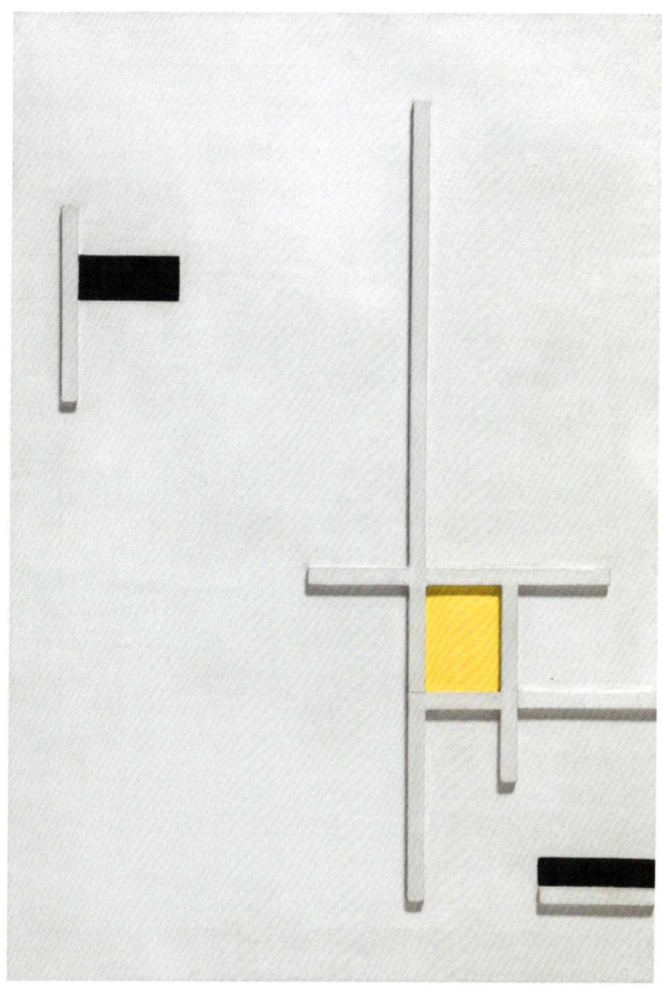

CLAUDE CAHUN

LINSEY YOUNG

Born in Nantes in 1894, Claude Cahun (born Lucy Schwob) was an artist, photographer and writer whose groundbreaking photographic self-portraits have become some of the most highly regarded and influential explorations of identity, gender and feminism, and whose impact can be traced in the work of subsequent artists such as Nan Goldin (b.1953) and Cindy Sherman (b.1954). Cahun used female pronouns but wrote in the autobiographical work, *Aveux non Avenus* (Disavowed Confessions), 'Masculine? Feminine? It depends on the situation. Neuter is the only gender that always suits me.' Since Cahun used feminine pronouns, we have elected to do the same, but do not in any way intend to preclude the queer possibilities of Cahun's gender identity.

The earliest known of her photographic portraits dates to 1912, when the artist was eighteen; she continued to work with the medium, creating highly staged shots in interiors, on the coast and in the grounds of her home.

Cahun enrolled at the Sorbonne in 1918 and settled in Paris with Marcel Moore (born Suzanne Malherbe, 1892–1972), her stepsister by marriage and the woman who would become her life partner. During the 1920s Cahun and Moore regularly held artist salons, which attracted many of the writers associated with the surrealists, such as Henri Michaux (1899–1994), Robert Desnos (1900–1945) and André Breton (1896–1966).

In 1930, Cahun published *Aveux non Avenus*. The book is illustrated with photomontages made in collaboration with Moore and takes the form of a compilation or collage of narrative text, poems and descriptions of dreams. It is here that Cahun articulates her 'neuter' understanding of gender. A copy was presented to the sexologist Havelock Ellis, 'who', according to the inscription,'has been a warm light on my desolate path, to the master I admire and love, to the friend who never failed me'.

While often considered solely in terms of her work on gender identity, Cahun's political interests and activism are perhaps as bold and striking as her portraits.

Formerly associated with left-wing political organisations such as the Association des Ecrivains et Artistes Revolutionnaires, in 1935 Cahun co-founded Contre Attaque, a group of artists and activists who protested against the rise of Hitler and the spread of fascism in France.

Having spent childhood summers on the island of Jersey, in 1937 Cahun and Moore moved to the island permanently. On moving to the island we can trace a shift in Cahun's practice, with many of her later photographs exploring the interaction between the body and the natural world, the beach, rockpools and the garden surrounding the house. Both Cahun and Moore became well known in the locality for their unorthodox behaviour, which included walking their cats on leads and wandering the coastline in costume.

When the island was occupied by German forces in 1945 Cahun and Moore waged a campaign of creative resistance against them, often at huge personal risk. Able to speak fluent German, Moore regularly translated news reports, which the couple would then handwrite and sign 'The soldier without a name'. These notes purported to be from a mutinous German officer and were designed to unsettle the troops on the ground. To distribute their work the pair often took the extraordinary step of dressing up as German soldiers to infiltrate marches and disseminate the texts by hand.

Cahun was arrested in 1944 and sentenced to death. Thankfully, the island was liberated before the sentence could be imposed, but the period of incarceration had an irrevocable effect on the artist, who never fully recovered from her treatment in prison and died in 1954.

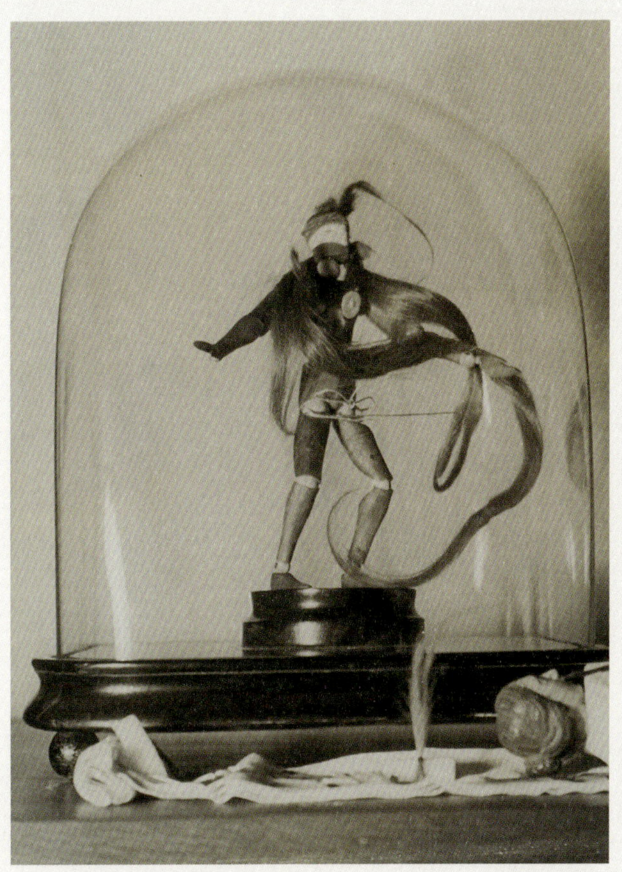

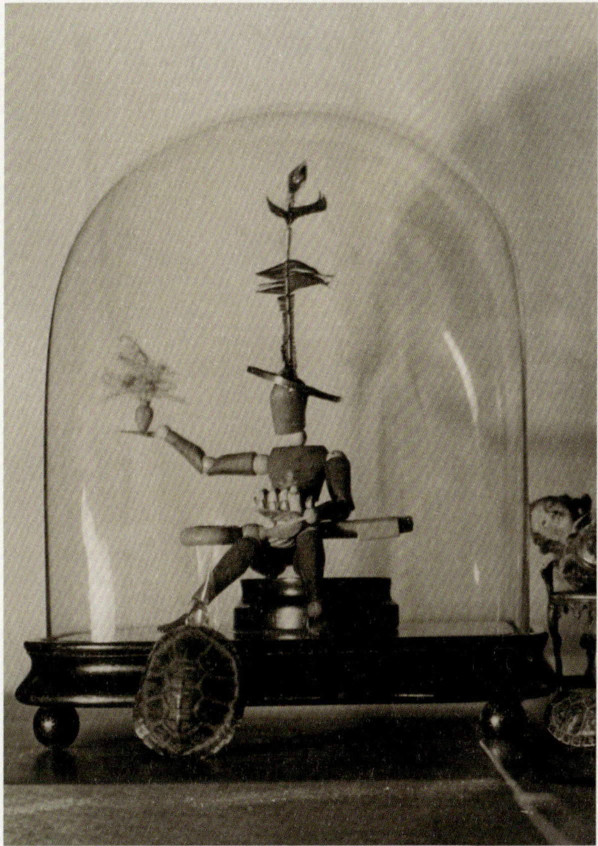

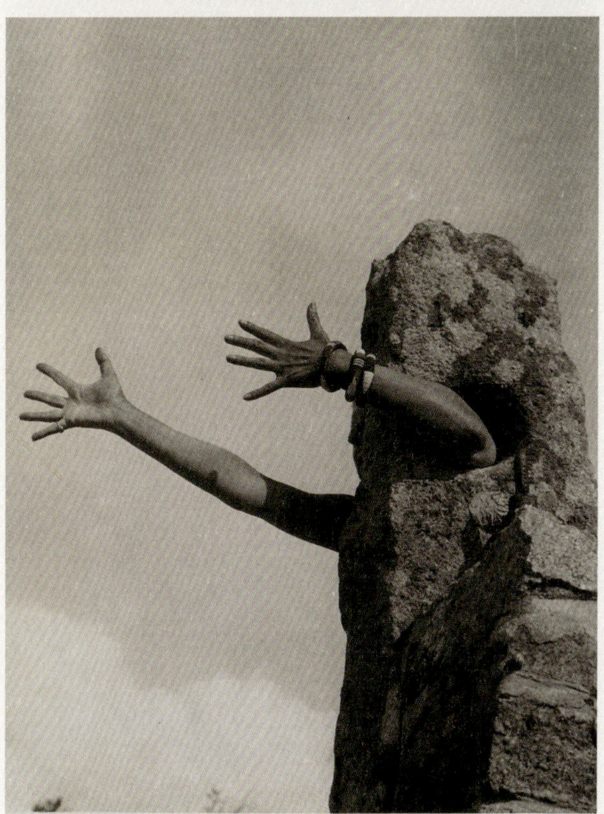

Untitled 1936
Photograph, gelatin silver
print on paper
23.8 x 18
Tate. Purchased 2007

Untitled 1936
Photograph, gelatin silver
print on paper
23.7 x 17.8
Tate. Purchased 2007

I Extend My Arms
Je tends les bras 1931–2
Photograph, gelatin silver
print on paper
21 x 15.6
Tate. Purchased 2007

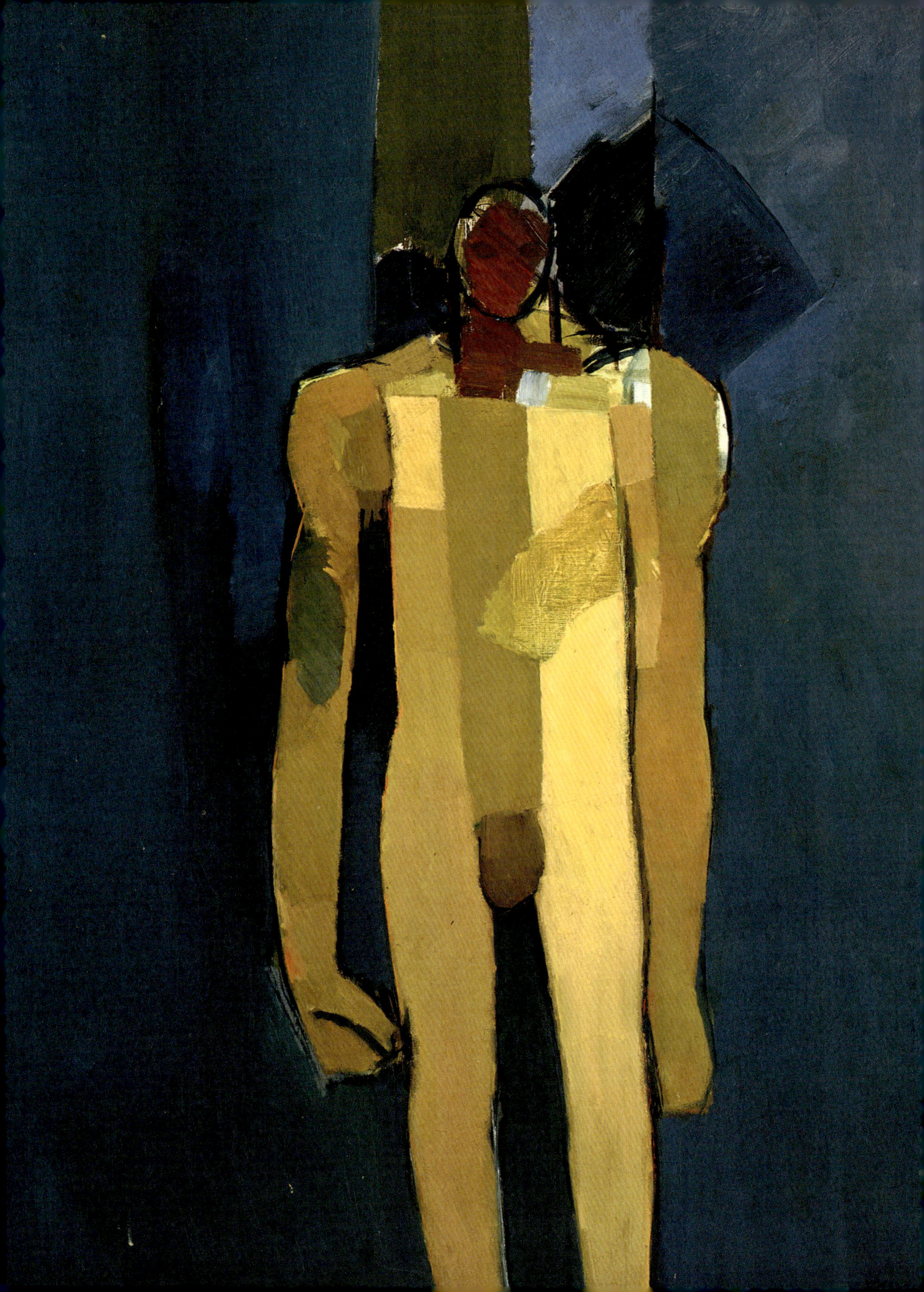

ARCADIA AND SOHO

ANDREW STEPHENSON

Keith Vaughan 1912–77
Kouros 1960
Oil on canvas
91.4 x 71.1
Private collection

WHEN THE LATE Victorian writer and cultural historian John Addington Symonds encountered a fellow admirer of male beauty, he recorded in his *Memoirs* that 'we soon became intimate and I discovered that he shared my Arcadian tastes'.[1] 'Arcadianism' in the developing homoerotic vocabulary was not only a reference to the search for an earlier pastoral idyll, but rather a way of signalling shared same-sex desires and tastes. It acted as a form of shorthand for a set of idealised codes and cultural interests through which the newly emerged male 'homosexual' community could identify fellow kindred spirits. For some British artists and intellectuals, especially in the late nineteenth century and early twentieth century, arcadianism took the explicit form of an idealisation of ancient Greece.

Greece exerted a continual fascination for many queer British artists, such as John Craxton (1922–2009) and Keith Vaughan, who acknowledged the exotic seduction of the Mediterranean life and climate, appreciated the beauty of its male inhabitants and valued its perceived greater 'authenticity' and sexual permissiveness. Craxton wrote that 'Greece was more than everything I had imagined and far more than I had expected'; an 'astonishing' and authentic place where 'it's possible to be a real person – real people, real elements, real windows – real sun above all' (p.142).[2] Attracted as much by Latin men's good looks and bronzed physiques as by the foreign beauty of the Mediterranean and Aegean landscapes, for Craxton the handsome, tanned Aegean sailor was inscribed not only by the democratic and athletic legacies valued by the ancient Greeks, but also embodied a compelling homoeroticism. Vaughan's *Kouros* 1960 (opposite, p.145) registers this fascination with male Greek physicality and it explicitly depicts the idealised nude youth, declaring in its title and adoption of stylised anatomical features its derivation from ancient Greek sculpture of the same name. Moving confidently towards the spectator, the young male, with his broad shoulders, deep chest, toned pectoral muscles and slim thighs, made more pronounced by emerging from a darkened background, represents an idealised and virile physique prized in classical Greek sculpture and highly appreciated by gay men.

For other artists such as Edward Burra, arcadianism was rooted in an appreciation of the art, literature, music and popular forms of French and Spanish Mediterranean cultures. The handsome male inhabitants of the South of France and Spain epitomised Latin beauty for the artist, and they carried a charged sexual passion evident in their good looks and relaxed manner. Indeed, the French naval ports of Marseille and Toulon were Burra's ideal destinations, and his work exploited the promiscuous connotations that the French sailor held in the 1920s and 1930s as a figure of homoerotic desire with a reputation for a lusty sexual appetite. Burra's design for the Creole Boy for Frederick Ashton's ballet, *A Day in a Southern Port – Rio Grande* (1931), adapted the sailor's outfit into a risqué and tight-fitting costume of fetching white drill cut-off trousers and a tight singlet with neck and armholes highlighted in silver sequins, to be worn with a strong fake tan, tight belt and flat cap by the artist's gay dancer friend, William Chappell (1907–94).

By contrast, it was ancient Celtic culture and the coastal landscapes of Brittany and Cornwall located on the geographical margins at 'the very edge of the world' that attracted Christopher Wood (p.138). Both Brittany and Cornwall formed part of a pan-European culture whose Celtic roots, seafaring folk cultures and rich mythology, set in opposition to the different cultural contours of Anglo-Saxon Englishness, were appreciated and highly valued. Wood's fascination with the rough physicality of Cornish and Breton fishermen was informed by the homoerotic writings and drawings of his friend and leading gay poet, Jean Cocteau (1889–1963). In July 1927, Wood wrote that 'the men are fishermen, great big, sometimes small, but beautifully proportioned, [with] bronze limbs [that] come out of their blue or white canvas trousers and striped vests'.[3]

Travel abroad also facilitated encounters with more racially diverse communities that offered up alternative models of masculinity, which stimulated and reconfigured modern same-sex imaginings derived from their vibrant Black, Arab and Latino-inspired cosmopolitanism. This expanding tourism facilitated first-hand experience of the thriving queer coteries of North America, notably New York, Harlem, San Francisco and Los Angeles, as well as those in the Caribbean Islands and North Africa, particularly Tangier and Casablanca. Such locations were prized for being socially informal and sexually fluid, and they appeared to test society's racial and sexual limits even if they often catered to exploitative sexual tourism. Reflecting these encounters, Burra's trip to New York, Harlem and Boston engaged with the lively low-life subcultures of the bars, speakeasies and nightclubs of these cities, and his fascination was captured in his painting of the popular Boston dance hall, *Izzy Orts* 1937 (p.139). Located in the Boston docks, 'Izzy Orts' attracted many on-leave American sailors including African-American men who, dressed in their conspicuous US navy uniform, highlighted the homoeroticism that such cross-racial encounters spawned.

Closer to home arcadianism carried the possibilities of an idealised social community with same-sex freedoms that transcended class barriers and facilitated democratic fusion. When the English socialist philosopher Edward Carpenter abandoned the urbane society of Cambridge and the 'gilded' youth of Cambridge University for the working-class community of Millthorpe near Sheffield, this relocation and the purchase of three fields to allow him to embark upon the career of a market gardener was motivated as much by a desire to establish comradeship with virile lower-class men as by the search to find an idyllic rural existence – 'a life close to Nature' – financed by his considerable private inheritance.

Wishing to break free from the respectability and sexual constraints of Victorian middle-class life, many queer 'back to Nature' enthusiasts, like Carpenter, espoused a utopian rejection of capitalism and consumerism that encapsulated a specific homoerotic component. 'My ideal of love', Carpenter wrote, 'is a powerful, strongly built man, of my own age or rather younger – preferably of the working class': a description that fits his subsequent northern lovers rather well.[4]

In a similar way, as a non-combatant, conscientious objector during the Second World War, Vaughan's journals make repeated reference to the appeal that cross-class homosociability between conscripts in the army barracks afforded. Living in close proximity to men coming from a range of class backgrounds, the forced experience of the war generated a sense of intimate comradeship. Valued as producing a social camaraderie that broadened class horizons and produced 'an atmosphere of tolerance', the war allowed Vaughan to experience at first hand the homoerotic attractiveness of the manly male working-class body and his relaxed, familiar sociability. The explicit attraction of muscular military masculinity is also referenced, albeit differently, in Burra's *Soldiers at Rye* 1941 (pp.140–1). Although based on sketches the artist made of troop activity around Rye during the Second World War in September and October 1940, Burra's figuration is given a more pronounced and sinister overtone by the soldiers' surrealist-inspired masks, hooked beaks and bird symbolism. Seen from behind, their close-fitting uniforms accentuate the enhanced physicality and bulbous nature of their military physiques, creating what one critic called the 'bulging husky leathery shape' of 'military ruffians',[5] and conveying the sense of a predatory masculinity that might register to some queer viewers as an appealingly virile, hyper-masculine, military homoeroticism with overtones of a sadomasochistic inclination.

Alternatively, the shared knowledge of arcadianism approached in its broadest terms provided a way of communicating the existence of open-air queer cultures. For Vaughan, the men-only bathing ponds at Hampstead Heath and at East London's Victoria Park and the Serpentine in Hyde Park offered opportunities for male exhibitionism that were part of London's public queer culture. They were sites where gay men congregated to admire youths swimming, diving or sunbathing and offered the possibilities for public sociability while watching juvenile nudity, occasionally encouraging cross-class cruising. For Vaughan, these ponds generated feelings of ' a brief and transitory perfection' even if, as he knew, any same-sex encounters could 'earn [him] at least life imprisonment if known & prosecuted'.[6]

Such environments, in which popular leisure pursuits and sports allowed men and women to interact informally, signalled the homoerotic appeal that the fit, athletic physique held for gay viewers. Giving licence to look closely and providing ample opportunities for voyeurism, leisure and sports activities afforded legitimate occasions for artists to watch the spectacle of trained athletic bodies in performance and at rest. As an example, Robert Medley's (1905–1994) *Summer Eclogue No. 1: Cyclists* 1950 (p.143) depicts the working-class cyclists who congregated on a popular riverside esplanade in a Gravesend park after working in paper factories

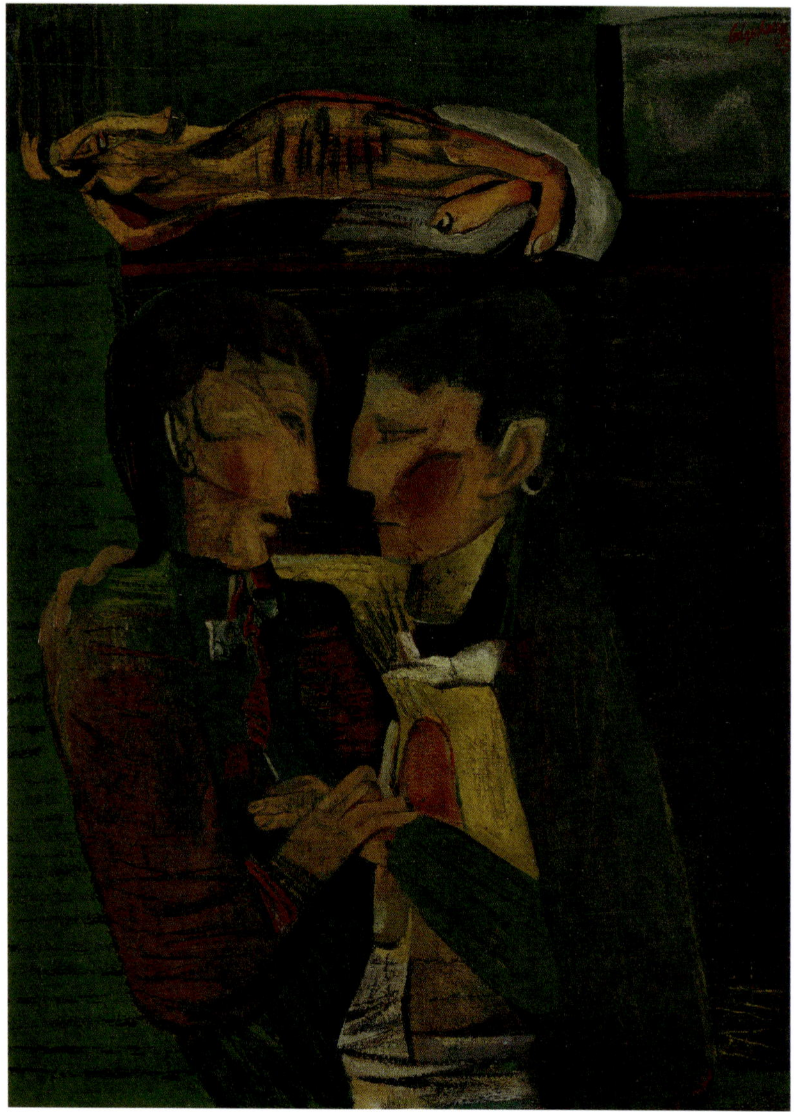

and cement installations, and it features the lover of Keith Vaughan, Ramsay McClure (1924–81), as the main male model for the cyclists.[7]

The modern theatre, like the ballet, opera and cinema, also explicitly made visible the male body in performance, focusing attention on a well-developed physique. Providing new ways of interrogating masculine sexuality and its performance, as Robert Colquhoun's *Actors on a Stage* 1945 (above) embracing in full make-up and costume underscores, the theatre opened up the conventions of what constituted normal masculinity and its manly codings to the varied interpretation of its queer admirers. Since many actors, dancers and performers were themselves gay men, the overly expressive movement, any excessive attention to the qualities of costume, make-up and decor, and any odd ambiguities in the narrative construction or delivery were carefully perused for evidence of transgressive sexual tastes and same-sex experience.

Robert Colquhoun
1914–1962

Actors on a Stage 1945
Oil on canvas
77.5 x 44.9
Private collection

Colquhoun's painting is one of a series of compositions from 1945–6 representing actors, spectators, clowns and fortune tellers, often as male pairs, sometimes shown embracing. Since 'being theatrical' was often associated with same-sex desire (pp.68–93), the embrace in this work, and the focus on costume and make-up, can be interpreted as referring to male same-sex desire. *Actors on a Stage* was highly significant for Colquhoun. His desires were bisexual but he had been in a long-term, if volatile, relationship with the Scottish painter Robert MacBryde (1913–66) since 1933. It is, then, difficult to avoid the autobiographical associations of this image. Homosexuality remained illegal in Scotland until 1980. Consequently, although their life together was 'an open secret' to friends, it was not widely known because of the risk of imprisonment. 'Acting' could therefore be seen as a metaphor for passing as 'straight' in public to avoid detection or blackmail.

However, it was urban culture that provided the greatest number of opportunities for gay men and women to congregate and to socialise, and cities generated the modern infrastructure for a vibrant, commercialised homosexual culture. As Hunter Davies claimed in 1966, 'London is the magnet which attracts queers in Britain',[8] and Soho stood at the epicentre of the metropolis's queer attractions, comprising what Francis Bacon called 'the sexual gymnasium of the city'.[9] Consisting of a complex warren of bustling West End streets, interconnecting courts and hidden alleyways, Soho held a reputation as the pre-eminent cosmopolitan and transgressive queer space. Attracted as much by its fictional, mass-media notoriety as a scandalous *demi-monde* as by its bohemian real-life experience, Soho's risqué reputation and criminal underworld enticed many gay artists, writers and intellectuals. Late-night bars, nightclubs and drug dens, as well as theatres, music halls and cinemas, provided rich source materials for gay consumers eager to experience the irresistible atmosphere and permissive social manners of the city's modern urban nightlife. At the same time, the raciness and eclecticism of 'the Square Mile of Vice', incorporating Old Compton Street, Dean Street and Soho Square, formed the updated contours of London's rapidly developing same-sex night-time economy and its highly fashionable and compelling queer culture.[10]

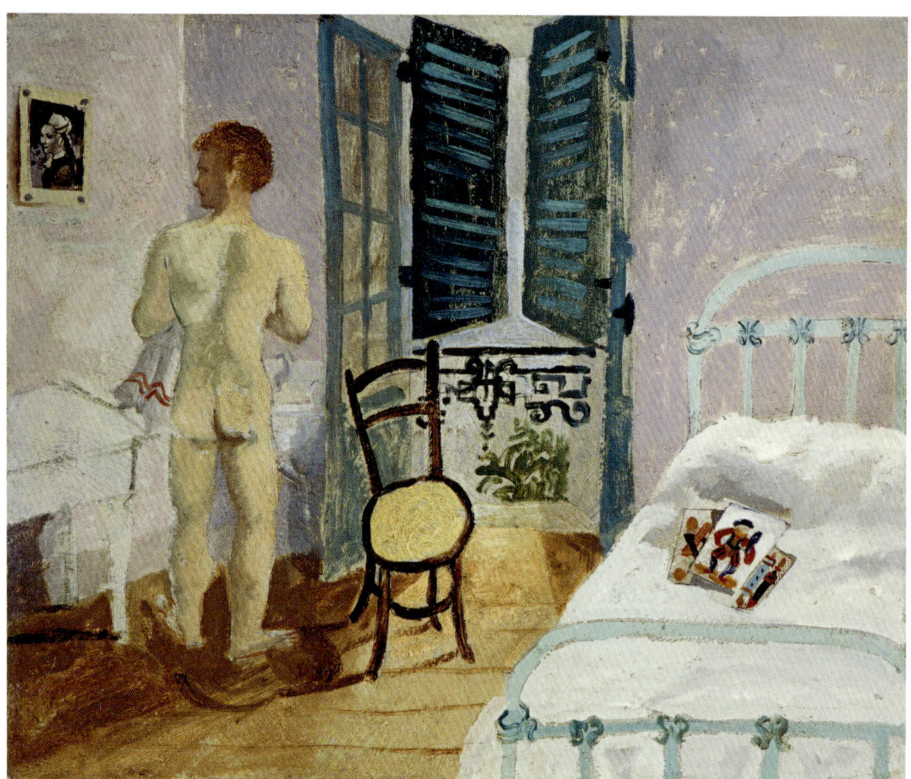

Christopher Wood 1901–30

Nude Boy in a Bedroom 1930

Oil on hardboard on plywood

53.8 x 65

Scottish National Gallery of Modern Art, Edinburgh

Christopher Wood's *Nude Boy in a Bedroom* represents the artist's friend and sometime lover, Francis Rose (1909–79), undressed and seen from behind in a French hotel bedroom with the shutters slightly open. The work is derived from Wood's trips to Brittany, which he first visited with four friends from July to October 1929. The group was later joined by Wood's female lover, Frosca Munster (1896–1963). On Wood's second visit, from June to late July 1930, to the Breton ports of Tréboul, Ploaré and Douarnenez, he stayed with Francis Rose and Max Jacob (1876–1944) at the Hotel Ty-Mad in Tréboul. During a nearly six-week period of feverish production, he completed more than forty paintings, including *Nude Boy in a Bedroom*, many of which featured Breton sailors and landscapes. According to Rose, the work 'is a nude painting of me washing at a basin' in which Wood 'scattered playing cards on the bed'.[11] The cards are clearly tarot cards and the top card shows the Page of Cups reversed, symbolising anxiety about a deception that will be soon discovered, or referring to someone incapable of making commitments – references perhaps to Wood's bisexuality at a time of his still ongoing sexual relationship with Munster, who was staying close by. It could also reference Wood's many failed attempts to cure his opium addiction and his persistent financial insecurities. Valued as anti-academic and intuitive, Wood's naïve style suggested an immediacy of expression and authenticity that many contemporary critics applauded. Even if the boy is looking towards the photograph of the young woman in traditional Breton dress pinned to the wall, there is an inescapable homoeroticism to the image derived from the representation of the muscular male body from behind. This has led some scholars to detect in the work a post-coital atmosphere.[12]

This painting once belonged to the actor Sir John Gielgud (1904–2000). [AS]

Edward Burra 1905–76

Izzy Orts 1937

Watercolour and graphite on paper

73.6 x 104.5

Scottish National Gallery of Modern Art, Edinburgh

Izzy Orts is derived from Edward Burra's second trip to
the USA in 1937, when he visited Boston, Springfield,
Washington, DC and New York as well as Mexico.
It underscores the artist's fascination with the
mixed-race subculture of American bars, speakeasies
and nightclubs previously examined in his earlier
paintings of Harlem and Spanish Harlem from 1933.
'Izzy Orts' was a popular dance hall in the Boston
docks to which Burra had been introduced by his
poet friend, Conrad Aiken (1889–1973), whom Burra
first met in 1924 when the American was living close
to Burra at Jeake's House in Rye. On his second
visit to Boston in 1937, Burra stayed with Aiken in
Charlestown and he painted the well-known, noisy
and crowded dance hall with its swing jazz band,
jiving dancers and array of social types. Given its
dockland location, the club was a popular site for
cross-race socialising, attracting many on-leave
American sailors, including African-American military
men, dressed in their conspicuous US navy uniforms.
Sailors were figures of great sexual attraction to their
many straight and queer admirers, and their racy
reputation was enhanced by their tight-fitting navy
uniforms, muscular physiques and well-known
portside promiscuity. [AS]

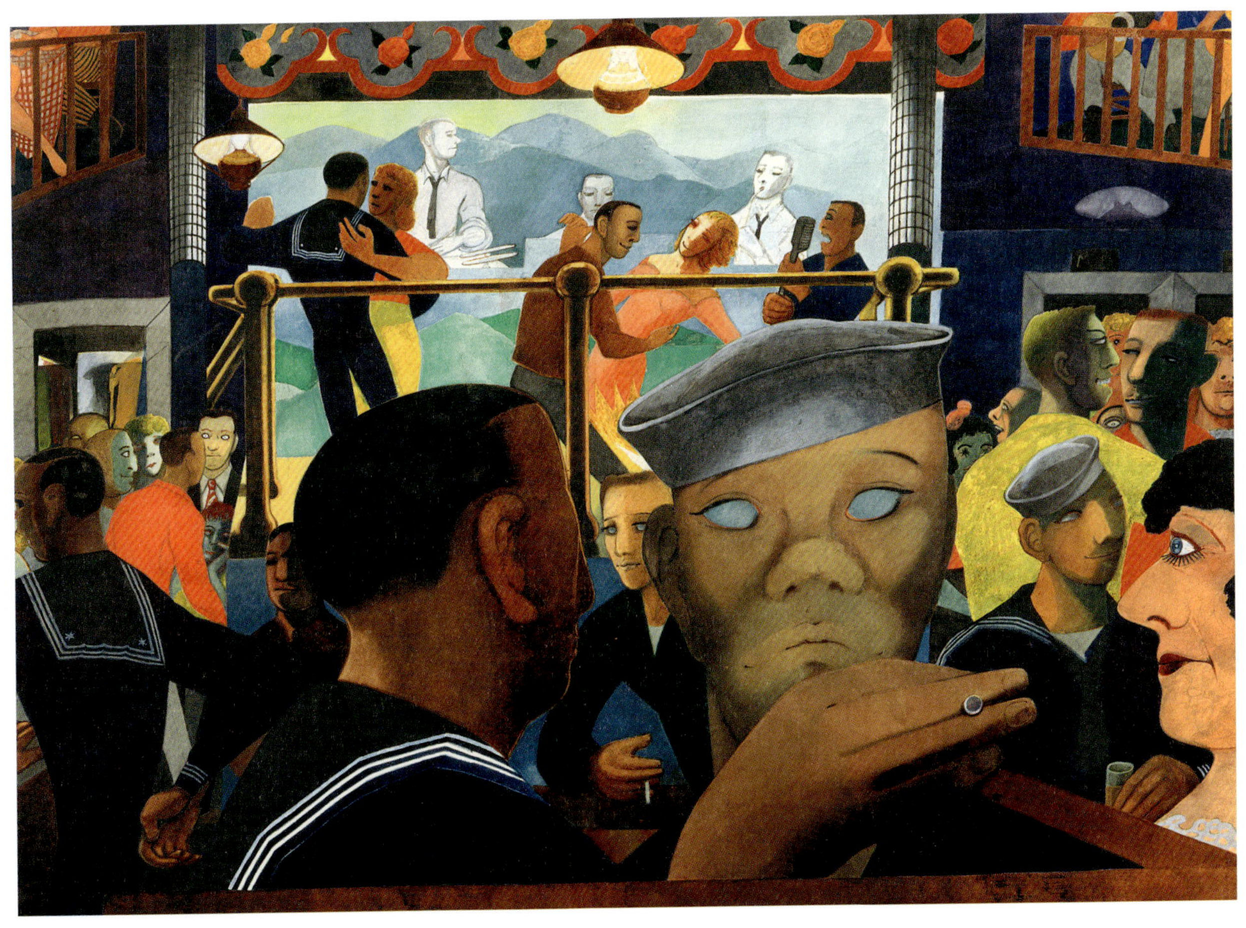

Edward Burra 1905–76
Soldiers at Rye 1941
Gouache, watercolour and ink on paper
124.8 x 228
Tate. Presented by Studio 1942

Soldiers at Rye is based on sketches the artist made
of troop activity around his home town of Rye
between September and October 1940. During the
Second World War, Edward Burra's fascination with
Elizabethan and Jacobean dramatic tragedies was
intensified by the access he had to the library of his
poet friend, Conrad Aiken, at Jeake's House in Rye.
However, Burra's depiction of soldiers rigging up
camouflage netting is not an accurate record of British
military preparations, even though they wear the
khaki and tin hats of conscripted British 'Tommies'.
Their red and yellow Venetian carnival masks are
reminiscent of seventeenth- and eighteenth-century
Commedia dell 'Arte actors' costumes, while their
theatrical gestures and pose and the elaborate red
material swirling across the bottom of the composition
add a theatrical effect derived in part from Burra's
interest in Spanish Baroque art, church furnishings
and ornamentation.[13] This taste for the dramatic and
the macabre was encouraged by Burra's frequent
visits to Spain from 1933 and informed by his
experience of the death and destruction he saw
during the Spanish Civil War. The bird symbolism
and hooked beaks that Burra employs underscores
the soldiers' predatory manner and was one that the
artist had developed from the early 1930s as part of
his surrealist engagement with the bird figures of Max
Ernst (1891–1976).[14] Seen from the back, the soldiers'
bodily bulk and close-fitting uniforms accentuate the
bulbous nature of their physique, producing a
figuration that one critic characterised as marking
out the 'bulging husky leathery shape' of 'military
ruffians'.[15] The ominous atmosphere of masculine
energy, drama and conflict captured in *Soldiers at Rye*
conveys a dangerous homoeroticism often identified
by queer viewers with the pleasures of a predatory and
perhaps sadomasochistic, military masculinity. [AS]

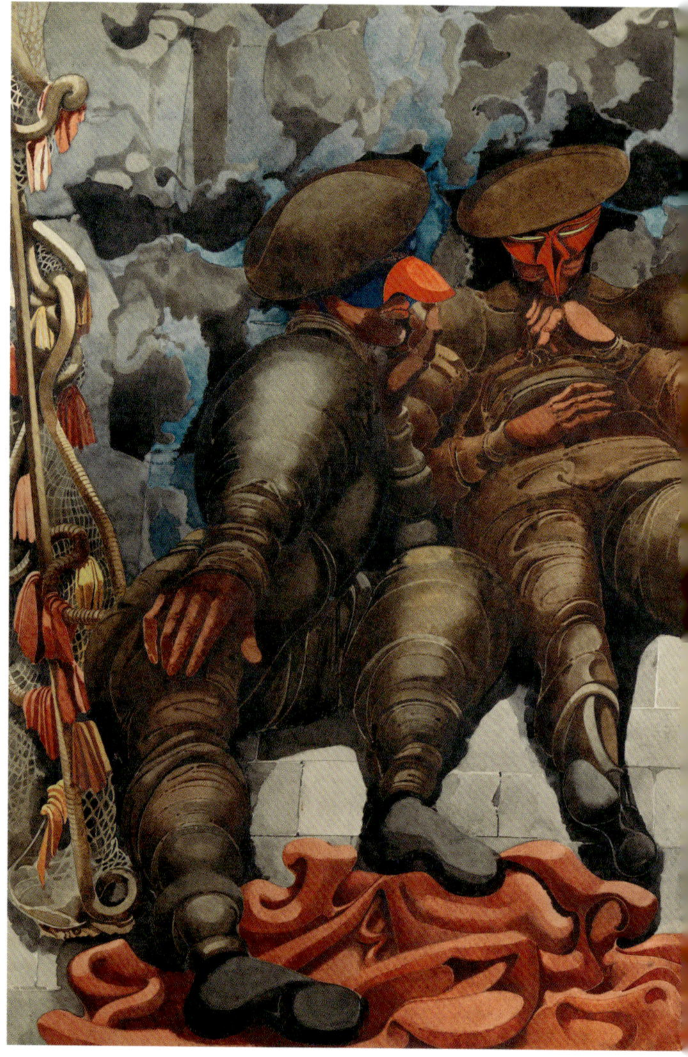

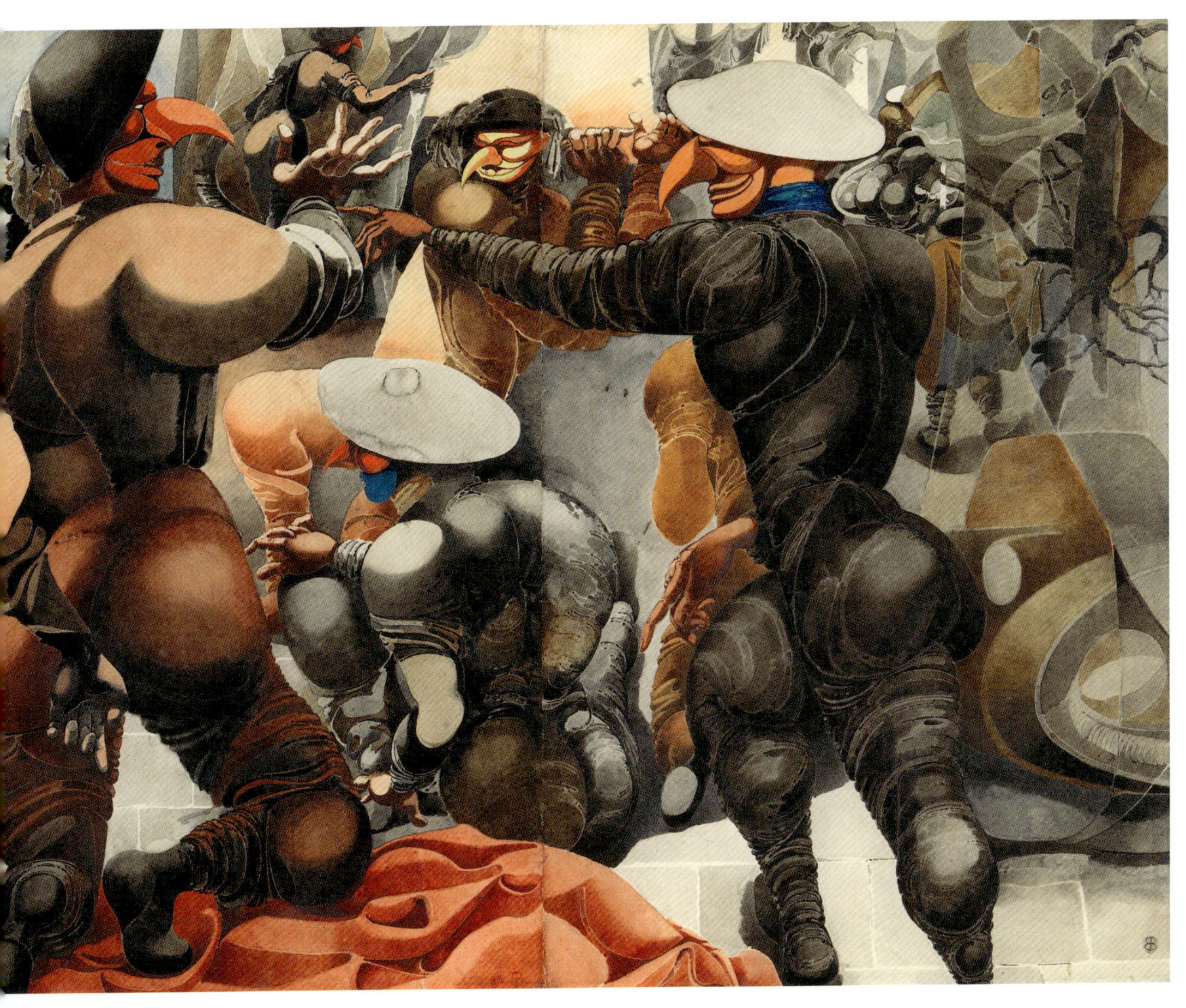

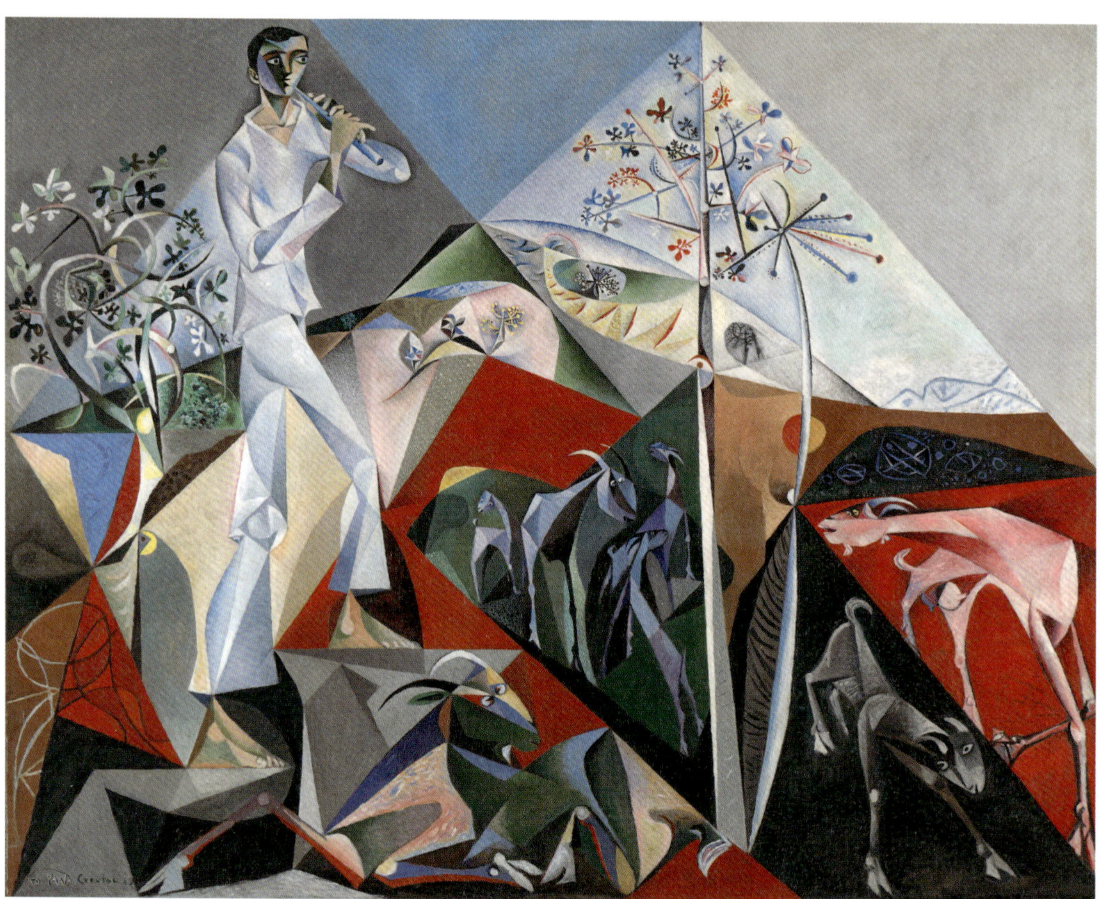

John Craxton 1922–2009
Pastoral for P.W. 1948
Oil on canvas
204.5 x 262.6
Tate. Purchased 1984

Pastoral for P.W. was a homage and gift dedicated to John Craxton's gay friend, Peter Watson (1908–56), whom he met in London in 1941 when the Scottish same-sex couple Robert Colquhoun and Robert MacBryde were temporarily living as lodgers in Watson's flat. Watson was a major art collector, aesthete, editor of the influential arts magazine *Horizon* and later co-founded the Institute of Contemporary Arts in 1947. The painting celebrates the power of music by depicting the goats being enthralled by the sound of the goatherd's flute. The scene is set in the brilliantly lit Cretan landscape that Craxton had first visited in 1947. Conceived of initially as a group of 'capricious portraits' of Watson's friends as 'goats' following Craxton's white-clad musician-goatherd, the painting's cubistic 'dislocated rhythms' and heightened colour signal a neo-romantic pastoralism, popular among British artists, writers and film-makers in the 1940s and 1950s, though transposed to the bright Greek landscape with its distinctive trees and foliage. Allured by the exoticism of Greece, first encountered by Craxton in 1946, with its Mediterranean climate and olive and citrus groves, it also held homoerotic overtones typified by the handsome, tanned Aegean sailors, shepherds and fishermen. Portrayed in many works from the late 1940s and early 1950s and inscribed by the compelling cultural legacies of the ancient Greeks and Hellenism, Craxton wrote that Greece was idyllic with islands 'where lemons grow & oranges melt into the mouth & goats snatch the last fig leaves off small trees, the corn is yellow and russles & the sea is harplike on volcanic shores'.[16] [AS]

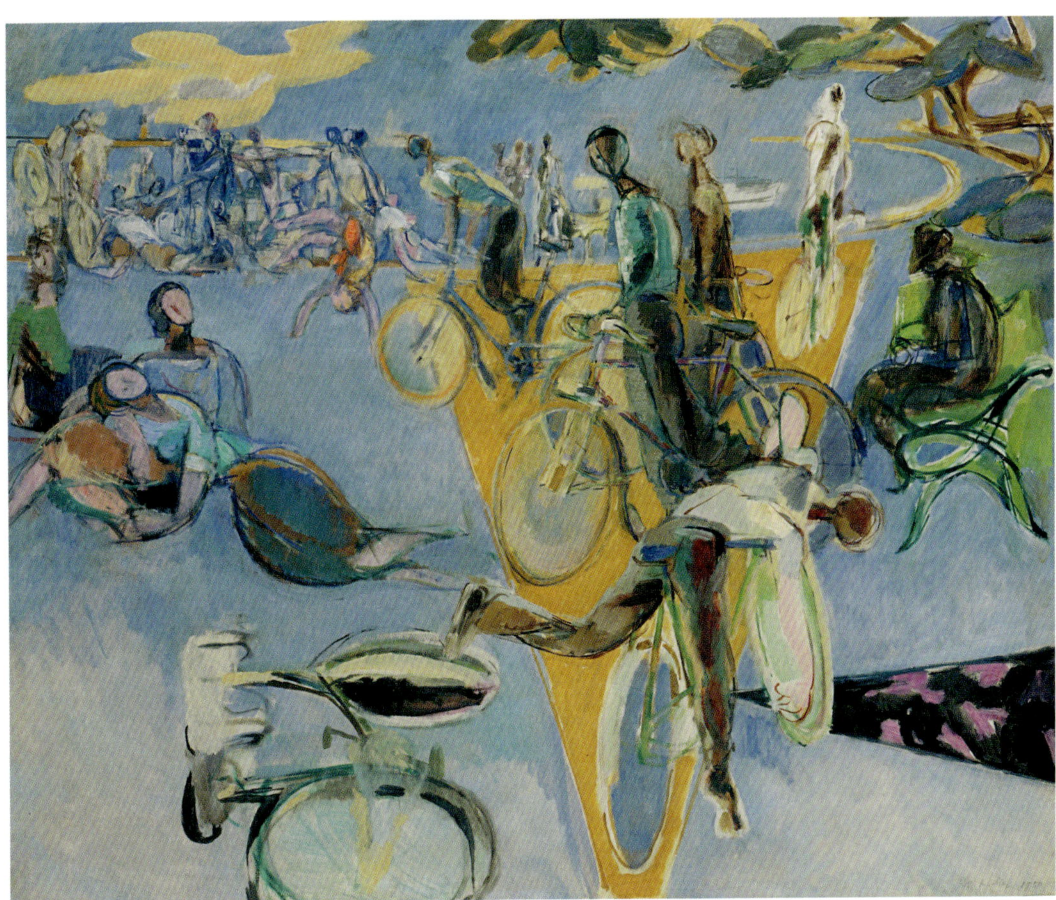

Robert Medley 1905–94
Summer Eclogue No. 1: Cyclists 1950
Oil on canvas
129.5 x 160
Tate. Purchased 1992

Robert Medley's painting of cyclists astride their bicycles on a summer's evening underscores the attractions that cross-class homosociability held as a subject for the modern gay painter. Exhibited at the Hanover Gallery in February 1950, the painting depicts groups of cyclists in motion and watching the goings-on around them in a Gravesend public park. Featuring a popular river esplanade where the workers from the paper factories and cement works congregated each summer evening, Medley portrayed young racing cyclists and their admirers, thereby providing a permissible means of perusing the muscular male bodies and taut limbs of the cyclists. In his

autobiography, Medley wrote that the eclogue theme, derived from the Latin poet Virgil's notion of idyllic scenes in which erotic forces disrupt an apparently bucolic atmosphere, provided for 'a more contemporary subject matter'.[17] Parks constituted 'a change of locale' from Medley's earlier works that relied on his memory of being in the Middle East during the Second World War. Influenced by Henri Matisse's (1869–1954) decorative paintings that used the convention of a uniform colour field, Medley believed that it was 'possible to evoke space without describing it' and without employing traditional linear perspective.[18] What the work achieved was an atmospheric composition that allowed ways of representing the human figure 'without deforming it' and it is significant that Medley's model was fellow artist Keith Vaughan's lover, Ramsay McClure.[19] [AS]

KEITH VAUGHAN

GERARD HASTINGS

Keith Vaughan was a self-taught painter. In the early 1930s he worked as a commercial artist, learning photography to study the male form in private. Some of his original photographs, taken at Hampstead Ponds and on Pagham Beach, West Sussex, have recently come to light. From 1939 he kept an extraordinarily frank journal revealing his sexual activities, emotional condition and, ultimately, the manner of his death.

During the Second World War Vaughan served as a non-combatant and fell in love with a heterosexual compatriot. This set up a lifelong habit of mismatched and agonisingly unrequited affairs. Despite wartime constraints he continued to paint and record the daily life of his fellow conscripts. Under the influence of Graham Sutherland (1903–80) he also produced a series of neo-romantic landscapes, peopled with melancholic figures. After the war Vaughan taught in London at the Camberwell School of Arts and Crafts, the Central School of Art and the Slade, while making a successful career as a painter. His journal reveals that he lived, like other gay men, in fear of blackmail:

> I ask myself which of my pictures would I be willing to stand beside in public, say Piccadilly Circus, for all to see. The least personal ones, I suppose, abstract landscapes. The continual use of the male figure… retains always the stain of a homosexual conception . …'K.V. paints nude young men'. Perfectly true, but I feel I must hide my head in shame. Inescapable, I suppose – social guilt of the invert.[20]

This insecurity extended into his personal life: 'It is difficult to bear in mind that with all one's honours, distinctions, success etc. one remains a member of the criminal class.'[21]

Nevertheless Vaughan published his *Journals and Drawings* the year before the decriminalisation of homosexuality, making public his sexual orientation. He lived with his partner, Ramsay McClure, for nearly thirty years despite it being a stormy and largely loveless union. However, it was his lover Johnny Walsh, a petty criminal, who became the subject of many photographs and paintings, including *Kouros* 1960 (opposite): 'A silver bromide image of Johnny standing naked in my studio, aloof, slightly tense, withdrawn like a Greek Kouros, gazing apprehensively at himself in the mirror, lithe, beautiful… it lies tormenting me on my table.'[22]

The two central subjects of Vaughan's work are male nudes and groups of male figures he referred to as 'assemblies'. Always reluctant to abandon figuration and pursue a purely abstract visual language, Vaughan experienced enormous frustration trying to achieve a balance between the representation of the object and the structural aspect of its expression. *Bather: August 4th 1961* (opposite) was a significant development:

> The Aug 4 Bather was the first break through. Every attempt up to then had finally resolved itself into another figure painting or an 'abstract'… I worked it by a slightly new procedure which consisted of painting towards an image – but destroying the image (with a paint scraper) every time it began to form and threatened to 'set' the picture. This kept it loose – but not abstract.[23]

Vaughan's process, by necessity, involved a degree of distortion and transformation to strengthen the image. His ability to describe the human anatomy and reconfigure it within a coherently constructed composition is, perhaps, his finest single achievement.

Three Figures 1960–1 (opposite) typifies Vaughan's approach to group figure painting. The lack of attire

Bather: August 4th 1961
1961

Oil on canvas

102.2 x 91.4

Tate. Purchased 1962

Three Figures 1960–1

Oil on board

43 x 40.5

Abbot Hall Art Gallery,

Lakeland Arts Trust,

Kendal, Cumbria

Kouros 1960

Oil on canvas

91.4 x 71.1

Private collection

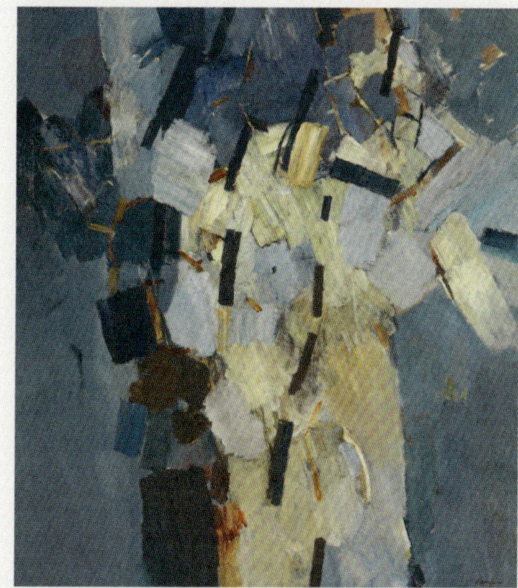

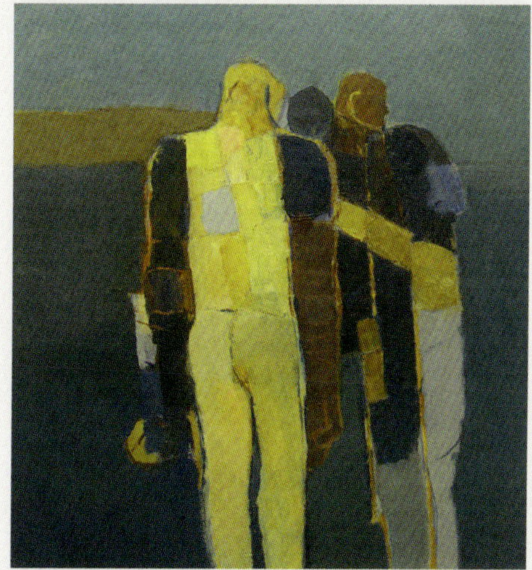

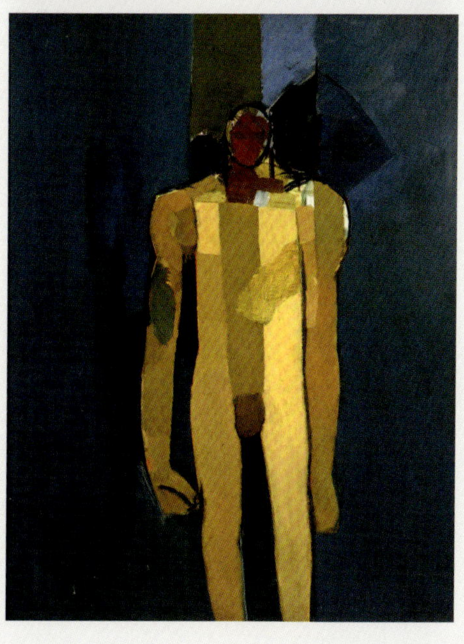

makes identification of the subjects, their social class or profession impossible to ascertain, as do the indeterminate environments. Neither can we interpret what activities the figures are engaged in, nor the purpose of their coming together. One may presume that they typify mankind in general: naked, vulnerable, sluggish and awkward in forging personal relationships and social associations.

In later life Vaughan was incapacitated by illness, cancer treatments and a colostomy operation, while suffering severe depression and dependency on barbiturates and alcohol. He spent much of his final year planning to terminate his life. He recorded his last moments of consciousness in his journal on 4 November 1977: 'The capsules have been taken with some whiskey… It wasn't a complete failure I did some good w….'

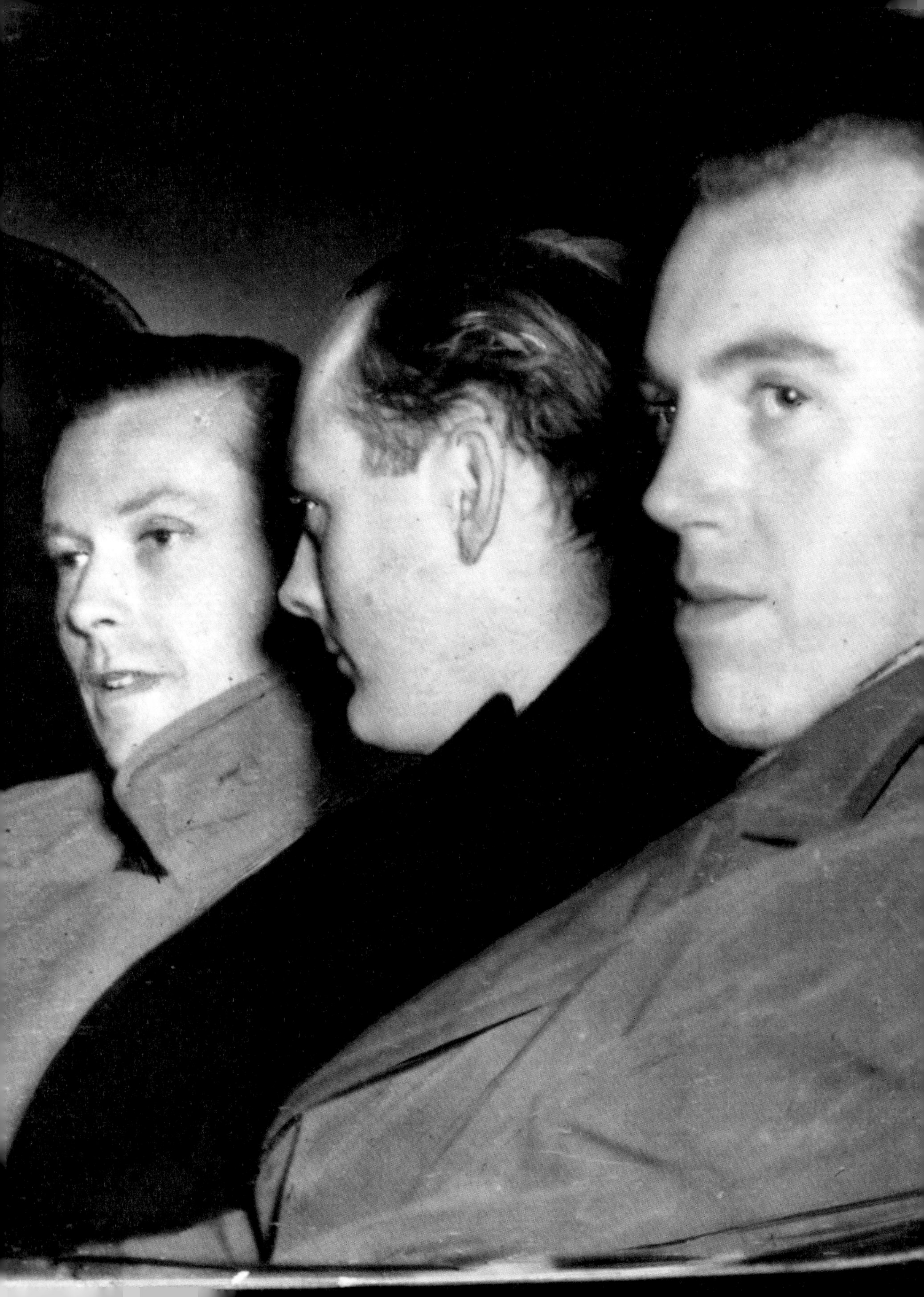

PUBLIC LIVES, PRIVATE PASSIONS

DOMINIC JANES

Unknown photographer
for Keystone Press
Agency Ltd
Michael Fox-Pitt-Rivers;
Edward Douglas-Scott-
Montagu, 3rd Baron
Montagu of Beaulieu;
Peter Wildeblood (detail)
24 March 1954
Photograph, bromide print
on paper
14 x 19.4
National Portrait Gallery,
London

MALE AND FEMALE homosexuality was regarded with great disapproval by a substantial part of the British public for much of the twentieth century, and the former was heavily criminalised. Many gay men and women either denied their own sexual tastes to themselves, or even if they admitted them, kept them secret from family and colleagues. Cities, London in particular, developed what might be termed queer subcultures in which those of like mind could meet. Romantic and sexual liaisons took place variously in discreet private clubs or through cruising in streets, parks and toilets. Both blackmail and arrest were very real threats. In these circumstances making queer art, or even appearing queerly dressed in public, could take considerable courage. There were, however, lesbians who dressed in men's clothes as a form of butch drag and gay men who found inspiration in the female beauties of the day. One such was Quentin Crisp (1908–99), who documented a private session of glamour photography in his autobiography *The Naked Civil Servant* (1968). 'Mr McBean longed to take photographs as fervently as I desired to be photographed', he commented.[1] Crisp worked from time to time as an artists' model, but his desire to be photographed by Angus McBean, whom he had first met in 1939, was about the wish to look fabulous in the mode of a contemporary female movie star, too (p.153).[2] Crisp also earned money, from time to time, by having sex with men who either took him for a woman or, more often, wanted sex with a 'queen' (an effeminate homosexual man). At a time when 'gay' still largely meant 'glad' rather than homosexual, there were more men who had sex with other men than who identified themselves, even in private, as queer. This was a world in which visual appearances provided vital clues to possible sexual availability.[3] The trick for many was to be visible to those one wished to attract without drawing the hostile gaze of others. This was not a balancing act in which the queens could participate and it was their very visibility that led to popular assumptions that gay men were, in essence, women in men's bodies.

It was in these circumstances that the public greeted the appearance of the 'Kinsey Reports' – notably, *Sexual Behavior in the Human Male* (1948) – variously with excitement, fascination and alarm. The news that American scientists had found that same-sex attraction was widespread in the general population led in the short term to a degree of panic and a stepping up of police activity, but in the long term paved the path to reform. A key stage in that process in Britain was marked by the publication in 1957 of the *Report of the Committee on Homosexual Offences and Prostitution*, which became known as the 'Wolfenden Report' (the

committee was chaired by Sir John Wolfenden (1906–1985), the Vice-Chancellor
of Reading University). Its key recommendation was that sex in private between
two men over the age of twenty-one should be decriminalised. This was no proud
exercise in identity affirmation, but rather an attempt to deal with what was felt to
be a pressing social problem and to allow men to come forward for treatment and
advice without the threat of arrest and blackmail. Evidence was gathered in private,
since 'only in [a] genuinely private session could our witnesses, giving evidence
on these delicate and controversial matters, speak to us with the full frankness
which the subject of our enquiry demanded'.[4]

One of those witnesses, the Anglo-Canadian journalist Peter Wildeblood
(1923–99), was exceptional in that not only had he become (in)famous for his
conviction for incitement to commit buggery in 1954, alongside the wealthy
Lord Montagu (1926–2015) and Michael Pitt-Rivers (1917–99) (p.146), but also
because unlike them he had unapologetically published his account of *identifying*
as a homosexual shortly thereafter.[5] In fact it seems likely that it was sensitivity
concerning the aristocratic milieu involved in this case that had forced the powers
that be to look at reform, since they feared the stereotyping of the Establishment
in the popular press as a bunch of decadent ex-public-school boys. The *Report*
was, therefore, commissioned and in due time made it clear that

> homosexuality is not, in spite of widely held belief to the contrary, peculiar
> to members of a particular profession or social classes; nor, as is sometimes
> supposed, is it peculiar to the *intelligentsia*. Our evidence shows that it exists
> among all callings and at all levels of society; and that among homosexuals
> will be found not only those possessing a high degree of intelligence, but also
> the dullest oafs.[6]

The popular association of male homosexuality with artistic and aristocratic circles
had a long history in Britain that was powerfully entrenched by Oscar Wilde's
conviction for gross indecency in 1895.[7] The *Report* did not deny that such raffish
locales as art colleges might contain a high proportion of homosexuals but that
was only because people might gravitate to certain professions where they could
meet others of like mind. Subsequent research sponsored by the Home Office
presented the interested reader with a complex variety of queer types, from the
boy lover to the bodybuilder and the 'sugar daddy'.[8] While much of this sociological
research was patronising it was not always wildly inaccurate. For instance, there
was a frequent element of cross-class attraction in same-sex affairs, in which an
older middle-class man sought the sexual attentions of working-class men and
youths. This was the case in some of Wilde's liaisons, and a similar impulse appears
in John Minton's (1917–1957) depiction of *Horseguards in Their Dressing Rooms at
Whitehall* 1953 (p.10), in which he tacitly referenced a long tradition of their sexual
availability for ready cash.

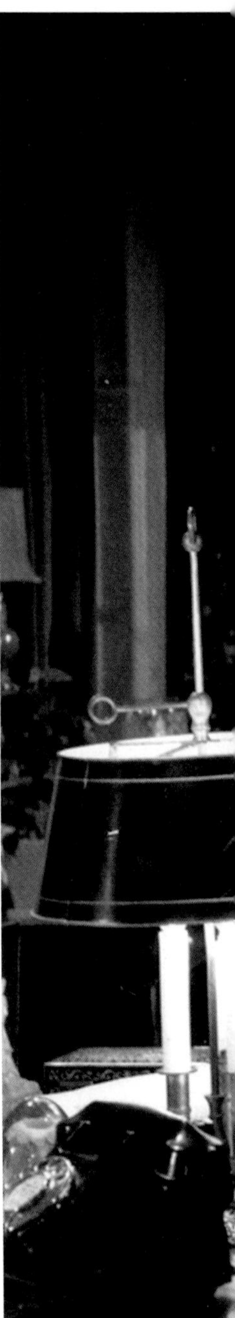

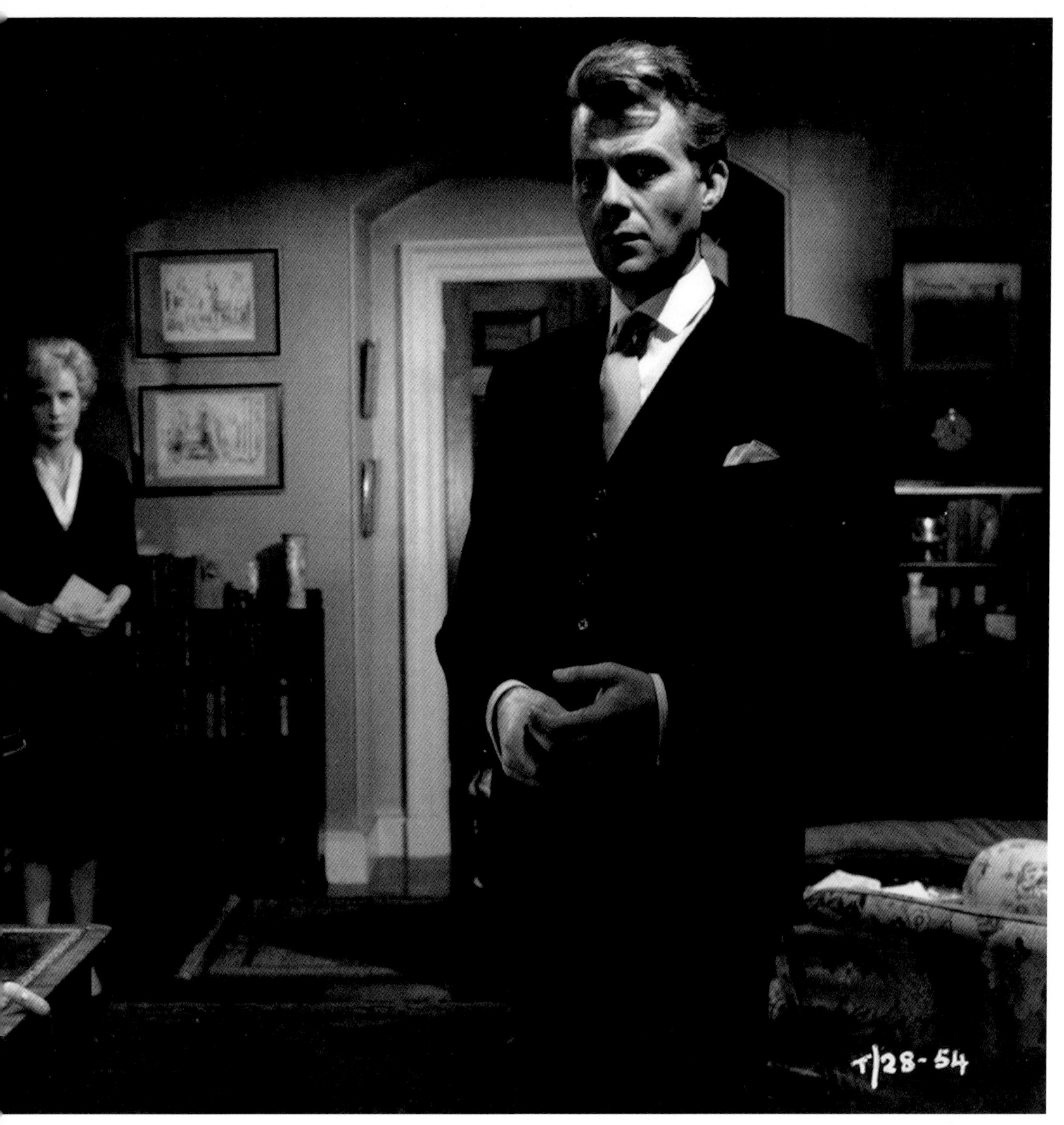

Victim (1961)
Directed by Basil Dearden

Those who advocated homosexual law reform did not spend much time on the question of lesbianism, but there were various attempts to reframe the gay man from being seen as a corrupter of youth to being a victim of societal injustice. This, in essence, was the agenda behind the important and pioneering *Victim* (dir. Basil Dearden, 1961) (p.149). In this film we see the suicide of the working-class (male) lover of a middle-class lawyer played by Dirk Bogarde (1921–99). He, in turn, is seen making a confession of his homosexual love affair to his wife played by Sylvia Syms (b.1934). She has spoken of the way in which Bogarde appeared so anguished when playing this scene that she thought he was also speaking about himself.[9] It is important to stress that he was a famous film star at the time and had played leading (heterosexual) romantic roles. He never publicly affirmed a sexual identity and his personal life has to be inferred from his long relationship with his manager, Tony Forwood (1915–88), with whom he shared his home.

Many of those who courted mainstream respectability in this period remained discreetly in the closet, but things were a little easier in the art world, which often situated itself in counter cultural relation to bourgeois mores. The younger generation of artists and writers was increasingly free, particularly as the sexual revolution began to gather pace, to be more open about its sexual interests. Men such as Patrick Procktor (1936–2003), Derek Jarman (1942–94) and Joe Orton (1933–67) started to make their names by bringing elements of queer eroticism into their art. While Crisp and McBean worked together in private for the love of imaging and being imaged, Procktor was commissioned to draw the thirty-four-year-old playwright Joe (originally John) Orton for a piece of theatre publicity. The latter described their meeting on 5 May 1967 by saying that

> Procktor was tall, thin, pallid. Rather Queerish. Willowy. I was wearing a green combat jacket, a forage cap, and a navy blue wooly... He drew me lying on the bed. I kept my socks on, nothing else. I kept my socks on because I think they're sexy. 'I've drawn you looking like a beautiful teenager', P. Procktor said. 'You'll get a lot of kinky letters after this, I'm sure.'[10]

Orton appeared to be all bravado and confidence, but bearing in mind the attitudes of the time it is hardly surprising that he was insecure about his own masculinity. 'Lamb posing as ram', was the caustic comment of Lewis Morley (1925–2013), when the playwright turned up at a photoshoot.[11] The results not only show Orton hiding his slim chest, but also camply posed in one shot so as to replicate Morley's famous image of Christine Keeler (b.1942) in the midst of the Profumo scandal of 1963 (p.154).[12]

The passing of the Sexual Offences Act (1967) saw the long-delayed implementation of the Wolfenden Committee's recommendations on the decriminalisation of certain forms of gay male sex. The Act received royal assent on 17 July 1967. It did not, however, bring about any immediate decline in public opprobrium; nor did it do away with the shame and stigma that went with that.

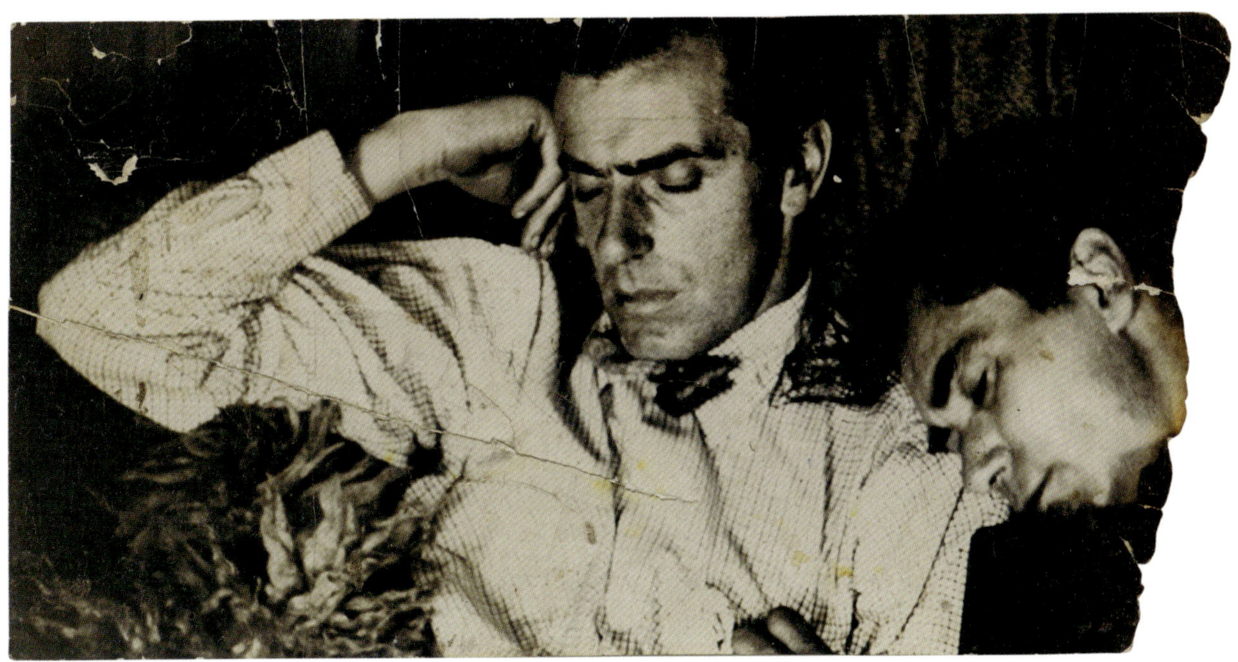

Scottish artists and lovers Robert Colquhoun (1914–62, left) and Robert MacBryde (1913–66) asleep, possibly at Tilty, the home of Canadian writer Elizabeth Smart, near Thaxted, Essex, c.1953. John Deakin Archive

Meanwhile, the public continued to be shown stereotypes of the tragic lives of queers in the theatre and in the cinema. It is the masculine older lesbian played by Beryl Reid (1919–96) in Frank Marcus's (1928–96) play, later a film, *The Killing of Sister George* (1964), whose life slides into failure and regret.[13] But, at the same time, directors recognised that there was a new popular appetite for seeing sexually attractive queers. Robert Aldrich (1918–83), who directed the film version, added a segment shot in a lesbian bar in London as well as a voyeuristic depiction of the seduction of Reid's young girlfriend by another middle-aged but considerably more glamorous woman. He commented at the time: 'What gets people into the theater? This scene...so it's an unavoidable must.'[14] That section garnered the film an X certificate on its release in the USA and led to it being extensively cut in the United Kingdom. A world of respectable public façades and private closeted passions was yet to evolve into one of private lives and public identities.

Angus McBean 1904–90

Quentin Crisp 1941

Photograph, bromide print on paper

43.4 x 34.4

National Portrait Gallery, London

Angus McBean met the writer and raconteur Quentin
Crisp while walking back from his studio in the blackout
in 1941. Crisp told in his acclaimed 1968 autobiography,
The Naked Civil Servant, how he had accosted McBean
when McBean overtook him on the pavement. McBean
offered to photograph him, leading to a session a few
nights later when this image was taken. The two became
occasional lovers and remained friends until the 1980s.
McBean later said of Crisp, 'He was really one of the
most beautiful people I have ever photographed.
It was a completely androgynous beauty and under
different circumstances it would have been difficult
to know what sex he was. He had this extraordinary
bone structure and there was this mop of coloured
hair. And all the time he kept up conversation in this
ornate language which was later dubbed Quentinese.'[15]

This androgynous beauty is captured in McBean's
photograph, which is posed so as to emphasise
Crisp's long lashes, glossy lips and elaborate ring,
held in such a position that it is suggestive of an
earring. Crisp's refusal to hide his sexuality or to
conform to norms of masculine appearance –
wearing bright make-up and often dyeing his hair
crimson – was courageous and unswerving in the
face of violence and hostility. [CB]

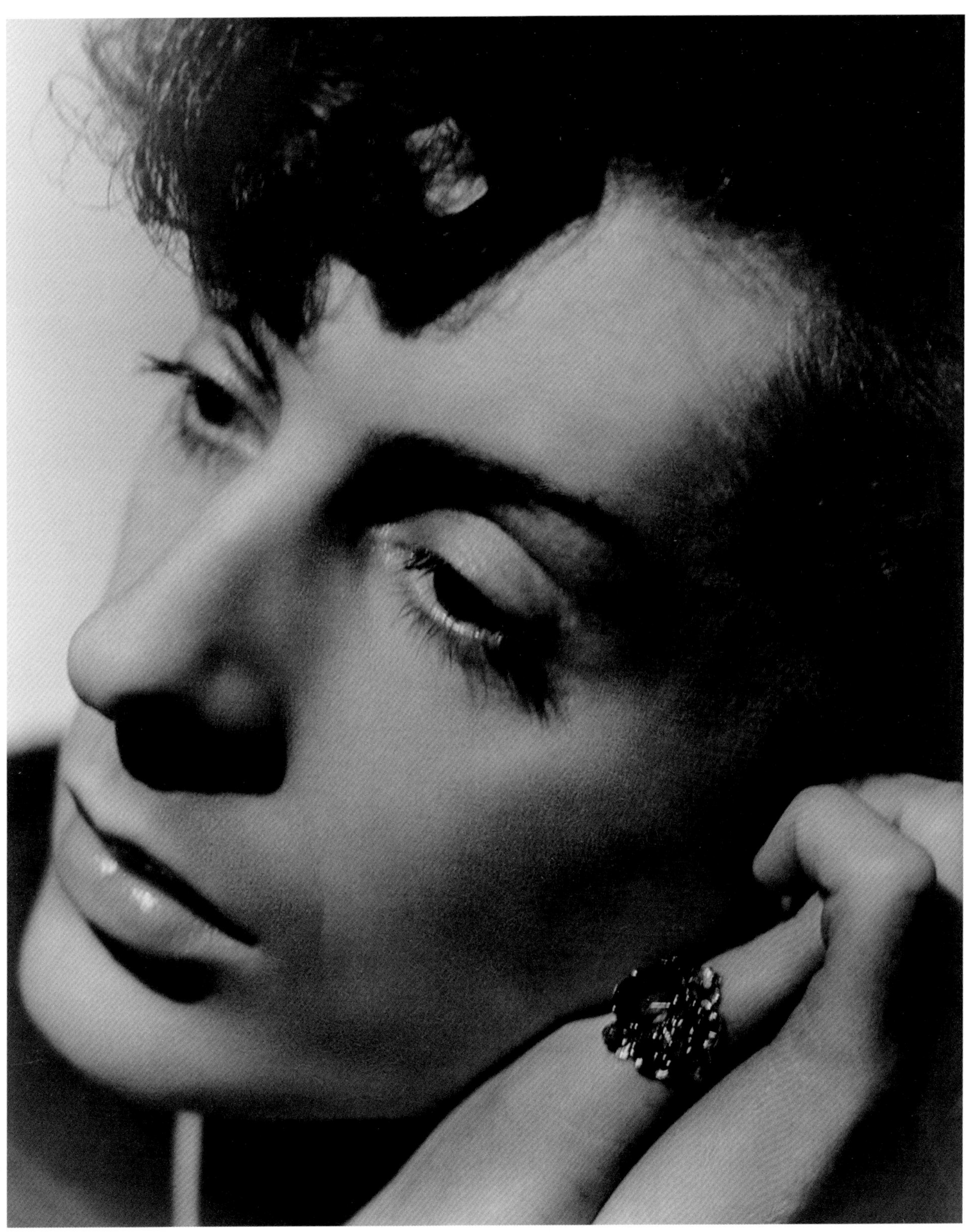

Lewis Morley 1925–2013
Joe Orton 1965
Photograph, bromide print on paper
30.4 x 25.1
National Portrait Gallery, London

This image was taken in a photoshoot for publicity
images to promote Joe Orton's play *Entertaining Mr
Sloane* (1964), which was transferring to the USA.
Lewis Morley later described this shoot in his
memoirs, *Black and White Lies* (1992): 'They were to
be body-building type shots, as he wanted it to be
known that he was the fittest, best built playwright
in the western hemisphere. In the interim I had met
Orton at the *Loot* photo call. I expected him to arrive
with the usual body-building gear that one sees
stretched over the highly oiled and over-developed
muscles in the body-building magazines. The spangled
jockstrap, the tiger-striped, hip-hugging, vee-cut
costume. At least a pair of trendy tight-fitting swimming
trunks. When I was finally confronted by a slim youth,
wearing a pair of ever-so-slightly stained Aertex
underpants, I was ever-so-slightly shocked... I had
misgivings about Joe's attire. I felt that the underpants
would somehow make a joke of his intentions, but he
appeared to be perfectly relaxed and completely at
ease, exuding the confidence that what he had chosen
for the session was absolutely right.'[16]

In this image, Morley's solution was to return to
one of his most famous compositions, his 1963
photograph of Christine Keeler. Keeler's relationships
with government minister John Profumo (1915–2006)
and Russian naval attaché Yevgeny Ivanov (1926–94)
caused a scandal. She was reluctant to pose nude so
Morley suggested that she hide her body behind the
back of a cheap imitation of a Jacobsen chair, which
Morley happened to have in the studio. Morley used
this pose for other sitters but this image of Orton is
its queerest iteration. In contrast to Keeler's more
seductive pose, Orton appears relaxed and at ease
with his apparent nudity. [CB]

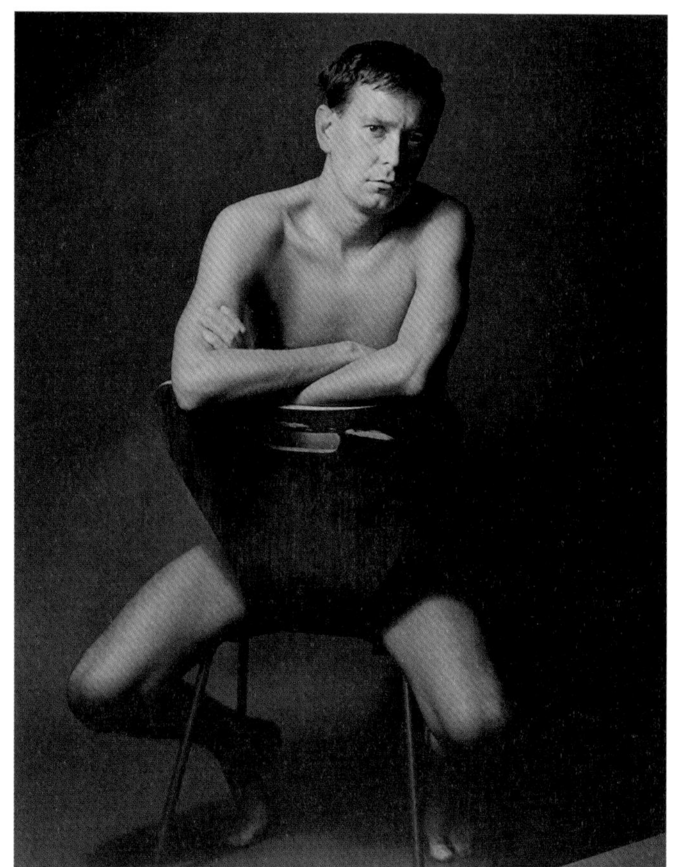

Patrick Procktor 1936–2003
Joe Orton 1967
Ink on paper
23.4 x 34.4
National Portrait Gallery, London

Naked except for his socks and lying on a bed, Patrick Procktor's drawing of Joe Orton seems to offer an intimate image of the playwright. The drawing was, however, commissioned by the Royal Court Theatre, to be reproduced in the programme for a double bill of Orton's short plays *The Erpingham Camp* (1966) and *The Ruffian on the Stair* (1964), which were staged under the title *Crimes of Passion*. As Ian Massey has argued, Procktor's overt engagement with his sexuality in his drawings and paintings from the period made him a natural choice for this commission.[17] The deft outline of Orton's body in the finished drawing, and careful depiction of details such as Orton's bird tattoo, contrasts with the dotted line of the bed coverings, suggesting the different textures of firm flesh and soft fabric. His gaze seems expectant and his hand between his thighs preserves his modesty but also hints at more erotic possibilities. Orton wrote in his diary for 5 May 1967: 'He drew me lying on the bed . . . I kept my socks on, because I think they're sexy. "I've drawn you looking like a beautiful teenager", P. Procktor said. "You'll get a lot of kinky letters after this, I'm sure."'

This was a period of great success for Orton: the 1966 London staging of *Loot* had received rave reviews and, in addition to revising the scripts for *Crimes of Passion*, he was writing *What the Butler Saw* and drafting a screenplay for The Beatles. Sadly, these would prove to be his final projects: on 9 August 1967 he was killed by his partner, Kenneth Halliwell. [CB]

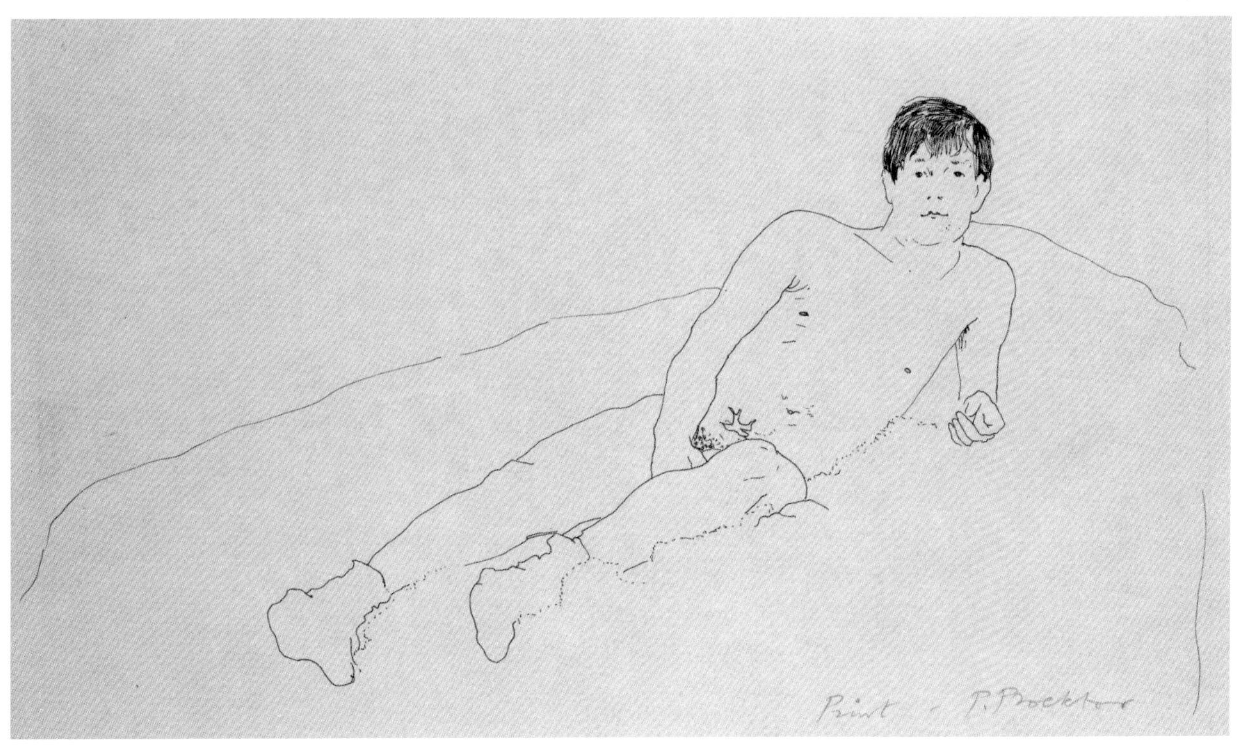

KENNETH HALLIWELL AND JOE ORTON

ILSA COLSELL

In the years 1959 to 1962, Kenneth Halliwell and John Orton (later known as Joe) visited the libraries of Islington, London, borrowing and stealing alike from their inventory. The couple attended together, browsing separately before returning home to show one another their haul. There they set about a series of collaged interventions: typed additions to interior texts, reconfigured image plates, front covers made anew and rewritten publishers' synopses. Rising up the walls around the two men as they worked were hundreds of previously excised large-scale image plates broadly sweeping through art's history and enveloping them both within their small bed-sitting room.

They had met and begun their relationship at the Royal Academy of Dramatic Art (RADA) in 1951. Writing together in a frugal yet methodically organised existence, they aimed to find a publisher to take them on jointly. Both were well read, their lives having been the cumulative formal and independent study of classical literature, Greek mythology, art history and theatre. Visiting Islington's libraries formed part of this ongoing education but where the shelves lacked in suitably intellectual reading material they prospered with other more anarchic possibility. Returning the altered books to these shelves and waiting to see them discovered became a source of satisfying private performance.

Their written work, sending up the ruling class and underlining its callous social hypocrisies, vividly reflected a London caught between postwar reserve and the beckoning of a more culturally permissive 1960s. Those that took themselves too seriously within this dwindling Empire edged forward as suitable prey and it was the cultural Establishment that suffered most in the library-book cover reworkings. Earnest theatrical portraits, such as of the inseparable acting couple 'The Lunts', were replaced with images of children's toys, and similar mocking stand-ins were inserted for others. The original

subtitle, 'An illustrated study of their work with a list of their appearances on stage & screen', was now attributed to these transposed frivolous playthings. Bringing together incongruous text and images made for quick wit on the page. Titles were co-opted and visually rewritten by creating half-rhymes on their suggestive meanings: *Queen's Favourite* was no longer the historical romance novel, but instead the scene of homoerotic embrace and a nod to the language of queer subculture. The careful addition of text also offered the opportunity to deride and subvert the sober intentions of authors and their publishers. Synopses were retyped and reimagined, offering more lewd alternatives. Titles humorously adjusted, Emlyn Williams's (1905–1987) oeuvre was altered so that his collected plays anthology, *Night Must Fall* (1935), was replaced by 'Knickers Must Fall'; *The Light of Heart* (1940) became 'Fucked by Monty'; and further titles were added, such as 'Up the Front', 'Up the Back' and 'Olivia Prude'. Other covers were reworked, forming entirely new and abstracted visual narratives that stood alone as discrete, reduced artworks.

These intensifying incisions were not unnoticed and though enjoyed by staff initially, the number of 'defaced' books mounted, costing the borough hundreds of pounds. The collaborators were eventually caught and handed a six-month custodial sentence. This was an abrupt intervention from the outside world into their own. Following their release from prison, both men continued to work creatively. Orton became the infamous playwright Joe, and Halliwell, his publicly absent editor, worked on larger-scale collages, developing his own distinct art practice.

Their tragic end brought a halt to sixteen years of shared life and collaboration. Halliwell, suffering a mental health breakdown in August 1967, murdered Orton and took his own life immediately afterwards.

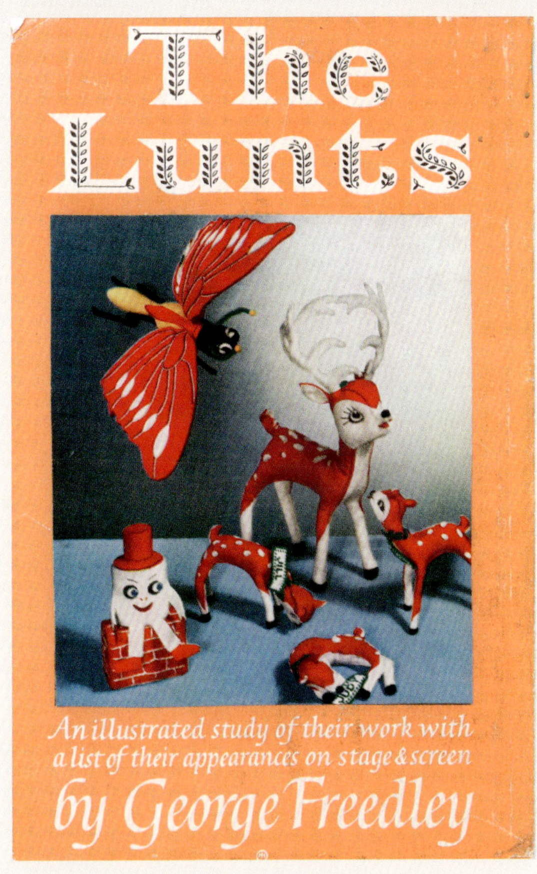

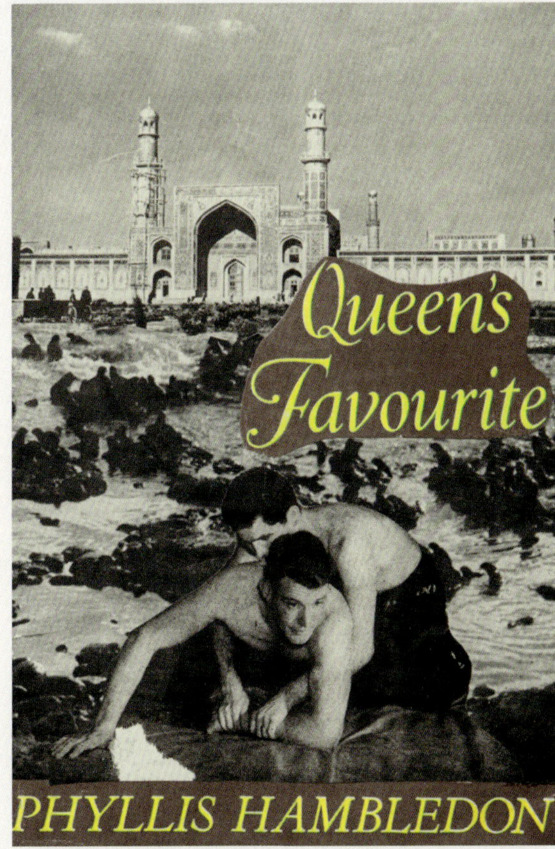

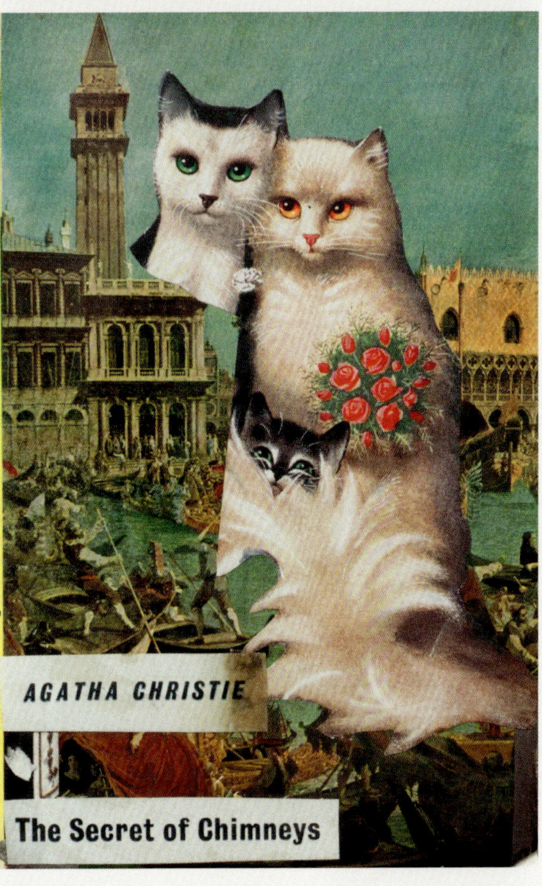

ABOVE LEFT

John Kingsley 'Joe' Orton
1933–67
Kenneth Leith Halliwell
1926–67
The Lunts by George Freedley
46 x 22.5
Islington Local History
Centre, London

RIGHT

John Kingsley 'Joe' Orton
1933–67
Kenneth Leith Halliwell
1926–67
The Secret of Chimneys by Agatha Christie
36.5 x 19
Islington Local History
Centre, London

ABOVE RIGHT

John Kingsley 'Joe' Orton
1933–67
Kenneth Leith Halliwell
1926–67
Queen's Favourite by Phyllis Hambledon
44.5 x 19
Islington Local History
Centre, London

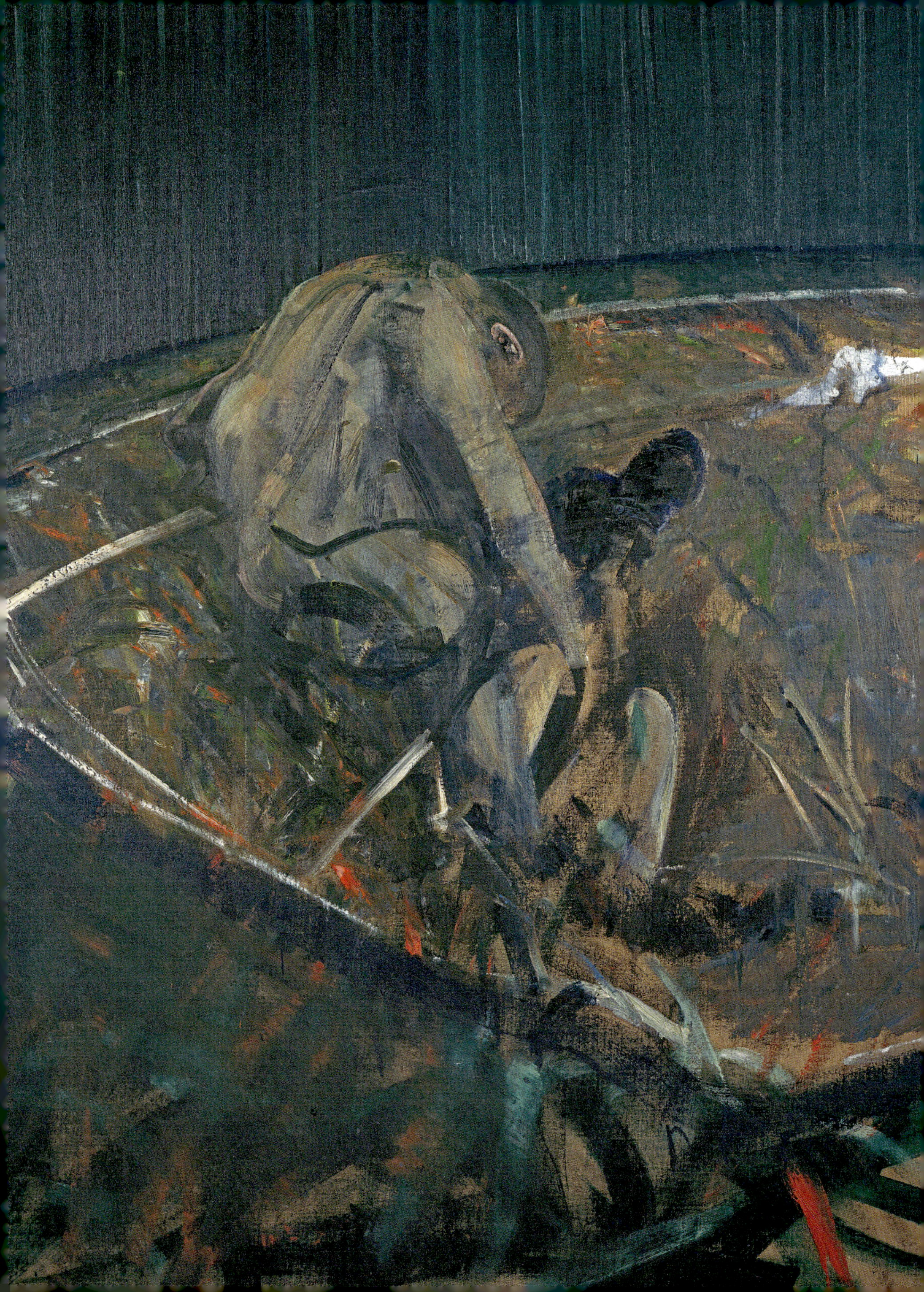

BEAUTIFUL BODIES

CATHERINE HOWE

Francis Bacon 1909–92

Figures in a Landscape

1956–7

Oil on canvas

150 x 107.5

Birmingham Museums
and Art Gallery

See also p.164

FRANCIS BACON AND David Hockney (b.1937) are two canonical figures in the history of twentieth-century British art. They are also crucial for queer art history, as daring men who explored their sexuality in their work prior to partial decriminalisation in 1967. Their art charts varying personal negotiations of desire and identity during a period of transition, from criminality to growing social and legal acceptance. Both responded to the legacy of same-sex desire in art before them, and its more widespread modes of representation within the contemporaneous queer community, drawing in particular from ambiguously erotic images of the male body, to convey the specifics of queer subjectivity.

Bacon knew that he was gay from a young age and his biography has been somewhat mythologised, especially since his death in 1992. He was at ease with his sexuality but told his close friend and leading biographer Michael Peppiatt (b.1941) that 'being homosexual is a defect… it's like having a limp',[1] a statement symptomatic of legal and scientific classifications to which he was subject throughout much of his life. In 1926, aged sixteen, Bacon's father found him trying on his mother's underwear and he was subsequently cast out of the family home in Ireland.[2] This prompted his move to London, where he quickly immersed himself in the city's covert gay culture, in between trips to Berlin and Paris.[3] By the 1950s, he was an infamous figure of queer Soho, known for his make-up, champagne and gambling habits.[4] A regular at the private members' club The Colony Room, he painted numerous portraits of its founder, Muriel Belcher (1908–79), an 'out' lesbian. His social circle included the photographers John Deakin (1912–72) and Cecil Beaton, the actor Paul Danquah (1925–2015), artists such as John Minton (1917–57),[5] and later Hockney himself.[6] He was also close friends with the painter Denis Wirth-Miller (1915–2010) and his partner, the designer Richard Chopping (1917–2008).[7] This queer community, coupled with his hedonistic lifestyle, had a direct impact upon his paintings.

Like Bacon, when Hockney moved to London to study at the Royal College of Art (RCA) in 1959, he soon came across and engaged with an established queer culture. The city provided a more open atmosphere for him as a gay man compared to his hometown of Bradford.[8] In 1960, he set about creating 'propaganda paintings', which dealt with subjects of great personal significance, including his homosexuality.[9] These were encouraged by fellow artists R.B. Kitaj (1932–2007) and Adrian Berg (1929–2011).[10] Hockney said, concerning his sexuality, that 'the moment you learn to deal with it in art, it's quite an exciting moment, just as in a sense when people "come out" it's quite an exciting moment. It means they become aware of their desires and deal with them in a reasonable honest way.'[11] Bacon's and Hockney's differing attitudes towards their sexuality seem circumstantial and of their time; the latter was far younger and had moved to London after the publication of the Wolfenden Report in 1957, which recommended a change in the law.[12]

Bacon later perpetuated generalised statements concerning the violence of reality, human presence and his sense of 'exhilarated despair',[13] in order to deter interpretation deduced from readable figurative content in his work. However, his imagery and sensory approach to painting resonate with queer experience, without recourse to a simplistic biographical narrative. He notoriously referenced Eadweard Muybridge's photographs of naked wrestlers c.1887 (opposite) as a cipher for the sexual encounter between two men, merged with the forms of Michelangelo Buonarroti's male nudes that were already associated with same-sex desire.[14] He was certainly not the first to adapt such a theme for queer ends, although his work has become one of the most famous examples. Bacon was probably aware that he was building upon aesthetic tropes of classical wrestling used since the nineteenth century as covert emblems of homosexuality or 'Uranian love'.[15] Wilhelm von Gloeden photographed muscular men wrestling (below), as well as the ambiguous youths for which he is well known. Likewise, Christopher Wood and Keith Vaughan explored the wrestling motif beforehand, with the latter continuing to do so even after Bacon's landmark paintings of the 1950s.[16] The uniqueness of Bacon's approach to the subject is that he captured a moment of violent tenderness and intimacy through figurative rupture, the sensations and atmosphere of the clandestine sexual experience symptomatic of his own desire and time.[17]

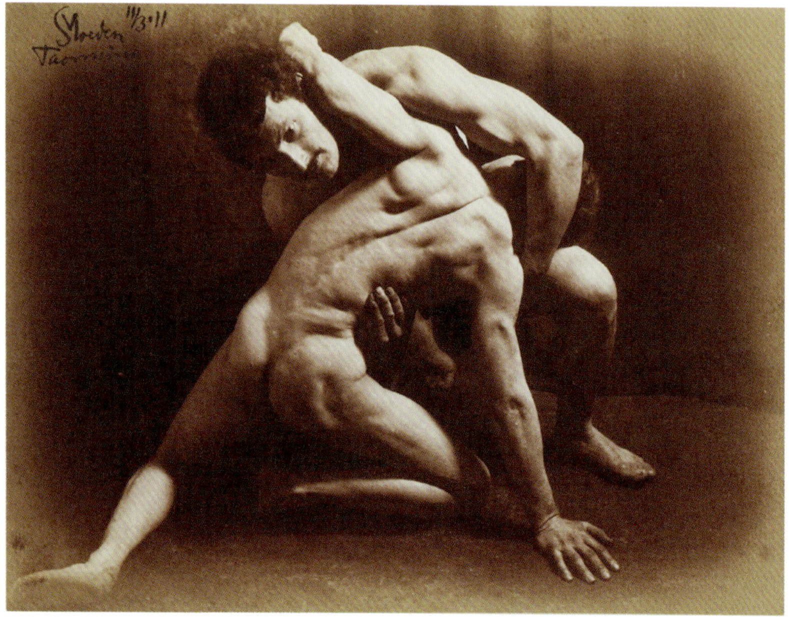

Wilhelm von Gloeden, 1856–1931
Wrestlers c.1903, printed 1911
Photograph, print on salted paper
18.2 x 24
Wilson Centre for Photography, London

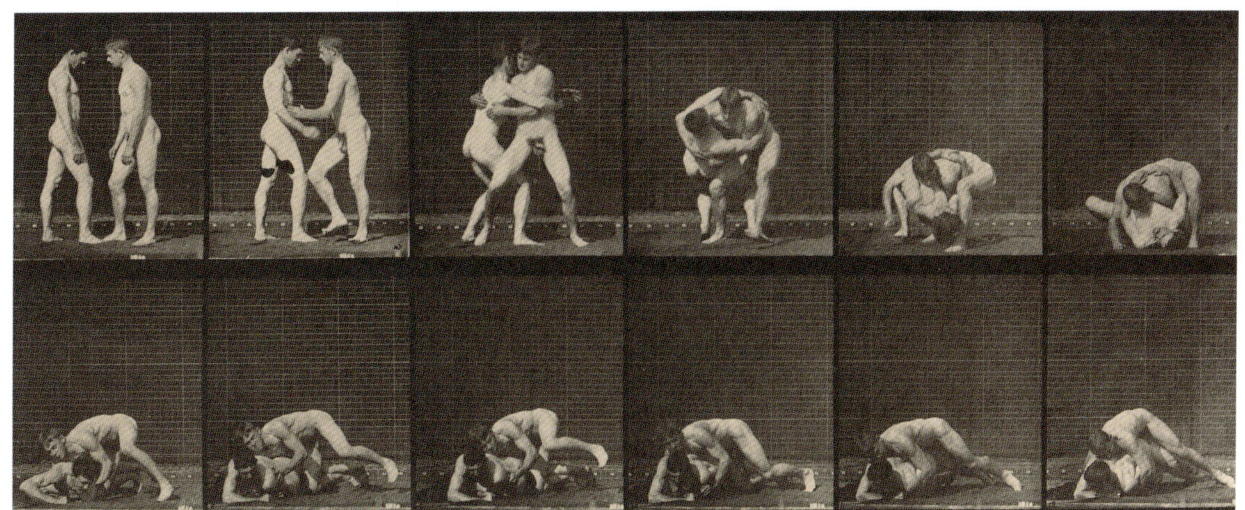

His queer content was evident enough to cause problems. *Two Figures* 1953 was shown out of public view at the Hanover Gallery,[18] probably due to its figurative hint of an erect penis.[19] When *Two Figures in the Grass* 1954, a development of the subject, was shown at a solo exhibition of Bacon's paintings at the Institute of Contemporary Arts in 1955 in full view, the police were called to investigate on grounds of obscenity.[20] The exhibition was supported by Peter Watson (1908–56), who was gay himself and patron to many other queer artists.[21] Both paintings have been seen to mark the peak of Bacon's relationship with Peter Lacy (1916–62), the violent love of his life.[22] Although the wrestling theme did not reemerge until 1967 in Bacon's work,[23] *Figures in a Landscape* 1956–7 (pp.158, 164) provides an ominous counterpoint to its predecessors, developing upon them far more ambiguously, the figures fragmented in a shadowy outdoor scene. The male body is both venerated and reduced to the status of animal; restricted yet liberated from societal conventions of desire.

Many of Bacon's other paintings from this decade feature suited male figures in darkened rooms, often relating to Lacy, such as the 1954 *Man in Blue* series.[24] *Seated Figure* 1961 (p.165) is in keeping with such preoccupations, though more stylistically experimental. Bacon continually explored concealment and revelation, along with conventions of masculinity, capturing his personal experience as a gay man.[25] He also worked from numerous photographs of those close to him and images that he found striking from publications such as *Paris Match* and *Picture Post*,[26] estranging the familiar and even queering it. Hockney's paintings from the early 1960s similarly draw from 'low' and popular culture in combination with high art to explore same-sex desire and stereotypes.[27] *Going to be a Queen for Tonight* 1960 (pp.166–7) is exemplary of the topics with which he was preoccupied throughout his time at the RCA and the strategies that he used to explore his sexuality and identity in art there. The painting privileges a disturbance of gender and heterosexuality and references graffiti upon male lavatory walls.[28] Cementing this connection, Hockney wrote a parody exhibition review titled 'The Latrine Gallery, SW7' of the men's toilets at the RCA.[29]

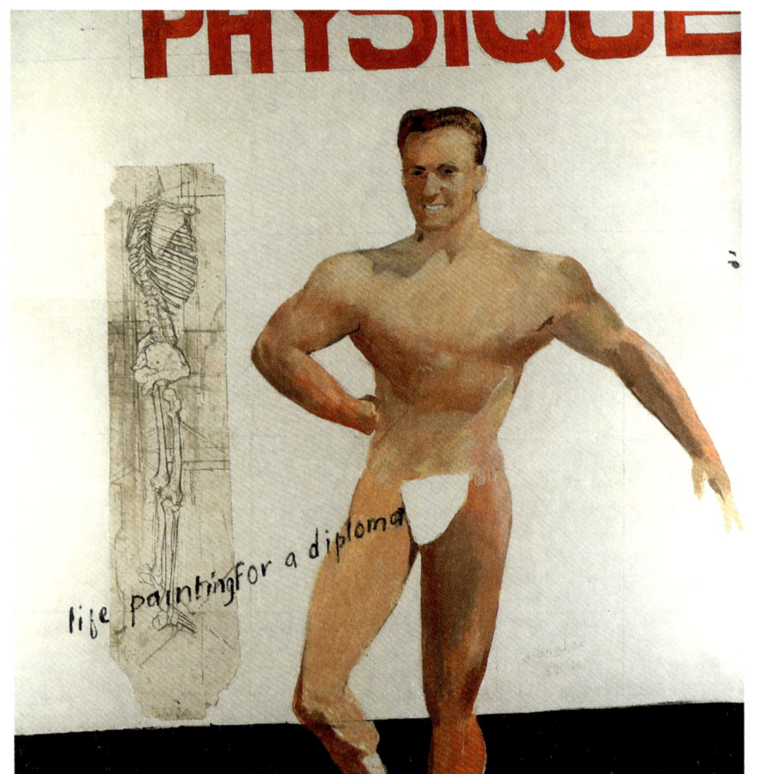

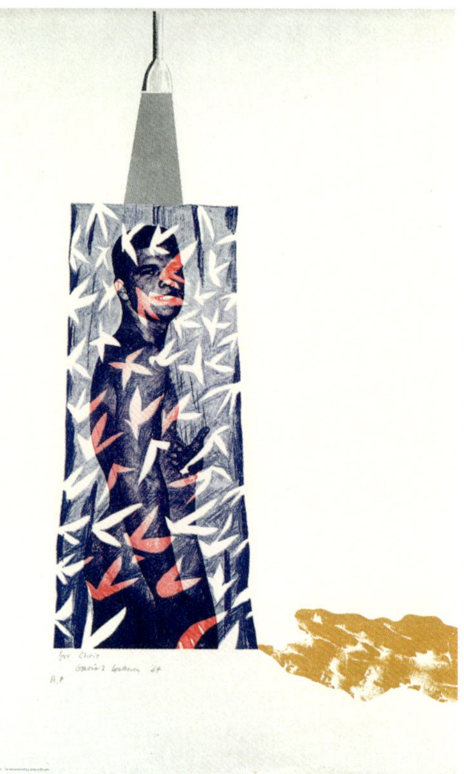

Painted the following year, *Bertha alias Bernie* 1961 (pp.168–9) explores gender conventions more figuratively, while the play of similar-sounding male and female names destabilises their difference.[30] Hockney himself proved no stranger to its subject of cross-dressing, appearing in drag at the RCA Christmas Revue that year.[31] Although Hockney developed his own personal idioms to explore his sexuality, Bacon certainly set an influential precedent for him.[32] He visited a solo exhibition of Bacon's paintings at the Marlborough Gallery in 1960.[33] Of the male nudes on display, he declared that 'one of the things I liked about them was that you could smell the balls'.[34] His sensory approach may well have influenced Hockney's own figurations, along with his interest in hiding and exposing the body. This can be seen not only in his violent handling of paint in the aforementioned works but also in his move towards depictions of the homoerotic nude. Hockney even bought a copy of Muybridge's *The Human Figure in Motion* (1887) in the early 1960s in the knowledge that his predecessor had used it as source material.[35]

Going further than Bacon's use of Muybridge, which queered an innocuous image, Hockney directly referenced photographs from physique magazines. They featured muscular men in various athletic scenarios and degrees of undress, produced to cater for homoerotic desires while legally passing as men's sports publications. They also often alluded to classicism, sculpture, Michelangelo and other established artistic ideals of the masculine body, fitting within the same tradition as Bacon's paintings.[36] As Emily Porter-Salmon has noted, a reader's letter to the editor published in *Physique Pictorial* even comments upon the queer potential of Muybridge's nude wrestlers, seemingly surprised that they were never subject to censorship.[37] The male figure in Hockney's *Life Painting for a Diploma* 1962 (opposite) was copied from a 1961 cover of the magazine *The Young Physique*.[38] Painted in order to satisfy the life study assessment criteria at the RCA, the work challenges the heterosexual pairing of male artist and female model, appealing to Hockney's own erotic interests.[39] In the artist's words, 'it's mocking their idea of being objective about a nude in front of you when really your feelings must be affected'.[40] The male body is rendered especially sensual in light of the context of the desiring male gaze. Placed alongside the skeleton, there is a clash of academic, popular and personal upon the canvas, as in Bacon's configuration of multiple sources in a single painting. It also similarly plays upon queer desire and its suppression, the posing pouch a void over the model's crotch.

Hockney stayed in California in 1964 and his work dealt more frequently with voyeuristic fantasies of men in showers and swimming pools.[41] He even visited *Physique Pictorial*, based in Los Angeles.[42] The screen print *Cleanliness is Next to Godliness* 1964 (opposite) borrows an image directly from this magazine.[43] The young macho model appears in a kitsch domestic setting, half-concealed by a patterned shower curtain. Its title is suggestive of advertising slogans and morality. The leaky puddle seems ejaculatory,[44] comparable to the shadowy expulsions that often seep from Bacon's figures, as in *Figures in a Landscape*. Paul Melia has claimed that 'had Hockney been born a couple of generations earlier, he would have gone to Capri rather than Los Angeles and have used photographs by Wilhelm von Gloeden',[45] pointing towards a tradition of queer iconography relevant to his own time and place. After Bacon's death, the contents of his studio were well documented, revealing that he owned copies of *Physique Pictorial* from the early 1960s.[46] This posits a shared interest and potential inspiration that Hockney could not have been aware of at the time, as proposed by Simon Ofield, that Bacon was engaging with contemporary gay visual culture alongside Muybridge and Michelangelo.[47] As he expounds, perhaps in reference to this, the artist revealed to David Sylvester in 1974 that 'I look all the time at photographs in magazines of footballers and boxers and all that kind of thing'.[48]

In the work of both artists, then, queerness is not simply reducible to biography but, in fact, integral to the disruptive aesthetic strategies that they used to convey the particularities of their experience. Their work addressed societal taboos and presented new possibilities in a time of upheaval, exploring and celebrating their desires in modern art. They drew from what was around them, as well as established queer visual motifs. The fact that both continued to pursue such themes long after 1967 attests to the importance of the change in law, which allowed for a greater openness towards queer desire in art and society. It equally proves that this was still a pressing subject demanding further attention, acceptance and equality.

Francis Bacon 1909–92

Figures in a Landscape 1956–7

Oil on canvas

150 x 107.5

Birmingham Museums and Art Gallery

Figures in a Landscape combines the homoerotic
themes of the 'crouching nude' and 'figures in the
grass' that Francis Bacon explored in multiple paintings
throughout the 1950s. He was inspired by Eadweard
Muybridge's photographs of wrestlers and athletes,
along with Michelangelo's drawings and sculpture.
Bacon adapted these to explore his homosexuality
with varying degrees of ambiguity. He later explained
that 'Michelangelo and Muybridge are mixed up in
my mind together' and 'I manipulate the Muybridge
bodies into the form of the bodies I have known.'[49]

At the time of painting *Figures in a Landscape*,
Bacon was involved in an intense and violent love
affair with Peter Lacy, who told him that 'you live in
a corner of my cottage on straw. You could sleep and
shit there.'[50] By 1956, their relationship had become
particularly difficult and this impacted upon his work.
Lacy was battling alcoholism and had moved to
Tangier, where the artist often stayed with him. The city
was seen as a liberal outpost for many gay men at this
time. In the painting, Bacon's use of an arena-like
circular framing device implies voyeurism and constraint,
the figures entrapped within the turbulent landscape
like wild animals. The more vibrant flecks of red and
green in the grass can be traced back to the effect
of the bright sunlight of Morocco. The scenery also
resembles the Essex countryside, as depicted in
paintings by Bacon's friend, Denis Wirth-Miller,
from around the same time. He introduced Bacon to
Muybridge's photographs and they shared a studio in
Wivenhoe sporadically throughout the decade. [CH]

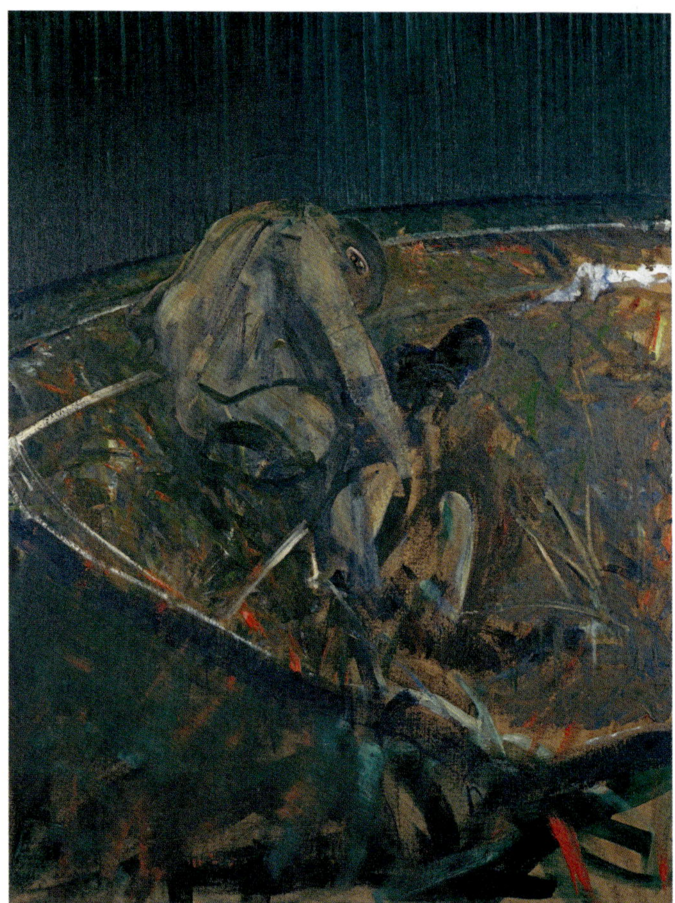

Francis Bacon 1909–92

Seated Figure 1961

Oil and sand on canvas

165.1 x 142.2

Tate. Presented by J. Sainsbury Ltd 1961

In *Seated Figure*, the man is identifiable as Francis
Bacon's former lover Peter Lacy, their troubled
relationship having ended by this date. The unbuttoned
shirt collar and thick neck resemble photographs of
him found in the artist's studio taken by John Deakin,
as well as Bacon's portraits of him from the previous
decade. It was painted the year before Lacy's death,
brought on by a long period of alcohol abuse. The exotic
rug may relate to their time spent together in Tangier.
Bacon spoke of his treatment of the people in his many
portraits as an 'injury'.[51] However, he considered
violence as an affirmation of human life.

In the late 1920s and into the early 1930s Bacon
also worked as an interior designer. This may account
for his adept rendering of the oppressive space
inhabited by Lacy in *Seated Figure*, including his use of
a geometric framing device. The partial detail of the
figure and furniture is at odds with the tempestuous
abstract backdrop, conveying both domesticity and
discomfort. In line with this, he later declared 'I hate
a homely atmosphere… I want to isolate the image
and take it away from the interior and the home.'[52]

Bacon never explicitly named Lacy in portrait
titles, referring to him as 'P.L.', if at all. Their same-sex
relationship had to be hidden from the law. Bacon
alluded to him as the subject of many works containing
solitary male figures, explaining in psychoanalytic
terms that 'this man was very neurotic and almost
hysterical'.[53] After 1967, Bacon was increasingly open
about his desires and the content of his paintings
became more sexually explicit. [CH]

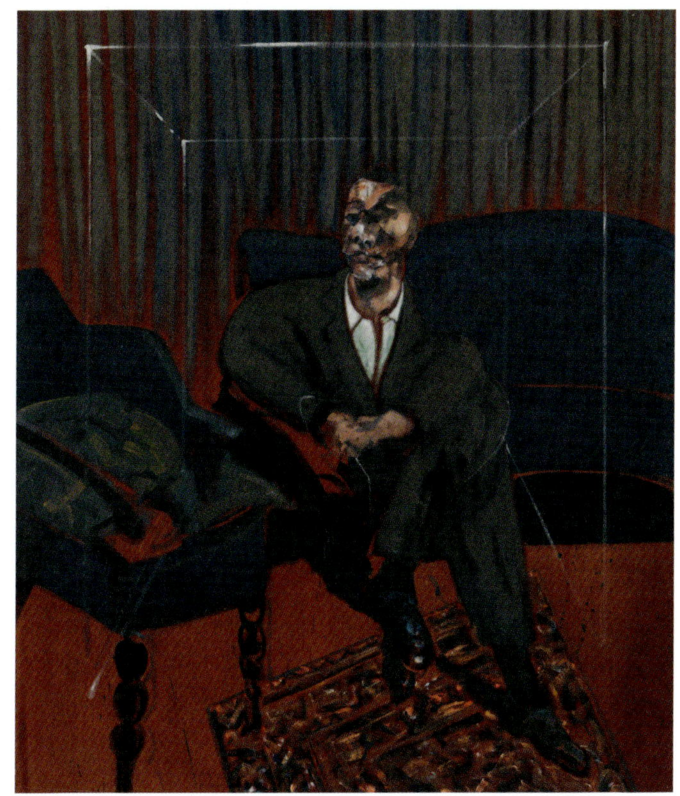

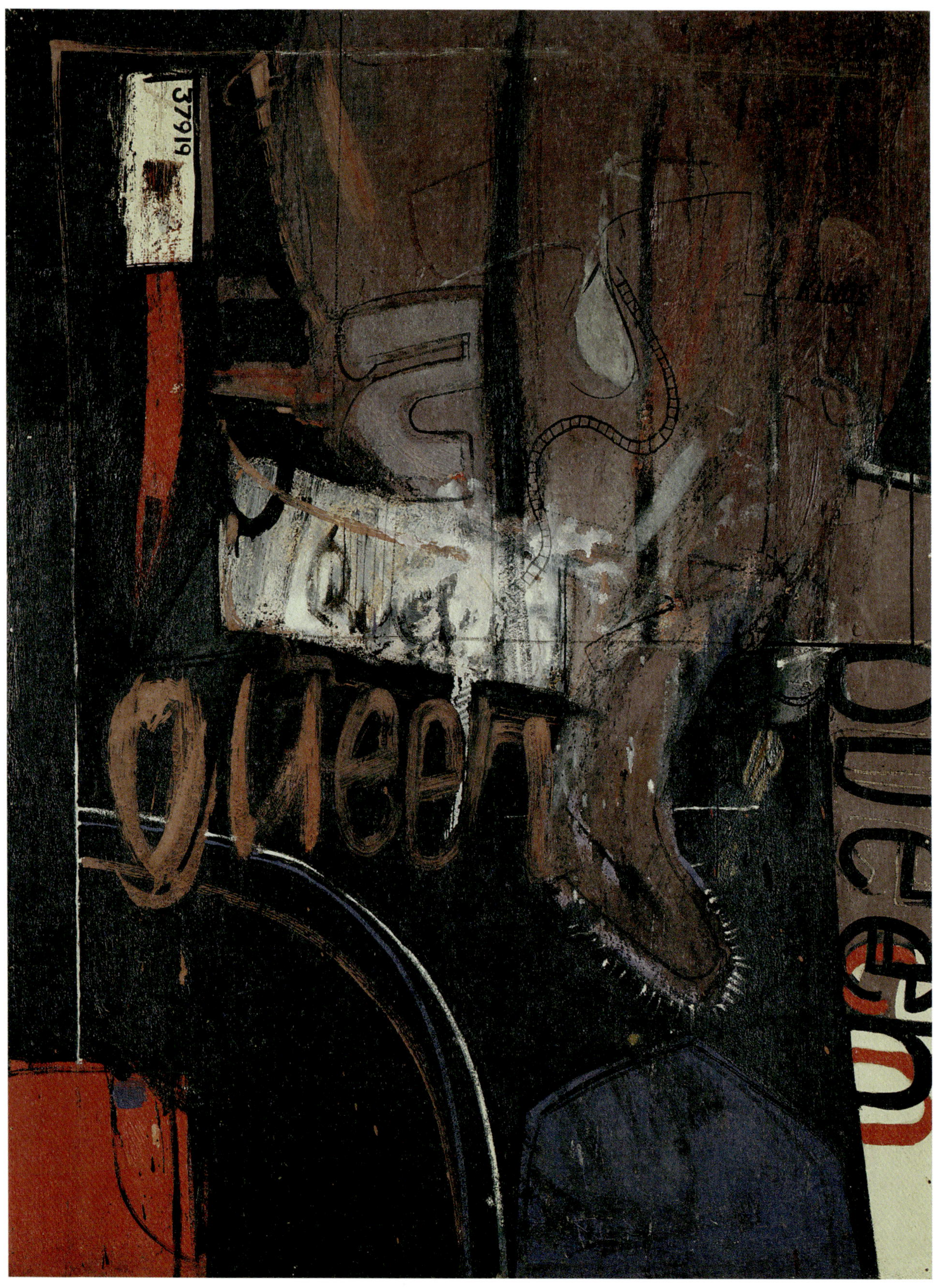

David Hockney b.1937
Going to be a Queen for Tonight 1960
Oil on board
120 x 85
Royal College of Art, London

David Hockney's *Going to Be a Queen for Tonight* was completed in 1960 after he had left his native Bradford and arrived to study at the Royal College of Art in London in September 1959. The artist's use of an expressionistic, graffiti-like style had been influenced by two shows of abstract paintings seen in 1958–9: the first by the Scottish artist Alan Davie (1920–2014) at the Wakefield City Art Gallery in March 1958; and the second at the Whitechapel Art Gallery in London in December 1959 of the American abstract expressionist painter, Jackson Pollock (1912–56). Hockney was also interested in the 'semi-figurative' abstract paintings of the British artist Roger Hilton (1911–75), with their allusive references, dirtied paint and scratched surfaces, and he recorded this through the winter of 1959–60: 'I did a few pictures… that were based on a kind of mixture of Alan Davie cum Jackson Pollock cum Roger Hilton.'[54] The work underlines Hockney's

homosexuality through the title's incorporation of 'Queen' and the recurrence in repeated large scrawled letters on its surface of the words 'queer' and 'queen', a gay slang term for an effeminate or outrageous gay man that can be used both pejoratively or in a celebratory way. Hockney's desire to make more explicit autobiographical allusions in his work was endorsed by his friendship with the openly gay fellow student Adrian Berg. Berg encouraged Hockney to read the work of the gay poets Walt Whitman and Constantine Cavafy (1863–1933), in which homosexuality was more openly declared and erotically charged exhibitionism applauded.[55] Nevertheless, the painting still incorporated overlapping shapes and unclear spatial forms alongside private numerical codes and crude inscriptions that are less easy to interpret. These coded languages signal Hockney's fascination with graffiti seen in the public toilets at Earls Court Underground station, which mixed messages about opportunities for casual sex with vulgar slogans and phallic designs,[56] and graffiti photographed close-up as a sign of urban ethnography by the French-Hungarian photographer, Brassaï (1899–1984). [AS]

David Hockney b.1937
Bertha alias Bernie 1961
Oil on board
118.5 x 89.2
Royal College of Art, London

Bertha alias Bernie takes as its main subject a drag
queen or a cross-dresser. It forms part of a series of
works that engaged more openly with David Hockney's
homosexual life including the drag balls that were a
feature of London's art school entertainment and
part of urban gay culture. The work employs a
self-consciously simplified and graffiti-like style in
its desire to exploit a sense of the untutored and
spontaneous, one that deliberately referenced the
French artist Jean Dubuffet (1901–85), whose spindly
figurative style inspired by children's art and outsider
art Hockney admired. He recalled, 'I got taken with
the deliberately childish thing and felt that I could use
it with a lot of subjects and ideas.'[57] The main figure
clearly inscribed as 'Bertha alias Bernie' stands
prominently against a dark background that focuses
attention upon her cosmetically enhanced features of
dyed blonde hair, conspicuous black mascaraed
eyelashes and tight red lips. Against a lighter painted
area, her breasts are outlined as a roughly sketched
figure appears to be bending over sideways in an
ambiguous way: one that could suggest voyeurism
with the figure furtively looking up her skirt, or it
might even imply a sexual act about to take place.
[AS]

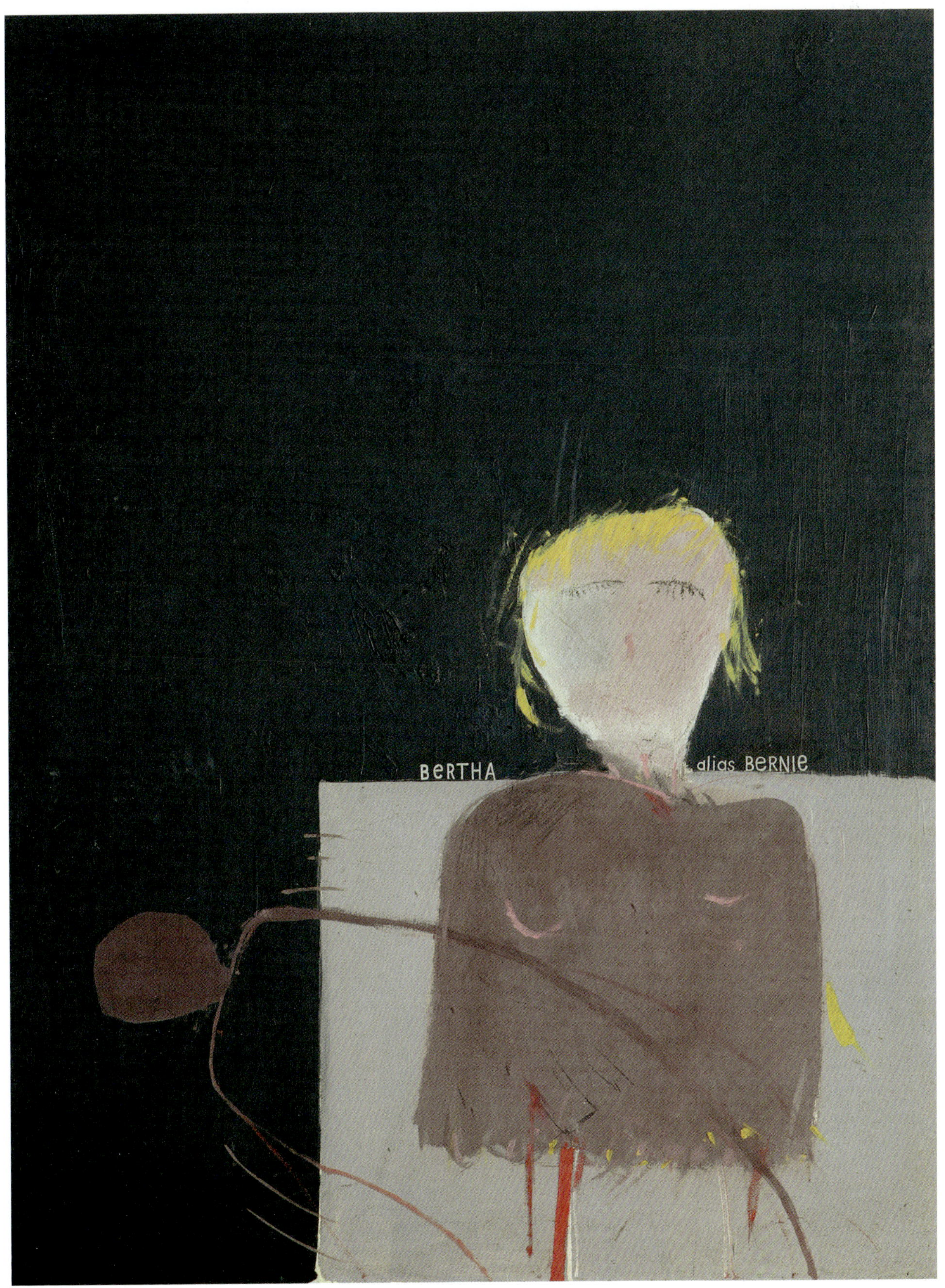

BERTHA
alias BERNIE

PHYSIQUE AND PHOTOGRAPHY

RUPERT SMITH

British gay photographers flourished in the period after the Second World War, creating work that documents same-sex desire and activity at a time of serious legal oppression. The growing popularity of bodybuilding, partly a result of training in the armed forces, created a huge number of young men eager to show off their physiques; photographic equipment was simpler and more affordable, providing their admirers with the means of recording them. As the government and police tried to stamp out homosexuality, leading to the high-profile prosecution of men such as Lord Montagu and Peter Wildeblood, gay culture adopted the disguise of sport and physical culture to survive and flourish. Physique photography not only made images of gay desire but also reached men all over the country, telling them that they were not alone, creating a community that could exist without legal harassment.

Physique culture operated on two levels: the legitimate and the underground. Magazines like *Health and Strength* and *Man's World* were available in newsagents, featured chaste photographs of bodybuilders in trunks and pouches, and ran articles about weight training and nutrition. To the general reader, they were innocent, specialist publications; if your mother found them in your room, she would not start screaming. Gay eyes saw more. The leading photographers whose work appeared in these magazines – Vince, Basil Clavering (alias 'Royale' and 'Hussar'), Scott, Lon of London, John Graham – were all gay men whose images emphasised the beauty, as well as the strength, of their models. If the bodies themselves were not alluring enough already, they were surrounded by classical trappings – columns, drapery, swords, etc. – referencing Greek sculpture and culture, a visual shorthand for homosexuality. The most popular models appeared over and over again, becoming stars in the physique world, their pictures avidly collected by fans.

Fans that wanted more could easily find it. A physique underground supplied material that was created, distributed and owned at considerable risk to all involved. Small ads in the bodybuilding magazines invited readers to send off for catalogues that enabled them to order full-frontal nudes, erection shots and action shots of their favourite models, produced by the very same photographers who were contributing to magazines sold in W.H. Smith. It was a risky business: selling or sending this material through the post landed many photographers in jail, and it was even seized in raids on private individuals. But that did not stop anyone. Throughout the 1950s and 1960s, the physique underground was big business. Maverick photographers like John S. Barrington (1920–91) dropped the bodybuilding pretence altogether, and sold their photographs of beautiful, naked young men directly to a burgeoning private market.

Physique culture died out as more openly pornographic material became available from America and Europe. Gay customers were increasing in confidence, and demanded a direct, explicit expression of their desires. The bodybuilding world retreated into a macho closet, with many of the models renouncing their gay following. The photographers either gave up, sick of the legal risks and unable to compete with more explicit material, or went into pornography themselves. The work that survives from the physique heyday bears witness to British gay life flourishing despite legal persecution, and captures a type of sexual fluidity – beautiful young men admired and desired by gay men, enjoying the attention and often engaging in same-sex activity – that predates by several decades the opening salvos of gay liberation.

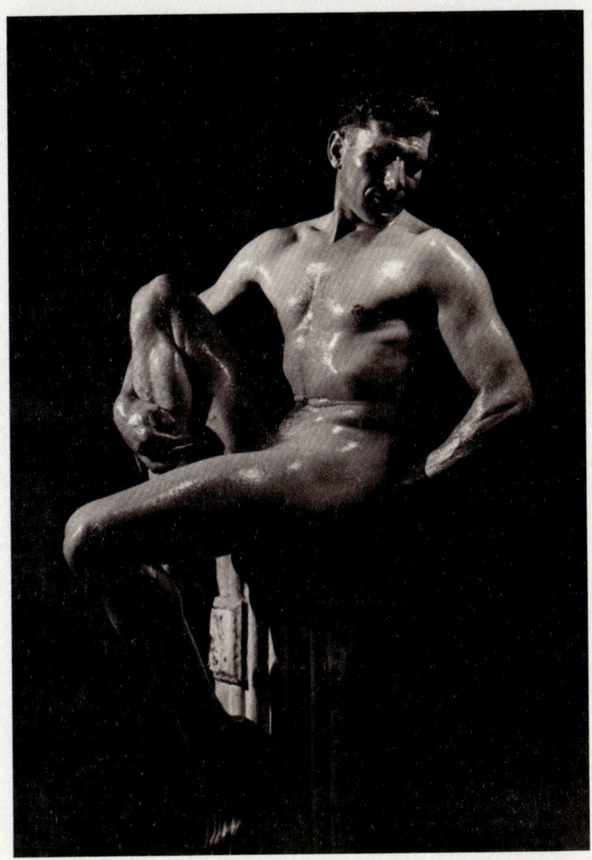

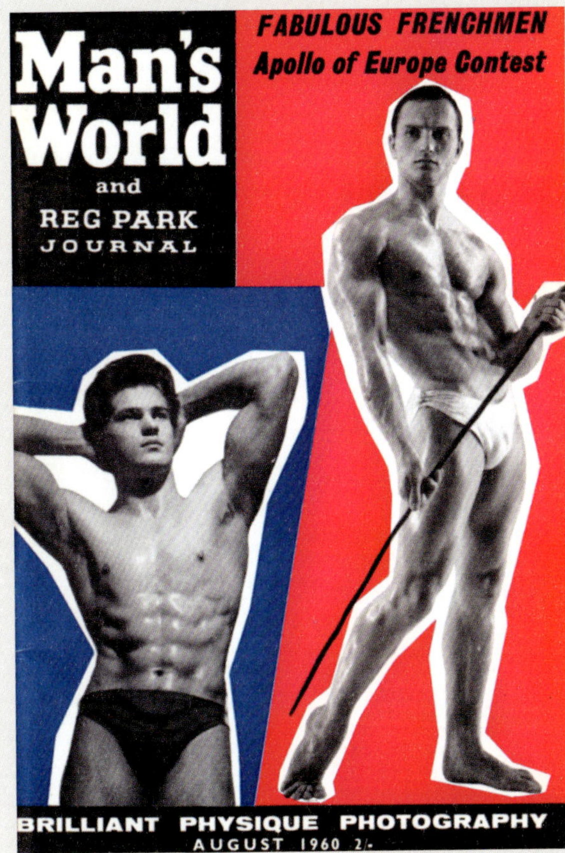

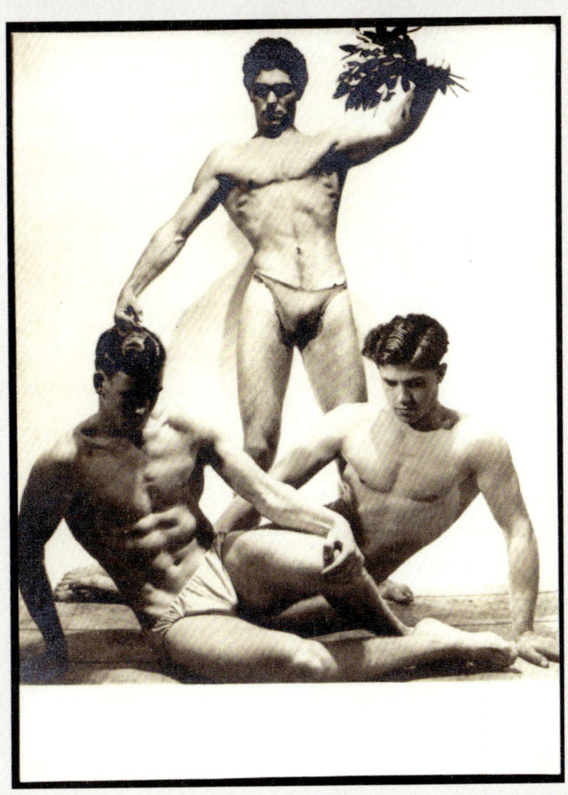

'Vince' Bill Green

Physique photograph:

private commission

c.1950s–1960s

20.6 x 15.4

Private collection

Man's World and Reg Park

Journal August 1960

Magazine

Private collection

Unknown photographer

Physique photograph

c.1950s

20.5 x 15.2

Private collection

NOTES

Introduction, pp.10–17

1. See, for example, Judith Butler, *Gender Trouble: Feminism and the Subversion of Identity*, New York 1990, and Eve Sedgwick, *Epistemology of the Closet*, Berkeley, CA 1990.
2. Sharon Marcus, *Between Women: Friendship, Desire, and Marriage in Victorian England*, Princeton 2007, p.141.
3. W. Graham Robertson, *Time Was*, London 1931, p.39.
4. Susan Sontag, *Against Interpretation and Other Essays*, New York, first edition 1961, this edition 1967, p.278.
5. Alan Crawford, *C.R. Ashbee: Architect, Designer & Romantic Socialist*, New Haven and London 2005, p.75.
6. Diana Souhami, *Gluck: Her Biography*, London 2013, first edition 1988, pp.5, 10.

Framing Queer British Art, pp.18–23

1. Jacob Simon, 'Women in Picture Framing' on *The Frame Blog*: https://theframeblog.com/2014/03/05/women-in-picture-framing/

1. Coded Desires, pp.24–47

1. *Pall Mall Gazette*, 13 February 1865, p.6.
2. *Spectator*, 19 February 1870, p.237.
3. *A Vision of Love Revealed in Sleep*, 1871, p.67.
4. W. Pater, *The Renaissance: Studies in Art and Poetry* (The 1893 Text), (ed.) Donald L. Hill, Berkeley, CA 1980, p.64.
5. Ibid., p.92.
6. Michael Hatt, 'Thoughts and things: Sculpture & the Victorian nude', Alison Smith (ed.), *Exposed: The Victorian Nude*, London 2001, p.48.
7. For an account of the charge and the case, see Carolyn Conroy, 'He hath Mingled with the Ungodly: The Life of Simeon Solomon After 1873, with a Survey of the Extant Works', unpublished PhD thesis, University of York 2009; for an account of the trial and its effects see Gayle Seymour, 'The trial and its aftermath', in *Solomon: A Family of Painters*, London 1985, pp.28–30.
8. *Manchester Guardian*, 28 April 1873, p.5.
9. For an account of this charge see William Peniston, *Pederasts and Others: Urban Culture and Sexual Identity in Nineteenth-Century Paris*, New York 2004, pp.77–8.
10. Arthur Symons, 'The Painting of the Nineteenth Century', *Studies in Seven Arts*, London 1906, pp.60–1.
11. 'Fine Arts', *The Morning Post*, 6 February 1868, p.5.
12. 'The Fourth General Exhibition of Water-colour Drawings. Dudley Gallery', *The Art Journal*, 1 March 1868, p.45.
13. Walter Pater, 'A Study of Dionysus', *Greek Studies*, London 1895, p.37.
14. Illustrating lines 65–7: '…leaning graceful from the ethereal car /Long did she gaze, and silently / Upon the slumbering maid.'
15. *The Athenaeum*, 2310, 3 February 1872, p.150.
16. *The Times*, Tuesday 13 February 1872, p.4.
17. For a discussion of the wider significance of periodical criticisms of Solomon's work at this time, see: Colin Cruise, 'Poetic, eccentric, Pre-Raphaelite: the critical reception of Simeon Solomon's work at the Dudley Gallery', *Writing the Pre-Raphaelites* (eds Tim Barringer and Michaela Geibelhausen), Aldershot 2009, pp.171–91.

18. Oscar Wilde, 'The Grosvenor Gallery', *Dublin University Magazine* 90, July 1877, pp.118–26.
19. Monday, 10 May 1886.
20. Walter Pater, *Studies in the History of the Renaissance*, London 1873, p.29.
21. Robert Aldrich, *The Seduction of the Mediterranean: Writing, Art and Homosexual Fantasy*, New York and London 1993, p.150.
22. W. Graham Robertson, *Time Was*, London 1931, p.39.
23. Ibid. See also: Alison Smith, *The Victorian Nude, Sexuality, Morality and Art*, Manchester 1996, p.197.
24. Walter Pater, *Studies in the History of the Renaissance*, London 1873, p.192.
25. W. Graham Robertson, *Time Was*, London 1931, p.39.
26. Michael Hatt, 'Near and far: homoeroticism, labour and Hamo Thornycroft's *Mower*', *Art History*, vol.26, no.1, February 2003, p.28.
27. I am grateful to Michael Hatt for drawing my attention to this poem.
28. Alan Crawford, *C.R. Ashbee: Architect, Designer & Romantic Socialist*, New Haven and London 1985, 2nd edn 2005, p.75.
29. For a discussion of Tuke's friendships see Emmanuel Cooper, *The Life and Work of Henry Scott Tuke*, London 1987, and Jongwoo Jeremy Kim, *Painted Men in Britain 1868–1918*, Farnham 2012.
30. There might be a subtle gay reference in referencing the caduceus of Hermes. Simeon Solomon incorporated it into his signature, as, for example, in *Love in Autumn* c.1860.
31. *Glasgow Herald*, 12 May 1900, issue 114, p.8.
32. Walter Pater, *The Renaissance: Studies in Art and Poetry* (The 1893 Text), (ed.) Donald L. Hill, Berkeley, CA 1980, p.189.
33. 'FJM', *The Speaker*, vol.6, no.136, May 1902, p.161.

2. Public Indecency: Portrait of an X, pp.48–67

1. 'Vision of Salome', *News of the World*, 2 June 1918, p. 3.
2. Edward Carpenter, *My Days and Dreams: Being Autobiographical Notes*, London 1916, p.321.
3. Ibid., p.30.
4. Denys Sutton (ed.), *The Letters of Roger Fry*, London 1972, vol.1, p.156
5. Ibid., p.159.
6. Jacques-Emile Blanche, *Portraits of a Lifetime*, trans. Walter Clement, London 1937, p.95.
7. Carol Blackett-Ord, *Later Victorian Portraits Catalogue*, National Portrait Gallery, http://www.npg.org.uk/collections/search/portraitExtended/mw00427/Aubrey-Beardsley (accessed 23/01/2017).
8. Susan Owens, 'Aubrey Beardsley, Salome and satire', unpublished PhD, London 2003.
9. Alison Pease, *Modernism, Mass Culture and the Aesthetics of Obscenity*, Cambridge 2000, p.130.
10. Linda Gertner Zatlin, *Aubrey Beardsley: A Catalogue Raisonne*, New Haven and London 2016, vol.2, p.30.
11. Ibid., p.322.
12. Neil McKenna, *The Secret Life of Oscar Wilde*, London 2004, p.157.
13. Martin Birnbaum, *Introductions: Painters, Sculptors and Graphic Artists*, New York 1919, p.25.

14. J.G.P. Delaney, *Charles Ricketts: A Biography*, Oxford 1990, p.25.

15. Matt Cook, *Queer Domesticities: Homosexuality and Home Life in Twentieth-Century London*, Basingstoke 2014, p.34.

16. Cecil Lewis (ed.), 'Self-Portrait', taken from *the Letters & Journals of Charles Ricketts*, R.A., collected and compiled by T. Sturge Moore, London 1939, p.325.

17. Delaney, *Charles Ricketts* (see note 14), p.138.

18. Emma Donoghue, *We Are Michael Field*, Bath 1998, p.34.

19. Ibid., p.43.

20. 'Madge Garland' (obituary), *The Times* (18 July 1990: 14), The Times Digital Archive (accessed 23 January 2017).

3. Theatrical Types, pp.68–93

1. Adrian Woodhouse, *Angus McBean: Face-Maker*, London 2006, p.115.

2. Frederic Woodbridge Wilson, *The Theatrical World of Angus McBean: Photographs from the Harvard Theatre Collection*, Boston 2009, p.144.

3. Black Cultural Archives, 'Ritchie Riley, Oral Testimony', interviewed in 1990, National Archives, BCA RROT/BCA, http://webarchive.nationalarchives.gov.uk/+/http://www.movinghere.org.uk/deliveryfiles/AMBH/BCA_RROT_BCA/0/3.pdf (accessed 27 January 2017).

4. Sarah Woodcock, 'Messel on stage', Thomas Messel (ed.), *Messel in the Theatre of Design*, New York n.d, p.58.

5. Quoted in Charles Castle, *Oliver Messel: A Biography*, London 1986, p.51.

6. Charles Silver, https://www.moma.org/explore/inside_out/2013/03/19/joseph-l-mankiewiczs-suddenly-last-summer/ (accessed 27/01/2017). *See also*: Boze Hadleigh, *The Lavender Screen: The Gay and Lesbian Films, Their Stars, Makers, Characters and Critics*, New York 2001, p.23.

7. *Daily Telegraph*, 30 April 1870.

8. *Curiosities of Street Literature, Comprising Cocks and Catchpennies*, London 1871.

9. Trial testimony of D. Richard Barwell, The Queen vs Boulton and Others before the Lord Chief Justice, 1871, The National Archives.

10. Indictment of Ernest Boulton and Frederick Park, 29 April 1870, The National Archives.

11. Sir Robert Heath, Attorney-General in the trial of the Earl of the Castlehaven for sodomy in 1631.

12. Lady De Frece, *Recollections of Vesta Tilley*, London 1934, p.25.

13. 14 August 1909.

14. Danny La Rue, *From Drags to Riches: My Autobiography*, London 1988, p.57.

15. Ibid., p.81.

16. Quoted in Roger Baker, *Drag: A History of Female Impersonation in the Arts*, New York 1994, p.202.

4. Bloomsbury and Beyond, pp.94–109

1. Christopher St John, *Edy: Recollections of Edith Craig*, (ed.) Eleanor Adlard, London 1949, p.32.

2. *The Times*, 12 November 1911.

3. *National Review*, December 1911.

4. Duncan Grant, letter to Paul Roche, ?June 1953, from the papers of Clarissa Roche. As quoted in Frances Spalding, *Duncan Grant: A Biography*, London 1997, p.414.

5. Paul Roche, letter to Duncan Grant, 30 January 1954, from the papers of Paul Roche. As quoted in Frances Spalding, *Duncan Grant, A Biography*, London 1997, p.417.

6. Glyn Warren Philpot, letter to Daisy Philpot, 'Wednesday' mid-October 1931, in J. G. P. Delaney, *Glyn Philpot: His Life and Art*, London 1999, p.119.

7. *The Scotsman*, 30 April 1932.

8. Quoted in J.G.P. Delaney, *Glyn Philpot: His Life and Art*, Aldershot 1999, p.135.

9. Quoted in J.G.P. Delaney, *Glyn Philpot* (see above), p.154.

10. See *Drawing Over the Colour Line: Geographies of Art and Cosmopolitan Politics in London, 1919-1939*, a research project led by Professors Caroline Bressey and Gemma Romain, University College London, https://www.ucl.ac.uk/equianocentre/projects/docl (accessed November 2016).

11. Walter Sickert, letter to Nan Hudson, 1913, Tate Archive TGA 9125/5, no.71.

12. Walter Sickert, letter to Nan Hudson, 1907, in Wendy Baron, *Sickert: Paintings and Drawings*, New Haven and London 2006, p.69.

13. Vanessa Bell, letter to Roger Fry, 21 July 1912, in Regina Marler (ed.), *Selected Letters of Vanessa Bell*, New York 1993, p.121, and Roger Fry, *Nation*, 1912, in Alicia Foster, *Tate Women Artists*, London 2004, p.161.

14. *The Westminster Gazette*, 1912, in Wendy Baron, *Miss Ethel Sands and her Circle*, London 1977, p.93.

15. Lytton Strachey, letter to Carrington, 23 March 1917, in David Garnett (ed.), *Carrington: Letters and Extracts from her Diaries*, London 1970, p.62.

16. Carrington diary entry, 1 January 1917, in Garnett, *Carrington: Letters and Extracts* (see above), p.52.

17. Quoted in Baron, *Miss Ethel Sands and her Circle* (see note 14), p.258.

18. Quoted in Alice Strang (ed.), *Modern Scottish Women: Painters and Sculptors 1885–1965*, Edinburgh 2015, p.104.

19. Grace English, 'Biographical Notes on Ethel Walker', Tate Gallery Archive. Grace English File, TGA 716/89.

5. Defying Convention, pp.110–31

1. Victoria Glendinning, *Vita: The Life of V. Sackville-West*, London 1983, p.93.

2. Alison Oram, *Her Husband Was A Woman! Women's Gender-Crossing in Modern British Popular Culture*, Abingdon 2007.

3. Bryher, letter to H.D., dated 20 March 1919, quoted in *Bryher: Two Novels: Development and Two Selves*, with an introduction by Joanne Winning, Madison and London 2000, xxviii.

4. Victoria Glendinning, *Vita* (see note 1), p.206.

5. Virginia Woolf, *Orlando: A Biography* (1928), (ed.) Rachel Bowlby, Oxford 1992, pp.180, 211.

6. Virginia Woolf, *A Room of One's Own* (1929), in *A Room of One's Own and Three Guineas,* (ed.) Anna Snaith, Oxford 1992, pp.61–3.

7. *Daily Telegraph*, 17 April 1914.

8. Woolf, *Orlando* (see note 5), pp.154–5.

9. Diana Souhami, *Gluck: Her Biography*, London 2013, c.1988, p.5.

10. Ibid., p.174.

11. Vineta Colby, *Vernon Lee: A Literary Biography*, Virginia 2003, p.2.

12. Richard Ormond, 'John Singer Sargent and Vernon Lee', *Colby Library Quarterly*, vol.9, no.3, September, p.166.

13. Alison Oram and Annmarie Turnbull (eds), *The Lesbian History Sourcebook: Love and Sex Between Women in Britain from 1780 to 1970*, London 2001, p.71.

14. Diana Holman-Hunt, *Latin Among Lions*, London 1974, p.96.

15. Claude Phillips, *The Daily Telegraph*, 17 April 1914, p.7. For discussion of this review see: Pamela Gerrish Nunn, 'Self-Portrait by Laura Knight (1877-1970), pp.53–7, *British Art Journal*, vol.8, no.2, p.54.

16. Frances Fowle, 'Cecile Walton's "Romance"', *Women's Art Journal*, pp.10–15, vol.23, no.2, Autumn 2002–Winter 2003, p.11.

17. Ibid., p.10.

18. Quoted by Antoinette H. Nijhoff, see Lucy Harriet Amy Howarth, 'Marlow Moss 1889-1958', unpublished PhD Thesis, University of Plymouth 2008, vol.1, p.103.

19. Quoted by Antoinette H. Nijhoff, see Lucy Harriet Amy Howarth, 'Marlow Moss 1889-1958', unpublished PhD Thesis, University of Plymouth 2008, vol.1, p.43.

6. Arcadia and Soho, pp.132-44

1. John Addington Symonds, *The Memoirs of John Addington Symonds*, (ed.) Phyllis Grosskurth, Chicago 1984, p.117.
2. John Craxton quoted from Geoffrey Grigson, *John Craxton: Paintings and Drawings*, London 1948, in Ian Collins, *John Craxton*, Farnham 2011, p.82.
3. Christopher Wood, letter to Winifred Nicholson from Villa Arlette, Cannes, 22 July 1927, TGA 8618/1/21.
4. Edward Carpenter, 'Self-analysis for Havelock Ellis', in Noel Grieg, *Edward Carpenter: Selected Writings, Vol.1: Sex*, London 1984, p.290.
5. Wyndham Lewis, 'The London Art Galleries', in *The Listener*, 9 June 1949, quoted in *Wyndham Lewis on Art: Collected Writings, 1913-1956*, (ed.) Walter Michel and C.J. Fox, London 1969, p.394.
6. Keith Vaughan from his journal quoted by Philip Vann, 'The Intimate Figurative Impulse', Philip Vann and Gerard Hastings, *Keith Vaughan*, Farnham 2012, p.23.
7. Robert Medley, *Drawn From The Life: A Memoir*, London 1983, pp.205-6.
8. Hunter Davies (ed.), *The New London Spy: A Discreet Guide to the City's Pleasures*, London 1966, p.222, quoted in Matt Houlbrook, *Queer London: Perils and Pleasures in the Sexual Metropolis, 1918-1957*, Chicago and London 2005, p.40.
9. Francis Bacon quoted in Daniel Farson, *Never a Normal Man*, London 1997, p.125.
10. The phrase is taken from Robert Fabian, *London After Dark: An Intimate Record of Life in London and a Selection of Crime Stories from the Case Book of Ex-Superintendent Robert Fabian*, London 1954, p.10 quoted in Frank Mort, *Capital Affairs: London and the Making of the Permissive Society*, New Haven and London 2010, p.223.
11. Quoted by Richard Ingleby, *Christopher Wood: An English Painter*, London 1995, p.245.
12. Ibid., p.246.
13. Burra's library collection included many of these authors listed TGA 771/6/3-5 and his scrapbooks contained in the Tate Archive include postcards, press cuttings and photographs of Spanish Baroque churches and religious carving, see TGA 939/9/2.
14. See Andrew Causey, *Edward Burra: Complete Catalogue*, Oxford 1985, pp.58-9, 65.
15. Wyndham Lewis, 'The London art galleries', *The Listener*, 9 June 1949, quoted in *Wyndham Lewis on Art: Collected Writings, 1913-1956*, (ed.) Walter Michel and C.J. Fox, London 1969, p.394.
16. Craxton in an undated postcard to E.Q. Nicholson, 1948, Tate Archive quoted by Ian Collins, *John Craxton*, Farnham 2011, p.99.
17. Robert Medley, *Drawn From The Life. A Memoir*, Faber and Faber, London 1983, p.205.
18. Ibid., p.205.
19. Ibid., p.205.
20. *Journal*, 22 December 1953.
21. Ibid.
22. *Journal*, 22 December 1953.
23. KV, 22 June 1962.

7. Public Lives, Private Passions, pp.146-57

1. Nigel Kelly, *Quentin Crisp: The Profession of Being. A Biography*, Jefferson, NC 2011, p.43.
2. Terence Pepper (ed.), *Angus McBean: Portraits*, London 2006, p.142.
3. Dominic Janes, *Picturing the Closet: Male Secrecy and Homosexual Visibility in Britain*, Oxford 2015.
4. Home Office, Scottish Home Department, *Report of the Committee on Homosexual Offences and Prostitution*, London 1957, p.7.
5. Peter Wildeblood, *Against the Law*, London 1955.
6. Home Office, Scottish Home Department, *Report of the Committee on Homosexual Offences and Prostitution*, London 1957, p.17.
7. Dominic Janes, *Oscar Wilde Prefigured: Queer Fashioning and British Caricature, 1750-1900*, Chicago, IL 2016.
8. Richard Hauser, *The Homosexual Society*, London 1962 and Chris Waters, 'The homosexual as social being in Britain, 1945-1968', *Journal of British Studies*, vol.51, no.3, 2012, pp.685-710, p.705.
9. Christopher Pullen, *Gay Identity, New Storytelling and the Media*, Basingstoke 2009, p.85.
10. Joe Orton, *The Orton Diaries* (ed.), New York 1988, p.152.
11. Lewis Morley, 'Joe Orton and Me: Lewis Morley, photographer', http://www.joeorton.org/Pages/Joe_Orton_andme_LM.html (accessed 6 September 2016).
12. Lewis Morley, 'Christine Keeler Photograph: A Modern Icon', http://www.vam.ac.uk/content/articles/c/christine-keeler-photograph-a-modern-icon (accessed 6 September 2016).
13. Frank Marcus, *The Killing of Sister George: A Comedy in Three Acts*, London 1965.
14. Robert Aldrich in Kelly Hankin, 'Lesbian locations: The production of lesbian bar space in *The Killing of Sister George*', *Cinema Journal*, vol.41, no.1, 2001, pp.3-27, p.5.
15. Adrian Woodhouse, *Angus McBean: Face-Maker*, London 2006, p.167.
16. Lewis Morley, *Black and White Lies. Self-Exposures: Some long, some short, some indecent*, Pymble, Australia 1992, pp.73-4.
17. Ian Massey, *Patrick Procktor: Art and Life*, Norwich 2010, p.87.

8. Beautiful Bodies, pp.158-71

1. Michael Peppiatt, *Francis Bacon: Anatomy of an Enigma*, London 2008, p.22.
2. Ibid., p.27.
3. Ibid., pp.28-53.
4. Ibid., pp.138, 186-96.
5. Ibid., pp.186-96. See also Daniel Farson, *The Gilded Gutter Life of Francis Bacon*, London 1994, pp.44-79.
6. Peppiatt, *Francis Bacon* (see note 1), p.352.
7. See Jon Lys Turner, *The Visitor's Book: In Francis Bacon's Shadow: The Lives of Richard Chopping and Denis Wirth-Miller*, London 2016.
8. Peter Webb, *Portrait of David Hockney*, London 1988, pp.23-4.
9. Ibid., p.23.
10. Ibid., pp.23-4.
11. Marco Livingstone, *David Hockney*, London 1996, p.21.
12. Similar points upon their differences are made in Andrew Sinclair, *Francis Bacon: His Life and Violent Times*, New York 1993, p.124, and Simon Ofield, 'Wrestling with Francis Bacon', *Oxford Art Journal*, vol.24, no.1, Oxford 2001, pp.115-30, p.115.
13. David Sylvester, *The Brutality of Fact: Interviews with Francis Bacon*, London 2009, p.83.
14. Ibid., pp.114-16. On same-sex desire in Renaissance art, see Emmanuel Cooper, *The Sexual Perspective: Homosexuality and Art in the Last 100 Years in the West*, London 1986, pp.1-23.
15. John Russell has also noted the similarity of the men in Bacon's *Two Figures* 1953 to a replica Greek third-century bronze in the Uffizi, titled *The Wrestlers*, although to his knowledge Bacon had never seen this exact work. See John Russell, *Francis Bacon*, London 1993, p.94. For an expansion upon the queer legacy of the wrestlers in Bacon's work, particularly concerning classicism and comment upon Russell, see Ofield 'Wrestling with Francis Bacon' (note 12), pp.117, 123, 129.

16. For Keith Vaughan's *Wrestlers* 1948, see Philip Vann and Gerard Hastings, *Keith Vaughan*, Farnham 2012, p.87.

17. For further study on this, see Rina Arya 'Constructions of homosexuality in the art of Francis Bacon', *Journal for Cultural Research*, vol.16, no.1, 2012, pp.43–61; Kenneth E. Silver, 'Master bedrooms and master narratives: Home, homosexuality and post-war art', Christopher Reed (ed.), *Not At Home: The Suppression of Domesticity in Modern Art and Architecture*, London 1996, pp.206–21, pp.206–8, and Ofield (see note 12).

18. See Ofield (note 12), p.129, and Peppiatt (note 1), p.197. For a further examination of public and private in Bacon's 1950s paintings, see Gregory Salter, 'Domesticity and Masculinity in 1950s British Painting', Unpublished PhD Thesis, University of East Anglia 2013, pp.82–7.

19. See also Ofield (note 12), p.119.

20. Martin Harrison (ed.), *Francis Bacon: Catalogue Raisonné*, London 2016, p.378 and Peppiatt (note 1), p.200.

21. Sinclair (note 12), p.87.

22. See Harrison (ed.) (note 20), p.360.

23. See *Two Figures on a Couch* 1967 and the entry on it in Harrison (ed.) (note 20), p.846.

24. Peppiatt (note 1), p.201.

25. See also Salter (note 18), pp.82–97, for further reading.

26. See Martin Harrison and Rebecca Daniels, *Francis Bacon: Incunabula*, London 2008.

27. A similar point is made in Simon Ofield, 'Comparative Strangers', Matthew Gale and Chris Stephens (eds), *Francis Bacon*, London 2008, pp.64–73, p.69.

28. For further examination of this, see Emily Porter-Salmon, 'Textual Cues, Visual Fictions: Representations of Homosexualities in the Works of David Hockney', unpublished PhD thesis, University of Birmingham 2011, pp.52–7, 61–7 and 81.

29. Webb (see note 8), p.27; also noted in Porter-Salmon (see above), p.63.

30. See Porter-Salmon (note 28), pp.55–8 for a greater theoretical examination of Hockney's approach to gender.

31. See Webb (note 8), ills 26, photo captioned 'David Hockney in the RCA Christmas Revue, 1961' and Porter-Salmon (note 28), p.51.

32. See also Porter-Salmon (note 28), pp.8, 164–5, and Livingstone (note 11), p.31.

33. Webb (note 8), p.28.

34. Ibid.

35. Nikos Stangos (ed.), *David Hockney by David Hockney*, London 1976, pp.90–1.

36. See Ofield (note 12), pp.125–30.

37. *Physique Pictorial*, vol.9, no.9, Los Angeles July 1959, p.7. This was first brought to my knowledge in Porter-Salmon (note 28), pp.165–6.

38. Porter-Salmon (note 28), p.146.

39. Stangos (note 35), p.88.

40. Ibid.

41. Webb (note 8), p.64. For further study, see Paul Melia, 'Showers, pools and power', Paul Melia (ed.), *David Hockney*, Manchester 1995.

42. Stangos (note 8), p.98.

43. Porter-Salmon (note 28), pp.154, 170.

44. Sexual metaphors of the shower have also been identified in Melia (see note 41), p.56.

45. Melia (see note 41), p.52.

46. Bacon's studio and book archive are held at Dublin City Gallery, The Hugh Lane. Included are two issues of *Physique Pictorial* dating from November 1961 and March 1962 (vol.XI–2 and vol.XI–3), RM98F235:4 and RM98F94:1. See also Harrison and Daniels (note 26), pp.26, 28. Bacon's interest in *Physique Pictorial* is also noted in Ofield (see note 12), p.64.

47. See Ofield (note 12), pp.124–30 for a closer examination of Bacon's engagement with the queer visual culture around him, including British physique magazines. In Ofield, p.64, he comments also upon *Physique Pictorial* but notes only one copy of it visible in a photograph of Bacon's studio. As he states, it is difficult to prove when exactly Bacon obtained such material.

48. David Sylvester, *The Brutality of Fact: Interviews with Francis Bacon*, London 2009, p.116. Quoted and discussed in Ofield (note 12), p.114, in the context of Bacon's interest in pre and post-war queer visual culture.

49. David Sylvester, *The Brutality of Fact* (see above), pp.114 and 116.

50. Michael Peppiatt, *Francis Bacon: Anatomy of an Enigma*, London 2008, p.178

51. David Sylvester, *The Brutality of Fact* (see note 48), pp.41.

52. Ibid., p.120.

53. Ibid., p.48.

54. David Hockney, *David Hockney: My Early Years,* London 1976, p.41.

55. Christopher Simon Sykes, *David Hockney: The Biography, 1937–1975. A Rake's Progress*, New York 2011, p.73.

56. Hockney, *My Early Years* (see note 54), p.44.

57. David Hockney interview with Christopher Simon Sykes, May 2010 quoted in Sykes, *David Hockney, The Biography* (see note 55), p.71.

TIMELINE

<table>
<tr><td>1533</td><td>Buggery Act – sodomy and bestiality are criminal offences, paired under this act.</td></tr>
<tr><td>1861</td><td>Offences Against the Person Act – abolishes the death penalty for sodomy.</td></tr>
<tr><td>1870</td><td>Frederick Park and Ernest Boulton, who perform as Fanny and Stella, are arrested while in drag outside the Strand Theatre for attempted sodomy.</td></tr>
<tr><td>1873</td><td>Simeon Solomon is charged with attempting to commit sodomy after being arrested in a male public toilet in London. Walter Pater's Studies in the History of the Renaissance is published.</td></tr>
<tr><td>1885</td><td>Labouchere Amendment, Section 11 of the Criminal Law Amendment Act – criminalises 'gross indecency' in 'public or private', including any consensual sexual activity between males aside from sodomy.</td></tr>
<tr><td>1889</td><td>Cleveland Street Scandal – police discover a homosexual male brothel in Fitzrovia, London, frequented by high-profile men and aristocrats.</td></tr>
<tr><td>1895</td><td>Oscar Wilde's trial starts on 3 April. On 25 May, he is convicted of gross indecency and sentenced to two years with hard labour in solitary confinement.</td></tr>
<tr><td>1897</td><td>Havelock Ellis's Sexual Inversion, co-authored by John Addington Symonds, is published. It is banned as an obscene publication the following year.</td></tr>
<tr><td>1912</td><td>Criminal Law Amendment Act – makes 'persistently importuning for an immoral purpose' an offence, impacting upon male prostitution, 'cruising' for sex or simply meeting in public spaces.</td></tr>
</table>

<table>
<tr><td>1918</td><td>The article 'The Cult of the Clitoris' by MP Noel Pemberton-Billing is published. This leads to the 'Black Book' libel trial concerning accusations of obscenity and lesbianism directed at the actress Maud Allan.</td></tr>
<tr><td>1921</td><td>Criminal Law Amendment Act – gross indecency is set to be extended to acts between women. It is, however, never passed into law, opposed by the House of Lords on the grounds that most women are not aware of lesbianism.</td></tr>
<tr><td>1928</td><td>Radclyffe Hall's The Well of Loneliness, prefaced by Havelock Ellis, is published. It is up for trial for obscenity by the end of the year, ironically raising public awareness of lesbianism that prosecutors sought to repress. Virginia Woolf's Orlando is published in the same year without controversy.</td></tr>
<tr><td>1951</td><td>Roberta Cowell (1918–2011) becomes the first trans woman in the UK to have gender reassignment surgery and a change of birth certificate.</td></tr>
<tr><td>1952</td><td>Alan Turing (1912–1954) is convicted of gross indecency and is subject to chemical castration as a result.</td></tr>
<tr><td>1953</td><td>John Gielgud is arrested on 20 October and fined for soliciting men in a public urinal in Chelsea.</td></tr>
<tr><td>1954</td><td>Michael Pitt-Rivers, Lord Montagu and Peter Wildeblood are charged and convicted for indecency relating to homosexual acts.</td></tr>
<tr><td>1954</td><td>Departmental Committee on Homosexual Offences and Prostitution, known as the Wolfenden Committee, is set up on 24 August.</td></tr>
</table>

1956	Sexual Offences Act – still condemns male homosexuality, and also recognises sexual assault between women.
1957	The Wolfenden Report is published on 4 December, recommending partial decriminalisation of homosexuality for consensual adult males in private.
1958	The Homosexual Law Reform Society is formed on 12 May, and campaigns for the recommendations of the Wolfenden Committee to be implemented.
1962	The first full and correct version of Wilde's 'De Profundis' is published, written while he was in prison in 1897.
1967	Sexual Offences Act – includes the partial decriminalisation of homosexuality in private and sets the age of consent at twenty-one in England and Wales.
1969	Stonewall Riots in the USA. Prompted by a police raid on the Stonewall Inn, New York, an openly gay establishment, this is a key event for the gay liberation movement in America.
1972	The first official UK Gay Pride rally is held in London.
1980	Homosexuality in Scotland between two consensual males over the age of twenty-one in private is decriminalised.
1981	The first recorded cases of AIDS in the UK and USA.
1982	Northern Ireland Homosexual Offences Order – decriminalises sex in private between two men over the age of twenty-one.
1983	Ban on homosexual men donating blood in the UK.
1985	Rock Hudson (1925–1985) is the first high-profile figure to die of an AIDS-related illness.
1988	Margaret Thatcher introduces Section 28 in the Local Government Act, prohibiting the promotion of homosexuality by schools and local authorities.
1992	Same-sex desire is no longer classed as a mental illness by the World Health Organization.
1994	The age of consent is lowered to eighteen for same-sex relations between men.
1998	The Bolton 7 are convicted for gross indecency for group sex and sex with a man six months under the legal age of consent (eighteen). Their claim that it breaches their right to a private life under Section 8 of the European Court of Human Rights is won and they are compensated by the UK government.
1999	The Admiral Duncan gay pub in Soho, London, is bombed, killing three people and injuring at least seventy.
2000	Sexual Offences Amendment Act – decriminalises group sex and lowers the age of consent to sixteen, the same as for heterosexual relationships.
2000	Ban lifted by the UK government on lesbian, gay and bisexual people serving in the armed forces.
2002	Same-sex couples are given equal rights to adoption.
2003	Section 28 is lifted in England, Scotland and Wales, which prohibited the promotion of homosexuality by local authorities and schools.
2003	Introduction of Employment Equality (Sexual Orientation) regulations.
2004	Civil Partnership Act – grants same-sex couples the same legal rights as married straight couples.
2004	Gender Recognition Act – allows trans people to have a new birth certificate, with the options of gender as male or female.
2011	Removal of the lifetime ban for blood donations from homosexual men – changed to twelve months' prohibition.
2014	Marriage (Same Sex Couples) Act 2013 comes into legal effect.

EXHIBITED WORKS

Page references to the works illustrated are given at the end of the entries.

1. Coded Desires

Walter Crane 1845–1915
The Renaissance of Venus 1877
Tempera on canvas 138.4 x 184.1
Tate. Presented by Mrs Watts
by the wish of the late George
Frederic Watts 1913
Illustrated p.43

Evelyn De Morgan 1855–1919
Aurora Triumphans 1877–8
Oil on canvas 114.5 x 187.8
Lent by the Russell-Cotes Art
Gallery & Museum, Bournemouth
Illustrated p.37

Wilhelm von Gloeden 1856–1931
Head of a Sicilian Boy 1890s
Photograph, gelatin silver print on
paper 21.1 x 16.8
Victoria and Albert Museum,
London
Illustrated p.29

Wilhelm von Gloeden
Three Nude Youths c.1900
Photograph, gelatin silver print on
paper 33 x 26
Victoria and Albert Museum,
London
Illustrated p.42

Frederic Leighton 1830–96
Daedalus and Icarus c.1869
Oil on canvas 138.2 x 106.5
Private collection
Illustrated p.38

Frederic Leighton 1830–96
The Sluggard 1885
Bronze 191.1 x 90.2 x 59.7
Tate. Presented by Sir Henry
Tate 1894
Illustrated p.39

Sidney Harold Meteyard
1868–1947
Hope Comforting Love in Bondage
exh.1901
Oil on canvas 104.2 x 109.2
Birmingham Museums and Art
Gallery, Birmingham
Illustrated p.36

William Blake Richmond
1842–1921
The Bowlers 1870
Oil on canvas 64.1 x 269.9
The Master, Fellows, and Scholars
of Downing College in the
University of Cambridge
Illustrated pp.140–1

Simeon Solomon 1840–1905
Corruptio Optimi Pessima: Medusa
c.1890s
Chalk on paper 40 x 31.5
Neil Bartlett and James Gardiner
Collection
Illustrated p.31

Simeon Solomon
Babylon hath been a golden cup
1859
Ink and graphite on paper
26.6 x 28.3
Birmingham Museums and Art
Gallery, Birmingham
Illustrated p.31

Simeon Solomon
Self-Portrait 1859
Graphite on paper 26.7 x 20.9
Tate. Presented anonymously 1919
Illustrated p.31

Simeon Solomon
*Sappho and Erinna in a Garden at
Mytilene* 1864
Watercolour on paper 33 x 38.1
Tate. Purchased 1980
Illustrated p.26

Simeon Solomon
The Bride, Bridegroom and Sad Love
1865
Ink on paper 25 x 19.4
Victoria and Albert Museum, London
Illustrated p.24

Simeon Solomon
Bacchus 1867
Oil on paper on canvas 50.3 x 37.5
Birmingham Museums and Art
Gallery, Birmingham
Illustrated p.33

Simeon Solomon
The Moon and Sleep 1894
Oil on canvas 51.4 x 76.2
Tate. Presented by Miss Margery
Abrahams in memory of Dr
Bertram L. Abrahams and Jane
Abrahams 1973
Illustrated p.34

Henry Scott Tuke 1858–1929
July Sun 1913
Oil on canvas 53.4 x 43.5
Lent by the Royal Academy of Arts,
London

Henry Scott Tuke
A Bathing Group 1914
Oil on canvas 90.2 x 59.7
Lent by the Royal Academy of Arts,
London
Illustrated pp.21, 47

Henry Scott Tuke
The Critics 1927
Oil on board 41.2 x 51.4
Courtesy of Leamington Spa Art
Gallery and Museum (Warwick
District Council)
Illustrated p.46

Unknown photographer
John Addington Symonds c.1850s
Photograph, collodion positive on
paper 7.4 x 5.5
Victoria and Albert Museum,
London

Walter Pater 1839–94
Renaissance
Book, fourth edition printed 1893
Private collection

Hamo Thornycroft 1850–1925
The Mower 1888–90
Bronze 58.5 x 33 x 18.5
Tate. Presented by Arthur Grogan
1985
Illustrated p.44

Charles Robert Ashbee 1863–1942
Twin-handled Cup 1893
Metal 8.2 x 16.1
Private collection
Illustrated p.45

2. Pubic Indecency

Beresford Egan
The Sink of Solitude 1928
Book
Lent by Lorna Booth

Oscar Wilde's prison door
Wood and metal
Kindly loaned by the National
Justice Museum, Nottingham
Illustrated p.61

*Programme for 'The Importance of
Being Earnest'* 1895
Victoria and Albert Museum,
London

*Visiting card and envelope for the
Marquis of Queensbury; Exhibit 'A'
in Oscar Wilde's Trial* 18 February
1895
Thin board, printed on both sides
in black ink and complex blue/
black ink handwriting on recto;
paper envelope with black border
and monogram on verso
3.7 x 7.7; 13.5 x 16.3
On loan from The National
Archives, UK CRIM 1/41/6 f.1,
CRIM 1/41 f.2

Aubrey Beardsley 1872–98
The Dancer's Reward from 'Salome'
c.1890s
Photo process print on paper
57.1 x 41.9 (framed)
Victoria and Albert Museum,
London

Aubrey Beardsley
Enter Herodias from 'Salome'
c.1890s
Photo process print on paper
28.6 x 22.4 (sheet)
Victoria and Albert Museum,
London
Illustrated p.58

Aubrey Beardsley
The Peacock Skirt c.1890s
Photo process print on paper
57.1 x 41.9 (framed)
Victoria and Albert Museum,
London

Aubrey Beardsley
The Examination of the Herald 1896
Ink on paper 27.8 x 19.4 (sheet)
Victoria and Albert Museum,
London. Purchased with the
assistance of The Art Fund

Aubrey Beardsley
The Lacedaemonian Ambassadors
1896
Ink on paper 27.8 x 19.4 (sheet)
Victoria and Albert Museum,
London. Purchased with the
assistance of The Art Fund
Illustrated p.59

Aubrey Beardsley
*Lysistrata Haranguing the Athenian
Women* 1896
Ink on paper 27.4 x 19.4 (sheet)
Victoria and Albert Museum,
London. Purchased with the
assistance of The Art Fund
Illustrated p.59

Robert Goodloe Harper
Pennington fl.1854–1920
Oscar Wilde c.1884
Oil on canvas 177.8 x 91.4
William Andrews Clark Memorial
Library, Los Angeles
Illustrated p.61

Cecil Beaton 1904–80
Stephen Tennant as Prince Charming
1927
Photograph, bromide print on

paper 19 x 26.4
National Portrait Gallery, London
Illustrated p.66

Cecil Beaton
Sylvia Townsend Warner 1930
Photograph, bromide print on
paper 30.2 x 23.5
National Portrait Gallery, London
Illustrated p.65

Cecil Beaton
Madge Garland 1927
Photograph, bromide print on
paper 20.3 x 20.3
National Portrait Gallery, London
Illustrated p.67

Roger Fry 1866–1934
Edward Carpenter 1894
Oil on canvas 74.9 x 43.8
National Portrait Gallery, London
Illustrated p.55

Henry Bishop 1868–1939
Henry Havelock Ellis 1890s
Oil on canvas 58.3 x 61
National Portrait Gallery, London
Illustrated p.54

Jacques-Emile Blanche 1861–1942
Aubrey Vincent Beardsley 1895
Oil on canvas 92.6 x 73.7
National Portrait Gallery, London
Illustrated p.57

Charles Buchel 1872–1950
Radclyffe Hall 1918
Oil on canvas 91.4 x 71.1
National Portrait Gallery, London
Illustrated p.48

Cecil Beaton
Cecil Beaton and his Friends
October 1927
Photograph, bromide print on
paper 14.2 x 24
National Portrait Gallery, London

Charles Ricketts 1866–1931
Pendant 1899
Gold, enamel, cabochon pearl,
amethyst
The Fitzwilliam Museum,
Cambridge

Charles Ricketts
Psyche's reception by the Gods 1901
Paper leaf 22.3 x 38.3
The Fitzwilliam Museum,
Cambridge

Charles Ricketts
The Sabbatai Ring 1904
Gold, cabochon star sapphire,
cabochon emerald, ambergris
The Fitzwilliam Museum,
Cambridge

Charles Ricketts
The Blue Bird Brooch 1899
Gold, enamel, garnet, cabochon
corals 4.7 x 4.8
The Fitzwilliam Museum,
Cambridge

Charles Ricketts
*Pendant: Pegasus Drinking from the
Fountain of Hippocrene for Miss
Edith Emma Cooper* 1901
Gold, enamel, pearls, graphite,
watercolour, gold on card
10.1 x 5.1 x 3.4
The Fitzwilliam Museum,
Cambridge
Illustrated p.63

Edmund Dulac 1882–1953
*Charles Ricketts and Charles
Shannon as Medieval Saints* 1920
Tempera on fine linen over board
38.7 x 30.5
The Fitzwilliam Museum,
Cambridge

Aubrey Beardsley
Cover Design for the 'Yellow Book'
1894
Ink on paper 26 x 21.6
Tate. Bequeathed by John Lane
1926

Gillman and Co.
*Oscar Wilde and Lord Alfred Bruce
Douglas* 1893
Photograph, gelatin silver print
13.6 x 9.7
National Portrait Gallery, London
Illustrated p.61

Unknown photographer,
published by J Beagles & Co.
*Maud Allan as Salome in 'The
Vision of Salome'* c.1908
Bromide postcard print
13.9 x 8.9
National Portrait Gallery, London.
Bequeathed by Patrick O'Connor,
2010
Illustrated p.51

Unknown photographer,
published by The Philco

Publishing Co.
Malcolm Scott in his 'Salome' dress
c.1905
Bromide postcard print 14 x 8.9
National Portrait Gallery, London.
Bequeathed by Patrick O'Connor,
2010
Illustrated p.89

3. Theatrical Types
Angus McBean 1904–90
Danny La Rue 1968
Photograph, bromide print on
paper 40 x 29.3
National Portrait Gallery, London
Illustrated p.93

Angus McBean
Beatrix Lehmann 1937
Photograph, bromide print on
paper 29.2 x 23.1
National Portrait Gallery, London
Illustrated p.74

Angus McBean 1904–90
Berto Pasuka 1946
Photograph, bromide print on
paper
37.4 x 29.9
National Portrait Gallery, London
Illustrated p.76

Angus McBean 1904–1990
*Binkie Beaumont, Angela Baddeley
and (George) Emlyn Williams* 1947
Photograph, bromide print on
paper 38 x 29.7
National Portrait Gallery, London
Illustrated p.77

Glyn Warren Philpot 1884–1937
Glen Byam Shaw as 'Laertes'
1934–5
Oil on canvas
75 x 62.2 (unconfirmed)
Kindly lent by the sitter's
grandson, Charles Hart
Illustrated p.78

Angus McBean 1904–90
Sir Robert Murray Helpmann 1950
Photograph, bromide print on
paper 50.8 x 40.3
National Portrait Gallery, London
Illustrated p.76

Francis Goodman 1913–89
Oliver Messel 1945
Photographic print from negative
56.6 x 56.6
National Portrait Gallery, London.

Bequeathed by Patrick O'Connor
2010
Illustrated p.81

Paul Tanqueray 1905–91
Douglas Byng 1934
Photograph, bromide print on
paper 23.9 x 19.3
National Portrait Gallery, London

Pink wig worn by Jimmy Slater
c.1930s
Pink raffia, cloth and netting
Sarah Moss
Illustrated p.90

*Diamante Earrings worn by Jimmy
Slater* c.1915
Sarah Moss

William Berry 'Willy' Clarkson
1861–1934
Tiara worn by Jimmy Slater c.1925
Sarah Moss

Poster for 'Soldiers in Skirts' 1945
Paper 31.8 x 25.5
Sarah Moss

Oliver Messel 1904–78
*Design for the King in Sleeping
Beauty* c.1946
Charcoal, graphite, gouache and
watercolour on paper 56.5 x 37.9
Victoria and Albert Museum,
London. Acquired with the
support of the Heritage Lottery
Fund, The Art Fund and the
Friends of the V&A.
Illustrated p.82

Oliver Messel
*Design for the Queen in Sleeping
Beauty* c.1946
Charcoal, ink, graphite, gouache
and watercolour on paper
43.2 x 35.3
Victoria and Albert Museum,
London. Acquired with the
support of the Heritage Lottery
Fund, The Art Fund and the
Friends of the V&A

Oliver Messel
Design for Suddenly Last Summer
1959
Charcoal, graphite, ink and wash
on paper 25.1 x 37.9
Victoria and Albert Museum,
London. Acquired with the
support of the Heritage Lottery

Fund, The Art Fund and the
Friends of the V&A
Illustrated p.83

Leslie Hurry 1909–78
Set design for 'Cat on a Hot Tin Roof'
1958
Ink, gouache and crayon on paper
41.9 x 57.1
Victoria and Albert Museum,
London. Purchased with the
assistance of the Linbury Trust

Printed by Echo Press
Poster advertising *'A Patriot for Me'*
1965 50.8 x 31.9
Victoria and Albert Museum,
London. Given by Mrs R. Russell

William Hargreaves 1880–1941
(composer); published by the
Lawrence Wright Music Company
Burlington Bertie 1915
Lithograph 28 x 21.5 (closed)
Victoria and Albert Museum,
London. Given by Mrs R. Russell

Unknown photographer, published
by Rotary Photographic Co. Ltd
Vesta Tilley 1900s
Bromide postcard print 13.8 x 8.7
National Portrait Gallery, London.
Bequeathed by Patrick O'Connor,
2010
Illustrated p.87

Published by Frank Dobson of
Liverpool; J. Beagles & Co.
*Frederick Jester Barnes in 'The Black
Sheep of the Family'* 1907
Bromide postcard print 13.8 x 8.9
National Portrait Gallery, London

Unknown photographer,
published by Star Music
Publishing Company Ltd
Frederick Jester Barnes 1914
Halftone reproduction 36 x 26
National Portrait Gallery, London

Unknown photographer,
published by Hana London
*George Robey in Character with
Sunbeam make-up* c.1910s
Photographic postcard 13.5 x 8.8
Wellcome Library, London

Unknown photographer
Julian Eltinge c.1907
Coloured photographic postcard
13.6 x 8.5

Wellcome Library, London

Unknown photographer
Terry Durham c.1960s
Photograph, silver gelatin print on
paper 13.4 x 8.3
Wellcome Library, London

Unknown photographer
Chris Shaw c.1960s
Photograph, silver gelatin print on
paper 14 x 9
Wellcome Library, London
Illustrated p.92

Unknown photographer
Tommie Rose 1948
Photograph, silver gelatin print on
paper 8.6 x 7.2
Wellcome Library, London
Illustrated p.91

Unknown photographer
Ronnie Stewart in 'Soldiers in Skirts'
1947
Photograph, silver gelatin print on
paper 13.8 x 8.8
Wellcome Library, London
Illustrated p.91

Unknown photographer
Jimmy Slater with Fan c.1925
Photograph, silver gelatin print on
paper 18.6 x 14
Sarah Moss
Illustrated p.68

Unknown photographer
Jimmy Slater with a Kitten 1923
Photograph, silver gelatin print on
paper 15 x 18.6
Sarah Moss
Illustrated p.90

Cynthia Tingey (dates unknown)
Costume design for Danny La Rue
1960
Crayon and gouache on paper
24.3 x 15.8
Victoria and Albert Museum,
London. Given by Cynthia Tingey

Unknown photographer
Lulu c.1870
Sepia photograph on paper
8.7 x 6.1
Victoria and Albert Museum,
London. Bequeathed by Guy Little
Illustrated p.88

Unknown photographer
Dan Leno in 'Mother Goose' Act 1
Postcard 13.6 x 8.6
Victoria and Albert Museum,
London

Unknown photographer
Dan Leno in 'Mother Goose' Act 2
Postcard 14 x 9.6
Victoria and Albert Museum,
London

Unknown photographer
*Kate Vaughan and Minnie Mario
in 'Cinderella'* c.1883
Photograph, print on paper
14.4 x 9.6
Victoria and Albert Museum,
London

Unknown photographer,
published by The Philco
Publishing Co.
Hetty King (Winifred Emms) 1910s
Bromide postcard print 13.7 x 8.7
National Portrait Gallery, London
Illustrated p.23

Programme for *The Blackmailers*
1894
Victoria and Albert Museum,
London
Illustrated p.71

Noel Coward's dressing gown
Silk with applique and machine
embroidery in white cotton
141.8 x 53
Victoria and Albert Museum,
London
Illustrated p.72

Oliver Messel
Mask c.1927
Paper, paint, glaze, glue and
synthetic hair 24 x 17 x 31
Victoria and Albert Museum,
London. Acquired with the
support of the Heritge Lottery
Fund, The Art Fund and the
Friends of the V&A
Illustrated p.82

Una Troubridge 1887–1963
Vaslav Nijinsky 1912
Plaster 48 x 23
Victoria and Albert Museum,
London. Given by Richard Buckle.
Illustrated p.80

Adolphe Beau fl.1864-98
Charlotte Saunders as 'Hercules'
undated
?Sepia photograph on paper
8.3 x 5.5
Victoria and Albert Museum,
London

Frederick Spalding
Stella (left) and Fanny (right)
c.1870
Essex Record Office

4. Bloomsbury and Beyond
Ethel Sands 1873-1962
The Chintz Couch c.1910-1
Oil on board 46.5 x 38.5
Tate. Presented by the
Contemporary Art Society 1924
Illustrated p.22

Ethel Walker 1861-1951
*Decoration: The Excursion of
Nausicaa* 1920
Oil on canvas 183.5 x 367
Tate. Purchased 1924
Illustrated pp.108-9

Duncan Grant 1885-1978
Bathing 1911
Oil on canvas 228.6 x 306.1
Tate. Purchased 1931
Illustrated p.99

Clare Atwood 1866-1962
John Gielgud's Room 1933
Oil on canvas 63.5 x 76.4
Tate. Presented by Mrs E.L.
Shute 1937
Illustrated p.94

Ethel Sands
Tea with Sickert c.1911-12
Oil on canvas 61 x 51
Tate. Bequeathed by Colonel
Christopher Sands 2000,
accessioned 2001
Illustrated p.105

Anna Hope Hudson 1869-1957
Chateau d'Auppegard after 1927
Oil on board 46.2 x 38.2
Tate. Bequeathed by Colonel
Christopher Sands 2000,
accessioned 2001
Illustrated p.107

Glyn Warren Philpot 1884-1937
Repose on the Flight into Egypt 1922
Oil on canvas 74.9 x 116.1 x 2.5
Tate. Purchased 2004

Edward Wolfe 1897-1982
Portrait of Patrick Nelson 1930s
Oil on canvas 94 x 73.1
Private collection
Illustrated p.103

Gluck 1895-1978
Lilac and Guelder Rose before
1932-7
Oil on canvas 109.2 x 109.3
Manchester City Galleries,
Manchester
Illustrated p.117

Dora Carrington 1893-1932
Lytton Strachey 1916
Oil on panel 50.8 x 60.9
National Portrait Gallery, London
Illustrated p.106

Gluck
Self-portrait 1942
Oil on canvas 30.6 x 25.4
National Portrait Gallery, London
Illustrated front cover, pp.18, 116

Duncan Grant
PC Harry Daley 1930
Oil on canvas 76 x 51
Guildhall Art Gallery,
City of London

Glyn Warren Philpot
Man with a Gun 1933
Oil on canvas 114.5 x 92
The Ashmolean Museum, Oxford.
Bequeathed by Jeffrey Daniels,
1986
Illustrated p.101

Glyn Warren Philpot
Henry Thomas 1934-5
Oil on canvas 52.5 x 36.4
Pallant House Gallery, Chichester
Illustrated p.103

Duncan Grant
Bathers by the Pond 1920-1
Oil on canvas 49 x 90
Pallant House Gallery, Chichester
Illustrated p.98

Duncan Grant
Paul Roche Reclining c.1946
Oil on canvas 57.2 x 78
The Charleston Trust, Lewes
Illustrated p.100

Duncan Grant
Drawing, group figure study c.1930
Ink on paper 22.9 x 17.7

The Charleston Trust, Lewes

Duncan Grant
Erotic embrace c.1950
Oil on paper 44.7 x 66.7
The Charleston Trust, Lewes
Illustrated p.96

Duncan Grant
Two men in an erotic embrace
c.1950s
Ink, graphite and watercolour on
paper 24.6 x 26.5
The Charleston Trust, Lewes

Duncan Grant
Erotic embrace c.1950s
Graphite and paint on paper
21 x 16.5
The Charleston Trust, Lewes

5. Defying Convention
Alvaro Guevara 1894-1951
Dame Edith Sitwell 1916
Oil on canvas 196.2 x 136 x 8
Tate. Presented by Lord Duveen,
Walter Taylor and George
Eumorfopoulos through the Art
Fund 1920
Illustrated p.120

John Singer Sargent 1856-1925
Vernon Lee 1881
Oil on canvas 53.7 x 43.2
Tate. Bequeathed by Miss Vernon
Lee through Miss Cooper Willis
1935
Illustrated p.119

Claude Cahun 1894-1954
Untitled 1936
Photograph, gelatin silver print on
paper 23.8 x 18
Tate. Purchased 2007
Illustrated p.131

Claude Cahu
Untitled 1936
Photograph, gelatin silver print on
paper 23.7 x 17.8
Tate. Purchased 2007
Illustrated p.131

Claude Cahun
I Extend My Arms 1931 or 1932
Je tends les bras
Photograph, gelatin silver print
on paper 21 x 15.6
Tate. Purchased 2007
Illustrated p.131

Marlow Moss 1889-1958
*Composition in Yellow, Black and
White* 1949
Oil and wood on canvas
50.8 x 35.6 x 0.6
Tate. Presented by Miss Erica
Brausen 1969
Illustrated p.129

Marlow Moss
*Balanced Forms in Gunmetal on
Cornish Granite* 1956-7
Metal and granite 22 x 33 x 28.5
Tate. Presented by Miss Erica
Brausen 1969

William Strang 1859-1921
Lady with a Red Hat 1918
Oil on canvas
129 x 103.4
Lent by Glasgow Life (Glasgow
Museums) on behalf of Glasgow
City Council. Purchased 1919
Illustrated p.111

Dorothy Johnstone 1892-1980
Rest Time in the Life Class 1923
Oil on canvas 121.5 x 106.2
City Art Centre, City of Edinburgh
Museums and Galleries
Illustrated pp.2, 17

Dora Carrington 1893-1932
Female Figure Lying on her Back
1912
Oil on canvas 50.8 x 76.2
University College London Art
Museum 5204
Illustrated pp.124-5

Cecile Walton 1891-1956
Romance 1920
Oil on canvas 100.6 x 150.9
Scottish National Portrait Gallery,
Edinburgh
Illustrated p.128

Dame Laura Knight 1877-1970
Self-portrait 1913
Oil on canvas 152.4 x 127.6
National Portrait Gallery, London
Illustrated p.122

Man Ray 1890-1976
Virginia Woolf 1934
Photograph, gelatin silver print
on paper 24.6 x 19.6
National Portrait Gallery, London
Illustrated p.113

Claude Cahun
*Aveux non avenus Claude Cahun.
Illustré d'hélio-gravures compsées
par Moore d'après les projets de
la'auteur. Préface de Pierre Mac
Orlan*
By permission of the British
Library

Virginia Woolf 1882–1941
Orlando: A Biography 1928
Book
Lent by Lorna Booth

6. Arcadia and Soho
Edward Burra 1905–76
Soldiers at Rye 1941
Gouache, watercolour and ink on
paper 124.8 x 228
Tate. Presented by Studio 1942
Illustrated pp.140–1

Keith Vaughan 1912–77
Bather: August 4th 1961 1961
Oil on canvas 102.2 x 91.4
Tate. Purchased 1962
Illustrated p.145

John Craxton 1922–2009
Pastoral for P.W. 1948
Oil on canvas 204.5 x 262.6
Tate. Purchased 1984
Illustrated p.142

Robert Medley 1905–94
Summer Eclogue No. 1: Cyclists 1950
Oil on canvas 129.5 x 160
Tate. Purchased 1992
Illustrated p.143

Edward Burra
Izzy Orts 1937
Watercolour and graphite on
paper 73.6 x 104.5
Scottish National Gallery of
Modern Art, Edinburgh
Illustrated p.139

Keith Vaughan
Three Figures 1960–1
Oil on board 43 x 40.5
Courtesy of Abbot Hall Art
Gallery, Lakeland Arts Trust,
Kendal, Cumbria
Illustrated p.145

Keith Vaughan
Kouros 1960
Oil on canvas 91.4 x 71.1
Private collection
Illustrated p.133, 145

Edward Burra
*Costume design for Billie Chappell in
Rio Grande* 1928–9
Watercolour on paper 62 x 50
James L. Gordon Collection

John Minton 1917–57
Cornish Boy at a Window 1948
Oil on canvas 75.6 x 51
Government Art Collection,
London

Robert Colquhoun 1914–62
Actors on a Stage 1945
Oil on canvas 77.5 x 44.9
Private collection
Illustrated p.136

Christopher Wood 1901–30
Nude Boy in a Bedroom 1930
Oil on hardboard on plywood
53.8 x 65
Scottish National Gallery of
Modern Art, Edinburgh
Illustrated p.138

John Craxton
Head of a Greek Sailor 1946
Oil on board 43.6 x 32.5
On loan from the London Borough
of Camden Council

Edward Burra
Design for 'Rio Grande'
1928–9 69.5 x 51.5 x 2.5
James L. Gordon Collection

Edward Burra
Design for 'Rio Grande' 1928–9
69.5 x 57.5
James L. Gordon Collection

Keith Vaughan
Drawing of two men kissing
1958–73
Graphite on paper 28 x 20.5
Tate Gallery Archive, The Estate of
Keith Vaughan, TGA 9013/1/114

Keith Vaughan
*Drawing of two nude males, one
bent over and nailed to the floor, and
a whip* 1958–73
Ink on paper 28 x 20
Tate Archive, The Estate of Keith
Vaughan, TGA 9013/1/118

Keith Vaughan
*Drawing of a group of five nude
males* 1958–73
Graphite on paper 28 x 20.5

Tate Gallery Archive, The Estate of
Keith Vaughan, TGA 9013/1/122

Keith Vaughan
*Drawing of two male nudes, one
seated, one with mouth open* 1963
Ink on paper 28 x 21.5
Tate Gallery Archive, The Estate of
Keith Vaughan, TGA9013/1/110

Keith Vaughan
*Drawing of a nude male
masturbating* 1963
Ink on paper 28 x 20.5
Tate Gallery Archive, The Estate of
Keith Vaughan, TGA9013/1/111

7. Public/Private Lives
John Minton
*Horseguards in their Dressing Rooms
at Whitehall* 1953
Lithograph on paper 42.3 x 30
Tate. Purchased 1990
Illustrated p.10

Kenneth Leith Halliwell 1926–67
Untitled 1967
Printed papers on hardboard
69.8 x 59.1
Tate. Purchased 2016

Lewis Morley 1925–2013
Joe Orton 1965
Photograph, bromide print on
paper 30.4 x 25.1
National Portrait Gallery, London
Illustrated p.154

Angus McBean 1904–90
Quentin Crisp 1941
Photograph, bromide print on
paper 43.4 x 34.4
National Portrait Gallery, London
Illustrated p.153

Patrick Procktor 1936–2003
Joe Orton 1967
Ink on paper 23.4 x 34.4
National Portrait Gallery, London
Illustrated p.155

Unknown photographer, for
Keystone Press Agency Ltd
*Michael Fox-Pitt-Rivers; Edward
Douglas-Scott-Montagu, 3rd Baron
Montagu of Beaulieu; Peter
Wildeblood* 24 March 1954
Photograph, bromide on paper
14 x 19.4
National Portrait Gallery, London
Illustrated p.146

Patrick Procktor 1936–2003
Derek Talking to me about Orpheus
1967
Watercolour on paper 29.2 x 22.8
Private collection

Box of buttons
Jon Lys Turner
Illustrated p.12

Letter from Prison
12 November 1944
Jon Lys Turner

Valentine Day's Card
Jon Lys Turner

Stephen Tennant 1906–86
*Lascar, a story of the Maritime
Boulevard* undated
Ink, watercolour and collage on
paper 37.5 x 27.5
Private collection

John Deakin 1912–72
Paul Danquah c.1950s
Photograph, black and white
negative 30.5 x 30.5
John Deakin Archive

John Deakin
Muriel Belcher in the Colony Room
c.1950s
Photographic print on paper
John Deakin Archive

John Deakin
*The Two Roberts Asleep - Colquhoun
and MacBryde* c.1953
Photograph, silver gelatin print on
paper 28 x 14
John Deakin Archive
Illustrated p.151

John Deakin
Francis Bacon 1958
Photograph, black and white
negative 30.5 x 30.5
John Deakin Archive

John Deakin 1912–72
Colin c.1950s
Photograph, black and white
negative 30.5 x 30.5
John Deakin Archive

John Deakin
Celia 'Sammy' Short c.1945
Photograph, silver gelatin print on
paper 30.5 x 25.4
John Deakin Archive

Unknown photographer
Photograph Album 23 x 18 (closed)
Neil Bartlett and James Gardiner
Collection

*Letter from Ralph to Montague
Glover*
Neil Bartlett and James Gardiner
Collection

Richard Chopping 1917-2008
The Fly 1965
Book 20.3 x 14
Jon Lys Turner

John Kingsley 'Joe' Orton 1933-67
Kenneth Leith Halliwell, 1926-67
The World of Paul Slickey
Paper 35 x 20.5
Islington Local History Centre

John Kingsley 'Joe' Orton
Kenneth Leith Halliwell
*The Secret of Chimneys by Agatha
Christie*
Paper 36.5 x 19
Islington Local History Centre
Illustrated p.157

John Kingsley 'Joe' Orton
Kenneth Leith Halliwell
Steel Cocoon by Bentz Plagemann
Paper 39 x 20.5
Islington Local History Centre

John Kingsley 'Joe' Orton
Kenneth Leith Halliwell
The Lunts by George Freedley
Paper 46 x 22.5
Islington Local History Centre
Illustrated p.157

John Kingsley 'Joe' Orton
Kenneth Leith Halliwell
*Queen's Favourite by Phyllis
Hambledon*
Paper 44.5 x 19
Islington Local History Centre
Illustrated p.157

John Kingsley 'Joe' Orton
Kenneth Leith Halliwell
*The Collected Plays of Emlyn
Williams, Vol.1*
Paper 47 x 20
Islington Local History Centre

Valentine Penrose 1898-1978
Dons des feminines 1951
Book
44 x 34 x 16 (open)

Victoria and Albert Museum,
London

*Report of the Committee on
Homosexual Offences and
Prostitution [Wolfenden Report]*
1957
Parliamentary Archives, London

Peter Wildeblood
Against the Law 1955
Book
Lent by Lorna Booth

8. Hockney/Bacon
David Hockney b.1937
Cleanliness is Next to Godliness
1964
Screenprint on paper 91.4 x 58.1
Tate. Presented by Rose and Chris
Prater through the Institute of
Contemporary Prints 1975
Illustrated p.162

Francis Bacon 1909-92
Seated Figure 1961
Oil on canvas 165.1 x 142.2
Tate. Presented by J. Sainsbury Ltd
1961
Illustrated p.165

Francis Bacon
Two Figures in a Landscape 1956
Oil on canvas 150 x 107.5
Birmingham Museums and Art
Gallery, Birmingham

David Hockney
Going to be a Queen for Tonight
1960
Oil on board 120 x 85
Royal College of Art, London
Illustrated p.166

David Hockney
Bertha alias Bernie 1961
Oil on board 118.5 x 89.2
Royal College of Art, London
Illustrated p.169

Keith Vaughan
Wrestlers 1965
Watercolour and ink on paper
47 x 39
York Museums Trust (York Art
Gallery). Gifted through the
Contemporary Art Society, as a
bequest from Dr Ronald Lande, in
memory of his life partner Walter
Urech, 2012

Eadweard Muybridge 1830-1904
Two Wrestlers c.1887
Photograph, collotype on paper
47.6 x 60.6
Wellcome Library, London
Illustrated p.161

David Hockney
Life Painting for a Diploma 1962
Oil on canvas with charcoal on
paper collage 180 x 180
Yageo Foundation Collection,
Taiwan
Illustrated p.162

Christopher Wood
The Wrestlers c.1920-30
Graphite on paper 43.2 x 27.3
Private collection
Illustrated p.21

Unknown photographer,
published by Rotary
Eugen Sandow, A Strongman 1909
Photographic postcard 13.7 x 8.8
Wellcome Library, London

Unknown photographer,
published by Rotary
*Ferdinand Gruhn and George
Hackenschmidt* c.1900s
Process print 8.6 x 13.8
Wellcome Library, London

Eadweard Muybridge
Wrestlers Plate 347 c.1887
Photograph, collotype on paper
47.6 x 60.6
Wilson Centre for Photography,
London

Wilhelm von Gloeden
Wrestlers c.1903, printed 1911
Photograph, print on salted paper
18.2 x 24
Wilson Centre for Photography,
London
Illustrated p.160

Health and Strength
24 December 1953
Magazine 21.5 x 13.7
Lent by Rupert Smith

Man's World August 1960
Magazine 18.3 x 12.4
Lent by Rupert Smith

Spencer Churchill undated
Photograph 14.1 x 9
Lent by Rupert Smith

Male Classics undated
Magazine 17 x 13.4
Lent by Rupert Smith

'Vince' Bill Green
Physique photograph c.1950s-
1960s
Photograph 20.6 x 15.4
Lent by Rupert Smith

John Barrington
Man-ifique! Spring 1959
Magazine 21.6 x 13.8
Lent by Rupert Smith

*Album of physique photography,
open at two images of Ron Parrott*
Undated
Photograph 21 x 14.3
Lent by Rupert Smith

Physique photograph c.1950s
Photograph 20.5 x 15.2
Lent by Rupert Smith

9. Other Spaces
David Medalla b.1942
*Cloud Canyons No. 3: An Ensemble
of Bubble Machines (Auto Creative
Sculptures)* 1961, remade 2004
Metal, Perspex, 2 compressors,
2 timers, water and soap
Dimensions variable
Tate. Purchased 2006

SELECTED FURTHER READING

Queer Art History

Matt Cook, *Queer Domesticities: Homosexuality and Home Life in Twentieth-Century London*, Basingstoke 2014

Emmanuel Cooper, *The Sexual Perspective: Homosexuality and Art in the Last 100 Years in the West*, London 1986

Whitney Davis, *Queer Beauty: Sexuality and Aesthetics from Winckelmann to Freud and Beyond*, New York 2010

Laura Doan, *Fashioning Sapphism: The Origins of a Modern English Lesbian Culture*, New York and Chichester 2001

Jack Halberstam, *Female Masculinity*, Durham and London 1998

Peter Horne and Reina Lewis (eds), *Outlooks: Lesbian and Gay Sexualities and Visual Cultures*, London 1996

Dominic Janes, *Picturing the Closet: Male Secrecy and Homosexual Visibility in Britain*, Oxford 2015

Jonathan D. Katz and David C. Ward, *Hide/Seek: Difference and Desire in American Portraiture*, exh. cat., Smithsonian Institution, Washington, DC, and National Portrait Gallery, London 2010

Catherine Lord and Richard Meyer (eds) *Art and Queer Culture*, London 2013

John Potvin, *Bachelors of a Different Sort: Queer Aesthetics, Material Culture and the Modern Interior in Britain*, Manchester 2014

Christopher Reed, *Art and Homosexuality: A History of Ideas*, New York and Oxford 2011

Claude J. Summers, *The Queer Encyclopedia of the Visual Arts*, San Francisco 2004

Queer History

Colin Baker, *Drag: A History of Female Impersonation in the Performing Arts*, New York 1994

Matt Cook, *A Gay History of Britain: Love and Sex Between Men Since the Middle Ages*, Oxford 2007

Laura Doan, *Disturbing Practices: History, Sexuality, and Women's Experience of War*, Chicago and London 2013

Matt Houlbrook, *Queer London*, Chicago 2005

Sharon Marcus, *Between Women: Friendship, Desire, and Marriage in Victorian England*, Princeton 2007

Nikki Sullivan, *A Critical Introduction to Queer Theory*, New York 2003

Martha Vicinus, *Intimate Friends: Women Who Loved Women, 1778–1928*, Chicago 2004

Biography

Neil Bartlett, *Who Was That Man? A Present for Mr Oscar Wilde*, London 1988

Adrian Clark and Jeremy Dronfield, *Queer Saint: The Cultured Life of Peter Watson*, London 2013

Emma Donoghue, *We Are Michael Field*, London 2014

Richard Ellmann, *Oscar Wilde*, London 1988

Philip Hoare, *Serious Pleasures: Life of Stephen Tennant*, London 1992

Neil McKenna, *Fanny and Stella: The Young Men Who Shocked Victorian England*, London 2013

Diana Souhami, *Gluck: Her Biography*, London 2013

Jon Lys Turner, *The Visitor's Book: In Francis Bacon's Shadow: The Lives of Richard Chopping and Denis Wirth-Miller*, London 2016

Hugo Vickers, *Cecil Beaton*, London 2002

Adrian Woodhouse, *Angus McBean: Face-Maker*, London 2006

PICTURE CREDITS

The publishers have made every effort to trace all the relevant copyright holders and apologise for omissions that may have been made. References are to page numbers

Copyright

© The estate of Clare Atwood 94

© The Estate of Francis Bacon. All rights reserved. DACS 2017 158, 164, 165

© The Cecil Beaton Studio Archive at Sotheby's 65–7

© Estate of the Artist, c/o Lefevre Fine Art Ltd, London 139

© Estate of Claude Cahun 131

© Estate of Robert Colquhoun/Bridgeman Images 136

© John Craxton 142

© The John Deakin Archive 151

© The Estate of Edmund Dulac. All rights reserved. DACS 2017 62

© The Estate of Gluck 117

© Estate of Duncan Grant. All rights reserved, DACS 2017 96–8, 100

© David Hockney 162, 166, 169

© The estate of Anna Hope Hudson 105

© Islington Local History Centre/Joe Orton Estate 157

© Keystone Press Agency/Getty Images 146

© Reproduced with permission of The Estate of Dame Laura Knight DBE RA 2017. All Rights Reserved 122

© Man Ray Trust/ADAGP, Paris and DACS, London 2017 113

Angus McBean Photograph.© Harvard Theatre Collection, Harvard University 74, 76 right, 77, 93

© Estate of Angus McBean/National Portrait Gallery back cover, 76 left, 153

© The estate of Robert Medley 143

© The estate of John Minton 10

© Lewis Morley Archive/National Portrait Gallery 154

© The Collection of Male Erotic Art/Basil Clavering 171 top right

© Estate of Marlow Moss. Reserved 129

© National Portrait Gallery front cover, 18, 48, 81, 116, 155

© James O'Connor 103 bottom

© Penguin Random House UK 157

© Alessandro Rossi Lemeni Makedon MD 80

© The estate of Ethel Sands 22 left, 105

© Studio Arax 171 top right

© Copyright by courtesy of Dr D A Sutherland and Lady J E Sutherland 2, 127

© Tate, 2017 99, 108–9, 120, 140–1

© The Estate of Keith Vaughan. All rights reserved, DACS 2017 132, 145

© Victoria and Albert Museum, London 82–3

© Vince of London top left, bottom

© Estate of Cecile Walton estate/Bridgeman Images 128

Photographic Credits

Aberystwyth School of Art Museum and Galleries, George E.J. Powell Bequest 34 bottom

Courtesy of Abbot Hall Art Gallery, Lakeland Arts Trust, Kendal 145

© Ashmolean Museum, University of Oxford 101

Birmingham Museums and Art Gallery/Bridgeman Images 158, 164

Photo © Birmingham Museums Trust 31 bottom, 33, 36

Charleston Trust, Lewes 96, 100

City Art Centre, City of Edinburgh Museums and Galleries 2, 127

The John Deakin Archive/Getty Images 151

By courtesy of Essex Record Office 85

© The Fitzwilliam Museum, Cambridge 62–3

© CSG CIC Glasgow Museums and Libraries Collections 110

Photo: Anthony Hepworth 132, 145 bottom

Islington Local History Centre 157

ITV/REX/Shutterstock 148–9

© Keystone Press Agency/Getty Images 146

(LEAMG : A4.1928) Image courtesy of Leamington Spa Art Gallery & Museum (Warwick District Council) 46

Manchester Art Gallery/Bridgeman Images 117

The National Justice Museum 61 bottom

© National Portrait Gallery, London front cover, back cover, 18, 22 right, 48, 51, 54, 55, 57, 61 top right, 65–7, 74, 76, 77, 81, 87, 89, 93, 106, 113, 116, 122, 146, 153, 154, 155

Pallant House Gallery 98, 103 top

Private collection 38

Private collection 136

Private collection/Photo © Christie's Images/Bridgeman Images 103 bottom

Private collection. Image courtesy of Prudence Cuming and Associates Ltd 21 right, 45

© Royal Academy of Arts, London; Photographer: John Hammond 21 left, 47

Royal College of Art, London, UK / Bridgeman Images 167, 169

Photograph reproduced with the kind permission of the Russell-Cotes Art Gallery & Museum, Bournemouth 37

Scottish National Portrait Gallery 128

Scottish National Gallery of Modern Art 138, 139

Sotheby's London 162 left

© Tate Photography, 2017 10, 22 left, 31 top right, 34 top, 39, 43, 44, 94, 108–9, 119, 120, 129, 131, 143, 162 right, 165; /Oliver Cowling 171; /Lucy Dawkins 26; /Mark Heathcote and Abbie Soanes 99, 105, 107, 142, 145 top; /Joe Humphrys 140–1; /David Lambert and Rod Tidnam 31 top left, 68, 78, 90

Jon Lys Turner Archive 12, 13

By kind permission of the Master, Fellows, and Scholars of Downing College in the University of Cambridge 40–1

© UCL Art Museum, University College London, UK/Bridgeman Images 124–5

© Victoria and Albert Museum, London 24, 29, 42, 58–9, 71, 72, 80, 82–3, 88

The William Andrews Clark Memorial Library. University of California, Los Angeles/Photograph by Gilles Jacob www.gilles-jacob-photo.com 61 top left

Wellcome Library, London 91–2, 161

Wilson Centre for Photography 160

SUPPORTING TATE

Tate relies on a large number of supporters – individuals, foundations, companies and public sector sources – to enable it to deliver its programme of activities, both on and off its gallery sites. This support is essential in order for Tate to acquire works of art for the Collection, run education, outreach and exhibition programmes, care for the Collection in storage and enable art to be displayed, both digitally and physically, inside and outside Tate. Please contact us at:

Development Office
Tate
Millbank
London SW1P 4RG

Tel: +44 (0)20 7887 4900
Fax: +44 (0)20 7887 8098

Tate Americas Foundation
520 West 27 Street Unit 404
New York, NY 10001
USA

Tel: 001 212 643 2818
Fax: 001 212 643 1001

Donations, no matter the size, are gratefully received, either to support particular areas of interest, or to contribute to general activity costs.

Legacies

A legacy to Tate may take the form of a residual share of an estate, a specific cash sum or an item of property such as a work of art. Legacies to Tate are free of inheritance tax, and help to secure a strong future for the Collection and galleries. For further information please contact the Development Office.

Offers in Lieu of Tax

Inheritance Tax can be satisfied by transferring to the Government a work of art of outstanding importance. In this case the amount of tax is reduced, and it can be made a condition of the offer that the work of art is allocated to Tate. Please contact us for details.

Tate Members

Tate Members enjoy unlimited free admission throughout the year to all exhibitions at Tate, as well as a number of other benefits such as exclusive use of our Members' Rooms and a free annual subscription to *Tate Etc*. Whilst enjoying the exclusive privileges of membership, members also help secure Tate's position at the very heart of British and modern art. Members' support actively contributes to new purchases of important art, ensuring that Tate's collection continues to be relevant and comprehensive, as well as funding projects in London, Liverpool and St Ives that increase access and understanding for everyone.

Tate Patrons

Tate Patrons share a passion for art and are committed to supporting Tate on an annual basis. The Patrons help enable the acquisition of works across Tate's broad collecting remit, support the staging of major exhibitions in the galleries, and also give their support to vital conservation, learning and research projects. The scheme provides a forum for Patrons to share their interest in art and meet curators, artists and one another in an enjoyable environment through a regular programme of events. These events take place both at Tate and beyond and encompass curator-led exhibition tours, visits to artists' studios and private collections, art trips both in the UK and abroad, and access to art fairs. The scheme welcomes supporters from outside the UK, giving the programme a truly international scope. For more information, please contact the Patrons Office on +44(0)20 7887 8740 or at patrons.office@tate.org.uk.

Corporate Membership

Corporate Membership at Tate Modern, Tate Britain and Tate Liverpool offers companies opportunities for corporate entertaining and the chance for a wide variety of employee benefits. These include special private views, special access to paying exhibitions, out-of-hours visits and tours, invitations to VIP events and talks at members' offices.

Corporate Investment

Tate has developed a range of imaginative partnerships with the corporate sector, ranging from international interpretation and exhibition programmes to local outreach and staff development programmes. We are particularly known for high-profile business-to-business marketing initiatives and employee benefit packages. Please contact the Corporate Partnerships team for further details.

Charity Details

The Tate Gallery is an exempt charity; the Museums & Galleries Act 1992 added the Tate Gallery to the list of exempt charities defined in the 1960 Charities Act. Tate Members is a registered charity (number 313021). Tate Foundation is a registered charity (number 1085314).

Tate Americas Foundation

Tate Americas Foundation is an independent charity based in New York that supports the work of Tate in the United Kingdom. It receives full tax exempt status from the IRS under section 501(c)(3), allowing United States taxpayers to receive tax deductions on gifts towards annual membership programmes, exhibitions, scholarship and capital projects. For more information please contact the Tate Americas Foundation office.

Art Fund
Artangel
Arts and Humanities Research
    Council
Arts Council England
The Artworkers Retirement
    Society
Charles Asprey
The Estate of Mr Edgar Astaire
Roger Ballen
Lionel Barber
The Estate of Peter and Caroline
    Barker-Mill
Margaret Bear
Corrine Bellow Charity
Big Lottery Fund
Anton and Lisa Bilton
Blavatnik Family Foundation
Bloomberg Philanthropies
Estate of Louise Bourgeois
Frank Bowling, Rachel Scott,
    Benjamin and Sacha Bowling,
    Marcia and Iona Scott
Sir Alan Bowness
Sophie Bowness
Pierre Brahm
Ivor Braka Limited
The Estate of Dr Marcella Louis
    Brenner
The Rory and Elizabeth Brooks
    Foundation
The Estate of Mrs KM Bush
Piers Butler
Jamal Butt
Mr and Mrs Nicolas Cattelain
Francise Hsin-Wen Chang
Trustees of the Chantrey Bequest
The Chaplaincy to the Arts and
    Recreation in North East
    England, Durham
CHK Charities Limited
City of London Corporation's
    charity, City Bridge Trust
The Clore Duffield Foundation
The Clothworkers' Foundation
Denise Coates Foundation
R and S Cohen Foundation
Sadie Coles
Pilar Corrias Gallery
Douglas S Cramer
Abraham Cruzvillegas
Sir Mick and Lady Barbara Davis
Mrs Tiqui Atencio Demirdjian
Department for Business,
    Innovation and Skills
Department for Culture, Media
    and Sport
The Estate of F.N. Dickins
Braco Dimitrijevic
James Diner
Anthony d'Offay

Peter Doig
Joe and Marie Donnelly
Peter Dubens
The Easton Foundation
Maryam and Edward Eisler
Carla Emil and Richard Silverstein
Tracey Emin
European Union
Eykyn Maclean
The Estate of Maurice
    Farquharson
The Estate of Mary Fedden and
    Julian Trevelyan
Wendy Fisher
Eric and Louise Franck
Freelands Foundation
The Estate of Lucian Freud
Gaia Art Foundation, UK
Laura Gannon
Garcia Family Foundation
Adrian Ghenie
The Hon HMT Gibson's
    Charitable Trust
The Giles Family
Estate of Kaveh Golestan
Sir Nicholas and Lady Goodison
Nicholas and Judith Goodison's
    Charitable Settlement
Marian Goodman Gallery
Antony Gormley
Lydia and Manfred Gorvy
Noam Gottesman
The Granville-Grossman Bequest
Greene Naftali Gallery
Dr Joana Grevers
Calouste Gulbenkian Foundation
The Estate of Mr John Haggart
The Hakuta Family
Paul Hamlyn Foundation
The Ray and Diana Harryhausen
    Foundation
Heritage Lottery Fund
Mauro Herlitzka
The Hintze Family Charitable
    Foundation
Damien Hirst
Robert Hiscox
David Hockney
Hazlitt Holland-Hibbert
The Alan Howard Foundation
Trustees of Lord Howard of
    Henderskelfe's Will Trust
Sally Hudson
Michael and Ali Hue-Williams
The J Isaacs Charitable Trust
IV. O Foundation
The Daniel Katz Gallery
Kikuji Kawada
Dr Martin Kenig
J Patrick Kennedy and Patricia A
    Kennedy

David Knaus
König Galerie
Andreas Kurtz
Mary Lambert
David Landau
The Estate of Jay and Fran
    Landesman
The Estate of Fay Elspeth Langford
The New York Community Trust
    AB/Avi and Maya Lavi Fund
The Leathersellers' Company
    Charitable Fund
The Leche Trust
Agnès and Edward Lee
Legacy Trust UK
The Leverhulme Trust
Ruben Levi
Lisson Gallery
London Art History Society
Lowell Libson Ltd British Art
LUMA Foundation
Lyndsey Ingram Ltd
Mace Foundation
Simon A Mackintosh
Robert Manoukian
The Estate of Sir Edwin Manton
The Manton Foundation
Rebecca Marks
Marlborough Fine Art
David Mayor
Lord McAlpine of West Green
The Mead Family Foundation
The Estate of Deborah Jane
    Medlicott
The Andrew W. Mellon
    Foundation
The Paul Mellon Centre for
    Studies in British Art
Sir Geoffroy Millais
The Henry Moore Foundation
Michael Moritz and Harriet
    Heyman
Marie-Louise von Motesiczky
    Charitable Trust
National Heritage Memorial Fund
Andrew Nikou Foundation
Simon Norfolk
Averill Ogden and Winston
    Ginsberg
Ordovas
Matthew Orr and Sybill Robson
    Orr
Outset Contemporary Art Fund
Pace Gallery
Midge and Simon Palley
The Pasmore Estate
Yana Peel
Jan-Christoph Peters
Catherine Petitgas
Clive Phillpot

Piano Nobile, Robert Travers
    (Works of Art) Ltd
Stanley Picker Trust
The Estate of R.V. Pitman
The Pivovarov Family
The Porter Foundation
The Porthmeor Fund
Mr Thibault Poutrel
Mrs Virginia Powell
Gilberto Pozzi
Massimo Prelz Oltramonti
Andrey Prigov
Emilio Prini
Laura Rapp and Jay Smith
The Redfern Gallery
Anthony Reynolds
The Estate of Michael Brinley
    Holmes Roberts
Valeria Rodnyansky
Barrie and Emmanuel Roman
The Estate of Eugene and
    Penelope Rosenberg
Judko Rosenstock and Oscar
    Hernandez
The Rothschild Foundation
Edward Ruscha
The Estate of Simon Sainsbury
Muriel and Freddy Salem
Julião Sarmento
John Schaeffer
Jake and Hélène Marie Shafran
Stephen Shore
Andy Simpkin
Vicky Hughes and John A Smith
Keren Souza Kohn, Francesca
    Souza and Anya Souza
Sterling Ruby Studio
The Estate of Michael Stoddart
Mercedes and Ian Stoutzker
Galeria Luisa Strina
T293, Rome
Tate 1897 Circle
Tate Africa Acquisitions
    Committee
Tate Americas Foundation
Tate Asia-Pacific Acquisitions
    Committee
Tate International Council
Tate Latin American Acquisitions
    Committee
Tate Members
Tate Middle East and North Africa
    Acquisitions Committee
Tate North American Acquisitions
    Committee
Tate Outreach Appeal
Tate Patrons
Tate Photography Acquisitions
    Committee
Tate Russia and Eastern Europe
    Acquisitions Committee

Tate South Asia Acquisitions Committee
Terra Foundation for American Art
The Estate of Mr Nicholas Themans
Phillip Trevelyan
Hiromi Tsuchida
The Estate of William Turnbull
Luc Tuymans
Cy Twombly Foundation
V-A-C Foundation
Alexa Waley-Cohen
Offer and Mika Waterman
Offer Waterman & Co
Matthew Westerman
Anthony Whishaw
Matthew Westerman
Jane and Michael Wilson
Wolfgang Wittrock
WME | IMG
The Lord Leonard and Lady Estelle Wolfson Foundation
Mr Nelson Woo
The Estate of Mrs Monica Wynter
Yuz Foundation
The Zabludowicz Collection
The Estate of Mr Anthony Zambra
and those who wish to remain anonymous

The 1897 Circle

Marilyn Bild
David and Deborah Botten
Geoff Bradbury
Charles Brett
Sylvia Carter
Eloise and Francis Charlton
Mr and Mrs Cronk
Alex Davids
Jonathan Davis
Professor Martyn Davis
Sean Dissington
Ronnie Duncan
Joan Edlis
V Fabian
Lt Cdr Paul Fletcher
Mr and Mrs R.N. and M.C. Fry
Tom Glynn
Richard S Hamilton
LA Hynes
John Janssen
Dr Martin Kenig
Isa Levy
Jean Medlycott
Susan Novell
Martin Owen
Simon Reynolds
Dr Claudia Rosanowski
Ann M Smith
Graham Smith
Deborah Stern
Jennifer Toynbee-Holmes
Estate of Paule Vézelay
D Von Bethmann-Hollweg
Audrey Wallrock

Professor Brian Whitton
Simon Casimir Wilson
Andrew Woodd
Mr and Mrs Zilberberg
and those who wish to remain anonymous

Tate Britain Corporate Supporters

Bloomberg
BMW
BP
Christie's
EY
Hildon Ltd
Hyundai Card
Hyundai Motor
IHS Markit
Microsoft
Qantas
Sotheby's
and those who wish to remain anonymous

Tate Britain Corporate Members

Baker & McKenzie
Bank of America Merrill Lynch
BCS Consulting
BlackRock
Bloomberg
Chanel
Clifford Chance LLP
The Cultivist
Deutsche Bank AG London
Dow Jones
EY
Finsbury
Hiscox
Holdingham Group
HSBC
Hyundai Card
Imperial College Healthcare Charity
JATO Dynamics
JCA Group
Linklaters
The Moody's Foundation
Morgan Stanley
Siegel + Gale
Tishman Speyer
and those who wish to remain anonymous

INDEX